# THE
# POSTMODERN
# PRESIDENCY

# THE POSTMODERN PRESIDENCY

### Bill Clinton's Legacy in U. S. Politics

Edited by

STEVEN E. SCHIER

UNIVERSITY OF PITTSBURGH PRESS

Copyright © 2000, University of Pittsburgh Press
All rights reserved
Manufactured in the United States of America
Printed on acid-free paper
10 9 8 7 6 5 4 3 2 1

Library of Congress Cataloging-in-Publication Data
The postmodern presidency : Bill Clinton's legacy in U.S. politics / edited by Steven E. Schier.
   p.    cm.
  ISBN 0-8229-4135-X (alk. paper)  ISBN 0-8229-5742-6 (pbk. : alk. paper)
  1. Clinton, Bill, 1946– Influence. 2. United States politics and government—1993– 3. Political leadership—United States—Case studies. 4. United States—Politics and government—Case studies. 5. Presidents—United States—Case studies. 6. Postmodernism—Political aspecs—United States—Case studies. 7. Clinton, Bill, 1946– I. Schier, Steven E.
  E885 .P67 2000
  973.929'092—dc21      00-009650

973.929 P858s

The postmodern presidency

To LEON D. EPSTEIN,

scholar, mentor, and friend

—*Steven Schier*

# CONTENTS

| | | |
|---|---|---|
| Introduction | A Unique Presidency   1 | |
| | STEVEN E. SCHIER | |
| PART I | The Presidency and Public Policy   17 | |
| Chapter 1 | Bill Clinton and the Institutionalized Presidency: Executive Autonomy and Presidential Leadership   19 | |
| | PERI E. ARNOLD | |
| Chapter 2 | Clinton, Class, and Economic Policy   41 | |
| | RAYMOND TATALOVICH AND JOHN FRENDREIS | |
| Chapter 3 | Clinton and Foreign Policy: Some Legacies for a New Century   60 | |
| | JAMES M. MC CORMICK | |
| PART II | The President and the Public   85 | |
| Chapter 4 | A Clouded Mirror: Bill Clinton, Polls, and the Politics of Survival   87 | |
| | JOHN F. HARRIS | |
| Chapter 5 | Courting the Public: Bill Clinton's Postmodern Education   106 | |
| | BRUCE MIROFF | |
| Chapter 6 | The Public's View of Clinton   124 | |
| | DIANE HOLLERN HARVEY | |
| PART III | Parties and Party Alignments   143 | |
| Chapter 7 | Clinton and the Party System in Historical Perspective   145 | |
| | JOHN J. COLEMAN | |

| Chapter 8 | Clinton and the Republican Party  167
JOHN J. PITNEY JR.

| Chapter 9 | Clinton and the Democrats:
The President as Party Leader  183
NICOL C. RAE

| PART IV | Cultural, Race, and Gender Politics  201

| Chapter 10 | Clinton, Impeachment, and the Culture Wars  203
JAMES L. GUTH

| Chapter 11 | Clinton and Racial Politics  223
SHARON D. WRIGHT

| Chapter 12 | The Clintons and Gender Politics  238
BARBARA BURRELL

| Conclusion | American Politics after Clinton  255
STEVEN E. SCHIER

*Notes*  267
*References*  271
*Contributors*  291
*Index*  293

INTRODUCTION

# A UNIQUE PRESIDENCY

STEVEN E. SCHIER

It is fitting to examine the impact of Bill Clinton, that most political of presidents, on American politics. The task is not a simple one, because the Clinton presidency is in several important respects unique. Of course, every presidency is in some sense "one of a kind." Only Woodrow Wilson could be the first president to deliver a State of the Union address on the floor of the House of Representatives; only Millard Fillmore could be the first to install an indoor toilet in the White House. Some presidential "firsts," like Wilson's, are politically consequential; many, like Fillmore's, are not. The Clinton presidency produced several remarkable and consequential political events: in electoral results, policy enactments, and presidential and congressional behavior. This chapter relates the distinctive characteristics of a presidency that is "marked by an unusual number of firsts." (Milkis and Nelson 1999, 371).

Scholars commonly acknowledge that the Clinton presidency is idiosyncratic. Descriptions of his tenure in office range from "unusual" (Rockman 1996, 356) and "puzzling" (Peri Arnold, in this volume) to "bizarre" (Skowronek 1997, 447). What accounts for the relative strangeness of Clinton's tenure in office? Perhaps, in part, the quirks of contemporary culture do. Bruce Miroff argues in his chapter that Clinton's "postmodern style"—involving multiple transformations of his political persona—fared well in a postmodern culture grounded in ambiguity, confusion, and irony. Most of the authors here assess aspects of this style, leading us to label his presidency as "postmodern" in the book's title. Stephen Skowronek, a leading scholar of the presidency, provides a more historical answer to the question.

The title of Skowronek's landmark book, *The Politics Presidents Make,* is a central topic of this volume. In it he argues presidents are forced to create new politics because the presidency is an order-creating institution. Chief executives try to "construct some new political arrangements that can stand the test of legitimacy with other institutions of government as well as the nation at large" (20–21). Creating new arrangements is a disruptive process, likely to induce pitched political battles over the president's efforts. In the late twentieth century, the persistence of large, stable governmental institutions made presidential attempts at political reconstruction more difficult: "More has to be changed to create a break from the past, and those adversely affected by the changes will be able to put up more formidable resistance" (56). The enhanced resistance to Bill Clinton's initiatives provided his presidency with several unique qualities. According to Skowronek, Clinton was a "preemptive president" working as an opposition leader to a resilient governmental regime (43).

What was this "regime" that Clinton challenged? Much of it involved the resistance of an independent Congress dominated in 1993 by a complacent Democratic majority and after 1994 by an insurgent Republican majority strongly opposed to Clinton, each supported by potent alliances of established interest groups. But beyond Congress and organized interests lay the "conventional wisdom" of the Reagan-Bush years, still powerful and resistant to major changes in national direction; America became more conservative from 1980 until the beginning of 1993. The Reagan-Bush agenda of lower taxes, smaller government, and increased defense spending had become the established national tendency by the early 1990s. As James Ceaser put it in 1988, "When it comes to the substance of his public philosophy, Reagan has succeeded for the moment in making his program the 'base' of American political discourse. Just as candidates once defined their position by reference to the New Deal, they now define themselves by reference to the Reagan Revolution" (206). Indeed, George Bush's apostasy from the Reagan creed when he raised taxes in 1990 helped to defeat him in 1992. The public ousted Bush, but it was not at all clear that they repudiated the twelve years of governance before 1992. Clinton, after all, received only 43 percent of the popular vote.

This produced an uncertain political environment for Bill Clinton in 1993, one in which he constantly had to improvise politically in order to survive. Preemptive presidents like Clinton are the "wild cards" of presidential history, who are prone to "zig-zagging" on policy in response to adverse political conditions (Skowronek 1997, 450, 453). Thus the Clinton presidency displayed several different political hues. From 1993 to 1994, Clinton tried to govern within the Democratic coalition and overcome Republican opposition. In 1995, he positioned himself rightward but also in opposition to the vehement new Republican majority in Congress. Then in 1996, Clinton cut deals with the Republican Congress that worked to their mutual electoral benefit that November. After 1997, he was forced into a survival mode as investigations surrounded him, culminating in impeachment.

In the uniquely turbulent politics of the 1990s, characterized by "weak partisan loyalties, divided government, and widespread distrust of the political process" (Milkis and Nelson 1999, 372), it is hardly surprising that a preemptive president would rack up an extraordinary number of political firsts. The ensuing sections discuss the often-distinctive characteristics of Clinton's political reign. First, I identify unique historical events and the remarkable electoral record of the decade. Then, Clinton's original governing style and some remarkable instances of presidential and congressional behavior receive attention. Finally, the distinctive policy results of the Clinton era are recapitulated. Bill Clinton's presidency was indeed no ordinary time.

## Historical Trends and Events

Several "firsts" of the Clinton presidency shaped the political tone of the 1990s. James Guth chronicles in his chapter the distinctive role the president played in sharpening the cultural conflicts of the 1990s. As the first babyboomer president, Bill Clinton had, along with many in his generation, found ways around the Vietnam draft, dabbled in drugs, and indulged in sex outside marriage. All these activities came to haunt Clinton with a vengeance, from the draft letter of the 1992 campaign to the Lewinsky scandal of 1998–1999. Media disclosures, resultant political attacks, and Clinton's evasive and at times false denials of such charges helped to give the politics of his time a distinctly nasty flavor. To borrow a phrase from feminists, "the personal became the political" in an unpleasant way for the president. As the initial First Lady strongly influenced by the feminist movement of the sixties and seventies, Hillary Rodham Clinton dramatically redefined the role of presidential spouse. Gone was the decorative and subordinate homebody; in her place was an assertive and independent political force working alongside her spouse. During Clinton's first term, she controversially spearheaded an abortive effort to reform health care, but she remained an important political adviser throughout his presidency. Indeed, her loyalty and discretion during the Lewinsky scandal saved his presidency. In 2000, Hillary again made history—

this time by running for a New York Senate seat while still serving as First Lady. In her contribution to this volume, Barbara Burrell details how the Clintons' generational experiences help to explain their emphasis on appointing women to the administration, addressing the policy concerns of women, and cultivating women as a political constituency.

The controversies surrounding the Clintons' pasts and their unorthodox political partnership intensified the combative political environment of national governance. The 1990s produced a close partisan balance in national politics, giving officeholders of each national party strong incentive to press differences and embarrass their partisan enemies. The Clintons became prime targets, due in no small part to their own political mistakes both before and during Bill Clinton's White House tenure. A public disaffected with parties produced (with the exception of 1992) election results that created divided government and resultant institutional warfare between president and Congress. As elections less conclusively determined who would govern, politics became dominated by forms of nonelectoral warfare aimed at destroying political enemies (Ginsberg and Shefter 1999). John J. Pitney in his chapter explains how the process of "revelation, investigation, and prosecution" begun in the 1970s reached its apogee in the Starr investigation and impeachment battles of 1997–1998 (41–44). The goal in this process is to control government not by winning elections but by politically disabling the opposition. Bill Clinton and his nemesis, Newt Gingrich, were the major targets and victims of the new scandal culture.

Washington scandals continued to rage because they had no great effect on most citizens' lives and did little to hamper the booming American economy of the 1990s. Though the president can claim some credit for the good economic results (because of his deficit reduction package of 1993 and appointments of Robert Rubin as Treasury Secretary and Alan Greenspan as chair of the Federal Reserve Board), the economy did more for him than he ever did for it. Several years of increasing economic growth, low inflation, and soaring stock prices aided his reelection and helped him to survive the Lewinsky scandal. The intense political jousting in Washington hardly encouraged public fixation on politics. In the 1996 presidential election, electoral participation dropped to below 50 percent for the first time since 1924 (shortly after women got the vote) and also declined during the off-year election of 1998 to 36 percent, the lowest since 1942 (which was in the midst of a world war). The stakes in Washington probably seemed small to many Americans because times were good.

Of all the historical circumstances of the 1990s, two had the greatest effect on presidential politics. One, already noted, is Skowronek's "institutional thickening" in Washington: "an ever thicker government" producing "greater institutional resilience" to attempts by presidents to alter established arrangements (1997, 413). This secular trend produced considerable difficulties for Clinton in the 1990s. In particular it placed him in a separated presidency with limited resources to employ in bending other Washington institutions to his wishes (Jones 1999, 75). Congress and the bureaucracy remained rival and competitive institutions supported by strong and enduring interest groups. Clinton's response, as we will see, was to manage public perceptions and create a personalized, postmodern presidency to help him deal with other Washington power centers and survive scandal.

The second grand historical circumstance of the 1990s, the end of the Cold War, importantly altered the president's job description. Lawrence Dodd describes the Olympian attributes expected of presidents during the Cold War era: "Military service, preferably a heroic performance in wartime, became a virtual necessity . . . personal problems became stigmas to be avoided or hidden at all costs, and significant symbols of personal success—in national politics, during wartime, or in business—seemed virtually mandatory" (1995, 259). Bill Clinton possessed none of these traits, and America seemed to no longer demand them from a president. Instead, Clinton redefined the presidency as an exalted governorship, aimed at solving the immediate domestic problems of citizens (Weisberg 1999). The public's interest in foreign policy shrank considerably, allowing domestic policy to dominate the presidential elections of the 1990s, a policy arena Bill Clinton knew well and in which he could excel. The end of the Cold War also produced great uncertainty over the course of American foreign policy. Without a great rival, how do we define American interests? How do we pursue them? These questions plagued Clinton and the rest of Washington during his presidency.

## The Electoral Record

The changing public expectations of the presidency, endemic institutional combat in Washington, and low incidence of party voting by the electorate all combined to produce a remarkably quirky series of national elections in the 1990s. The electoral arena for the first time in this century featured close competitive balance between the two parties at both presidential and congressional levels in an environment in which individual elections centered not around party labels but on the personal traits and campaigns of individual candidates. The following facts and interpretations demonstrate that elections in the 1990s involved Clinton in an electoral roller-coaster ride unlike anything encountered by previous presidents.

- Clinton's election and reelection as a Democratic president was unusual. He became the first two-term Democratic president since Franklin Roosevelt and the first two-term president never to win a majority of the popular vote since Woodrow Wilson. Clinton is also the only two-term president in the twentieth century to win election twice with less than four hundred electoral votes. In 1992, Clinton won the presidency while running well behind all but a handful of congressional Democrats in their districts and although Democrats lost ten House seats. While the House experienced only small partisan change, it underwent the biggest turnover of its membership in forty years—due to retirements, redistricting, and public disaffection resulting from the House banking scandal. The combination of a Clinton victory, Democratic House losses, and great member turnover in the House caused Gary Jacobson to describe the 1992 congressional elections as "most peculiar" (1993, 154). Bill Clinton thus shattered recent precedents by winning twice without either time receiving a strong electoral mandate from the public.

- The 1994 election, described by Walter Dean Burnham as "very likely the most consequential off year election in one hundred years" (1996, 363), produced fifty-two additional Republican House members and eight new senators, giving Republicans unified control of Congress for the first time in forty years. Burnham argues the 1994 election was so great a shift toward Republican voting that it may betoken an incipient partisan realignment (1996). The administration suffered the largest congressional losses since 1922, in the wake of the Teapot Dome scandal. The election also led to the "unique" rise of Speaker Newt Gingrich, who attempted to assert the powers of a prime minister during the heady days of the congressional Republican revolution of 1995 (Campbell 2000, 50). The overreaching by the Gingrich-led congressional Republicans led to budget stalemate and two government shutdowns that rekindled Clinton's popularity and contributed to his reelection in 1996.

- The 1996 elections made Clinton the first Democrat ever to win reelection while Republicans retained control of Congress and made him the first Democratic president to serve more than two years with a Republican Congress. Democrats picked up nine House seats but lost two Senate seats; Clinton's personal victory did not translate into a broader party victory.

- The 1998 elections produced results described as "very unusual" by political analyst Charles Cook (1998, 1). Though the elections occurred in the midst of an impeachment investigation by the House of Representatives, Democrats nevertheless gained six House seats, the first time a president's party had picked up seats during the midterm election of a president's second term since 1822, while no net change resulted in the Senate. Not since 1934 had Democrats gained any House seats in a midterm election when their party held the White House. The overall change in seats in 1998 was the second lowest of post–World War II midterms (Shafer 2000, 28). Together, the congressional election results of 1996 and 1998 produced "remarkable stasis" given the turbulence of national politics during this time (27).

- The elections of the 1990s produced new presidential voting alignments. In both 1992 and 1996, Clinton effectively targeted swing voters largely concentrated in America's suburbs and presented a carefully tailored agenda suited to their concerns (Stengel and Pooley 1996; Schier 2000), thus producing new electoral inroads for a Democratic presidential candidate.

- Clinton also assembled an Electoral College base of states from America's northeast, west, and northern border states that may serve as the basis for future Democratic success in presidential elections. Clinton is also the first president to make female and black voters so central a component of his electoral coalition in important swing states (Sapiro and Canon 2000). The administration's record regarding women and racial minorities, discussed by both Barbara Burrell and Sharon Wright in this volume, was mixed, but better in the eyes of advocates than that of any recent predecessor. Women and blacks "emerged from the periphery to help shape the last presidency of the twentieth century," a development with many possible implications for the future of American politics (170).

John Coleman in this volume finds a pattern underlying the seemingly confusing electoral results of the 1990s. He argues that the 1968 election produced a party realignment that resembled more a "dealignment" in which Democrats had an advantage among a less partisan electorate that increasingly elected divided national governments. In 1994, a similar realignment resulted, one in which Republicans now gained the advantage in national elections. But the public clearly preferred neither party as a normal majority party, as Clinton's reelection in 1996 and the stalemate verdict in 1998 revealed. In such a fluid situation, according to Coleman, "there are several paths for party development." The volatility of the 1990s gives us no strong clues as to which possible path will actually result.

An additional Clinton-era electoral innovation receives fuller discussion in the following section, which is concerned with the president's governing style. Clinton's governance can be termed "hyperpolitical," due to his uniquely strong concern with using the presidency to maximize both his reelection chances and his job approval among the public. Other presidents, such as Lyndon Johnson, devoted much attention to such matters. Clinton, though, elevated the cultivation of personal political success to a near-obsession.

## Governing Style

George Edwards and Stephen Wayne argue that a president's governing style involves two distinct sorts of leadership activities. First, a president must at times be a "director of change, creating opportunities to move in new directions and leading others where they otherwise would not go." And in other circumstances, a president must be a "facilitator of change, exploiting opportunities to help others go where they want to go anyway" (1994, 14). Bill Clinton, characteristically, developed a governing style that frequently permitted him to "have it both ways" with the public—acting as a director and facilitator of change at the same time. Clinton and his advisers perfected this method in 1995 and 1996 while preparing for his reelection campaign. First, his pollsters surveyed swing voters on various small-scale domestic politics they might prefer. Once these were identified, Clinton then publicly emphasized the policies. The public would not have gone for these policies had they not been first discovered by surveys. The polling thus directed attention to new directions that might prove popular, once discovered. Clinton could then direct public and congressional attention to the policies, and engage in leadership by facilitation once the public discovered the president's agenda and expressed approval. This merger of direction and facilitation is no small political achievement and is unmatched among recent presidents. When a president can create opportunities for people to move in new directions that appear the directions they want to go anyway, the political costs of public presidential leadership shrink. Only Ronald Reagan achieved this political ideal on occasion, but his more emphatic ideological convictions produced fewer opportunities for conflating the direction and facilitation of change. The ideologically much more flexible Clinton made the discovery of such opportunities the core of his governing style.

How did Clinton do it? He initially learned from painful experience. After his first hundred days, he was less popular than was any president in the history of polling. Yet by his sixth year, in the midst of the historically unprecedented Lewinsky scandal, he had the highest job approval ever of any president at that point in his term. Given the limited resources and opportunities available to presidents due to the decline of parties, the rise of congressional assertiveness, divided government, and the interest group intransigence of "permanent Washington," this is a remarkable political achievement. His governing style successfully aimed at public approval and entailed many components.

Clinton raised the importance of pollsters as presidential advisers to new heights. No other American president has demonstrated Bill Clinton's interest in opinion polls (Edwards 2000, 37). In his chapter, John Harris explains how in 1995 and 1996, pollster Dick Morris gained unprecedented authority in framing domestic policy for Clinton with an eye toward reelection. Morris helped to direct public attention to poll-discovered policies so that Clinton could lead through facilitation—a novel conflation of direction and facilitation (Morris 1997). Clinton also often resorted to pure facilitation. Even during the war in Kosovo, Clinton relied on pollster Mark Penn's daily survey results, which consistently revealed support for aerial bombing but opposition to ground troops. Clinton followed this advice to military victory and popular success in the conflict (Harris 1999c).

"Governing by campaigning," which appeared first during the Reagan presidency, became a constant under Clinton (Jones 1999, 278). From the beginning of his presidency, Clinton set a new pace by engaging in more public appearances than any previous president (Ragsdale 1996, 176, 179). As part of his triangulation strategy of 1995–1996, in which he attempted to place himself near the political center and equidistant from congressional Republicans and Democrats, Clinton engaged in innovative use of presidential advertising. For the first time in a nonelection year, the White House supervised spending some $18 million in television ads on the president's behalf (Woodward 1996, 344). The legality of the "soft money" spending by the Democratic National Committee was questionable, but the ads helped to frame issues for the 1996 election in ways favorable to the president.

The result was a governing strategy combining rhetoric and administrative actions to create personal ties with the public. This created distance between the president and his own party, as Nicol C. Rae notes in his chapter. It also did not encourage popular debate or discussion of issues in any depth.

Instead, it attached the president to popular policies. This personal relationship between the president and targeted parts of the public proved helpful in the short run for Clinton, particularly when he was under frequent political assault from scandal and investigation; an effective governing strategy eventually became a vital survival strategy.

Though it is difficult to overstate the effectiveness of Clinton's governing strategy with the public, that approach proved of only limited effectiveness when the separated president faced the other power centers of Washington. Though often popular with the public, Clinton's initiatives fared less well in Washington. His proposals often came in great quantity and complexity, allowing Congress to ignore many of them without great political cost. Presentation of a few simple, popular initiatives might have a promising chance of success, but Clinton could not restrain himself from overloading his agenda, giving overly long State of the Union addresses stuffed with dozens of small policy proposals (Rockman 2000).

A deeper problem for his governing style, discussed further in the next section, was his reputation within Washington, defined by Richard Neustadt as "impressions within the Washington community about how he will put his powers to use" (1990, 185). As his presidency proceeded, Clinton's reputation gradually suffered, for several reasons. His long and diffuse agenda and frequent shifts in priorities gave uncertain signals. He also developed a reputation among legislators as a president who could not be trusted to keep his word (Penny 1999). Bob Kerrey, fellow Democrat and senator from Nebraska, even publicly referred to him as "an unusually good liar—unusually good" (Will 1997). In 1993, for example, House Democrats took a political risk in voting for an administration-sponsored increase in energy taxes, only to have the president drop the proposal when negotiating with the Senate. Actions like this lingered long among Democrats on Capitol Hill, though most continued to support his initiatives in 1993 and 1994.

The arrival of a Republican Congress and the onset of the Lewinsky debacle dramatically worsened the president's reputation problems in Washington. The new Congress disagreed with the president on policy and seldom trusted him to keep his word. As a result, congressional support for presidential initiatives tumbled further during a two-year period than ever before since *Congressional Quarterly* started the calculations in 1953, from an impressive 86.4 percent success in 1994 to an abysmal 36.1 percent in 1995 (Doherty 1996, 3427). Though Clinton's congressional support grew later in his term, it never again approached the level of his first two years.

## Institutional Behavior

The president's reputation problems help to explain the unique combination of his public popularity and the widespread suspicion Washington accorded him during most of his presidency. Add an unusual level of partisan polarization in Congress, and the result is a climate in which policymaking becomes extraordinarily difficult. Washington in the nineties witnessed several government shutdowns, record use of the filibuster as an obstructive device in the Senate, and an unparalleled invasive investigative assault on the president by independent counsel Kenneth Starr.

The rancorous partisanship in Congress during the 1990s can hardly be overstated. Shortly after Clinton took office, the filibuster became a new tool of partisan warfare in the Senate. It was previously used only by a few senators to obstruct Senate business at the end of a session. Minority Leader Bob Dole managed to unify Senate Republicans behind an unprecedented party-line filibuster of the economic stimulus component of Clinton's economic plan in 1993. As a result of their success, the minority party in the Senate has gained new clout through threatening and executing filibusters, thus slowing down the pace of Senate work and empowering minorities who seek to make partisan points. Though the majority party continues to direct House business without effective minority obstruction, that chamber as well has confronted poisonous partisanship, from the ethics investigation of Speaker Gingrich in 1995–1996 to the impeachment debate of 1999.

President Clinton, lacking Washington reputation and finding unending combat on Capitol Hill, spent most of his second term resisting forays by congressional investigative committees on Whitewater, campaign finance, the Lewinsky matter, and the loss of nuclear secrets to the Chinese. His battles with independent counsel Starr became an unprecedented struggle for presidential survival. Clinton became the first president subpoenaed by a prosecutor while in office and the first to testify before a grand jury—which he did twice, once regarding charges of sexual harassment towards Paula Jones and once concerning a possible obstruction of justice regarding his affair with Monica Lewinsky. The administration asserted an immunity from prosecution claim in the Jones case and a series of executive privilege claims in the Lewinsky situation, leading to several historic federal court decisions that promise to circumscribe such claims by future presidents. In *Clinton v. Jones* (117 S. Ct. 1636) the Supreme Court ruled in 1997 that the president has no immunity from sexual harassment prosecution while in office, holding that "the doctrine of separation of powers does not require federal courts to stay all private actions against the president until he leaves office." The process of discovery proceeded in the Jones case, leading to revelations of a sexual affair between the president and a young White House intern, Monica Lewinsky.

Independent counsel Starr, seeking evidence of possible obstruction of justice by the White House in the Jones case, subpoenaed the president, his secret service officers, and White House attorneys for evidence about the Lewinsky matter. The administration appealed the subpoenas of secret service agents and White House lawyers, arguing that executive privilege shielded them from testifying. In each case, a federal appeals court ruled against the White House. Testimony before grand juries proceeded, and the presidential zone of privacy shrank further for Clinton and future presidents.

The culmination of the testimony involved the first impeachment proceedings against a popularly elected president. The House of Representatives on December 19, 1998, approved two articles of impeachment by narrow, partisan margins. One accused the president of lying under oath before the Starr grand jury, and the other charged him with obstruction of justice in the Jones civil case. This occurred despite public opposition to impeachment in opinion polls and the surprising Republican losses in the midterm elections the month before. The Senate trial failed to muster majority votes for either article.

The future of impeachment politics remains uncertain. Skowronek notes that preemptive presidents like Clinton have faced torrents of personal abuse while in office—Andrew Johnson, the only other president impeached, also ranks as a preemptive president (1997, 44). In her chapter, Diane Harvey suggests that Clinton's behavior may have "desensitized the public to presidential scandals—particularly sex scandals." Much hinges on the political consequences of impeachment in the 2000 elections; a large political penalty imposed on Republicans would lessen enthusiasm for impeachment investigations in the future. At this point, however, impeachment's impact on the 2000 elections seems limited, which may make impeachment a more frequent tool of political combat in Washington. Harvey demonstrates, however, how popular suspicion of Clinton's accusers helped him through the crisis, which might deter similar future assaults. But partisan and principled motivations can overcome such tactical calculations. Should the competitive, evenly matched, and poisonous partisanship of the late 1990s persist, impeachment may well be invoked again soon. In this most dramatic sense, the Clinton presidency has produced unprecedented institutional behavior in Washington.

## Policy Legacy

The Clinton record on policy is hard to assess because he presented so many small initiatives—some of which became law, but none of which changed American life fundamentally. A few major policy initiatives do promise to mark the Clinton presidency as distinctive. First, as Peri Arnold and John Coleman note herein, the president can claim partial credit for an unprecedented turnaround in government finances. No president has seen the national budget move from such deep deficits to such strong surpluses during his time in office. In Fiscal Year 1993, Clinton faced a deficit amounting to 3.9 percent of Gross Domestic Product (GDP), totaling $300 billion dollars (Council of Economic Advisors 1999, B-79). By Fiscal Year 1999, that deficit had reached a surplus equal to $99 billion, 1.2 percent of GDP (Pianin and Harris 1999, A1). The budget turnaround under Clinton promises to restructure spending politics, so long constrained by the shadow of large deficits.

Another major action of the Clinton presidency, discussed by Raymond Tatalovich and John Frendreis in this book, was the 1996 disentitling of welfare. Clinton reached a compromise with a Republican Congress over welfare policy, shifting its focus from income maintenance through entitlement to limited-term assistance and mandatory training and employment. Aid to Families with Dependent Children, an entitlement since the days of FDR, was abolished, the first such eradication in this century. The successful economy, accompanied with this reform, helped to shrink welfare rolls dramatically in the late 1990s (Quirk and Cunion 2000, 200–201). The fate of the poor under these new laws during an economic downturn, however, has yet to be known.

A third major legacy may be the successful military action in Kosovo. James McCormick notes in his chapter how the Kosovo war reflected the administration's strong commitment to many forms of international engagement. The terms, however, have changed; for the first time, America participated in an offensive military action by the North Atlantic Treaty Organization (NATO). The underlying logic of the action was innovative as well. No vital national interest lay behind the American military action; rather, the action sought to improve the humanitarian lot of the Kosovars by defeating Serb repression and thus bringing new stability to the region. Instead, the initial effects of the operation produced the displacement of hundreds of thousands of Kosovars. Whether stability will come to the Balkans at last remains to be seen. The action did open the possibility, however, that foreign and defense policy will pursue humanitarian goals beyond the traditional strategic objectives of America's national interests. In the short run, this produced a surprising bipartisan consensus in support of additional defense spending, as many liberals responded positively to the prospect of a military policy driven more by humanitarian concerns (Pianin 1999, A1).

A fourth and more ambiguous policy impact lies in the growing domestic and international salience of trade policy, emphasized by the Clinton administration as an important element of its international strategy. The successful passage of the North American Free Trade Agreement in 1993 and of permanent normal trade relations with China in 2000 marked the major administration triumphs in trade policy. Even so, a majority of House Democrats opposed these trade liberalizations. Between the two triumphs, the administration suffered a series of trade policy setbacks, failing to win congressional support for expanding NAFTA to Latin America and extended "fast track" presidential negotiation powers. The tumultuous failure of the Seattle round of World Trade Organization talks in 1999, amidst tens of thousands of anti-WTO protestors, dramatized the higher political stakes in trade policy. As several authors in this volume note, Clinton did not convince key components of his party's coalition—environmentalists and labor unions—of the utility of his administration's push for market liberalization. Thanks in part to Clinton's own emphasis on it, trade policy promises to remain a more important and controversial part of foreign policy than it has been in recent decades (Greenhouse 1999).

## The Important "Firsts"

The above summary of the many remarkable and unprecedented occurrences during the Clinton presidency raises the question of their ultimate significance for American politics. Some of the "firsts" seem to have few lasting implications. Clinton's plummet in congressional voting support from 1994 to 1995, for example, seems very much a specific product of the times with few long-term political impacts. New facts make new politics, however, and the policy changes listed above promise repercussions into the twenty-first century. Other "firsts" reflect lasting changes in our politics. The role possibilities for First Ladies, for instance, seem to have been permanently widened by Hillary Clinton's pioneering assertiveness, and the presidential office has been redefined in a lasting way, as well. As Peri Arnold explains in his chapter, the federal courts have constricted executive privilege and presidential immunity from civil suits in ways that surely will affect future occupants of the Oval Office.

One innovation of the Clinton presidency, however, deserves a final, special mention. It's likely that future presidents will employ more campaign styles and approaches to governing as a result of Bill Clinton's efforts in this regard. Clinton found it possible, through careful assessment of public opinion and shrewd campaigning while in office, to create public approval of his job performance without a stable governing coalition supporting him in Washington or widespread policy consensus on the role of government among the public. This is no small accomplishment in the treacherous politics of the 1990s. His survival of impeachment is the ultimate testament to the efficacy of this governing style for personal presidential survival and success, and it is a lesson that will not be lost on his successors. Clinton's remarkable ability to reinvent himself in such threatening circumstances earns him the label of "postmodern" president—one able to successfully alter his identity as the political context shifted.

## The Plan of the Book

Unlike most "legacy" books, which primarily recapitulate what happened, this book assesses the impact of Bill Clinton's presidency on the future of American politics and public policy. Each author evaluates Clinton's record in the context of its likely effects on future events. A prospective focus supplies an expansive perspective for examining Clinton's record and will stimulate many constructive speculations among the book's readers. The authors here offer varying hypothetical speculations as well. This does not always produce consensus among them, but does add to the liveliness of the volume.

Reflecting Clinton's affinity for policy substance, this volume begins with three pieces that examine his stewardship of the institutional presidency and his impact on economic and foreign policy. Peri Arnold emphasizes Clinton's personalization of his presidential role in his conduct of the institutional presidency. Raymond Tatalovich and John Frendreis explain how Clinton's economic policies departed from those of previous Democratic presidents by deemphasizing economic redistribution. James McCormick reveals how the Clinton administration heavily weighed domestic political considerations in its conduct of foreign policy. Uneven presidential attention to foreign policy, he argues, hindered its coherence.

Clinton's great emphasis on directing and facilitating public opinion then receives attention from three quite differing viewpoints. John Harris, from the perspective of a White House reporter, explains the politicized nature of the Clinton presidency's daily operations, with particular attention to the unprecedented influence of pollster Dick Morris in 1995 and 1996. Bruce Miroff's cultural analysis reveals the convergent "postmodern" traits of Clinton the politician and American culture in explaining his successful courtship of the public. Diane Harvey systematically analyzes public opinion data to discover the sources of Clinton's public popularity and its impressive durability during the impeachment ordeal.

Clinton devoted much time and energy to electoral politics, and the next three chapters examine the future implications of his masterful conduct of that role. John Coleman explains how Clinton affected the pattern of party alignments in the electorate through his efforts as a preemptive president and his impact on economic policy. John Pitney, also reflecting the "preemptive" theme, notes the many ways that Clinton's actions toward the Republican Party resembled Richard Nixon's tactics toward Democrats. Both, he argues, had large impacts on national politics through their handling of the opposition. Nicol C. Rae notes the distance Clinton placed between himself and his party in pursuit of reelection and in the policymaking of Dick Morris–inspired triangulation.

The final chapters in the book examine Clinton's effects on important divisions within America's politics. James Guth reveals the many ways that Clinton's presidency aggravated the culture war, contributing to his ultimate impeachment. Barbara Burrell examines the important effects of both Bill and Hillary Clinton on the politics of gender, through appointments, electoral strategies, and public policy. The complex impact of race on Clinton's politics and policy receives assessment by Sharon Wright. Clinton emphasized racial reconciliation more than previous presidents, she argues, and also came to depend heavily on support among racial minorities during the impeachment trauma.

Bill Clinton's presidency, with its many distinctive qualities, promises important consequences for America's political future. Each of this volume's contributing authors presents several of these likely consequences. Added together, they make an intriguing set of possible effects. Bill Clinton wanted to make a difference as president. In many ways, including several he surely did not intend, he has.

PART
I

# The Presidency and Public Policy

The Clinton presidency initiated new directions in public policy while contending with unprecedented problems in presidential government. Peri Arnold explains how Clinton distanced his presidency from other Washington institutions, producing frustrations for Clinton that contain lessons for future presidents who choose this path of governance. Raymond Tatalovich and John Frendreis reveal how Clinton's centrist economic policies led to a new governing formula for Democratic presidents, far removed from the more redistributionist and interventionist methods of Roosevelt, Truman, and Johnson. The authors speculate on the lessons Clinton's divergence will offer future presidents. Though Clinton leaves an economic legacy of success, his foreign-policy impact is far more ambiguous. James McCormick discusses how Clinton could indulge his lack of interest in foreign policy because of the lower stakes of the post–Cold War world and discusses how domestic factors influenced his foreign-policy–making and his choice of foreign enemies. Ultimately, McCormick finds large policy and political legacies in Clinton's variable foreign-policy record.

CHAPTER 1

# BILL CLINTON AND THE INSTITUTIONALIZED PRESIDENCY

Executive Autonomy and Presidential Leadership

PERI E. ARNOLD

Bill Clinton's presidency was one of extreme paradoxes. His blunders were huge, but his ability to recover was remarkable. He was the second president in American history to be tried for impeachment. Yet during the Senate trial to remove him, nearly 70 percent of Americans approved of his job performance. By contrast, at the same time in his second term, Ronald Reagan's approval rating was only 48 percent (Cook 1999). In opinion polling, Americans reported that they did not respect President Clinton's character, yet they approved of his performance in office. Commentators attribute his political resiliency to his character. Critics accuse him of sleights-of-hand and dishonest rhetoric. Journalists read like drama critics and pop psychologists as they explain Clinton. But solving the puzzle of the Clinton presidency requires us to understand that there is more to presidential leadership than an incumbent's personal characteristics.

Presidents act within the institutional role of the presidency. That role is formed from precedents and public expectations about the office, its authority, its symbols, and its organizational system (Burke 1992; Arnold 1993). Describing the institution's effect on the behavior of incumbents, Hugh Heclo wrote: "In terms of its *deep structure* . . . the office is largely a given." It is the "exposed ganglion of government where immense lines of force come together. . . . The total effect is to program the modern president" (Heclo 1999, 24–25). Thus, on the one hand, an incumbent's personal qualities, and on the other, the constraints, expectations, routines, and possibilities of the presidential office make up presidential leadership.

And it is not only the office's "structure" that is a given. The president's options are formed in a political reality, its mood, possibilities, and problems. This chapter examines President Clinton's use of the institutional presidency to address the problems of his political context. My guiding assumption is that when presidents act in ways that are consistent with expectations of the office, its authority, and consistent with precedents for its use, they have the advantage over other actors and institutions.

The presidency is a complex role, and, as Richard Neustadt teaches, it "is no place for amateurs" (1990, 152). Those who enter the office face a steep learning curve to grasp their responsibilities and learn how the institution can be used to meet those responsibilities. For a young governor from Arkansas, inexperienced in Washington, this was a large challenge. As I shall show, Clinton's successes, and his abilities to overcome personal political calamities, were related to his own learning curve about the presidency's institutional resources.

After a brief introduction to the institutional presidency, I shall survey Clinton's use of it over time in several key dimensions of his responsibilities. First, I address his experience in taking control of the institutional presidency. Second, I examine his leadership in health care, welfare reform, and budget policies. Then I compare the president's performance in two successive foreign policy crises in the Balkans. Finally, I look ahead to Clinton's legacy for the way future presidents will use the office.

By way of a caveat, I do not mean to imply that personal character is irrelevant to the presidency. However, I do aim to convince the reader that to understand presidential leadership, one must conceptualize it within the institutions that form it. Only then can we meaningfully consider the role of character in leadership.

## The Presidency's Political Autonomy

Were a president's leadership dependent on a disciplined majority party in Congress and consistently high public approval ratings, Bill Clinton would have had few successes. He was often at odds with congressional Democrats when they were in the majority, his main policy initiatives were criticized widely, and his popular approval sagged, dropping to 37 percent in June 1993 (Cook 1999). After Republicans won a majority in both houses of Congress in the 1994 election, Clinton seemed marginalized; his public approval rating was 42 percent in February 1995 (Goley 1997).

Modern presidents are *not* dependent simply on their political party or high popular approval for political efficacy. The Constitution's system of checks and balances endows the presidency with some independent capacity, distinct from Congress and popular sentiment, the veto for example. However, the office's constitutional independence is generally passive and insufficient for executive leadership in the twentieth century. Consequently, presidents sought more robust autonomy during the twentieth century.

With new challenges for governance, twentieth-century presidents sought means of increased leadership effectiveness. The Executive Office of the President (EOP) was one consequence of that impulse (Arnold 1998, 81–117). Sidney Milkis observed that the presidency has been "emancipated" from domination by political parties and Congress through "the transformation of the executive office from an institution of modest size and authority into a formidable institution invested with formal and informal powers" (1993, 12). The White House and EOP staffs constitute a kind of presidential government in themselves (Greenstein 1988). Within the institutional presidency the incumbent gains political and policy advice, personnel services, communication staff and facilities, and a travel organization to whisk the president, staff, and the attentive press anywhere on short notice (Hart 1995).

The presidency's autonomy is a function of more than staff organization. The presidency has disconnected from the other institutions that were once binding on it—parties, Congress, and stable alignments of interest groups. American politics is more fluid; parties are weaker, interest groups are more numerous and nimble in forming tactical alliances, the media focus intensely for short periods on ephemeral issues, and political life is awash in money (Kernell 1993; McWilliams 1997).

Modern presidents built autonomous resources of organization and authority to circumvent the weaknesses of parties and partisan coalitions. Among these resources is the presidency's symbolic status in American political culture, making it an unparalleled platform from which to appeal for support (Hargrove 1998). Theodore Lowi wrote: "The decline of institutionalized restraints and of clear legislative rules [regarding the presidency] has not been compensated for by any strengthening of informal restraints" (1985, 157). The consequence of all this is a presidency that responds to high public expectations through an autonomous organizational apparatus and generates support by stimulating public approval.

## Bill Clinton Meets the Institutional Presidency

A president joins personal characteristics to the office's structure. This marriage is made in the transition between the election and inauguration. In that period a president-elect chooses staff and high officials and sets priorities. An effective transition should align an incumbent with the presidency's "deep structure." How effective was Clinton's transition?

### Clinton's Transition to the Presidency

James Pfiffner observed that Clinton's transition "could not be characterized as well planned, and he did not hit the ground running" (1996, 148). The pace of nominations and appointments gives a hint about the progress of a transition effort. Comparing the dates of public announcement for four senior roles in the Clinton, Bush, and Reagan administrations, one sees that Clinton's dates are generally similar to Reagan's, whose transition also represented party turnover. However, Clinton's chief of staff appointment stands out as an exception to the pattern.

Clinton selected his White House chief of staff, Thomas McLarty, a month later than his predecessors had chosen their chiefs of staff, announcing McLarty and his cabinet between December 10 and December 24, 1992. Clinton's senior White House staff appointments, beyond McClarty, were not chosen until just before the inauguration (Pfiffner 1996, 148). Even communications director (George Stephanopoulos) and press secretary (Dee Dee Myers), those responsible for portraying Clinton to the world, were not designated until January 14, 1993. Months past the inauguration, Clinton's White House organization still was vague, his staff operations uncoordinated, and access to the president unmediated by a strong chief of staff (Putzel 1993).

Why did Clinton announce his cabinet appointments before he declared his White House staff? Did he intend to make his administration cabinet-centered rather than White House–focused? In fact, the White House would be Clinton's major forum for advising and policy development. In the transition,

Table 1
Announcement Dates for Selected Senior Appointments in Transitions, by Administration

|         | State         | Treasury      | Chief of Staff | Budget        |
|---------|---------------|---------------|----------------|---------------|
| Clinton | Dec. 22, 1992 | Dec. 10, 1992 | Dec. 12, 1992  | Dec. 10, 1992 |
| Bush    | Nov. 16, 1988 | Nov. 16, 1988 | Nov. 16, 1988  | Nov. 16, 1988 |
| Reagan  | Dec. 16, 1980 | Dec. 11, 1980 | Nov. 14, 1980  | Dec. 11, 1980 |

Clinton paid more attention to representing his approach to government publicly than to the task of entering the institutional presidency. His cabinet appointments exhibited his commitment to diversity; four women, three African Americans, and one Hispanic were among the nominees. While choosing cabinet nominees, Clinton put off organizing White House operations. Remaining in Little Rock throughout the transition, he had a political rationale for staying physically and psychologically apart from Washington. In a time of popular hostility to government, Clinton had won with only 43 percent of the popular vote—while Ross Perot, running against government as usual, managed to gain 18.9 percent of the vote. What incentive did the president-elect have for identifying closely with Washington?

There is the sense of a political campaign by other means in Clinton's transition. His single-mindedness about his campaign pledge to reduce the White House staff by 25 percent indicates the priority of his symbolic aims entering office. Instead of ensuring the staff's capacity to serve his aims, Clinton promised to reduce government's purported excesses. In his third week in office he announced a reduction of 350 mostly lower level positions among the White House and Executive Office staff (Solomon 1993, 19). John Hart observed that Clinton was not responding to any political or functional requirement for this reduction beyond "his own desire to send a symbolic message" (Hart 1995, 48).

The lack of clear policy focus was another consequence of Bill Clinton's haphazard transition. He did not use it to translate his preferences into developed proposals (Pfiffner 1996, 173). The hostile reception to Clinton's early initiative to end discrimination against gays in the military was a reflection of poor agenda setting and preparation by the White House. However, after the inauguration, Clinton was in a new and different role. Presidential status and authority would now color his proposals. Clinton the campaigner could be idiosyncratic and rhetorical, but after the inauguration his language and action would have heavy consequences.

### Loyalty Trumps Institution: The Travel Office Controversy

Bill Clinton was responsible for filling 3,466 appointive positions in government. About four hundred of these were significant positions in the White House and Executive Office of the President (Twentieth Century Fund Task Force 1996, 43). Presidents tend to look within their campaigns, and to their early supporters, for those who will serve them in the White House, and Bill Clinton's reliance on loyalty was true to form. The White House chief of staff and communication director are the two most prominent cases illustrating

Clinton's underestimation of experience and qualifications in his appointments. His first chief of staff, Arkansas utilities executive Thomas "Mack" McLarty, was an old friend but lacked Washington experience. Clinton's director of communications, George Stephanopoulos, a close adviser during the campaign, had served earlier on a congressional staff but had no media experience. Acute problems appeared quickly in White House staff organization and in media relations. Admitting his errors in appointments management, Clinton later said to reporters: "I've never operated here before, and there are some things that are very different about the way Washington works" (Putzel 1993). By late spring both these loyalists were replaced by old Washington hands; former congressman Leon Panetta moved from budget director to chief of staff, and David Gergen, an adviser from the Nixon and Reagan administrations, became communications adviser to the president.

Clinton's over-reliance on loyalty created the travel office debacle. The president's assistant for management and administration is responsible for administrative housekeeping functions in the White House and EOP units, including the White House travel office; which purchases services from airlines and charter companies for White House staff and press travel. Clinton named David Watkins, an Arkansan and a campaign official, to that position. On May 19, 1993, the White House announced the firing of the supervisor and six staff members of the White House travel office, all longtime, nonpolitical employees (Devroy and Kamen 1993). Explaining the dismissals, the White House suggested that the travel-office employees were guilty of financial mismanagement. It was also announced that a Clinton relative, Catherine Cornelius, would become the new travel-office supervisor.

A day later the travel-office story grew more complicated. The White House admitted that friends of the president had complained to Watkins that the travel office was not responsive to their interest in White House air-charter contracts (Devroy 1993). A week after this, a chagrined White House press secretary Dee Dee Myers announced that the dismissals were rescinded. Furthermore, Chief of Staff McLarty was described as investigating the situation. At Congress's request, the General Accounting Office eventually issued a report on the matter, finding David Watkins responsible for the improper firings and attributing his actions to "inexperience and ineptitude" (Marcus 1994). Watkins remained Clinton's assistant for management and administration until May 1994, when he was fired for creating another very public embarrassment by using a presidential helicopter for a personal golf outing (*Weekly Compilation* 1994, 1169).

## Learning the Possibilities of the Institutional Presidency: Health, Welfare, and the Budget

Bill Clinton's actions on health-care reform and welfare reform offer glimpses of his learning curve within the institutional presidency. In an effort at comprehensive reform of health care during 1993–1994, Clinton's initiative extended far beyond the resources available to his role. By contrast, reshaping Republican efforts at welfare reform in 1995–1996 and blunting Republican budget initiatives, Clinton discovered the presidency's autonomous political leverage.

### The Health-Reform Failure

After decades of debate about health-care policy, 1993 seemed ripe for comprehensive health-policy reform. Polling showed Americans supporting reform. In the 1992 campaign, Clinton had promised reform. Once in office, health-care reform was a major goal for 1993 (Woodward 1994, 89). Of course, the president's eventual plan failed to even gain a floor vote in either house of Congress and died in 1994.

Candidate Clinton had promised health-care coverage for all Americans without increased taxes or an expanded federal deficit. After his inauguration, President Clinton promised a health plan in a hundred days. He appointed his wife, Hillary Rodham Clinton, to chair a planning task force. Ira Magaziner, a business consultant and adviser during the campaign and transition, headed an advisory staff to the task force. The ad hoc advisory staff eventually included five hundred participants, drawn from the executive branch, congressional staffs, the research community, and the private sector. The task force worked in secrecy and was distrusted by many of the stakeholders in the health-care industry. From January into early summer (missing the hundred-day mark), this complex planning process worked to square the circle, assuring health coverage for all Americans without producing new costs or deficits. President Clinton presented the plan in a September 23, 1993, speech to a joint session of Congress. He said, "We must make this our most urgent priority, giving every American health security; health care that can never be taken away, health care that is always there" (*Weekly Compilation* 1993, 1837).

After the health-reform effort failed, commentators criticized its substance, its complexity, and Mrs. Clinton's and Magaziner's roles; however, the failure was more than a piece of bad execution by an inexperienced president (and his wife). Clinton might have pursued reform differently. Yet this case also reveals the limits of Clinton's political context and the constraints of the institutional presidency within that context. Bill Clinton entered office evoking images of Franklin Roosevelt's "hundred days, and favorably compared himself to two plurality presidents of famed achievement, Lincoln and Wilson" (Hacker 1997, 118).

However, Bill Clinton misread his political context and its prospects for innovation. His misjudgment was not simply tactical in nature, as if more consistent advocacy on his part would have brought success (Skocpol 1997, 76–83). Rather, Clinton's error was in his reading of the presidency's capacities in the context he occupied. As Jacob Hacker has observed, Clinton faced a strategic context that made it unlikely that he could effect large policy innovations. First, the Senate's Democratic majority was too small to block filibusters, and the party lost House seats in the 1992 election. Second, the budget deficit was at its apex in 1992, and government was not ripe for major, new extensions of health policy. Third, Clinton was a plurality president whose victory was more an expression of a negative vote for Bush than it was a mandate for his campaign promises (1997, 117). Entering the presidency, Clinton evoked Franklin Roosevelt as an exemplar; Roosevelt's Depression-era context was receptive to innovation, but, alas, Clinton failed to recognize how different his context was from Roosevelt's 1930s.

## Ending Welfare as We Know It

The Republican victory of 1994 changed the context in which Clinton governed. Using Clinton's health plan as the very image of domineering government, Republicans mobilized Americans against government and won control of both houses of Congress for the first time in forty-two years (Skocpol 1997). In 1995, Congress set out to shrink the national government's roles in social policy and regulation, guided by the Republican "Contract with America." The elimination of federal welfare policy was a prime Republican goal.

In the 1992 campaign Clinton had promised to "end welfare as we know it." Yet Clinton did not specify what he meant by welfare reform until late in 1994, when he offered a bare outline of a plan. Welfare payments to individuals would be limited to two years, and recipients would be required to seek work. Supporting that requirement, the reformed program would provide job training and child care. What the Republicans meant by ending welfare was harsher.

The House Republicans proposed abolishing Aid to Families with Dependent Children (AFDC) and transforming welfare into a block grant to the states, giving each state maximum freedom to construct its own program for moving people off welfare. At the same time, the Republican bill, introduced early in 1995, made no provision for adjusting the size of the block grant to accommodate changing economic conditions. The Republican bill eliminated an entitlement to welfare, and it did not require states to maintain existing payment levels to the poor. Unwed mothers under the age of eighteen were not to be eligible for welfare, and states would be prohibited from increasing payments for additional children born to women already on welfare. The bill provided no funds for job training or child care, and it rewarded states for decreasing the number of welfare recipients without discriminating between those moved to work and those simply eliminated from the welfare rolls. By getting rid of a number of federal entitlement programs for the poor, the bill envisioned saving up to $200 billion that could pay for the tax cuts promised by the Contract for America (Cammisa 1998).

Empowered by the 1994 election results, the Republicans sought comprehensive change, and Clinton had to react to their initiatives. Welfare reform gave him the opportunity to find in the presidency political leverage to blunt the Republicans' policy innovations and demonstrate that he was not irrelevant. Clinton's approach here would be called "triangulation" by political consultants and journalists. He adopted positions more moderate than those of the congressional Republicans and to the right of those of most congressional Democrats. His success at taking positions that separated him from his party is itself a manifestation of the political autonomy of the institutional presidency.

The Republican bill was an anathema to the liberal Democrats in Congress, but the president was open to some of the Republican proposals. Yet he sought a reform that would balance help for welfare recipients with work requirements and negative incentives. His problem was to determine how much of the Republican reform he could accept and how he would use his presidential capacities to affect the outcomes of this reform.

In early 1995 Clinton was elusive about welfare, appearing inconsistent. He criticized the harshness of the Republican bill, describing it in as "too tough on children and too weak on work" (*Weekly Compilation* 1995a, 403). However, he did not offer an alternative. Democrats, journalists, and the Republican opposition speculated about where Clinton stood, and he seemed to have little leverage over the process of welfare reform (Drew 1996, 89). That changed in April, with the shocking bombing of the federal building in Oklahoma City. Speaking somberly of the tragedy and deaths, Clinton's weight in the welfare policy reform equation was increased as he castigated extremism and politicians who encourage it.

The congressional Republicans were themselves conflicted over their welfare bill. The House produced a bill that turned welfare into a block grant but attached strings, reflecting the demands of the Republican social conservatives. The Senate produced a cleaner bill, but the House-Senate conference report reflected the House's priorities on out-of-wedlock births, ineligibility for legal immigrants, and inclusion of other federal programs, such as foodstamp benefits, in the block grant. Congress approved the conference report in early December 1995 and included it in a deficit reduction appropriations bill that it sent to Clinton for his signature.

How was Clinton to assert his priorities? He reached for his institutional capacities, and on December 6, 1995, he vetoed the budget reconciliation bill in which the Congress had inserted welfare reform. When Congress returned for its next session in early 1996, it passed the same welfare program as a freestanding bill, daring another veto—a challenge Clinton met. On August 22, 1996, Clinton finally signed a welfare bill that moderated provisions of the earlier bills he had vetoed. It retained the food-stamp entitlement and extended Medicaid eligibility to those leaving welfare. The president's policy experts urged a veto on the bill, but his political advisers recommended that he sign it. Clinton's decision to sign was a triangulation in which he found institutional capacities to fashion a policy outcome distinct from both Republican and liberal Democratic preferences (Cammisa, 85–90).

Clinton discovered capacities to stand against the invigorated Republican majorities of the House and Senate. First, the presidential veto allowed him to overcome the Republicans of both houses because they held under two-thirds of each. Second, the presidency gave him a podium from which to make principled and policy declarations to justify his vetoes. In fact, in the wake of the 1994 Republican congressional victory, the presidential veto became part of Clinton's governing strategy, demonstrating to the electorate that preventing unwise policy was a presidential responsibility; he could present himself as a protector of the public interest against the intemperate passions of the congressional Republicans.

*Budget Politics*

A strategy combining vetoes and public communication also served Clinton in his battle with Congress over the Fiscal Year 1996 federal budget. The budget struggle during 1995–1996 was driven by policy aims expressed in budgetary terms as well as by concerns over budget deficits themselves. The Contract for America promised balanced budgets. At the same time, the new Republican majority also sought to use the congressional budget reconciliation and appropriations processes to reconfigure policy priorities and reduce discretionary domestic spending.

Clinton entered the presidency to find a 1992 deficit of $290 billion; an even larger deficit was projected for the coming year (Clinton 1998, 373). Throughout the 1992 campaign he promised an economic stimulus package, responding to the sluggish economy at the end of the Bush presidency. What is easily uttered on the campaign hustings, however, haunts the successful candidate once in office; during early 1993 the difficulty of both achieving deficit reductions and creating an economic stimulus package became apparent (Novak 1993). As Frendreis and Tatalovich explain in the following chapter in this volume, Clinton's most influential economic advisers stressed to him the primacy of deficit reduction while recommending against a fiscal stimulus.

The legislative vehicle of Clinton's initial economic program was his 1993 Omnibus Budget Reconciliation bill. It projected savings of $490 billion over the next five years through a combination of increased taxes, budget reductions, and a more modest stimulus package than Clinton originally conceived. Under attack from Republicans for its tax increase on upper-level incomes, the bill barely passed Congress, and in the process, Clinton's stimulus package was stripped away from it (Schneider 1993).

Clinton's 1993 tax increases gave campaign fodder to Republicans in the 1994 election. The subsequent Republican takeover of Congress in 1995 set the scene for a struggle over the scale and purposes of federal spending, and the FY 1996 budget was the new majority's first opportunity to shape a budget. The Republicans targeted Medicare and Medicaid for substantial reductions in projected expenditures, $270 billion for the former and $182 billion for the latter over five years. As well, they aimed to either radically reduce or end appropriations for a number of domestic programs (Fraley and Rubin 1995). The proposed cuts gave President Clinton a political opportunity, and he threatened to use his veto power against bills containing what he characterized as extreme budget cuts. In a November 1, 1995, meeting with the Republican congressional leaders on budget issues, Clinton said: " If you want somebody to sign your budget you're going to have to elect someone else . . . because I'm not going to do it" (Woodward 1996, 317).

On October 1, 1995, working under a continuing resolution that extended government spending after the beginning of the new fiscal year, Clinton and the Republicans negotiated without agreement; and the continuing resolution ran out. Renewing it, the Republicans attempted to trump Clinton by incorporating in the resolution many of their spending reductions. Surprising many observers, and the Republicans especially, Clinton vetoed the continuing resolution, and on November 14 a partial shutdown of government began that lasted six days.

Forcing the Republicans into a clean continuing resolution to reopen government, Clinton again confronted them over their budget package when it passed through both houses, vetoing it on December 6. The next day Clinton issued his own seven-year plan for balancing the budget. It seemed that Clinton had submitted to the Republican timetable; however, the Republicans were outraged because Clinton's budget plan contained far fewer reductions in domestic social spending and made more optimistic assumptions for growth and future government revenue than did the Republican plan. Again, Clinton seemed to be outwitting the Republicans by agreeing with them (Rubin 1995).

In mid-December, Clinton forced the Republicans to a deadlock and another shutdown of government. Throughout this period the public blamed Republicans for government's inability to perform its budget tasks, and the president presented himself as a defender of responsible government and programs important to all Americans. In his December 6 veto message on the Republican budget-reconciliation bill, Clinton said that the bill "seeks to make unacceptable changes in Medicare and Medicaid, and to raise taxes on millions of working Americans. . . . I have profound differences with the extreme approach that the Republican majority has adopted" (1995c, 3762). The Republicans surrendered to President Clinton in late January 1996. Recognizing that the public was blaming them for the shutdown of government, and realizing that Clinton would not back down, the Republican's leaders began to cooperate with Clinton to pass FY 1996 appropriations. The war was over; "the GOP effectively sued for peace" (Hager 1996).

How had a president with approval ratings below 50 percent won the budget war? He used his institutional advantages to block the Republicans and to embarrass them. He stopped their legislative momentum with the veto and used the presidency's visibility and symbolic stature to justify his actions in terms of the public interest. He attacked the Republicans for seeking to harm average Americans with their budget plan, and he made them the cause of the government shutdown. And by January 1996, according to the *National Journal*'s "Opinion Outlook" of January 13, 1996, 78 percent of Americans reported that they thought the shutdown was bad. In short, while politically weakened, Clinton could find institutional resources to win the budget war, if he had the skill and will to use them. Journalist George Hager wrote: "Instead of a waffling . . . president they might have thought they could bully . . . Republicans encountered a determined chief executive who had been badly wounded by accusations that he was a spineless flip-flopper" (1995, 3503).

## The Presidency as a Protective Cloak

The scandal surrounding his relationship with Monica Lewinsky created the most extreme threat Bill Clinton faced in his presidency. That situation, compounded with Paula Jones's civil suit, led to Clinton's impeachment in December 1998 and his Senate trial in early 1999. One would expect these events to have greatly burdened Clinton's ability to lead; remarkably, however, he was able to overshadow those proceedings with his own presidential activity. Over the course of the impeachment and trial, his public approval ratings rose to the highest levels of his presidency. Puzzling over this phenomenon, the journalist Jacob Weisberg observed that what historians of the future "will have to ponder is not how [the impeachment and trial] shook the country, but why it didn't" (1999, 30). Immediately after the House impeachment vote, Clinton prepared a strategy for countering the Senate trial by busily governing within the presidency. As James Bennet wrote in the *New York Times* on December 20, 1998: "The White House is planning . . . aggressive defense . . . before the Senate . . . alongside a blaze of campaign-style events early next year to promote [Clinton's] policies" (A31).

Clinton's public response to the impeachment drama was to conduct a presidency of high visibility and grand gestures. As the House managers argued the case for Clinton's removal from office, Clinton acted out the lofty role of the presidency, welcoming Pope John Paul II to St. Louis. The Senate trial was about tawdry affairs, but Clinton's public actions in St. Louis reinforced the grandeur and appropriateness of the presidency. With insight into the presidency's symbolic power, a journalist observed that while the trial was about the cover-up of Clinton's affair, "the President demonstrated again . . . his most potent cover-up is the political one he had conducted, all year, in plain sight" (Bennet 1999, A1).

Clinton turned the struggle into a question of whether a president who was performing well should be removed for actions unconnected to his official duties. His ability to dominate public attention was not merely a trick of his personal skills or of his wiliness. He directed attention, rather, through his understanding of the meaning of the institution of the presidency in American political culture. Clinton's political enemies may have underestimated his political wiliness, but they also underestimated the institutional presidency as a source of his power and stature. Despite our checked and balanced constitutional regime, the presidency is the natural point of public focus for Americans.

The anthropologist Clifford Geertz wrote that at "the political center of any complexly organized society there is both a governing elite and a set of symbolic forms... that mark the center as center and give what goes on there its aura of being not merely important but in some odd fashion connected with the way the world is built" (1983, 124). Bill Clinton's use of his office during the Lewinsky affair was a reminder that he occupied and articulated this society's central political role. Implying the pettiness of his enemies, Clinton addressed important problems, spoke to values we share, and represented the nation in reaching out to the world. Clinton's use of the presidency during the impeachment and trial might provide no better illustration of Geertz's conclusion: "The extraordinary has not gone out of modern politics, however much the banal may have entered; power not only still intoxicates, it still exalts" (143).

## Clinton, the Foreign Policy Presidency, and the Balkans

The president's foreign policy role is institutionalized in several respects. An organizational apparatus supports it, and it is formalized also in responsibilities distributed among several cabinet departments, which the president must coordinate in light of a new administration's goals and personalities. Not least, the presidency's foreign policy role is also structural in the sense that at any given time there are policy precedents and, even more broadly, presumed outlooks—doctrines—that make up the compass for an incumbent's foreign policy decisions (Burke and Greenstein 1991, 2–25; Walcott and Hult 1995, 159–81).

Bill Clinton entered the presidency at a time when the Cold War alignment of forces that guided U.S. foreign policy for fifty years no longer obtained. It was an office with few relevant precedents to guide decision-making in a world that was loosed from the dangers of the Cold War but also confused by the demise of the Cold War's bipolar symmetry. Nothing about Clinton's own background prepared him for his foreign policy role, yet foreign policy issues were prominent in his campaign. He criticized Bush for inattention to human rights issues in China, Bosnia, and Haiti and promised to address in the economic dimension of international issues.

Once in office, President Clinton seemed indecisive in foreign policy. His national security team, Secretary of State Warren Christopher and national security adviser Anthony Lake, provided guidance insufficient to make up for his own inexperience. Particularly embarrassing was Clinton's continued reversal in action of his campaign charges against Bush. In the case of China, Clinton seemed committed to trade over human rights. And he, like Bush, quickly realized he could not tolerate high levels of Haitian refugee flows into the United States. Finally, regarding the ongoing tragedy of ethnic cleansing in Bosnia, Clinton seemed to dither.

*Bosnia*

Instead of decisive action in Bosnia as Clinton had promised, within several months of taking office Secretary of State Christopher rejected the possibility of the United States stopping ethnic killing. He said: "The United States simply doesn't have the means to make people in that region . . . like each other" (Friedman 1995, A5).

Events in Somalia reinforced the Clinton administration's sense of danger in foreign adventures. On October 3, 1993, serving as part of a United Nations force in Somalia, eighteen U.S. Army Rangers were killed, and the body of one was filmed dragged through the streets of Mogadishu. Consequently, Clinton was all the less eager to commit U.S. forces into Bosnia, and the administration conducted recurring consultations with European allies over the Bosnia crisis, to no resolution. The distance between President Clinton's rhetoric about human rights in Bosnia and events on the ground came to a head in July 1995, when Serbs slaughtered Bosnian Muslims sheltered in what were the United Nations' "safe areas." Increasingly, critics pointed to the president's inconsistency. Finally, in August 1995, the administration and the North Atlantic Treaty Organization (NATO) allies agreed on limited bombing of Bosnian Serb forces.

The NATO bombing, along with a Croatian offensive against the Bosnian Serbs, created conditions for peace talks (Judah 1997, 298–304). In the subsequent Dayton talks agreement was reached for a tri-ethnic Bosnian federation. However, the accord could not erase the inconsistencies in Clinton's foreign policy. As one critic wrote of Clinton's first term foreign policy: "The Clinton team failed to set forth a post–Cold War vision for America's role in the new global order" (Henriksen 1996, 38).

*Kosovo*

A comparison of the Kosovo and Bosnia cases suggests that Clinton took on Kosovo in a more orderly way, relying more clearly on the expectations and resources of the institutional presidency. Responding to Kosovo as the crisis emerged, Clinton articulated a U.S. national interest in the matter. In this case Clinton also had precedent to follow; in December 1992 President Bush had threatened intervention should the government of Yugoslavian President Milosevic act against ethnic Albanians in Yugoslavia's Kosovo province (Kitfield 1999).

In early 1998 Serbian military and police used indiscriminate force to battle the ethnic Albanian Kosovo Liberation Army. As Clinton coped with the Lewinsky scandal, the expansion of the special prosecutor's inquiry to cover the Lewinsky case, and the impending impeachment crisis, he also negotiated consensus among NATO members about Kosovo. As the Lewinsky matter threatened his presidency, Clinton reminded the public that as president he was responsible for peace and security.

In October 1998 the Clinton administration planned an intensifying bombing campaign against the Serbs, should President Milosevic continue violence in Kosovo (Sciolino and Bronner 1999). Later the administration and NATO conducted negotiations with an alternately cooperative and belligerent Milosevic. In mid-January 1999, the Senate began the trial on the impeachment charge. Simultaneously, Clinton sharpened the threat to Milosevic, whose forces violated a ceasefire to which he had agreed (Priest and Trueheart 1999). During January and February of 1999, Secretary of State Madeleine Albright coordinated NATO's policy on Kosovo (Cohn 1999).

On January 29, 1999, the day after the Senate defeated the impeachment charges, Clinton announced a NATO plan for Kosovo. In his January 29 radio talk, he repeated President Bush's rationale that violence in Kosovo could spill over to include Albania and Macedonia and then Greece and Turkey. He added a second reason for action: the United States should prevent humanitarian crises where that is possible. He said, "Our experience in . . . Bosnia . . . teaches us a sobering lesson. Where you have ethnic hatreds, where you know they can get out of hand and destabilize millions of millions of other people . . . if you don't oppose the violence, it just gets worse and worse" (Lippman 1999, A27).

The Serbs' eventual rejection of the NATO peace initiative triggered the air war against Yugoslavia, with American forces carrying out the bulk of the action. The campaign lasted over two months, during which time the Serbs conducted a brutal ethnic cleansing of Kosovo. When Milosevic finally submitted, NATO forces entered Kosovo along with returning ethnic Albanians.

President Clinton's policies in both Bosnia and Kosovo were successful in that in each situation they ended ethnic slaughter and resulted in the beginning of stabilization efforts. Yet the cases differed in important ways. Clinton developed a response to the Kosovo crisis as it unfolded, rather than playing catch-up as he had in Bosnia. The Bosnia policy took several years to formulate, although Clinton had made campaign promises to intervene. He learned from his hesitancy in Bosnia and felt that further delay would make the situation worse. He also took guidance from his predecessor's commitment to Kosovo. While his advisers were divided in this case as well, his secretary of state, now Albright rather than Christopher, was an interventionist. Finally, Kosovo unfolded during the year of the Lewinsky situation. Clinton must have been distracted, but the most effective way he could respond to scandal-related attacks on himself was to seek the shelter of the presidency's gravity and responsibilities.

This chapter has argued that Bill Clinton's successes in office were directly related to his ability to use the presidency's institutional advantages and that his stumbles in office were frequently related to his misunderstandings of the office's limitations. Following Hugh Heclo's image of the presidency's "deep structure," we can say that Clinton's successes and failures in using his role exemplify the institution's tendency to shape the behavior of incumbents; his leadership was most effective when he acted harmoniously with the presidency's advantages. Now, we may ask, what will be the influence of his use of the office on the future presidency?

## Clinton's Legacy and the Institutional Presidency

Bill Clinton's legacy is constituted by his embarrassments and stumbles as well as by his successes and innovations. His early gaffes in office may forewarn his immediate successors of the transition's importance, and his political and policy successes will direct their attentions to the association between the office as pulpit for rhetorical leadership and its political autonomy within the American system. And not least, Clinton's legacy in the presidency will include the consequences of his search for immunity from legal investigation and the courts.

There is an element of speculation in considering Clinton's legacy, but this is not mere guesswork. We know that a successor in office is going to be affected by routines and expectations that accumulate and constitute the institution. Our job of informed speculation is to identify what of Clinton's use of the presidency will affect his successors' uses of the office, in the near term as well as at a greater distance in time.

*Be Prepared to "Hit the Ground Running"*

Bill Clinton's transition into the presidency should become an object lesson for his successor. The consequences of Clinton's failure to quickly build an effective team in the White House underline the importance of the transition for the president-elect. It is likely that his successors will use Clinton's experience to see the utility of calling on the experience of Washington insiders. The conditions in American politics that seem to favor "outsiders" for presidential nominations and election increase the importance of future presidents learning from the Clinton legacy the significance of Washington political experience as a job qualification.

However, if past experience is a guide, the power of this lesson will be strongest in the short run and will diminish over time. Transition planning is not routinized in the modern presidency; each new president approaches the transition task differently, guided by little in the way of institutional memory, and the experiences most likely to affect the president-elect's choices are those that are closest in time. Rough start-up experiences are likely to alert a successor administration to the value of a well-orchestrated turnover of office. However, over time, the attraction of personal loyalties in assembling presidential staffs is likely to outweigh concerns for the importance of transitions.

*Presidential Leadership Is Communicative*

In his use of the presidency as a "bully pulpit," Clinton was responding to Ronald Reagan's lesson that, independently of other institutions, the president can generate political and policy support through rhetoric and gesture. Without his ability to articulate a distinctive voice within the cacophony of national politics, Bill Clinton could never have successfully triangulated between the congressional Republican majority and the congressional liberal Democrats. Both Reagan and Clinton thrived on the basis of their sense of the institution as a communicative role. Highlighting that lesson through negative example is George Bush, the one-term president separating Reagan and Clinton: inarticulate about growing economic problems and seemingly inattentive to them, Bush saw his political fortunes sink.

The pattern of failed presidential nominees in recent elections further reinforces the importance of presidential communication. For instance, Michael Dukakis seemed stiff and unsympathetic in 1988, and Bush was elected. In 1992 George Bush could not, as he admitted, articulate "the vision thing," and he lost the election. In 1996 a deeply inexpressive Bob Dole seemed incapable of communicating why he was seeking the presidency, and

Clinton was reelected. Presidents long after Clinton are likely to read these lessons as meaning that their presidencies must be actively communicative. One consequence of this legacy will probably be the continuing expansion of the White House's public liaison and communication staffs.

## How Big a Bite of the Policy Apple Does a Context Allow?

The stalemates that affect American politics currently will be with us for the foreseeable future. We are a society of many focused interests with large amounts of money and effective means for shaping public opinion and influencing politicians. As President Clinton demonstrated in his failed effort at health-care reform, large-scale policy change is very difficult in any sector containing diverse, powerful interests as stakeholders. And as he learned in welfare reform, it will be easier for presidents to introduce incremental changes and to use their positional advantages for shaping initiatives that begin elsewhere. Clinton's immediate successor is likely to understand the presidency as a place for incremental policy initiatives rather than as a leverage point for comprehensive change.

Furthermore, Clinton's failure at health-care reform reinforces the importance of political context in defining the possibilities of a president's agenda. Bill Clinton took his election as a mandate for comprehensive policy reform in health care. Yet 1993 was not a Rooseveltian moment, so to speak. Successors in office are likely to take this example as instructive of the limits of one's political situation.

## A Politics of Budget Surplus

President Clinton entered office at a time of huge budget deficits. With a year left in his presidency, the Congressional Budget Office projected an accumulating budget surplus of $861 billion over the next ten years, assuming that future budgets remain within the established spending caps (Parks 2000, 231). Albeit, those spending caps were already being violated by the president and Congress in creating the fiscal year 2000 budget.

Overcoming the budget deficit was one of those issues that President Clinton made his own through triangulation as well as through his budget actions. He raised taxes and blunted the Republican drive to cut the budget. He protected his spending priorities, and, in the face of a looming budgetary surplus, he introduced the link between that surplus and funding future shortfalls in middle-class entitlement programs. While these entail policy and economic matters, not the institution of the presidency per se, it is useful to think of budget politics as having a structural dimension.

Budget deficits and surpluses structure radically different policy contexts. Deficits work against new government initiatives and impose tight strictures on government; surpluses, on the other hand, allow questions of what priorities most demand new spending, given new resources. To have shaped the structure in which future presidents will engage in budget decisions and budget politics will be part of Clinton's legacy. His stress on funding entitlements with budget surpluses represented a first move on his part to set the framework within which a successor will make budget decisions. And his veto of large, Republican-sponsored tax reductions impressed his priorities onto the continuing debate about the uses of the projected surplus.

A last question about Clinton's budget legacy is, will he be satisfied to have as his legacy that he ended the deficit and saved Social Security and Medicare? Or, before leaving the presidency will he have attempted to impose some priorities for domestic policy, such as education and health care, onto the future use of whatever budget surplus actually materializes?

## A Clinton Doctrine?

Scorched by Somalia, Bill Clinton stumbled in slow motion into his Bosnia policy. Clinton's strategy on Kosovo was a steadier march, with decisions reflecting lessons learned in Bosnia, attention to Bush's verbal commitment regarding Kosovo, and a sense that intervening in humanitarian tragedies, when possible, is a U.S. national interest.

Clinton's interventionist policies in Bosnia and Kosovo were successful in ending ethnic slaughter and bringing some stability, with relatively light costs for the United States. It is likely that a succeeding president will find a presumption in American foreign policy that reflects Clinton's humanitarian rationale for intervention. Whether or not Clinton finally articulates a "Clinton doctrine," his actions in office may serve as a justification for an implied new doctrine in U.S. foreign policy. Of course, the limits to an enlarged U.S. understanding of a national interest in ending humanitarian catastrophes are not yet clear. The eventual outcomes of the conflicts in Bosnia and Kosovo will go far towards defining those boundaries.

## Eroding Presidential Immunity

Inescapably, Clinton's legacy also includes the consequences of his use of the institutional presidency as a bulwark against legal threats. The institutionalized presidency has a presumptive dimension; a penumbra of untested assumptions and claims of presidential authority and privileges surround it (Fisher 1997; Pious 1996). The foundation of these presumptive presidential qualities rests in the shifting ground of institutional checks and balances within the American constitutional system, which itself often works best when the authorities and privileges of the separate institutions are respected rather than challenged, assumed rather than defined crisply.

Simultaneously, President Clinton was the target of an independent counsel's investigation and a federal civil suit charging him with sexual harassment in the workplace, *Jones v. Clinton*. Both matters focused on events that were alleged to have occurred while Clinton was governor; however, both increasingly probed Clinton's behavior within the presidency. Thus the ongoing investigation by the special prosecutor, Kenneth Starr, as well as the civil suit, touched on Clinton's activities in the presidency and his communications with members of his staff, in particular the White House counsel.

President Clinton's defense against the special prosecutor and the Jones lawsuit tested a set of presumptions of immunities surrounding the presidency. Can a president be subject to civil law suit for actions outside his official duties? Is communication between the White House consul and president covered by the lawyer-client relationship if not by a broader protection of privilege for communication between a president and presidential staff? Can members of the president's protection service, the U.S. Secret Service, be compelled to testify in a legal proceeding about presidential communications and activities? Bill Clinton claimed each of these presumptive immunities against the Starr investigation and the Jones case, losing each claim in a court test.

The presumption of immunities itself is protective and creates an aura that encourages a degree of comity between the presidency and other institutions. Therefore, Clinton's failed claims of presumed presidential immunities weaken the presidency. The resulting decrease of presumptive privilege leaves Clinton's successors more vulnerable to civil suits and to investigations that seek information about the incumbent's confidential White House relationships.

## Conclusion: Clinton's Overall Legacy

Clinton's most important legacy might be his example of governing through the institutional presidency in a context of multiple political disadvantages, a preemptive condition, in Stephen Skowronek's terms. Skowronek observes that contemporary American presidential politics may be in "a state of perpetual preemption" in which presidents face resilient conditions that are oppositional to their own partisan loyalties and policy goals. The indicators of that political condition, he notes, "have been the cultivation [by presidents] of independent political identities, the exploitation of ad hoc coalitions, and the high risk of suffering the ultimate disgrace of impeachment" (Skowronek 1993, 444).

Clinton entered the presidency in a time of declined trust in government, little policy consensus, massive budget deficits, intense interest group activity, weakened parties, and divided government (Shogan 1998, 289–319). Yet he entered office promising to emulate presidents of achievement. Clinton's early stumbles in office signaled his misreading political context and his misuse of the advantages of the institutional presidency. As this chapter reveals, over time he learned that his political context had few openings for grand innovations and that his party was an insufficient base for presidential governance. The shock of the 1994 Republican victory left him politically vulnerable—without majority party support, without substantial public approval, without a policy agenda, and without a clear identity. Of course he was further burdened by his own personal misdeeds, reputed as well as real.

In the face of his disadvantages, Clinton learned that his office itself contained the means for establishing presidential governance in a context of oppositional politics. His degree of success in this endeavor, despite the overlay of personal scandal that plagued him, is a legacy to future presidents as they seek an approach to governance in a preemptive era.

CHAPTER 2

# CLINTON, CLASS, AND ECONOMIC POLICY

RAYMOND TATALOVICH AND
JOHN FRENDREIS

As the United States begins the twenty-first century, the American economy seemingly stands supreme not only domestically but also within the global economy. Was this achievement good policy by William Jefferson Clinton, and what does it portend for the future of class politics in America? Our thesis is that class politics of the industrialized era will give way to a postmaterialist age. To be sure, pockets of poverty will remain, just as a wage gap has widened the income disparity between the rich and the poor, but it seems unlikely that the Democratic presidential contender any more than his Republican counterpart will raise the level of class rhetoric in any campaign in the near term. Many observers point to the Truman-Dewey contest of 1948 as the last class based election in America, and the experience under "New Democrat" Clinton suggests that the old class politics of Roosevelt's New Deal, Truman's Fair Deal, and Johnson's Great Society may not survive Clinton into the twenty-first century.

Any judgment about Clinton's place in history must assess his effect on the presidency and his policy legacy. Clinton understood why George Bush lost the 1992 election and how prosperity could salvage his own presidency, and, while he made pledges (favoring a middle-class tax cut) and offered hints (having protectionist sympathies) that were later abandoned, he did not articulate a coherent vision of economic policy, like Reagan did in 1980. The record suggests that the bounty of the 1990s resulted less from Clinton's personal stewardship of prosperity than from his willingness to follow the learned advice of others and, more fundamentally, from economic forces beyond his control. While being an opportunist is not exactly a character virtue, in economic policy it served the country well.

What about the future? Under President Reagan, it was argued that any welfare programs that survived his domestic cuts were so legitimized that they would never be threatened again, and the same logic may apply to the policy legacy of Clinton. More important than continued economic growth and budget surpluses may be the long-term influence of Clinton's "post-Keynesian" macroeconomics (free trade, global capitalism, and competitive markets) on the Democratic Party. No less important is the likelihood that redistributive politics have yielded to a post-materialist era that will accept income inequalities without finding dire implications for class conflict.

## The Economic Mandate

According to one observer, "The story of the 1992 campaign is fundamentally shaped by the failure of Bush's campaign to address voter concerns about the economy" (Arterton 1993, 86–87). Indeed polling data indicated to Gerald Pomper (1993, 145–46) that "instead of self-interest, the key element of the economic issue was a concern for the national welfare." Bush was judged to be overly attentive to foreign affairs and disconnected from the economic realities of everyday life, a theme repeatedly hammered on by the Clinton campaign. As a friendly reminder, George Stephanopoulos posted a now-famous sign in Clinton's campaign headquarters proclaiming, "It's the economy, stupid."

President Clinton did not inherit a robust economy from President Bush, though the seeds of recovery were there. Two problems for Bush were that the 1990–1991 recession was wide but shallow in effect and, more important, that the macroeconomic indicators did not point to a decisive turning point in the business cycle. In fact, the National Bureau of Economic Research, which tracks the peaks and troughs of business cycles, was uncertain until December 22, 1992—more than a month *after* election day—that the recession had bottomed out in March 1991 (Frendreis and Tatalovich 1994, 192).

However, unemployment averaged 7.5 percent in 1992 and remained above 6 percent through 1993 and 1994. It was this statistic that influenced the Clinton campaign to promise an economic stimulus package immediately after he would be inaugurated. Yet Clinton's economic stewardship did not win accolades from the American people as compared to his second term. During

1993–1996 Clinton often got less than majority approval, and even fewer people credited his handling of the economy (Daynes, Tatalovich, and Soden 1998, 132); since then Clinton's popularity rarely has fallen below 50 percent. It took a while for the economy to improve and even longer for the credit to President Clinton to accrue. The continued sluggishness of the economy during 1993–1995 helped the GOP capture both houses of Congress. At that time 54 percent of Americans told *New York Times*/CBS News pollsters that the "economy, jobs, or inflation" was the most important problem facing the country. Moreover, its tracking polls indicated that the last time so many people felt that way was in 1980 (59 percent), dropping to 41 percent with Reagan's reelection and further to 17 percent in 1988 with Bush's election. In contrast, by the time President Clinton faced reelection in 1996, that polling statistic was 23 percent (Rosenbaum and Lohr, 1996).

When compared with those in the eleven presidential administrations since 1948, the economy during the first Clinton term was not all that remarkable (Table 2.1). The standard macroeconomic indicators are unemployment, inflation, economic growth, productivity, and the current account balance on international transactions. The composite score based on four-year averages for these five measures ranks Clinton's first term seventh, much better than Bush, Carter, Reagan-I, and even Reagan-II (who ranked twelfth, eleventh, tenth, and eighth respectively).

The political significance of any such measure, however, depends on public perceptions, and Americans generally pay much less attention to productivity and international transactions (like trade deficits) than to unemployment, inflation, and economic growth. The term *misery index* was coined by liberal economist Arthur Okun (a member of Kennedy's Council of Economic Advisers) to measure the combined impact of unemployment and inflation. By this standard, Clinton's first term was markedly better than any president's since Lyndon Johnson. To these indicators, economist Robert Barro adds interest rates and economic growth, and his new composite misery index catapults Reagan-I into first place and Reagan-II into third place, whereas Clinton respectably is ranked fifth. However Barro's calculation for 1997 and 1998 shows that Clinton placed only marginally lower than Reagan-I, leading him to speculate that Clinton is "still a contender to overtake Reagan," based on the Barro Misery Index (1999, 22).

These varied measures of economic performance show how the precise mix can affect presidential rankings. Nonetheless, Clinton's first term was superior to those of Nixon-Ford, Carter, and Bush on all three indices, and our indicators for his second term—should those patterns continue through

Table 1
Measuring Economic Performance from Truman to Clinton

|  | Presidential Economic Scorecard[a] | | | | | | Overall Misery Index[b] | Barro Misery Index[c] |
|---|---|---|---|---|---|---|---|---|
|  | U | I | EG | P | CAB | Rank | | |
| Truman 1949–1952 | 4.4% | 2.5% | 5.7% | 4.3% | +0.6 | 2.5 | 6.9 (3) | −0.8 (6) |
| Eisenhower 1953–1956 | 4.2 | 0.6 | 2.6 | 2.3 | +2.0 | 4 | 4.8 (1) | +3.1 (11) |
| Eisenhower 1957–1960 | 5.5 | 2.2 | 2.3 | 2.7 | +7.1 | 5 | 7.7 (5) | +1.9 (10) |
| Kennedy/Johnson 1961–1964 | 5.8 | 1.2 | 4.3 | 3.9 | +18.4 | 2.5 | 7.0 (4) | −2.5 (4) |
| Johnson 1965–1968 | 3.9 | 2.9 | 4.6 | 2.8 | +11.6 | 1 | 6.8 (2) | +1.3 (8) |
| Nixon 1969–1972 | 5.0 | 4.7 | 2.5 | 1.8 | −4.5 | 6 | 9.7 (7) | +1.6 (9) |
| Nixon/Ford 1973–1976 | 6.7 | 8.0 | 2.1 | 1.1 | +31.4 | 9 | 14.7 (11) | +8.0 (12) |
| Carter 1977–1980 | 6.5 | 9.8 | 3.1 | 0.3 | −29.8 | 10 | 16.3 (12) | +9.4 (13) |
| Reagan 1981–1984 | 8.6 | 6.0 | 2.4 | 1.5 | −138.1 | 11 | 14.6 (10) | −4.9 (1) |
| Reagan 1985–1988 | 6.5 | 3.3 | 3.3 | 1.3 | −554.1 | 7 | 9.8 (8) | −3.1 (3) |
| Bush 1989–1992 | 6.2 | 4.4 | 1.0 | 0.6 | −257.6 | 12 | 10.6 (9) | +0.5 (7) |
| Clinton 1993–1996 | 6.0 | 2.9 | 2.6 | 0.5 | −561.6 | 8 | 8.9 (6) | −2.4 (5) |
| Clinton 1997–1998 | 4.7 | 2.0 | 3.9 | 1.7 | −369.9 | 6 (est) | 6.7 | −4.5 |

[a]The data and overall ranking for 1949–1992 were calculated in Frendreis and Tatalovich (1994, 308–9). The data for Clinton were calculated by the authors. The five macroeconomic indicators were rank-ordered, and the overall ranking was the average, based on the five individual ranks. The codes represent these five macroeconomic indicators: U = Unemployment, or the four-year average unemployment rate; I = Inflation, or the four-year average percentage changes in Consumer Price Index over each year; EG = Economic Growth, or the four-year average percentage change in real gross national product over each year; P = Productivity, or the four-year average percentage change in productivity (real output per hour per employee) over each year; CAB = Current Account Balance, or the net surplus or deficit over four years.

[b]The Misery Index is simply the four-year average unemployment rate and the four-year average percentage changes in Consumer Price Index over each year, or U + I. The rank is listed from lowest to highest misery.

[c]The Barro Misery Index was developed by economist Robert J. Barro (1999, 22). It includes unemployment and inflation but also gross domestic product and interest rates and was calculated as follows: (1) the change in the rate of the CPI is the difference between the average for the term and the average of the last year of the previous term; (2) the change in the unemployment rate is the difference between the average value during the term and the value from the last month of the previous term; (3) the change in the interest rate is the change in the long-term government bond yield during the term; (4) the GDP growth rate is the shortfall of the rate during the term from 3.1 percent per year (the long-term average value). The change in the Barro Misery Index is the sum of these macroeconomic indicators, and the rank is listed from lowest to highest misery.

2000—would rank Clinton-II sixth, an overall better performance than any term since President Johnson in 1965–1968. The trough of the business cycle in March 1991 yielded the longest period of economic expansion since World War II.

*Economic Advisers: Staying a Pro-Business Course*

After election day, on ABC's *Nightline* president-elect Clinton said that he was "going to focus like a laser beam on the economy" (quoted in Destler 1996, 8). He proceeded to announce his economic team before his choices for national security or domestic policy. By Executive Order 12835, on February 1, 1993, President Clinton established the National Economic Council (NEC), with an eighteen-person membership chaired by the president, to "coordinate the economic policy-making process" involving domestic and international economic issues, "coordinate economic policy advice to the President," "ensure that economic policy decisions and programs are consistent with the President's stated goals, ensure that those goals are being effectively pursued," and "monitor implementation of the President's economic policy agenda" (*Weekly Compilation* 1993, 95).

A millionaire entrepreneur and solidly on the side of big business, Senator Lloyd Bentsen (D-Tx.), who chaired the Senate Finance Committee, accepted the position of secretary of treasury on condition that he be the administration's economic spokesman. Bentsen's chief competitor was Robert Rubin, Assistant to the President for Economic Policy, who had been co-chairman of Goldman Sachs, a Wall Street brokerage firm, and a Democratic fundraiser. Clinton picked Leon Panetta, former congressman (D-Calif.), to be director of the Office of Management and Budget.

As Rubin recalled his conversation with the president, Clinton told him "to replicate on the economic side what George Bush had done on the foreign-policy side" (*Economist* 1994, A28), and thus Clinton wanted the NEC to have a stature similar to that of the National Security Council. Clinton later remarked: "I think when the history of this administration is written, one of the most significant organizational changes we will have made, and one that I predict all future administrations will follow, is the creation of the National Economic Council and the development of a coordinated, disciplined national economic policy for global economy" (*Weekly Compilation* 1995, 282). Undoubtedly, with the expansion of world trade, the growing financial interdependence of nations, and the rise of multinational corporations, mechanisms for economic policymaking will have to integrate more fully the domestic and international arenas.

Clinton appointed Rubin to reassure Wall Street but he also expected that Rubin would be a masterful "honest" broker who would operate through a collegial decision-making apparatus just as he had at Goldman Sachs. However, the NEC's "process" model did not preclude Rubin from promoting his own "pro-business, pro-free trade" opinions (*Economist* 1994, A28). In short order Rubin's economic views came to be highly regarded and arguably the strongest influence on President Clinton.

No decision-maker ranked higher in expertise and stature than Chairman of the Federal Reserve Board Alan Greenspan. He was a Reagan appointee, and eventually Clinton, too, saw the wisdom of reappointing Greenspan in 1996, and again in 2000, to continue as "Fed" chairman. The 2000 decision is more prophetic because the Federal Reserve Board had announced a series of interest rate hikes over 1999 and was expected to continue tightening credit into 2000, on the basis of its inflation fears. Greenspan had a close working relationship with Clinton, but, nonetheless, Clinton "was also bowing to the reality that Mr. Greenspan has become an institution in his own right, one whose support runs so broadly and deeply in Washington and on Wall Street that the White House was under increasing pressure to make its decision known" (Stevenson 2000, A1, C8).

If Clinton was blessed by an economic mandate, a mediocre Bush record against which he would be judged, and superbly qualified and judicious economic advisers, more problematic was his leadership style. He seemed more opportunistic than principled in his policy choices, and it was not long before observers began to doubt whether Bill Clinton held any "core" beliefs, though by instinct he may have been a closet liberal. Elizabeth Drew noted that "Clinton's self-definition as 'a new kind of Democrat' was designed, among other things, to camouflage his big government tendencies, which were real enough" (1994, 60).

Clinton's latent liberalism was not manifested on the economic front, and the best policy outcomes resulted when Clinton followed the recommendations of conservative advisers like Rubin, Greenspan, Panetta, and Bentsen. It is no paradox that the one major policy initiative—health-care reform—that was beyond the reach of his economic-advisory network (Destler 1996, 23) led to disastrous political consequences (see Arnold, this volume). In critical instances Clinton even owes a political debt to congressional Republicans for derailing misguided economic policies and forcing his hand on balancing the budget. Another example, called "truly historic" by President Clinton, was the legislation that fundamentally overhauled the Glass-Steagall Act of 1933, which had prohibited banks, securities firms, and insurance companies from merging and selling those various financial services. It was backed by the Clinton administration, but more credit goes to the Republicans and notably to

Senator Phil Gramm (R-Texas), who wrote the law along with GOP cosponsors in the House.

Fred Greenstein observes that President Clinton's pragmatism "appears to come into play only after outside forces have humbled him" (1993–1994, 596), and Stanley Renshon, author of the award-winning psychobiographical study of Clinton, agrees that "there were no countervailing forces within the president's psychology, and few in his administration, for the political restraint of his ambitions. Therefore, paradoxically, the best hope for his presidency was a Republican Congress." At base, Renshon believes that "President Clinton has become a policy-moderate by political necessity, not by personal inclination" (1998, xiii).

The resignation of Treasury Secretary Lloyd Bentsen in December 1994 and Clinton's nomination of Rubin to be his successor were widely anticipated; one commentator noted that Rubin who "emerged as the most influential adviser in Mr. Clinton's economic team . . . is about to become the most visible adviser as well" (*Economist* 1994, A28). No replacement was named for Rubin at the NEC for eleven weeks, until Council of Economic Advisers (CEA) Chair Laura Tyson was appointed. "Put simply, they botched it [the transition] badly," concludes Destler (1996, 43). That Tyson would abandon the CEA as chair signifies the reduced influence and prestige of the CEA, yet Tyson could not begin to compete with Rubin who, according to commentators, "continued to dominate economic policymaking from the Treasury, along with his deputy secretary, Lawrence Summers" (*Economist* 1997, 71).

*Deficit Reduction*

At the end of 1992, Fed chair Alan Greenspan met with Clinton to explain the relationship between the federal deficit and high long-term interest rates, arguing that a credible plan to reduce future deficits would persuade Wall Street and eventually yield lower interest rates. During the 1992 presidential campaign, however, Clinton had promised to reduce the federal budget deficit and enact an economic stimulus package during his first hundred days, which would include increased spending on education and the infrastructure; and he claimed that he could achieve both goals by raising taxes on the wealthy and cutting military spending. Even so, the FY1994 budget that President Clinton submitted to Congress on April 8 projected a deficit of $262 billion for FY1994, declining to $205 billion in FY1996, but then climbing again to $241 billion for FY1998.

When the pessimistic projections of future deficits appeared, Rubin persuaded Clinton to focus on deficit reduction and defer any public investment expenditures. Rubin was the leader of a deficit-cutting "gang of four" (along with Panetta, Deputy Office of Management and Budget [OMB] Director Alice Rivlin, and Bentsen) who were opposed by Labor Secretary Robert Reich and CEA Chair Tyson. Rubin echoed the previous arguments by Greenspan, and it was Rubin's Wall Street experience that carried the day, Tyson recalls: "At that point, it was very important that he could say that based on his own [Wall Street] experience it would work" (Judis 1993, 21). Adds John Judis: "Rubin won the argument. . . .Tyson, a stalwart Keynesian, was sounding Rubin's neoclassical themes. So was Clinton" (21).

*Economic Stimulus*

The economic-stimulus package was a policy blunder, and the NEC was partly responsible because it failed "to question the need for the stimulus: with the unexpectedly strong economic surge in late 1992, [when] the economy was far less in need of a boost than it seemed during the campaign" (Destler 1996, 20). On February 19, 1993, President Clinton recommended to Congress a $30 billion stimulus package for highway construction, extended unemployment benefits, and community block grants, another $230 billion in spending and tax breaks for infrastructure improvements (*1993 Congressional Quarterly Almanac* 1994a, 7D–12D). The plan, however, was attacked not only by Republicans who called its expenditures "pork barrel" and who opposed the tax increases but also by some "deficit hawks" among the Democrats who demanded that the leadership finalize a deficit-reduction plan before considering any economic stimulus package. Clinton and the congressional leadership capitulated, and on March 18 the House voted first for the budget resolution and later for the supplemental appropriations bill. Only three Republicans voted for the stimulus package. In the Senate, Republican opposition was assisted by some southern Democrats but ultimately it was a GOP filibuster that killed this legislation. According to Sinclair "the complexity of Clinton's program put him at a disadvantage vis-à-vis the simple Republican message of deficit reduction and opposition to pork, especially with a cynical public primed to believe that most government spending is wasteful" (1996, 104).

*NAFTA and Trade Policy*

Another early misstep involved the North American Free Trade Agreement (NAFTA). President Bush had negotiated NAFTA with Canada and Mexico, but the task of getting congressional approval was left to Clinton. Though personally sympathetic to free trade (Woodward 1995, 49), Bill Clinton wanted "to support free trade, to protect . . . against charges of protectionism that have plagued Democratic candidates" yet "raise enough questions to maintain the loyalty of labor and environmental groups that generally oppose the pact" (Stokes 1993, 1161).

On NAFTA, Clinton's economic advisory system was not all that helpful. Rubin acted to facilitate Secretary Bentsen's strong advocacy of NAFTA, but the NEC "did not prevent serious adverse spillover from this division, which effectively ceded the public and congressional debate to NAFTA's adversaries for six long months" (Destler 1996, 20). Even though more Americans opposed than favored NAFTA (actually the plurality had no opinion; see Cohen 1997, 323), Clinton and his congressional allies undertook "a campaign to build public support, compromises and deals to win commitments from groups of members, and an enormous amount of one-on-one lobbying" (Sinclair 1996, 110). Congress enacted NAFTA on November 17, 1993, thanks to lopsided Republican and southern Democratic support. The majority of (northern) House and Senate Democrats voted no.

Another Republican legacy was GATT, or General Agreement on Tariffs and Trade. President Bush wanted to get congressional approval before he left office, but he failed, and thus GATT fell to Clinton's agenda. Because of anti-trade sentiments among Democrats from Frost Belt districts, the 103rd Congress did not act, and there was pressure to postpone any vote on GATT until after the 1994 midterm elections. The pact was scheduled to be considered by a rare special session of Congress after election day, but then Republicans unexpectedly won majorities in both houses of Congress. Speaker designate Gingrich was behind GATT, but key to its success was the prospective Senate majority party leader Bob Dole (R-Kans.), and contender for the GOP presidential nomination. Dole negotiated with the White House a "trigger mechanism" allowing Congress to vote to withdraw from GATT if the United States was subjected to unfair rulings by a newly created Court of International Trade. Once agreed to, both House and Senate voted for GATT by huge bipartisan majorities. That bipartisanship did not extend to "fast-track" presidential authority to negotiate trade agreements under which Congress has a deadline for considering the pact and is limited in its ability to add legislative amendments. Since Gerald Ford in 1974, all presidents have had "fast-track" authority, but it lapsed in 1994 and Congress has never reauthorized it. In June 1993 Congress did enact an extension effective through April 16, 1994.

Later in 1994 President Clinton withdrew his request for its continuation. He had made a strategic error of coupling fast-track with GATT, and now business groups and some Republicans joined in opposition fearing, as a spokesman for the U.S. Chamber of Commerce put it, that Clinton might use his authority to "legislate liberal social policies" (which seemingly would favor labor and environmentalists) into future trade deals (Stepanek 1994, A2). Seeing the threat to GATT, Clinton agreed to forgo fast-track and focus instead on GATT. But the support of organized labor was not firm, and yet another presidential attempt in 1997 ended when President Clinton asked that fast-track legislation be dropped rather than face defeat in the House. His instincts were prophetic insofar as the House of Representatives in 1998—one month before the midterm elections—did defeat fast-track, with the majority of Republicans supporting Clinton (151-71) but more Democrats opposing him (29-171).

A final trade issue harked back to the 1992 presidential campaign, when candidate Clinton persistently attacked President Bush for his China policy in the wake of the 1989 Tiananmen Square massacre of pro-democracy demonstrators. It was assumed that President Clinton would demand that China guarantee human rights before the United States would grant trade privileges. Yet it was Robert Rubin who favored decoupling the issue of human rights from trade policy with the People's Republic of China.

To grant a temporary "most favored nation" status for China, executive authorization has to be reaffirmed each year pursuant to legislation requiring human rights reports to Congress. On seven previous occasions Congress acquiesced to Clinton's decision, but the matter became further complicated by allegations that the Chinese government had funneled funds to the Clinton-Gore campaign and accusations that Chinese agents stole nuclear secrets from American research installations. Congress might not be sympathetic to his pleas should President Clinton request legislation to permanently authorize normal trade relations (NTR) with China. Ending the deadlock over China trade eluded the administration until President Clinton and President Jiang Zemin personally met in 1999 for discussions on how to gain the admission of China into the World Trade Organization (the successor organization to GATT). Once again, however, Clinton was forced into acting decisively.

What re-ignited Clinton was a five-day road trip by Chinese prime minister Zhu Rongji in April of 1999, when he warned American business leaders that their hopes to access the Chinese market could vanish until a trade deal was completed soon. According to news reports, "what really stung the White House was harsh criticism from the business community" whose executives began "a campaign of E-mails and phone calls to each other about how to make Mr. Clinton quickly finish the accord" (Sanger 1999b, A6). In November U.S. and Chinese negotiators agreed on a pact, which U.S. Trade Representative Charlene Barshefsky said had "profound and historic importance" (McCutcheon and Nitschke 1999, 2795), but organized labor and its congressional allies were opposed and the WTO's own reputation was soiled when its leadership met in Seattle in early December. The WTO conference provoked street demonstrations and violent protests and, in the end, achieved nothing. President Clinton tried to have it both ways. It was he who pushed for the WTO to meet in Seattle, yet he gave a speech critical of the WTO for its secretive procedures. Approval of permanent NTR for China finally gained approval by Congress in 2000.

### Balancing the Budget

A plan to balance the budget was another instance, like welfare reform (see Arnold, this volume), in which Clinton was forced into a political corner by congressional Republicans. One centerpiece of the 1994 GOP Contract with America was a constitutional amendment requiring a balanced federal budget. Such an amendment passed the House in 1995 by the requisite two-thirds vote but fell one vote short of that margin in the Senate (its defeat was due to the defection of Republican Senator Mark Hatfield of Oregon). Thereupon the GOP shifted tactics designed to force President Clinton to accept a balanced budget timetable.

In 1995 President Clinton sent Congress a stand-pat budget with little deficit reduction and no new programs, essentially daring the Republicans to draft their own balanced budget package. They did, proposing to balance the budget by 2002 through cuts in domestic spending coupled with tax relief. OMB Director Alice Rivlin (who succeeded Panetta after he became the White House chief of staff) argued at NEC meetings that a ten-year balanced budget was achievable without program cuts or tax hikes. Dick Morris, Clinton's political guru, backed Rivlin, but George Stephanopolous and Leon Panetta resisted. By spring President Clinton came to believe that he needed his own balanced budget plan, and in June he made a five-minute television appearance offering a plan to erase the deficit in ten years, by 2005. However his proposal was based on lower deficit projections by the OMB. "He's lowered the bar and then cleared it comfortably," said former Congressional Budget Office (CBO) director Robert D. Reischauer (*Congressional Quarterly Almanac* 1995b).

Congressional Republicans pretty much ignored Clinton and proceeded to fashion their own tax and spending plans to achieve a budget in seven years. Because most of the appropriations bills had not been approved by the start of FY1996, Congress had to approve a continuing resolution to keep the government running. But Clinton vetoed the resolution, and this impasse precipitated the first government shutdown, which lasted from November 14 to November 19. As part of a new continuing resolution that ended the shutdown, GOP leaders and Clinton seemingly agreed in principle to language that committed him to balance the federal budget in seven years based on CBO economic projections. On this happy note, the temporary spending bill reopened the government through December 15.

But optimism gave way to pessimism as GOP leaders and the White House began budget negotiations on a reconciliation bill for FY1996. Talks broke down amid accusations of bad faith, because Clinton was unwilling to submit his plan based on the seven-year timetable and CBO economic projects as preconditions for budget negotiations. The reconciliation bill that Congress enacted was vetoed on December 6, and the next day President Clinton presented his third budget plan—this time proposing a balanced budget in seven years based, however, on the more optimistic economic assumptions of the OMB. The CBO "calculated that Clinton's plan was $115 billion to $175 billion short of a balanced budget" that "seemed to make Republicans angrier. They saw it as little more than political posturing and denounced Clinton for using economic projections they said were phony" (*Congressional Quarterly Almanac* 1995a). While House-GOP negotiations remained stalled, in mid-December Clinton revised yet again his offer, but GOP rank-and-file believed Clinton untrustworthy and held fast to their bottom line, that a balanced budget be achieved by 2002 based on CBO economic projections. The collapse in talks led to a second government shutdown on December 16.

President Clinton emerged from the budget battles in better shape politically than the GOP (see Arnold, this volume), and by the end of January 1996, when Congress reconvened, the GOP was thoroughly frustrated. "We do not believe it's possible now to get a budget agreement," said Speaker Gingrich. "I don't expect us to get a seven-year balanced budget with President Clinton in office" (*Congressional Quarterly Almanac* 1995a). Even before the FY1996 budget was finalized in April 1996, however, one month earlier President Clinton had shifted gears when he submitted his FY1997 budget to Congress. It was "proof of how far the Republicans had moved Clinton and the budget debate since sweeping into control of Congress in 1995" because now President Clinton proposed to balance the budget by 2002 on the basis of the more pessimistic CBO forecasts, a long-standing Republican demand (*Congressional Quarterly*

*Almanac* 1997, 2–4). The process was messy, and the Republicans lost the "PR" battle, since they were blamed for the government shutdowns, but ultimately they won the war over a balanced budget.

## Short-Term Impact: "New Vision" Economics?

It was not until 1997 that the Clinton CEA outlined its economic philosophy. Says James K. Galbraith, "The 1997 report joins the 1962 report of the Kennedy council and the 1982 report of the Reagan council in the scale of its ambition. After three years of tacking one way and another, the Clinton council has here made its most serious attempt to define how it thinks and what it stands for" (1997, 45). Written by CEA Chair Joseph Stiglitz, who succeeded Tyson once she went to the NEC, his views were caricatured by Galbraith (the son of liberal economist John Kenneth Galbraith) as "New Vision Economics" with a "profound anti-Keynesianism," based on how Stiglitz arbitrarily divides economics into two camps. Stiglitz later elaborated that the CEA tried "to articulate a new economic agenda for the Democrats that is somewhere between the New Deal and Reaganomics. On the one hand, we must acknowledge that the world has changed. The kind of strong government intervention associated with the New Deal is clearly inappropriate now. On the other hand, Reaganomics led to its own problems—such as deregulation. To a large extent, the banking crisis of 1989 was related to regulatory lapse. Maybe more important, the implicit assumptions of trickle-down economics and social Darwinism clearly have problems for the long-run strength of the country. Arriving at an economic philosophy that lies between these two represents an achievement in the sense that it lays a new course, a direction for our time" (1997, 22).

For liberal critics, the post-Keynesian posture of Clinton's economic advisers was not much better than what the CEA touted during the Reagan-Bush era in terms of deliberate counter-cyclical policy. When Berkeley economist Janet Yellen was named to be CEA chair in 1997, Galbraith called her "the first macroeconomist and the first even approximate Keynesian in nearly twenty years to chair the Council of Economic Advisers" (Galbraith, 1998, 87), yet Yellen did not deviate much from Clintonomics. But was there a "Clintonomics" akin to the deliberate tax cutting policies of Reaganomics? No!

President Clinton deserves political credit for *not* acting in ways that could have retarded economic expansion at a time when the American economy was primed for a period of growth without inflation. According to Robert Kuttner, "economic events handed Clinton a rare opportunity. But not fumbling an opportunity is harder than it looks" (1999, 22). Liberal critic Galbraith would agree that, even though the White House took credit for economic growth and declining unemployment, more realistically the Clinton "administration benefited from an ordinary cyclical rebound not of its own making, abetted by low interest rates between 1991 and 1993" (1997, 45). Economic fundamentals may have been largely responsible for the 1990s expansion—surely more so than deliberate counter-cyclical policy—but the invisible marketplace is not the entire answer. Even if Clinton cannot take much credit for *positive* leadership, Fed Chair Alan Greenspan can. The *New York Times* editorialized that "most economists believe Alan Greenspan is more responsible for the economy's spectacular performance than Congress, Presidents Bush and Clinton or any other identifiable factor" (2000, A24).

The only apt comparison with Greenspan is his predecessor, Paul Volcker, who held fast to a tight monetary policy during the 1981–1982 recession, allowed unemployment to rise sharply, but ultimately broke the back of inflationary pressures. Greenspan achieved the reverse. "To me, Greenspan's greatest contribution has been his willingness to let the unemployment rate ratchet downwards without quickly jumping on the brakes," observes C. Fred Bergsten, director of the Institute for International Research. "It's a truly historic contribution that has changed the face not just of monetary policy but of our economy and its prospects" (cited in Stevenson 2000, C8).

Fiscal frugality earmarks the end of President Clinton's tenure yet, in retrospect, two early policy decisions by Presidents Bush and Clinton set the groundwork for restraining federal deficits. They were the spending caps legislated as a result of the bipartisan 1990 budget summit agreement between the White House and leaders of the Democratic 101$^{st}$ Congress and the entirely partisan enactment by the Democratic 103$^{rd}$ Congress of Clinton's 1993 income-tax hike. It was at the 1990 budget summit that President Bush abandoned his "Read my lips, no new taxes" pledge of 1988, allowing taxes on the wealthiest Americans to rise from 28 percent to 31 percent, but in return, the Democrats were forced to accept caps on discretionary spending. "The major heavy lifting was done by George Bush and the 101$^{st}$ Congress," said Robert D. Reischauer, then CBO Director, who calculated that the five-year savings from the 1990 deal was $580 billion in 1997 dollars as compared to the savings of $474 billion from the 1993 Clinton deficit-reduction package (Rosenbaum 1997, A17).

Most controversial in 1993 was the creation of a fourth income-tax bracket —by increasing the marginal rate to 36 percent—and adding another 10-

percent surtax on incomes above $250,000, to yield an effective top rate of 39.6 percent (*Congressional Quarterly Almanac* 1994a, 120). Because Clinton's deficit-reduction package relied heavily on tax hikes, it squeaked through the House (218-216) and the Senate (on a tie-breaking vote by Vice President Gore). Every Republican voted no.

## Long-Term Outcome: Inequality Amid Surpluses

Liberal pundits roundly condemned President Reagan, almost personally, for the rising income inequality that accompanied the 1980s prosperity, and even some defenders of Reaganomics follow the politically correct route of not defending the Reagan record on that score (see Sloan 1999, 246–62). But the reality is that the trend towards increasing income inequality began before Reagan and has continued—indeed accelerated—under Clinton, yet liberals often have refrained from criticizing the Clinton administration. The bottom line is that, based on total household income, the lowest quintile controlled 4.4 percent of the income in 1976, 3.9 percent in 1986, and 3.7 percent in 1996. The 60 percent representing the middle-income earners held 52 percent of the income in 1976, lost some ground in 1986 (falling to 50 percent) and dropped even more by 1996 (47 percent). Meanwhile, the share of household income controlled by the top quintile rose steadily from 43 percent in 1976 to 46 percent in 1986 and to nearly half (49 percent) in 1996 (James and Kleiman 1997). A reanalysis of CBO data by the liberal Center on Budget and Policy Priorities painted an even worse picture, arguing that in 1999 the lowest fifth controlled 4.2 percent of all income, whereas the top fifth held 50 percent of all income. Moreover, between 1977 and 1999 the lowest quintile income share dropped 12 percent while the highest quintile increased its income share by 38.2 percent (Johnston 1999).

Jared Bernstein, economist with the Economic Policy Institute, a liberal think-tank, observed in 1996 that "widespread wage erosion persists in this economy" and pointed to a "disconnect" between the ongoing economic expansion and the incomes of most people. Bernstein also viewed the CEA analysis of job growth as "bogus," because the CEA has no data on what those new jobs are paying and, moreover, because real wages have been falling in many sectors of the economy (Francis 1996, 1). Lawrence Mishel, research director at the Economic Policy Institute and co-author of "The State of Working America," echoed those sentiments: "Bill Clinton has presided over a recovery from recession, but not a solution to most people's long-term problems" because "the problems of falling wages and eroding benefits among the vast majority have yet to be turned around" (Gosselin 1996, A1).

Statistics released by the Census Bureau, and publicized by the Clinton Administration, focused on the good news that median household income rose overall and among minority groups and that the percentage of Americans under poverty in 1998 fell to the lowest level since 1989. Actually, this comparison is quite damning of the Clinton record, by suggesting that the poverty rate was as low at the end of Reagan's tenure. For families below the poverty line, the four-year average was 11.8 percent during the recessionary Reagan first term, dropped markedly to 10.9 perceent during his second term, rose slightly to11.1 percent under President Bush as recession resurfaced, and jumped again to 11.4 percent during the Clinton first term (*Economic Report of the President* 1999, 366).

President Clinton tried to minimize the fact that the 1998 data confirmed the growing trend towards inequality. "Finally we have stemmed the tide of rising inequality," he said, "and this new report documents the strong income growth among all groups of people." But Jared Bernstein of the Economic Policy Institute took issue. "If the strongest economy in 30 years is unable to ameliorate this serious economic and social problem, there is a strong rationale for public policy that addresses these concerns" (Uchitelle 1999, A22).

As almost an afterthought, in mid-1999 President Clinton embarked on a four-day tour of the nation's poorest communities, first in Kentucky and Mississippi, then the Pine Ridge Indian reservation in South Dakota, and ending in an inner-city neighborhood of Los Angeles. He chose not to propose any LBJ-styled war on poverty but rather advocated federal incentives to encourage private capital to invest in those areas. His trip was ridiculed as "cosmetic" by a former assistant secretary in the Department of Health and Human Services (HHS), who had resigned to protest Clinton's signing the 1996 welfare reforms, saying that "he should stop referring to them as 'pockets' of poverty," because "persistent poverty is endemic in cities and rural areas and is increasingly present, if less visibly so, in suburbs" (Edelman 1999, A25). This failed-policy legacy is likely to become a standard criticism in liberal post-mortems on the Clinton-Gore administration. The latest book by presidency scholar James MacGregor Burns, an icon for Democratic liberalism, chastises the "moderation" of the Clinton-Gore leadership and points specifically to "the grotesque income gap between the rich and the poor in America" and states that "Clinton failed to exhibit the moral outrage that could have put inequality at the top of the nation's agenda" (Burns and Sorenson 1999, 338).

## Conclusion

The federal budget achieved a surplus of $69.2 billion for FY1998 and one of $79.3 billion for FY1999 (*Economic Report of the President* 1999, 419). That a balanced budget actually has been achieved earlier than anticipated by President Clinton or the Congressional Budget Office was largely the result of our unprecedented economic expansion. There is now pressure in Congress, from both parties, to remove the 1990 spending caps, otherwise the surplus cannot be spent. The contours of the upcoming political battles seem a replay, despite the changed economic context, because congressional Republicans favor a massive tax cut, whereas President Clinton wants to use the windfall to "save" two expensive middle-class entitlements that face bankruptcy—Social Security and Medicare—as well as increase spending for defense, education, child care, health, and other domestic programs. "With our economy expanding and our surplus rising, we have confidence that we can now look to the long-term challenges of our country to fulfill our obligations to twenty-first-century Americans, both young and old," said Clinton on February 1, 1999, as he unveiled his FY2000 budget (Taylor 1999, 290).

After his budget message, Clinton affirmed his commitment to fiscal frugality by announcing that he wanted to draw down the national debt by having the Treasury refinance older, higher yielding government bonds. Undeterred, the Republican Congress ignored Clinton's budgetary game-plan and passed a sweeping $792 billion tax cut, arguing that there was enough money to save Social Security and Medicare, provide for domestic programs, and give Americans tax relief. President Clinton stuck to his priorities and, in September of 1999, dutifully vetoed it. Now it was President Clinton who was arguing that huge tax cuts risked a return to crippling budget deficits of the past.

The more long-term they are, the more problematic are economic forecasts, but current projections show budget surpluses into the next century. Cynics have speculated that President Reagan deliberately engineered triple-digit deficits to forge a "politics of subtraction" where constituency pressures would cause Congress to think twice before creating any expensive new social-welfare programs. The Reagan anti-tax legacy dates back to his 1980 campaign and became political gospel after he beat Democratic candidate Walter Mondale in a landslide (Mondale admitted he would raise taxes once elected) and continued with Bush's "Read my lips, no new taxes" pledge (until his ill-fated 1990 budget summit). Taxes are no more popular today, but the unprecedented peacetime prosperity may yield a new "politics of addition" in the future, albeit with zero-sum properties, given the divergent budgetary priorities of Republicans and Democrats. Still, making compromises on what spending to increase and which taxes to cut is much less distasteful to politicians than the reverse.

One commentator observed that "for Clinton, whose presidency opened with a politically costly deficit-cutting effort and is currently stained by impeachment, the budget and its surplus predictions represent an opportunity to establish a legacy that could redeem his place in history" (Taylor 1999, 29). Yet that interpretation may not fly with liberals like economist James K. Galbraith, who editorialized that Fed Chairman Alan Greenspan "did more–by doing nothing. By not raising interest rates after 1995 while unemployment fell, ignoring dire warnings that inflation would spiral out of control, Mr. Greenspan helped to create the budget surpluses" (1999, A25).

Liberal criticisms notwithstanding, the New Democratic economic legacy of William Jefferson Clinton will include not only budget surpluses and fiscal integrity but also a post-Keynesian commitment to pro-business growth strategies, to market-based solutions for policy problems, and to free trade. Surely Bill Clinton has been the most committed free trader of any Democrat since Franklin D. Roosevelt, who signed the Reciprocal Trade Agreements Act of 1934, beginning the process of lowering barriers to international trade.

But there may be something much more fundamental to the Clinton policy legacy. When Clinton assumed office, his more liberal instincts prevailed as he announced his economic stimulus program, submitted an FY 1993 budget that anticipated future triple-digit deficits, and later authorized his wife to undertake a radical transformation of the health-care system. All these initiatives were upended, and, after the health-care debacle and the 1994 midterm elections that gave the GOP control of Congress, no explicit *redistributive* policies have emerged from the Clinton Administration.

In 1981, when OMB Director David Stockman publicly disparaged Reaganomics as being nothing more than old-fashioned "trickle-down" economics, designed to rationalize cutting income taxes, his candid interview was a political bombshell, not only angering President Reagan but also confirming the worst suspicions of Democrats (Greider 1981, 46). The phrase "trickle-down" economics has a pejorative meaning that was a public relations miscue for the Reagan administration, yet as economic policy it seemingly has survived in the Clinton administration. How else can we explain the Clinton administration's political tolerance for income inequality and the growing wage gap between the rich and poor?

In the 2000 presidential campaign, and neither Vice President Al Gore nor former contender Bill Bradley raised the call for income redistribution, although both men were campaigning further to the "left" than Bill Clinton did in 1992. Of course Gore may not be able to defeat the Republican frontrunner in 2000, but, whatever the electoral outcome, the concerns about "sharing the wealth" and economic justice that dominated political discourse and public policy during much of the twentieth century may simply disappear from future policy agendas. The advent of the twenty-first century may be post-materialist primarily in this non-redistributive sense.

CHAPTER 3

# CLINTON AND FOREIGN POLICY

Some Legacies for a
New Century

JAMES M. McCORMICK

On the first day of the NATO air campaign against Serbian forces in Kosovo in March 1999, President Clinton addressed the American people and justified American participation in those air strikes by asserting, "We are upholding our values, protecting our interests, and advancing the cause of peace." The United States, Clinton declared, was acting out of a "moral imperative" to help the people of Kosovo, but he also justified America's actions as an effort to defend its "national interest" by preventing the conflict from spreading into the rest of Europe and by demonstrating the effectiveness of the NATO alliance in the post–Cold War era (Clinton 1999b). By early 1999, foreign policy was an important issue for the administration, and its policy rationale at this point exhibited elements of both idealism and realism.

Six years earlier, the U.S. foreign policy approach was different in at least two ways. First, foreign policy was not a central concern for the administration. Indeed, Clinton came to office with little foreign-policy experience and with little interest in foreign affairs. Anthony Lake, Clinton's first national security adviser, was told to "keep foreign policy from becoming a problem—keep it off the screen and spare Clinton from getting embroiled as he went about his domestic business" (Drew 1994, 38). Second, to the extent that foreign policy was an issue, the Clinton approach was steeped in idealism. Two fundamental premises shaped its initial strategy of enlargement as the administration sought to create a more peaceful global community: enlarge the number of democracies, since "democracies don't fight one another," and expand the number of market economies and global prosperity, since prospering nations do not have time to fight one another. According to this design, global peace and security would be pursued indirectly—and without an emphasis on the alliances, force, and threat of war that had marked the previous forty-five years.

Despite a change in emphasis during the Clinton administration's time in office, a common thread held its foreign-policy process together: a concern for linking American domestic politics and American foreign policy. At the outset of its term, for instance, the emphasis on the growth of market democracies was driven by candidate Clinton's commitment to following a foreign policy "grounded in America's democratic values" (Clinton 1992) and by the desire to pursue a foreign policy that would assist the American economy. At the time of the Clinton administration's actions in Kosovo, the impact of domestic politics had not diminished. Because of the American public's opposition to the use of U.S. ground forces abroad, President Clinton (1999b) felt compelled to eschew sending troops to Kosovo in his March 1999 address.[1] Furthermore, he had to proceed cautiously since Congress was divided over the wisdom of Kosovo policy.[2]

I will here discuss the evolution of the Clinton administration's approach to foreign policy, assess the effect of international and domestic politics in shaping its approach over the course of the administration, and identify several legacies of the administration for the new millennium. I begin by outlining the initial approach of the administration and by describing how it changed over time. Next, I discuss several international and domestic challenges that the Clinton administration faced in the foreign-policy arena and their impact on its foreign-policy approach. I use several major crises (for example, Somalia, Bosnia, and Kosovo) to illustrate the international challenges the administration faced, and several domestic disputes over foreign-policy issues to illustrate the effects of Congress, political parties, interest groups, and public opinion on Clinton's foreign-policy approach.

Several themes thus shape this analysis. First, these domestic and international challenges focused greater presidential attention and involvement on foreign policy; these challenges altered the Clinton administration's heavy foreign-policy idealism and produced a greater sense of political realism by its second term; and the domestic constraints—whether from Congress, interest groups, and the public—were often crucial in the Clinton administration's foreign-policy responses. On the basis of this analysis, I conclude by identifying several short- and long-term legacies of the Clinton administration for American foreign policy—legacies for both the policy priorities that the administration pursued and the policymaking process that it employed.

## The Clinton Foreign-Policy Approach: Strengths and Weaknesses

Bill Clinton came to office under some unusual foreign-policy circumstances and with several apparent foreign-policy disadvantages. As he assumed the presidency, the fundamental rationale for American foreign policy over the past five decades had been lost, the importance of foreign policy was in question, and the level of public support for foreign-policy actions seemed uncertain. Furthermore, unlike his two immediate predecessors, Bill Clinton came to office with neither a strong ideological view on foreign affairs nor much foreign-policy experience. In addition, he promised to focus on the domestic economy, not on foreign policy.

Despite these disadvantages, Bill Clinton also enjoyed a major advantage: The Cold War was over, and he had some margin for error in shaping and conducting American foreign policy. As such, he announced that he wanted to change American foreign policy from the ad hoc approach of the Bush years and establish one based on American values. That is, instead of a policy that had been "rudderless, reactive, and erratic" under the Bush administration, from its outset, Clinton would have a foreign policy that was "strategic," "vigorous," and compatible with American values (Clinton 1992).

### Key Principles

The administration started by identifying three key principles to serve as guides to its foreign policy—achieving economic security for the United States, maintaining an appropriate defense posture for the post–Cold War era, and promoting democracy (Christopher 1993b). In addition, these principles were expected to serve as means for linking the foreign and domestic arenas.

The first principle, achieving economic security, was an especially important initial policy guide and a crucial link between the two arenas. In his campaign for the presidency in 1992, candidate Bill Clinton declared that the United States "must tear down the wall in our thinking between domestic and foreign policy" (1992). The isolation of one policy arena from the other was hampering America's ability to build an effective policy for the United States as a whole, especially in light of the dramatic changes in global politics and in light of the stagnant domestic economy. Hence, the United States would take several domestic actions to improve America's global competitiveness and several international actions to open foreign markets (McCormick 1998a, 217–18). Moreover, these foreign economic actions would be pursued as vigorously as the United States had waged the Cold War (Christopher 1993b, 2).

The second principle, maintaining an effective defense, emphasized downsizing and reshaping America's military for a new era. The Clinton administration's Bottom-up Review outlined the kind of new military that it sought—a military that was smaller, more mobile, and more capable of new missions for the changing threat environment. This new military, too, would produce savings on defense expenditures. The result of this effort, and a follow-on study in 1997, the Quadrennial Defense Review, was to produce a smaller, more technologically sophisticated military with the ability to fight two major regional conflicts (MRCs) simultaneously (or nearly simultaneously) and to undertake several new tasks, such as international peacekeeping.

The third initial principle, promoting democracy worldwide, was an effort to move away from the status quo approach that the administration claimed the Bush administration followed and to embrace global democratic reform. "My administration," Bill Clinton declared, "will stand up for democracy" (Clinton 1992). The emphasis on democracy was embraced not only to espouse American values but also as a mechanism to achieve a more peaceful world. As noted above, the more democracies in the world, the more likely peace would be maintained (Clinton 1991).

A synergistic relationship existed among these principles for American foreign policy. As America's economy rebounded, a strong and flexible defense posture would be possible, albeit one that would not burden the American economy. A sound American economy, bolstered by a solid defense, would allow the United States to promote democracy across the world. In all, the creation of more democracies globally would produce a safer international environment.

*The Strategy of Enlargement*

By September 1993, these initial principles were expanded and incorporated into a broader statement, labeled the "strategy of enlargement."[3] This strategy was designed to replace the containment strategy and to give a more dynamic vision to the overall Clinton administration's approach. The strategy of enlargement meant the "enlargement of the world's free community of market democracies," in the words of Anthony Lake, Clinton's first national security adviser (1993, 659). The strategy had four major components: "strengthen the community of major market democracies . . . foster and consolidate new democracies and market economies where possible . . . counter the aggression—and support the liberalization of states hostile to democracy and markets . . . [and] pursue our humanitarian agenda not only by providing aid but also by working to help democracy and market economies [develop]" (660).

As this strategy was outlined, Lake, and other key foreign-policy officials (Clinton 1993; Christopher 1993a; Albright 1993), reiterated several other foreign-policy principles that would shape administration policy: The United States was committed to a global role; it would act unilaterally or multilaterally, depending on the circumstances, to achieve its goals; and it would use American force when necessary. Responding to critics who argued that Clinton policy had been driven too much by global considerations and not enough by U.S. interests, Lake maintained that American national interests would always be the guide to policy actions.

*Some Concerns about the Initial Approach*

Despite the effort to refocus and reshape American foreign policy in a more coherent way with this strategy, it soon became a source of weakness when the strategy of enlargement did not gain much support at home (also see discussion by Peri Arnold in chapter 1 on the difficulties that Clinton faced in formulating foreign policy). The overall approach was criticized outside the administration as being less a strategy and more a statement of principles, as overly ambitious and lacking "operational terms" (Kissinger 1994, 74) and as approaching "foreign policy as if it were on a supermarket shopping spree, grabbing whatever it takes a fancy to" (Szamuely 1994, 393). A congressional critic (Senator John McCain) characterized the approach as lacking "a conception of what they want the world to look like in ten or twenty years" (Quoted in *Economist* 1995, 23). It was even viewed skeptically inside the administration. Secretary of State Warren Christopher saw the strategy of enlargement simply as "a trade policy masquerading as foreign policy" and not as a way to address significant international problems that required attention on a case-by-case basis. Moreover, as one official said, "Christopher just refused to use the 'E' word" (Brinkley 1997, 121).

Furthermore, this strategy did not provide a very clear guide to American policy in several key policy arenas that the Clinton administration faced. For instance, how did the strategy suggest specific policy direction for American actions in Bosnia or Somalia? How did it help specify the actions that the United States ought to pursue toward the changes in Russia and China? How did it guide policy for the new kinds of strategic and transnational threats, whether from the bombing of the World Trade Center or from the perfidy posed by Saddam Hussein?

*Some Revisions in Approach*

By early 1995, therefore, Secretary of State Christopher (1995, 41–45) sought to give more concrete definition to the administration's foreign policy. He did so by outlining several specific policy principles and linking them to American actions in key areas of the world. While Christopher once again committed the United States to global engagement and leadership, he also indicated that America would pursue cooperative ties with other powerful nations, seek to adapt and build sound economic and security institutions in the international community, and support democracy and human rights. In turn, these principles would lead to focusing on opening up the global trading order, building a new security system in Europe, seeking a comprehensive peace in the Middle East, halting the spread of weapons of mass destruction, and combating international crime. These principles and proposed actions would also do something else; they would increasingly emphasize the political/security arena, even as the economic policy focus remained, and involve the president directly in policy direction.

Two years later, in March 1997, near the beginning of the second term, the new national security adviser, Samuel (Sandy) Berger gave an even more pronounced security focus to the Clinton administration's foreign policy. Berger now identified "six key strategic objectives" that the Clinton administration would seek to address in the new term: "working for an undivided, democratic peaceful Europe . . . forging a strong, stable Asia Pacific community . . . embracing our role . . . as a decisive force for peace in the world . . . building the bulwarks through a more open and competitive trading system . . . and maintaining a strong military and fully funded diplomacy" (1997, 2–3). These kinds of objectives appeared to be much more concrete than the original strategy of enlargement and were more typical of American objectives in earlier decades as well.

Two months later the Clinton administration also reported to Congress on its "National Security Strategy for a New Century" (U.S. Executive Office of the President 1997, 2) and, significantly, inverted two of the three policy principles originally identified in 1993. It now identified America's new strategy's core objectives as seeking "to enhance our security with effective diplomacy and with military forces that are ready to fight and win, to bolster America's economic prosperity [and] to promote democracy abroad." In essence, the traditional political/military emphasis gained increased primacy among the key objectives or policy principles, even as the economic security and democracy goals remained important objectives. By this time, too (and most likely dating back to 1994 over Haiti and Bosnia), President Clinton had become fully engaged in the foreign affairs arena and the direction of policy.

Finally, in February 1999, President Clinton (1999a, 3–10) again outlined a new foreign-policy direction by identifying five major challenges that the United States faced at the dawn of the millennium. Significantly, the first two challenges revealed the continued emphasis on political/military concerns by calling for building "a more peaceful twenty-first century" by renewing alliances, whether through NATO expansion or renewed alliances with Japan and Korea, and by bringing "our former adversaries, Russia and China" into international policy "as open, prosperous, stable nations." The third challenge, too, had a security ring to it, although it was directed more toward the new threats and dangers in the international arenas than the past ones. The United States must seek "to build a future in which our people are safe from dangers that arise . . . from proliferation, from terrorism, from drugs, from the multiple catastrophes that could arise from climate change." Only the fourth and fifth challenges reflected the kind of emphasis that the administration originally brought to foreign policy in 1993. They focused on creating "a world trading and financial system that will lift the lives of ordinary people on every continent around the world" and keeping "freedom as a top goal for the world of the twenty-first century." In short, security relations and state-to-state relations were now receiving a greater emphasis from the administration than was the restructuring of the global society through democratic enlargement that marked the beginning of the administration.

## International and Domestic Policy Challenges: Sources of Policy Revisions

These revisions in foreign-policy priorities—moving from the original three principles and the strategy of enlargement, and then to Christopher's, Berger's, and Clinton's reformulations—may be perceived by some as refinement of policy direction, or they may be viewed as a more significant transformation from idealism to realism. Whatever one's ultimate assessment, these changes do reveal two important modifications: The president now saw foreign policy as a crucial area of policy interest; and the emphasis in foreign policy had shifted from the earliest days of the administration.

These changes, of course, did not occur in a vacuum; instead, they were the result of policy successes and failures in both the international and domestic arenas for the Clinton administration. By examining key foreign-policy actions in these two arenas, we can gain a better sense of how these changes in policy priorities came about and can begin to judge the likely stability of these changes for American foreign policy at the start of a new millennium.

## International Challenges

Early on in the Clinton administration, several international challenges required the administration (and the president) to focus more fully on foreign policy and to rethink its initial approach. As noted, the three key principles and the strategy of enlargement proved less-than-adequate foreign-policy guides for addressing specific problems in Somalia, Bosnia, Rwanda, Russia, and Central Europe. As a result, policy became somewhat ad hoc and often driven by domestic political considerations. In fact, one critic (Mandelbaum 1996) characterized the early Clinton approach as foreign policy by "social work" and not as an approach protecting American interests. Such criticism only added to the budding controversy over foreign policy and accelerated the call for policy reformulation.

The cases of Somalia and Bosnia in particular serve to illustrate the uncertainty in policymaking during the early years of the Clinton administration. Although the Bush administration had intervened in Somalia in December 1992 to provide humanitarian assistance to those suffering from the warring tribal clans, the Clinton administration sought to expand the mission there. The new administration enlarged the mission to include a nation-building goal in which the United States would help to restore order and a functioning government in Somalia. By the fall of 1993, the new mission had failed, owing to the sustained resistance of some clans and the ambivalence of the Clinton administration over how much force it wanted to use. In October 1993, the killing of eighteen Army Rangers, the dragging of a dead American through the streets of Mogadishu, and the public display and ridicule of a captured American produced a sharp response from both the U.S. Congress and the American public. The Clinton administration and Congress moved quickly to end American involvement there; the direction of American foreign policy was very much in doubt.

The effectiveness of the administration's initial policy towards Bosnia proved equally troubling. Bosnia, a former republic of Yugoslavia, had declared its independence in 1992, an action that precipitated a civil war among ethnic Serbs, ethnic Croats, and Muslims living there. While the Bush administration had largely adopted a hands-off stance regarding that conflict, Bill Clinton asserted that it would take decisive action by adopting a "lift and strike" policy—lifting the arms embargo for the Bosnian Muslims to allow them to defend themselves and striking the Serbs with American air power.

Once in office, Clinton did neither. Instead, the administration's initial inaction was caricatured as one of "rift and drift"—a rift with its European allies over appropriate policy and a drift because of its indecisiveness over what to do next (Drew 1994, 159). Clinton administration policy changed toward Bosnia by mid-1995, due to the increased atrocities that occurred in Bosnia and to prodding by Congress in lifting of the American arms embargo. As President Clinton became more fully engaged and as the situation changed on the ground due in part to NATO bombing, the Dayton Accords were eventually negotiated and signed in Paris among the conflicting parties. In essence, a more detached policy from early on in the administration had evolved into a policy of substantial American engagement by late 1995.

Several other international crises in the administration's early years also illustrate the difficulty that it faced in providing a clear and firm direction in foreign policy. On the one hand, the Clinton administration did very little when Rwanda erupted in genocide in April 1994, even though the administration's human-rights concerns seemingly would have driven it toward substantial involvement. The reason was that the Somalia experience paralyzed the administration, producing a reassessment of how and when American military power should be used. On the other hand, the Clinton administration acted more robustly when Saddam Hussein sought to challenge the no-fly zones imposed on Iraq by the international community. In October 1994 the administration ordered 36,000 American forces into Kuwait to serve as a deterrent to any contemplated Iraqi action. Similarly, in September 1994 the administration adopted an interventionist policy toward Haiti, when its earlier diplomatic and economic measures failed to budge the military leaders from power.

Several other international issues also pulled the administration toward greater involvement in foreign policy. In post-Communist Russia, for example, the situation was quite unsettled, and the stability of the new government of Boris Yeltsin was in doubt. The Clinton administration thus moved to provide substantial amount of economic assistance to Russia and diplomatic support to Yeltsin. Similarly, while the negotiations in the Middle East peace process had produced agreements between Israel and the Palestinians and between Israel and Jordan by 1993 and 1994, the administration quickly saw that further progress would require sustained attention by the president.

Two other important policy issues—most-favored-nation (MFN) status for China and the question of NATO expansion—also prompted the Clinton administration to address foreign policy, but the two cases also revealed the difficulty that the administration faced in reconciling some of its foreign-policy principles to its actions with its actions. The issue of granting China MFN, of course, was not a new one. It had vexed past administrations, especially in light of documented human-rights violations by China (e.g., the Tiananmen Square massacre of June 1989). Indeed, the Democratic Congress challenged the Bush administration over its granting of MFN and nearly passed a resolution overriding a presidential veto on at least one occasion. What was new was that candidate Bill Clinton asserted he would stand up to the tyrants in Beijing and promote democracy. In a quick policy reversal shortly after his election in November 1992, though, Clinton announced that he would continue the past Bush policy. Indeed, in May 1993 he granted China provisional renewal of MFN status, but he required that China make real progress in the human-rights area for subsequent renewals. In May 1994, however, the Clinton administration not only decided to renew MFN, but the administration delinked future renewals from human-rights considerations. Since then, the Clinton administration routinely renewed MFN, arguing that a free trading relationship is the most practical way to promote long-term political (democratic) change. At least in the short run, its economic principle trumped its democratic reform principle.

The issue of NATO's future was hardly new either. The Bush administration had already sought to enhance consultation and cooperation with the countries of Central Europe after the end of the Cold War. The Clinton administration, however, needed to decide how far NATO change would go, especially in light of its effort to nurture better ties with Russia. Its initial NATO proposal called for creating "Partnership for Peace," a kind of "junior membership" for states of Central and Eastern Europe and including Russia, in which individual states would complete an agreement with NATO on cooperative and "confidence-building" measures between them. Some countries of Central Europe were not satisfied with the partnership idea and desired full membership instead. As a way to put a firmer stamp on Clinton-administration foreign policy (and perhaps to appeal to Americans of Central European descent), several advisers within the administration urged the president to offer full membership to some states (see Goldgeier 1999). The proposed new NATO states, Poland, Hungary, and the Czech Republic, wanted full membership to insure their own security, while the United States saw it as a way to facilitate democracy in the region (Albright 1999). Russia objected strongly to this initiative because NATO expansion represented yet another kind of encirclement and as another way to divide up Europe. After several maneuvers, the United States and its NATO alliance announced at the Madrid Summit in July 1997 that it would go ahead with the expansion plan in April 1999, the fiftieth anniversary of the alliance. Thus, the Clinton administration ultimately opted for promoting democracy (and security) in Europe rather than focusing so singularly on solidifying American-Russian relations.

## Domestic Challenges

A number of domestic challenges over foreign policy also encouraged greater presidential attention to international issues and, ultimately, some change in policy direction. The first and most difficult domestic challenge on a foreign-policy issue was the administration's effort to gain approval from Congress for the North American Free Trade Agreement (NAFTA). Although the American public had consistently supported efforts to provide greater economic security through international actions (see Rielly 1995, 1999b), domestic critics raised serious questions about NAFTA. Substantial opposition to NAFTA came from members of the president's own party, especially from labor unions, who were anxious about the loss of jobs to cheaper labor in Mexico, producer groups (for example, citrus and fruit growers), who would suffer from the trade pacts, and environmentalists, who were concerned about the enforcement of pollution and water standards along the Mexican border. As a result, the administration spent a considerable amount of time bargaining to gain congressional approval. In the end, the Clinton administration was forced to rely more on Republicans than Democrats to ensure the passage of NAFTA in the House of Representatives (McCormick 1998a, 226–28), as they did for the passage of permanent normal trade relations with China in 2000. In chapter 2 of this volume, Tatalovich and Frendreis discuss these and other difficulties that the Clinton administration had with NAFTA.

A second area of domestic foreign-policy challenge emerged over American military involvement abroad. The public's view of such actions had been quite stable—and quite negative—for some time. That is, the public was generally opposed to interventions by the Clinton administration that sought to change domestic regimes or interventions that might entangle the United States into ongoing civil wars (Jentleson 1992; Jentleson and Britton 1998). Further, the public was not very supportive of foreign-policy efforts that emphasized the promotion of democracy and human rights (Rielly 1995, 15–16 ; 1999b, 16–17), though it was generally sympathetic to the suffering of the peoples in these countries. Hence, the Clinton administration faced an uphill battle in gaining public support for undertaking military measures, be they in Somalia, Bosnia, or Haiti. Moreover, the level of public support for President Clinton's foreign-policy leadership during the first two years of his administration suffered as a result.[4] Indeed, public caution over the use of American troops continued to influence the administration's actions, as evidenced by its reluctance to discuss this option during the war in Kosovo.

Domestic political opposition on foreign policy crystallized when Republicans won control of both Houses of Congress in the 1994 congressional elections. Unsurprisingly, Republicans were skeptical of the Clinton administration's domestic-policy priorities, but they were also at odds with much of the administration's foreign-policy goals and actions. To be sure, most Republican members of Congress supported the Clinton administration's efforts at liberalizing trade around the world, but they generally opposed undertaking humanitarian interventions, participating in United Nations peacekeeping efforts, promoting sustainable development, and cutting the defense budget and the size of the American military. Hence, the new congressional majority rather quickly undertook actions to trim America's foreign-assistance and international-affairs budget, stop the sending of American forces abroad, and reverse the cuts in defense spending that the administration had initiated. Congress's overall record on these efforts was mixed, but the Republican majority did take some actions that stopped, slowed down, or questioned some Clinton administration foreign-policy initiatives. In this sense, Congress had an effect on the direction of foreign policy during the Clinton years.

In the economic area, for instance, three significant actions illustrate the Congress's efforts to alter the Clinton agenda. First, Congress objected to an American bailout of the Mexican government after the peso plunged in late 1994 and early 1995. The Clinton administration saw this assistance as vital to the success of NAFTA and to the economic health of the United States, but Congress saw it as leading to rescuing other insolvent countries around the world at America's expense. The Clinton administration eventually used its own executive authority to fashion a $50 billion assistance package. Second, Congress was most reluctant to refinance the International Monetary Fund (IMF) after the 1997 Asian financial crisis had engulfed several nations there—Thailand, Indonesia, and South Korea, among others. Congressional debate and discussions in various forums surrounded this executive branch request for $17.9 billion. Finally, after extensive White House, business, and farm group lobbying, the Congress did approve a $17.9 billion appropriation to replenish the IMF, albeit more than twelve months later, in October 1998. Congress did so, only after adding several conditions on IMF actions (M. Pomper 1998, 2833). Third, and perhaps most significantly, the Congress failed to renew fast-track negotiating authority for the executive branch in November 1997. Under fast-track authority, Congress empowered the president to negotiate trade agreements with other countries, leaving Congress only the right to vote the pacts up or down, without benefit of any amendments. The authority offers the executive (and other nations) a considerable advantage, since once a pact is completed, it could not be changed. Ironically, Democratic opposition in the House to fast-track authority ultimately doomed congressional action on this measure.

In the security area, Congress also took actions that challenged the Clinton approach. Perhaps the most dramatic measures occurred over Somalia, Bosnia, and, more recently, Kosovo. After the October 3, 1993, incident in which eighteen Americans were killed in Somalia, Congress quickly voted to require that American troops be withdrawn from there by March 31, 1994. As the Dayton Accords over Bosnia were being completed in November 1995 and the president announced that American forces would be sent to that troubled country, both chambers of Congress passed resolutions supporting American forces in Bosnia but opposing the Clinton policy toward that country. In March 1999, just as the NATO operation was about to begin over Kosovo, the U.S. Senate passed a resolution of support, but it did so only by a very weak margin (58-41), with most senators voting along party lines. At the same time, the House backed the American military personnel involved in the air attacks virtually by unanimity (424-1), but it did not debate the merits of the air attack as such (M. Pomper 1999, 763). In April 1999 on a tie vote (213-213), however, the House rejected a resolution authorizing American participation in the air war (Towell 1999, 1037).

More generally, Congress sought to reshape defense spending away from the priorities of the Clinton administration. Under the Clinton defense plans, for instance, the American military was trimmed back significantly with each service undergoing personnel reductions. The Army and Air Force had the biggest cuts, each with a 45 percent reduction since 1989, and the Navy and the Marines had smaller reductions, with the former reduced by 36 percent and the latter by 12 percent (Pins 1999, 1B). Similarly, overall spending on defense had also been cut during the Clinton years, although near the end of its term the Clinton administration had begun to recommend some increases. When the Republicans gained majority control of the Congress, they called for increases in spending on defense preparedness—additional training for personnel and modern weaponry—and questioned whether the U.S. military is currently equipped to fight two MRCs simultaneously. In addition, the Republican Congress and the White House continually clashed over a variety of other issues—an anti-defense missile system for the United States, the extension of the Nuclear Non-Proliferation Treaty, the passage of the Chemical

Weapons Convention, and the ratification for the Comprehensive Test-Ban Treaty. Although Congress only enjoyed limited victories with several of these measures, it still successfully made it more difficult for the administration to continue its foreign-policy direction unimpeded.

Perhaps Congress's major effect on the Clinton administration's foreign policy occurred on two recent security questions related to nuclear weaponry. On one issue, the Republican Congress prodded the administration toward its favored position on a national missile defense system, and on the other, it stymied the administration's effort in gaining approval for a ban on nuclear testing. On the former, despite opposition from the Clinton administration, Congress succeeded in keeping a theater missile defense program alive in the mid-1990s, and ultimately it enacted the National Missile Defense Act in 1999, with President Clinton's signature. Under this legislation, the United States must deploy a limited system "as soon as technologically feasible" and the Clinton administration has promised a decision by June 2000 (Quoted in Lewis, Gronlund, and Wright 1999–2000, 122). On the latter, the Senate rendered a stinging foreign-policy defeat by recommending against the ratification of the Comprehensive Test-Ban Treaty because it was viewed the treaty as flawed (*New York Times* 1999b, A13). While the treaty passed the Senate by a narrow margin (51-48) largely along party lines, that margin was still sixteen votes short of the necessary two-thirds support required. The defeat was characterized as a "humiliating setback" of a treaty that "was supposed to be the crowning achievement of his foreign policy." (Sanger 1999a, A1). In this sense, Congress sought, and succeeded in, redirecting American foreign policy toward its own priorities in these areas.

Finally, a domestic issue also contributed to greater attention to foreign policy—the impeachment of President Clinton by the House of Representative and the ensuing trial in the Senate in late 1998 and early 1999. Although these actions resulted from President Clinton's involvement with a White House intern, Monica Lewinsky, and his lying about this affair to the American public and federal authorities, it also had an indirect foreign-policy effect. During the lengthy investigations and hearings over this matter, the president seemed to take on more foreign-policy duties—including travel overseas—to illustrate that he was continuing to conduct the matters of state, to present a sense of normalcy, and to downplay this issue. In short, foreign policy received more and more attention by the administration and the president by 1998 and 1999.

## The Long- and Short-Term Foreign-Policy Legacies

While it is difficult to assess fully the foreign-policy influence of the Clinton administration at close range, let me suggest some possible short- and long-term legacies that the administration likely leaves.[5] For analytic purposes, these legacies will be divided between the administration's likely influence on *policy priorities* toward other nations and on the *policymaking process* within the United States, but, in essence, they are intertwined because domestic politics continue to play a prominent role in the shaping of American foreign policy.

### Policy Priorities

On the policy side, the first—and perhaps most important—legacy of the Clinton administration is the commitment to continued American involvement in global affairs after the end of the Cold War. Voices from several different political quarters—and ranging all along the political spectrum—called for various forms of isolationism or unilateralism with the end of the Cold War (e.g., Kristol and Kagan 1996; Nordlinger 1995; Steel 1995), but the Clinton administration never wavered in its commitment to maintaining a global role for the United States. Presidential- and executive-branch statements throughout the administration's two terms, virtually without exception, confirmed (and reinforced) this commitment to global involvement.[6]

The commitment to sustained international engagement was manifested more fully through the several significant economic and military actions that the administration undertook. The passage of NAFTA and the General Agreement on Tariffs and Trade (GATT) are important indicators of this engagement, as are the continued presence of American military personnel in Europe (roughly at 100,000) and in Asia (also at roughly 100,000 in Japan and Korea). Specific American military actions, however, provide an even greater sense of the commitment to a sustained global role. Whether enforcing the "no-fly zones" over Iraq, sending a significant military component for the peacekeeping operations in Bosnia, conducting the war with Serbia against Kosovo (and subsequently sending in peacekeeping forces), or proposing (and achieving) NATO expansion—the Clinton administration consistently sought engagement over non-engagement after the Cold War. In this sense, the commitments and engagements initiated by the Clinton administration seem to ensure a global role for the United States, both in the short and long term.

A second policy legacy—and the one that will likely represent its greatest long-term, specific policy bequeath—is the placement of foreign economic policy at the center of America's international-policy agenda. While global economic security issues have always been an important concern for post–World War II administrations, the Clinton administration placed an even higher policy priority on those issues with the end of the Cold War. In this sense, the bilateral and multilateral free-trade agreements negotiated by the administration are, and will remain, a significant policy legacy. The maintenance and expansion of these agreements will necessarily continue as a high priority for future administrations as global economic interdependence accelerates and America's economic hegemony continues to be challenged. If an enduring legacy of the Franklin Delano Roosevelt administration was for American presidents to assume more responsibility for assisting in managing the American domestic economy, a likely legacy of the Clinton administration will be for future American presidents to assume more responsibility in managing the global economy.

There is also an important global corollary to this economic legacy: Through its bilateral and multilateral economic actions, the Clinton administration bequeathed a more liberal global trading order to the international community than existed when it took office. The ratification of the GATT accords was particularly significant, since it created a new successor global economic organization, the World Trade Organization (WTO). This organization is more fully committed to enforcing the principle of free trade than ever before. Other multilateral actions—whether through passing NAFTA and permanent normal trade relations with China, prodding the Asia-Pacific Economic Cooperation (APEC) to create a free-trade area, or initiating Western Hemisphere discussions on free trade—contributed to this more open trade environment, too. Further, the Clinton administration signed over 270 trade liberalization pacts with other countries during its tenure (Clinton 1999a, 8).

This free-trade legacy, however, continues to be controversial. The massive demonstrations at the WTO's meeting in Seattle in December 1999 illustrate the concerns and anguish of many groups across many nations over the expansion of free trade. While some nations benefit from these efforts at opening global markets, both in the long- and short-run, other nations fear that they may be left behind. In addition, many environmental and labor groups fear that their interests will be seriously damaged if some limits are not placed on these free-trade agreements. Nonetheless, President Clinton reaffirmed his commitment to the free-trade principle and to the WTO in Seattle, even as he called for some organizational reform within that organization (Sanger 1999b, A1, A14; *New York Times* 1999a, A15).

A third long-term policy legacy is in the redefinition of the threat environment faced by the United States after the Cold War. Unlike the previous post–

World War II administrations, the Clinton administration had to contend with a global threat environment that was now more diverse and more diffuse than during the Cold War. While that period had represented largely a singular threat from the Soviet Union with its arsenal of nuclear weapons, the new environment presented new threats ranging from new (or old) regional and communal conflicts to any old (or new) great-power rivalries (Nye 1999a). As regional powers seek regional dominance and acquire a variety of weapons of mass destruction (whether they be nuclear, biological, or chemical), they potentially pose dangers for the national interests of the United States. As communal conflicts within and between states over religious, cultural, and ethnic identities increase, they, too, present the prospect that the United States might be drawn into them. The fighting over Kashmir between the newest nuclear-power states, India and Pakistan, in the summer of 1999 illustrates the former, while the seventy-eight-day war over Kosovo, also in 1999, illustrates the latter. American quarrels with Russia over Kosovo or Bosnia or American disputes with China over Taiwan or spying within the United States illustrate the continuity of great power conflicts, too.

A fourth, and more troublesome, policy legacy flows from the third: While the Clinton administration recognized these new threats, it was less successful in developing a "strategic consensus" (Hoffmann 1981 on this term; also see Goldman and Berman 2000; Naim 1997–1998) around them and in restructuring the military in a way to deal with them. That is, the administration failed to define and rank-order these threats and to outline a strategy (or set of strategies) to deal with them. Leading analysts, both implicitly and explicitly, touch on this policy shortcoming. Joseph Nye recently outlined the need to redefine the "new national interest" in the information age and specified alternate responses to differing American interests and threats (1999b). Earlier, Samuel Huntington worried about "the erosion of the American national interests" and was pessimistic that the United States could move beyond the current "foreign policy of particularism," which was largely driven by ethnic and commercial interests (1997). As such, future administrations face at least a short-term Clinton legacy in seeking to put together a coherent policy consensus to deal with these differing threats.

To be sure, the Clinton administration sought to do so, but it largely did not succeed, as evidenced by the great gulf between opinion leaders and the public across a wide array of foreign-policy issues (Rielly 1999b).[7] While creating a policy consensus has many dimensions and represents a formidable task for any administration, two components will remain particularly vexing in the short term for future administrations. The first focuses on the appropriate American response to regional and communal conflicts, and the second deals with devising the appropriate strategy for managing great-power conflicts in the new millennium, especially with an emerging great power such as China.

The first component encompasses both reshaping the American military in a way that will enable the United States to respond to regional and communal threats *and* developing a clearer decision calculus of when and what kind of force should be used in these conflicts. For the former, the Clinton administration initially moved toward a considerable downsizing of the military and a substantial reliance on the "revolution in military affairs" to address emerging threats. While the administration has recently proposed greater funding for military preparedness, including some weapons modernization, resolving the debate over the size and shape of the military for the new century is an immediate short-term legacy for any new administration. For the latter, the administration issued Presidential Decision Directive 25 (or PDD-25) after the Somalia debacle. This directive identified specific conditions that needed to be met for American participation in multilateral peacekeeping operations. Although these conditions represent an attempt to establish a closer linkage between domestic politics and foreign policy, they are hardly ironclad guides to policy, since they allow considerable judgment on the part of decision makers.

The second component of any effort to build a policy consensus requires a fuller strategy for dealing with great-power conflicts. While Russia will continue to pose some uncertainty for the United States, China, as an emerging great power, poses a greater policy challenge for American administrations in the new millennium. The Clinton administration embraced a policy of "constructive engagement," a variety of continuing contacts and interactions between the two countries. The rationale for this policy was that these contacts would stimulate Chinese economic and political reforms in ways compatible with American interests. This approach, however, created substantial domestic controversy. The Chinese have been accused of engaging in a litany of activities that jeopardize this relationship—whether it be spying within the United States, contributing illegal campaign funds in the 1996 elections, engaging in unfair trade practices, committing continuous human-rights violations, promoting abortions, or threatening Taiwan. Thus in the short term future administrations will be faced with how to manage this relationship effectively as part of a more general effort to develop a new foreign-policy consensus.

*Policymaking Process*

Many of the Clinton administration's policymaking legacies flow from these foreign-policy priorities and reveal more fully how domestic politics and foreign policy are closely linked today. While these legacies generally broaden domestic participation in foreign-policy decision-making, they also represent a continuation (and sometimes an acceleration) of trends begun under previous administrations. In this sense, they generally connote incremental long-term changes in the policymaking process, rather than abrupt short-term trends tied to a particular administration. For convenience of discussion, these policymaking legacies may be divided between those that have developed within the executive branch and those that have developed beyond it.

In the executive branch, the Clinton administration leaves at least three policymaking legacies. The first two—the number of issues constituting the foreign-policy agenda and the number of participants addressing them in Washington—emanate from the changing global-threat environment in international politics today. While security issues remained an important component of the foreign-policy agenda, especially as the Clinton administration's policy approach evolved, the breadth of the issues that fall under the foreign-policy rubric broadened to include global environmental, economic, and social issues. As these kinds of issues expanded, the number of foreign-policy participants within the executive branch (and beyond) necessarily grew as well. Now virtually all cabinet departments and offices within the executive branch can place some claim on a foreign-policy issue.

Consider, for example, a relatively new foreign-policy issue, such as international drug trafficking from a South American country, and the array of agencies involved in addressing various aspects of that issue. The Department of State, Department of Commerce, and the Office of the U.S. Trade Representative would likely be involved in addressing the political and economic aspects of the relationship with the country in which the drugs originate. The U.S. Customs Bureau, the Drug Enforcement Administration, the Central Intelligence Agency, and the Department of Defense would likely be involved in efforts to control the transference of drugs into the United States. Finally, the Department of the Treasury, the FBI, and, more generally, the U.S. Department of Justice would likely be involved in tracking the attempts to launder the drug profits and in bringing those responsible for these activities to justice.

A third policymaking legacy flows from the first two and reflects the economic-policy priority underpinning the Clinton approach to foreign policy: the substantial increase in the number of individuals and institutions with economic expertise in the foreign-policy–making machinery of government at the start of the new millennium. At least four significant changes illustrate this enhanced economic role developed by the Clinton administration. First, the administration established a National Economic Council (NEC), in theory to be equivalent to the National Security Council, to provide economic advice on domestic- and foreign-policy concerns (Rosati and Twing 1998, 5; also see Tatalovich and Frendreis in chapter 2 of this volume on the NEC and the general role of economic policymakers). Second, the administration formally included economic advisers as members of the committees forming the national security council decision-making system.[8] Third, the administration restructured the Department of State to give a greater role to economic issues (for example, the creation of the Office of the Coordinator for Business Affairs within the Undersecretariat for Economic, Business, and Agricultural Affairs). Fourth, and finally, the Clinton administration has given increased prominence to the Department of Treasury (and particularly, the Secretary of Treasury) in formulating economic policy and to the Department of Commerce in promoting trade policy around the world (McCormick 1998a). While this legacy may be short term (since a new administration largely has substantial latitude to restructure the executive branch as it sees fit), the changing global economy and the sustained involvement of "domestic" bureaucracies in foreign-policy issues in earlier administrations suggest that these structural and process changes are more likely to be long term.

Outside the executive branch, several policymaking legacies from the Clinton administration remain, but they, too, largely reflect an acceleration of trends already underway. The first one centers on the increasing role of Congress in dealing with foreign-policy issues, and the second focuses on the increasing partisan divisions over the direction of American foreign policy. On balance, the intensities of these trends probably are short-term legacies of the Clinton administration that may be ameliorated by a new administration or a new Congress, although the general directions of these trends are unlikely to be reversed any time soon.

While an increased congressional role in foreign policy is hardly a new phenomenon, it quickened during the Clinton years, especially as the foreign-policy issue agenda widened and as political differences surfaced. These institutional divisions ranged across the entire foreign policy issue spectrum—from security to economic to environmental to social issues. Witness the extended debate between the branches on such issues as NAFTA, Bosnia, foreign assistance, global human rights, and global warming. Since many of these issues permeate the foreign-policy/domestic-policy divide and affect constituencies in a differential way (that is, the passage of NAFTA helps some members' districts but it hurts others'), members of Congress are more likely to act independently on these issues, regardless of party affiliation or presidential leadership. Hence, the "domestication of foreign policy" has really come home to many lawmakers through these new international issues.

Second, and following from the first, the partisan and ideological foreign-policy divisions intensified between the White House and Congress and within political parties during the Clinton years. Arms-control issues, such as the Chemical Weapons Convention and the Comprehensive Test-Ban Treaty (Schmitt 1999, A8), and foreign aid issues have particularly sparked partisan (and ideological) debate between Democrats and Republicans. Some issues, too, (for example, the NAFTA vote in 1993, the fast-track vote in 1997, and the vote on permanent normal trade relations with China in 2000) produced a sharp intra-party debate (among Democrats) by exacerbating ideological divisions over the direction of American trade policy. As one study (McCormick, Wittkopf, and Danna 1997) demonstrates, partisan and ideological voting on foreign-policy issues in both Houses of Congress became more acrimonious in the Bush and Clinton years, with the level of executive/legislative bipartisanship lower than at any time since the beginning of the Cold War.

Two other policymaking legacies of the Clinton administration are likely to have more long-term effects and involve the incorporation of more and more domestic actors into the foreign-policy process. One trend includes a greater role for interest groups in foreign policymaking, the other a greater role for public opinion. Over the past decade, for instance, the number of interest groups—and particularly interests lobbying on behalf of foreign nations (including apparently illegal campaign contributions from abroad)—has grown significantly. Virtually all the countries that were republics in the Soviet Union have representatives in Washington as do Russia, China, and a myriad list of smaller countries. These foreign lobbies are now standard fare in the nation's capital (McCormick 1998b, 182–84). In addition, lobbying by economic interest groups (for instance, over policy toward China) and new ethnic groups (for example, the Central and East European Coalition over NATO expansion or aid to Central Europe) continue apace and actually have accelerated in recent years.

The role of public opinion in the foreign-policy process has been enhanced also, especially since the Clinton administration relied so heavily on public opinion polling to shape or restrain its foreign-policy actions. As foreign-policy opinions remained remarkably stable after the end of the Cold

War, especially toward American military involvement abroad (see Jentleson 1992; Jentleson and Britton 1998), the degree of decision latitude for policymakers narrowed. The restraining effect of public opinion (or the public mood) on the Clinton administration was especially evident over its reluctance to send American ground forces abroad in civil conflicts and its concern about the possible loss of American lives in foreign lands. To be sure, the Clinton administration did on occasion act in opposition to the public mood (such as in the case of the intervention in Haiti), but it was still careful to assess the direction of the public on key foreign-policy questions, especially as evidenced over the war in Kosovo. Whether these public constraints will be as confining for future leaders, of course, remains an open question, but the legacy of increased attention to the public's views remains.[9]

Finally, the greater involvements of interest groups and of public opinion represent opposite kinds of restraints on the foreign-policy process as a legacy of the Clinton years—one directing policy toward narrower individual interests, the other aiming it toward societal interests. Such conflicting policymaking legacies are a mixed blessing for any future administration as it seeks to develop a coherent and consistent policy approach after the Clinton years. Yet, this, too, represents a long-term contribution of the Clinton administration to the new millennium.

## Conclusion

President Clinton came to office with limited interest in foreign policy but with a goal to change the direction of American foreign policy. Buffeted by both international and domestic challenges, the Clinton administration soon gave greater prominence to foreign affairs and adjusted its foreign policy approach as well. While its initial approach had a strong dose of idealism, the administration moved toward a sense of realism by the end of its time in office. Security concerns increasingly gained pride of place—whether dealing with changing relations with Russia or China or with the instability in the Balkans or the Middle East—over its commitment to economic and democratic concerns. To be sure, the administration's commitment to democratic enlargement and economic liberalism remained important and prominent goals, but by the end of its tenure the political/military requirements of several pressing international issues often trumped these concerns.

Still, the Clinton administration left several important policy legacies for future administrations. These included a commitment to a sustained role for the United States in global affairs after the Cold War, an enhanced position for economic issues on the foreign-policy agenda, and a redefinition of the global threat environment that the United States faces as it enters the new millennium. Another legacy, however, also remains. The administration did not succeed in developing and gaining widespread domestic support for a strategic consensus for when and how the United States should address regional and communal conflicts. Put more generally, the larger question of how values and interests should shape American foreign policy remains unresolved.

On the domestic front, the Clinton administration leaves several important legacies for the foreign-policy-making process. Importantly, the Clinton administration broadened the number of issues and actors involved in foreign policy within the executive branch and also incorporated more economic participants into the foreign-policy decision-making apparatus of the government. More troublesome, perhaps, are other lingering legacies in the decision-making arena. Foreign policy became an increasingly contentious issue between Congress and the executive branch (as witnessed most dramatically with the vote on the Comprehensive Test Ban Treaty), and more and more interest groups lobbied to influence the direction of American foreign policy, including an increasing number of foreign groups (as evidenced over trade policy with China). Finally, and in line with a more democratic emphasis on foreign affairs, public opinion and public polling also played a part in policymaking during the Clinton years. In short, then, domestic politics and foreign policy will be increasingly linked in the new millennium.

As we gain some distance from the Clinton administration, its foreign policy impact will come into sharper relief, and its short- and long-term legacies will become more recognizable. That is, future administrations will likely have to grapple with a similar mix of policy and policymaking concerns as that faced by the first post–Cold War administration, and succeeding administrations' answers to those concerns will go a long way toward assessing more fully the legacies of the Clinton years. Some of the key questions to use in evaluating the effect of the Clinton administration on them include the following: How do those administrations mix political idealism and political realism in an era facing multiple foreign-policy threats? How do those administrations define the appropriate role for the United States in a world without a single opponent to shape its policy? How do those administrations incorporate domestic politics to shape American foreign policy? How effective are those administrations in developing a domestic consensus in a time when regional and communal conflict dominate the global agenda? While each succeeding administration will answer these in a different way, especially as the international context changes, the approach of the Clinton administration offers a useful starting point in understanding the direction of American foreign policy after the Cold War.

PART

II

# The President and the Public

Bill Clinton's obsessive courtship of public opinion is unprecedented in the annals of the modern presidency. The following chapters analyze Clinton's relations with the public from three varying perspectives. John Harris, writing from the "inside" viewpoint of a White House reporter, explains how no administration has relied as heavily and consistently on polls and media management as this one. The influence of pollsters broadened beyond problems of "packaging" to include the actual formulation of public policy, an innovation that Clinton's successors may well copy. Assessing broader cultural trends, Bruce Miroff examines the postmodern style of Clinton's public presidency and how it helped him to survive the 1994 elections and impeachment. Once the public views the president as merely another celebrity, the parameters of permissible behavior in the White House broaden considerably, a transformation with several implications for future presidential behavior. Employing survey research, Diane Hollern Harvey assesses public support for Clinton, demonstrating how he was blessed by the unpopularity of his enemies. Clinton's survival, she argues, may well desensitize the public to future presidential sex scandals.

CHAPTER 4

# A CLOUDED MIRROR

Bill Clinton, Polls, and the
Politics of Survival

JOHN F. HARRIS

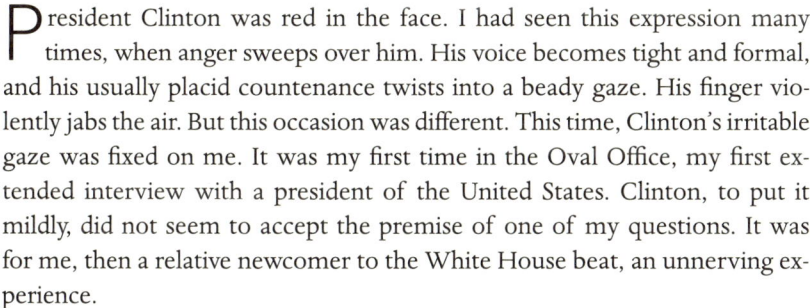

President Clinton was red in the face. I had seen this expression many times, when anger sweeps over him. His voice becomes tight and formal, and his usually placid countenance twists into a beady gaze. His finger violently jabs the air. But this occasion was different. This time, Clinton's irritable gaze was fixed on me. It was my first time in the Oval Office, my first extended interview with a president of the United States. Clinton, to put it mildly, did not seem to accept the premise of one of my questions. It was for me, then a relative newcomer to the White House beat, an unnerving experience.

This interview was in January 1996, just days after Clinton in his State of the Union address famously declared, "The era of big government is over." I prompted a presidential storm, brief but intense, by drawing his attention back to his first speech to Congress, made three years earlier. Then, Clinton had declared, "Tonight I want to talk with you about what government can do, because I believe government must do more." He had gone on to outline an immediate $30 billion appropriation "to put people to work now, to create a half a million jobs—jobs to rebuild our highways and airports, to renovate housing, to bring new life to rural communities." Was the rhetoric of these two speeches, I ventured, perhaps a bit inconsistent? "Only if you have that kind of selective quotes," Clinton shot back. Warming to the subject, he proceeded to explain how over the course of his administration his governing philosophy had been "remarkably consistent" (Devroy and Harris 1996).

The president's irritation with me was of no lasting significance. He probably forgot the exchange by the end of the day. But the episode now comes back to mind as a cautionary reminder: Bill Clinton almost certainly would object vigorously to a notion that is the foundation of this chapter and is in fact one of the animating themes of this volume.

Clinton's presidency should be understood as an exercise in perpetual reinvention—a constantly evolving response to new circumstances and to new emergencies threatening his political survival. He executed this feat by using, to a degree unmatched by any predecessor, the modern techniques for managing public opinion: polling, advertising, and constant recalibration of presidential rhetoric. It probably would not assuage Clinton's feelings much that I offer this assessment as praise—at least in part. This president has been a signal innovator in the ways he has merged his political tactics with his governmental strategy, and he has prospered as a result.

What did prosperity mean for the Clinton White House? In the most immediate sense, it signified public support—in the form of consistently high approval ratings for Clinton's job performance, if often not for Clinton personally. These ratings were critical to helping him transcend the Republican effort to render his presidency irrelevant after the 1994 congressional elections and to end his presidency altogether during impeachment. Voters liked Clinton's issue positions even as many chafed at the process by which he arrived at them. Each tactical maneuver that Clinton executed to win a short-term victory exacerbated the common perception—one that in my view was not entirely justified—that his presidency represented the triumph of tactics over policy. And while Clinton often complained about the news media's constant reductionism, the tendency to examine everything through the prism of tactics and political process, his own acrobatics encouraged this practice.

Political maneuvers crafted for the daily Washington brawl had consequences over the long haul. The most favorable one was a recasting of the image of the national Democratic Party. In relocating himself in response to Republican attacks, Clinton also moved his party away from its historic stereotype of profligate spending and showing undue sympathy to criminals and welfare recipients. But this achievement seems tentative. Beneath the new image, it remains unclear how complete the substantive transition has been; on some issues, such as free trade and restraining the costs of entitlement programs, it seems plain the party's historic positions scarcely have moved at all.

To the extent that Clintonism is a coherent philosophy, it is questionable that it could be sustained by a successor Democrat lacking Clinton's gifts for tactical improvisation.

Most of all, Clinton's political style, focused as it was on day-to-day victories, carried enormous long-term costs that he seemed to little comprehend. Clinton never engendered the trust and respect of the majority in the ways that the most successful presidents do (ABC News/Washington Post poll 1999).[1] This failure prevented him from commanding a popular majority in his two presidential elections and, more importantly, limited his effective range of influence in national debate on issues that hinged on questions of values or personal responsibility. There were many reasons for the blot on Clinton's popular standing. But in an age of great popular skepticism of politicians, Clinton's often-deserved reputation for calculation, glibness, and equivocation is an important one. "Slick Willie" was the name an unadmiring Arkansas editorialist tagged Clinton with in the early 1980s, and nearly two decades later, he continued to protest the accusation, though even many people once among his closest aides have essentially endorsed similar interpretations (Reich 1997; Stephanopoulos 1999).

This criticism puts Clinton's political techniques at the center of a debate long since underway and certain to echo long into the future. Can a presidency so focused on reading and responding to public opinion summon the constancy of purpose needed to produce a genuine policy legacy? Does the Clinton political style provide a model successors will be tempted to emulate?

The argument presented here is that Clinton's polling-based political style did yield some important successes, beyond mere survival in office. It helped him craft a centrist ideological consensus that dominated national politics as the race to succeed Clinton began in earnest. This is no minor accomplishment; most presidents and presidential contenders, of course, yearn to define and occupy the political center, but the ideological and special-interest factions that dominate both major parties make this goal persistently difficult to obtain. In 1996 Clinton became the first Democrat not to face a contest for his party's presidential nomination since Lyndon B. Johnson in 1964. At the end of his term, when public attention is focused more on the unstable Republican coalition—cultural conservatives and establishment moderates tugging for control, both sides lacking ideological confidence—it requires a mental leap to remember that it used to be the Democrats who seemed on the verge of a crack-up from within. They were sharply at odds on the merits of deficit reduction, and also on proposals to overhaul welfare so that it would require work and place time limits on benefits. Clinton enacted (with varying degrees of enthusiasm on his own part) policies that eliminated annual budget deficits and imposed the most far-reaching changes since the New Deal era in the way the federal government ministers to the poor. There was dissension within Democratic ranks but never an open revolt. At the same time, Clinton responded to the most potent GOP assault on activist federal government in sixty years—the Newt Gingrich–led "revolution" that took control of Congress in the 1994 elections—by reinvigorating public support for many of this government's central tasks. The GOP revolutionaries found that the public did not share their enthusiasm for curbing middle-class entitlements or sharply pruning environmental regulations. On other issues, where a majority was broadly sympathetic to GOP goals, Clinton prevailed by making tactical concessions that recast the debate in terms more favorable to him. Against the GOP's proposed abandonment of all racial preferences, Clinton offered a "mend-it, don't-end-it," alternative that involved only minor retreats from existing affirmative-action policies. Against the GOP's broad-based tax cuts, Clinton offered more limited reductions, targeted to policy goals such as subsidizing higher education, that proved more appealing to the public.

Little wonder, then, that presidential contenders in both parties—most notably Democrat Vice President Gore and Republican Texas governor George W. Bush—began the 2000 election race borrowing elements of the Clinton model. There are clear limits, however, to how much they or any other national figures would want to borrow from the Clinton experience.

That is because Clinton's political tactics were at their core a manifestation of presidential weakness. A variety of factors left Clinton persistently on the defensive during his White House tenure (and much of his career before it). He faced a remorseless Republican opposition bent on his destruction. He arrived in Washington at a time when the pursuit of scandal by the news media, congressional panels, and independent prosecutors, had become ritualized and unceasing. He had more cause than his predecessors to worry constantly about public opinion, since it came to be the most important part of his defense from these forces of attack.

To this unforgiving Washington arena, moreover, Clinton brought personal idiosyncracies. From an early age, as numerous biographers have demonstrated, Clinton possessed an uncommonly strong desire to win the approval of others. (Maraniss 1995, 139–41, 239–40; Renshon 1998). Unlike most of his predecessors, Clinton had spent virtually none of his adult life outside electoral politics. He arrived in the White House not so much with an ideology as with a loosely bound bundle of good intentions, some of them at odds with each other. Confronted with difficult policy tradeoffs, Clinton's instinct was invariably to find a way to avoid a clear choice. On spending, he wanted to "cut and invest"—that is, accommodate the needs of both those in favor of deficit reduction and those for increased domestic spending. Accused of wanting it both ways, Clinton would invariably complain about "false choices." He was the leader of a political movement that rejected right and left to search for a third way. Clinton's amorphous philosophy is in part a reflection of his accommodating personality. Both factors combined to leave him uniquely susceptible to outside influences, which he quantified and ranked through constant polling.

The point here is by no means that Clinton was bereft of governing principles. Amid the excursions, detours, and contradictions of Clinton's presidency there are plainly unifying themes. He is unquestionably a man of progressive instincts, who believes that activist government can be an instrument of social betterment. He believes in open trade borders and an assertive economic and security role for the United States overseas—a foreign policy agenda he has pursued on occasions in defiance of his own short-term political advantage. Ironically, at times when Clinton did do this—such as his sponsorship of two U.S. military interventions in the Balkans in the face of skeptical public opinion—his personal confidence, presidential stature, and popular support all seemed to grow. (Harris 1996; 1999b). More irony: While Clinton was the consummate politician, the most capable and widely respected of his appointees—such as Defense Secretary William J. Perry and Treasury Secretary Robert E. Rubin—were thoroughly apolitical men.

This leads to the real point about Clinton's penchant for political tactics: his obsession with reading the public mood blurred his vision nearly as often as it clarified it. The public was eager for a president liberated from the orthodoxies of both parties and able to fashion remedies for problems—crime, welfare, insolvent federal budgets—from the political center. Clinton filled this need, often masterfully. The public also seemed to yearn for a leader who could speak the language of command. Clinton feared Gen. Colin Powell as a potential political rival. (Morris 1999a, 156). But he did not seem to grasp the elements of Powell's appeal; it was Powell's candor, his seeming aversion to posturing and rhetorical cant, that made him so intriguing to an electorate that had come to see through political tactics more than the politicians realized. At a time when many Americans were concerned above all about issues of values, there was a premium granted leaders would could convey confidence in their own values and judgment. In the early 2000 campaign, Democrat Bill Bradley conveyed some of this same appeal, as did Republican

John McCain, though both men failed to win their parties' nominations. The electorate, as some of Clinton's own advisers had earlier concluded, was hungering for someone who could speak in the voice of national father. This was the need Clinton never did fill; his polls were of no help.

And so the Clinton era, though marked by episodic national plunges into prurience and even farce, raises issues of first principles for students of democratic theory: What do voters want from a leader? Do successful modern presidents follow public opinion or lead it? These timeless questions have grown lately more acute, as technology has accelerated democratic communication. In the age of CNN, voters have instantaneous access to news and debate. In the age of the Matt Drudge and Don Imus, they have instantaneous access also to all manner of rumor, speculation, and commentary calculated to diminish the mystique of any leader. Meanwhile, as polling has grown more sophisticated and ubiquitous, the politicians can monitor with more immediacy than ever what these voters are thinking. They can also isolate and classify voters—which ones are likely to vote on which issues, which ones respond to which types of ads and rhetorical appeals, and which ones aren't likely to cast a ballot under any circumstances—in a practice that Steven Schier has identified as "the political variant of niche marketing" (1999, B2).

So far, it is too early to know what to make of this clamorous, and often quite manipulative, brand of democracy. Some people—most notably, Dick Morris, an apostle of polling and Clinton's 1996 political guru—anticipate with approval the imminent transformation of American politics into a virtual plebiscitory democracy. As polls and referendums proliferate, so the theory goes, American politics will become something approximating the "pure democracy" that Madison spoke of in the Federalist Papers.

This prospect doesn't excite everyone. "Interactivity encourages instant responses, discourages second thoughts, and offers outlets for demagoguery, egomania, insult, and hate," writes historian Arthur Schlesinger Jr. "In too interactive a polity, a 'common passion,' as Madison thought, could sweep through a people and lead to emotional and ill-judged actions. . . . The Internet has done little thus far to foster the reasoned exchanges that in Madison's words 'refine and enlarge the public views'" (1997).

More than this, many people will find something base and unappealing about a leader who is fixated too intently on the views of his audience. Leadership is supposed to be about public persuasion, not propitiation. A president as poll-following improvisationist offends our idealistic notions of what leaders do. Clinton, a man whose pragmatic and idealistic sides are chronically in tension, is himself plainly offended by the suggestion. Little wonder, then, that in January 1996 he turned red with irritation at my impertinent question as he readied himself for a reelection campaign marked by pragmatic compromises at every turn.

## Clinton and the Morris Model of Politics

Months later in 1996, I had another conversation with Clinton. The discussion returned, more congenially this time, to our old theme—the relationship between tactics and principles for political leaders. Clinton asserted, as he had often in the past, that the cynicism felt by so many voters was misplaced. He said he wished that the public could sit in while government decisions were being made. The result, he felt certain, was that people would be surprised and impressed by how conscientious and idealistic the process really is.

I pressed him: Is public cynicism really so unjustified? If people could look inside his operation, or that of his Republican opponents, wouldn't they see a process dominated by political consultants and pollsters? Yes, Clinton answered, they would find pollsters. But, he argued, there was nothing wrong with that. Any smart politician wants to know what people are thinking, not necessarily to echo their views, but to tailor his own arguments. "Every president since Franklin Roosevelt has used pollsters," Clinton said.

Clinton had a point—one this chapter has an obligation to confront. If all modern presidents have used polls, what after all was so noteworthy about Clinton's reliance on them? The difference is one of degree and of kind. There were simply more polls in the Clinton White House, and they covered more subjects. In fact, we know from the testimony of people who served with Clinton that they covered everything. The Clinton team wanted to know more than the traditional presidential approval rating or the horse-race match-ups between candidates. They wanted an extensive portrait of the cultural values espoused by Americans, particularly the crucial "swing voters" aligned with neither major party. They wanted to test slogans for possible use in Clinton speeches. And they wanted to test voter reaction to every possible policy idea, in either the foreign or domestic arena, that was linked to or might in the future become linked to Clinton. This was the difference of degree.

The difference of kind was the central role that pollsters and political consultants played in the policymaking process in the Clinton White House. Historically, pollsters and media advisers have played supportive roles for the presidents and senior policy officials. They let these people know how their ideas were playing in Peoria and suggested ways of tailoring the presidential message for maximum support. In the Clinton White House, pollsters were often the source of policy ideas. In numerous other instances they were the vital force either stopping policy preferences advanced elsewhere in the administration or in pushing policies onto Clinton's agenda over the wishes of a recalcitrant bureaucracy.

This new primacy for pollsters in the Clinton White House coincided with the arrival—in late 1994 after the Democratic rout in the midterm congressional elections that year—of consultant Dick Morris. Morris had been a Clinton adviser in his Arkansas years but, after a falling out in the early 1990s, was not an important figure in the first years of the Clinton White House. After the 1994 disaster, President Clinton and First Lady Hillary Rodham Clinton, their backs against the wall, brought the politically ambidextrous Morris back onto their team. (Morris had worked for many Republicans and called himself a centrist). At the same time, an existing group of advisers—including, notably, pollster Stan Greenberg—was evicted from the Clinton inner circle.

There were important differences between the Greenberg polling model and the new model that Morris and pollster Mark Penn brought to the White House after the midterm humiliation. These differences are critical to understanding the evolution of the Clinton presidency. One person who watched this evolution with a jaundiced eye was Harold Ickes, the deputy White House chief of staff, a traditional and unabashed liberal. Ickes had known Morris for years from New York City politics and despised him.

But Ickes, in an interview with the author, was frank in acknowledging how Morris transformed the Clinton White House in 1995 and 1996. The Greenberg model of polling, as Ickes and others described it, was fairly conventional. Greenberg would monitor public opinion on such topics as Clinton's approval rating and the standing of such initiatives as the 1994 proposal to overhaul health care. His tasks were not so different than those that pollsters such as Robert Teeter performed for George Bush or Richard Wirthlin for Ronald Reagan. Greenberg, by most accounts, was an important presence in the early Clinton White House, but he was never a dominant figure in actually fashioning the content of its agenda.

Morris indisputably was such a figure. Ickes recalled political meetings, at which Morris held forth on the latest polling data, and offered his ideas of what Clinton should say and do next. Clinton would sit silently and listen. "I have never seen such a role reversal," said Ickes. "Bill Clinton dominates every other conversation I have witnessed, including with other heads of state. But with Morris it was almost as if he had some supernatural hold on him. He would sit for 30 minutes, not saying a word" (1999). Clinton did not always take Morris's advice, Ickes added, but he was nonetheless in 1995 and 1996 the president's most important domestic adviser, and also weighed in freely on the political dimensions of foreign policy decisions about Bosnia and countering terrorism. Clinton, according to Morris, once praised him with a comparison to his earlier pollster: "Greenberg never told me what to do" (Morris 1999a, 41).

Morris inaugurated the custom of weekly political meetings with the president in the White House residence. These meetings, which have no obvious precedent in previous presidencies, were the principal vehicle by which policy and political strategies were merged. In addition to consultants such as Morris and Penn, and media adviser Robert Squier, the sessions grew to include Vice President Gore, cabinet secretaries such as Labor Secretary Robert Reich, Education Secretary Richard Riley, and then-deputy national security adviser Samuel Berger. The weekly political meetings outlived Morris, who was banished from the 1996 campaign following disclosure in the *Star,* the tabloid, of his relationship with a prostitute. In the second term, the meetings included such figures as White House senior adviser Douglas Sosnik and the White House's two senior domestic policy aides—National Economic Adviser Gene Sperling and Domestic Policy Adviser Bruce Reed (Berke 1996; Harris 1997a). Morris has been voluble on the way in which his political input shaped the 1995 and 1996 agenda. The consultant was a critical voice in urging Clinton to take a leading role—through either rhetorical pronouncements or policy initiatives—on a blizzard of subjects.

Several times a week during 1996, Clinton would emerge with a new executive action or policy endorsement. Many of these initiatives carried a plain subtext: they were part of the so-called values agenda that was fashioned in order to persuade middle-class swing voters that Clinton shared their everyday concerns about children, families, paying for education, and countering the coarsening effects of modern culture. Items backed under Morris's advocacy included Clinton's prodding of the television industry to adapt a ratings system for violent and sexually explicit content; new regulations to help the government track fathers who don't pay child support across state lines; a new tax credit to help offset the cost of college tuition; and a broad campaign to align the federal government against the tobacco industry, with proposed new taxes on and new regulations of cigarette manufacturing.

Some of the initiatives Morris pushed were easy to lampoon—"small bore," in the phrase critics routinely invoked that year. Even some on Clinton's own staff questioned whether prodding corporations to donate cell phones to neighborhood-watch groups was the best way for a commander-in-chief to exert his influence. But Morris's role was also enormous on more consequential issues. In the summer of 1996, the consultant was perhaps the dominant voice in an emotional White House debate about whether Clinton should sign what was arguably the most significant piece of domestic legislation of his term, the Republican-drafted law to overhaul federal relief to the poor. Clinton backed welfare reform as a general concept but worried that the GOP version was too punitive toward the poor and objected to its abandonment of assistance for legal immigrants. Prior to signing the bill that became law, he had vetoed two similar bills. Centrist policy aide Bruce Reed favored signing this version, but few other administration officials shared this view. Health and Human Services Secretary Donna Shalala, and then–senior adviser George Stephanopoulos were both opposed; first Lady Hillary Rodham Clinton expressed deep skepticism; but Morris carried the day with his warning that a veto of welfare reform was the last major threat to Clinton's reelection, the only way that Republican nominee Robert J. Dole could revive his anemic campaign. According to Morris, Clinton called him an hour after he signed the bill to say, "I want you to know I signed that bill because I trust you" (Morris 1999a, 304).

Aware of Morris's critical role, and of Clinton's addiction to polling, other Clinton aides began to tailor their own bureaucratic strategies accordingly. Labor Secretary Reich, for instance, has written that he often used Morris as a vehicle to push previously ignored items onto the presidential agenda (Reich 1997). Shalala, too, learned that it did not pay to back ideas in the Clinton White House unless she could demonstrate that there was polling data to suggest they would help Clinton politically (1999).

The Clinton White House's obsession with political advantage was sometimes a source of comic relief. Once White House officials held a briefing to announce a new initiative to require federal tracking of guns used in crimes, and it fell to me in the next day's *Washington Post* to remind the White House that the administration had announced precisely the same program months earlier. A Morris aide recalled to me how he thought he had devised a clever initiative, suggesting new federal rules requiring public disclosure when paroled child abusers move into a community. But polling results were highly unfavorable; it turned out that voters were appalled that child abusers are ever paroled in the first place. The proposal was dropped.

On other occasions, the White House's political preoccupations were less amusing. At Morris's urging, in July 1996 Clinton once overrode his own Justice Department in endorsing a constitutional amendment that would guarantee rights to crime victims. Something that was so important in July that it merited revising the nation's founding document was never mentioned again after November. I recall conversations in which White House aides indignantly denounced cynical reporters for suggesting that the president might be seeking political gain by his handling of the bombing of the federal building at Oklahoma City. It was not until three years later, when Morris made available the agendas from the weekly political meetings, that I saw how the strategy was laid out coldly just a week after the tragedy: "Temporary gain: boost in ratings," read the agenda for a meeting on the aftermath of Oklahoma City bombing. "Permanent possible gain: sets up Extremist Issue vs. Republicans" (Morris 1999a, 419). It makes one wonder about Clinton's admonition that the public would be taken aback by the idealism of politics, if only people had the chance to sit on the meetings.

*The Origins of the Clinton Style*

David Maraniss, a Clinton biographer and one of my *Washington Post* colleagues, has an axiom for those seeking to understand the personal and political idiosyncrasies of President Clinton: Return to Arkansas. Clinton's distinctive brand of presidential politics took shape in 1995 and 1996, as he sought to claw his way back from the policy and political disasters of 1994 and win reelection. But the origins of this style are rooted firmly in Clinton's Arkansas experience. How was it that Clinton came to be a president who relied more on polling and TV advertising than his predecessors? Part of the answer is psychological, reflecting a family upbringing that, by Clinton's own testimony, left him with a powerful attentiveness to winning the approval of others. Part of the answer is practical, underscoring the special challenges facing an essentially liberal politician trying to succeed in a state more culturally and ideologically conservative than he was.

Psychobiography is treacherous terrain for journalists and political scientists alike; there is no need to dwell in this fundamentally speculative realm for long. Still, there is considerable evidence suggesting that Clinton is in a literal sense a natural politician; the instincts he brings to the task of winning approval predate his own consciousness of them. Clinton's early home life was difficult. His mother and grandmother (a surrogate parent for part of his childhood) had a famously antagonistic relationship; his adoptive father, Roger Clinton, was a charming man who turned violent during frequent drinking binges. Amid this turmoil, the young boy assigned himself the role of mediator and kept private problems hidden from the world, even from close friends like Carolyn Staley and David Leopoulos (Harris 1998b). In the 1992 campaign video, the Democratic nominee himself acknowledged that his family background sometimes inclined him to try too hard to please people.

(I had a humorous glimpse of this side of Clinton in 1996, when the president traveled to the 1996 Democratic National Convention in Chicago by train. Clinton was in the caboose, and the press corps had seats up front. Soon, we heard Clinton's disembodied voice from a loudspeaker, yelling to the people in backyards bordering the tracks. "Nice dog," he yelled to one family. "I love your garden," he shouted to another. I always thought this was Bill Clinton's ultimate fantasy, or at least his ultimate political fantasy; here he was rolling through middle America, being cheered by strangers, lavishing them with praise, seducing the public one house at a time [Harris and Baker 1996].)

Stanley Renshon, a psychologist and political scientist, believes that Clinton's background helped shape one of the "core elements" of his character: "a distinct and powerful turn toward others in his interpersonal relationships, motivated by his strong need for validation of his somewhat idealized view of himself" (1998). Dick Morris has the same assessment but puts it more squarely in the political context. "Typically, much of Bill Clinton's self-image comes from the feelings reflected by others around him," he writes. "In a room, he will instinctively, as if by canine sense of smell, find anyone who shows reserve toward him, and he will work full time on winning his or her approval and, if possible, affection. . . . America is the ultimate room for Clinton. For him, a poll helps him sense who doesn't like him and why they don't. In the reflected numbers, he sees his shortcomings and his potential, his successes, and failures" (Morris 1999a, 11).

It is noteworthy that Morris notes Clinton's need for polls is essentially defensive, a warning sign about political danger. Arkansas, where Clinton began his career, is a place fraught with dangers for a politician of his ideological stripe. After winning the State House in 1977, Clinton was the youngest governor in America. Two years later, he was the youngest former governor in America, after voters reacted against the increase in car taxes he passed and concluded that he was too politically and culturally liberal. In Clinton's comeback election two years later, he and Morris fashioned the political style that would dominate the rest of his governorship. After extensive polling, Clinton broadcast an advertisement apologizing for the tax increases of his first term. In the years thereafter, Clinton would poll and advertise heavily over issues, even when elections were not imminent. The "permanent campaign" was underway (Morris 1999a, 42–69).

There are two noteworthy points about the Arkansas origins of Clinton's political style. One is that Clinton's adaptation to circumstance follows a model others have used. Look at the centrist Democratic Leadership Council, which Clinton helped found in the mid-1980s. Its core group was made up of southern Democrats, like Senators Charles S. Robb of Virginia and Sam Nunn of Georgia, people who needed to escape their party's liberal national reputation if they were to survive in their home states. The second point is that Clinton, as president, proved to be a recidivist. The mistakes of his first two years were echoes of the mistakes he made in his first term as governor. So, too, were the techniques he used to revive himself echoes of the ones he used for prospering in Arkansas in the 1980s.

*Presidential Communication in the Clinton Era*

Governing in the modern era is above all a task of communication. Presidents seek to lead by having the words they speak, and the images of leadership they project, set the terms of national debate. The persistent challenge of the Clinton White House was to communicate in a climate of unusual adversity. With its emphasis on polling and television advertising, the Clinton political style was a response to this challenge.

The adversity sprang from several sources, including a Congress that, for three-quarters of Clinton's tenure, was in the hands of a hostile Republican majority that showed him little of the deference, or even the routine courtesy, that legislators have historically extended to all presidents regardless of party. This surliness doubtless reflected the fact that the Republicans represented that significant minority of the electorate who not only opposed Clinton's policies but also despised him personally and never accepted the legitimacy of his presidency. (Several times a week, my mail would bring correspondence from this sullen faction. "Stop covering up for this lying traitor!" one typical letter chided me during 1999, after I had written a favorable, if hardly effusive, piece about Clinton in the wake of NATO's successful military intervention in Kosovo. "It appears that Monica Lewinsky has given her 'presidential kneepads' to you!") Other sources of adversity included the independent counsel statute, which bedeviled all presidents since its post-Watergate founding but reached its dubious apogee during the Clinton years. The law, with its low standards for triggering independent prosecutors and the loose measures of accountability it imposed on them, ensured that at any given moment of his presidency Clinton and his appointees would be the targets of numerous ethical investigations.

And there was Clinton's adversarial relationship with the news media, a subject on which I have a personal vantage point. This sour history could easily be a subject of a book itself (and in fact has been already, written by my

*Washington Post* colleague Howard Kurtz). Suffice to say here that there were practical reasons, as well as deeply rooted psychological ones, why the two sides got along less than swimmingly.

From the press's perspective, the practical reason was often that Clinton wrongly withheld information or shaved the truth on difficult subjects. From Clinton's perspective, the press was comprised of shallow reductionists—obsessed always with process and political motives, bored and cynical about his policies and their real-life impacts. But these practical grievances scarcely explained the emotion—and lack of proportion—on both sides. White House press secretary Michael McCurry once perceptively told John F. Kennedy Jr. that the press tended to see Clinton as the sort who was high school cheerleader—peppy, full of himself, a bit two-faced (Kennedy 1999). Most reporters, by contrast, were the sort who spent school sitting at the back of class, offering tart commentary and wisecracks.

For his part, Clinton is someone who his entire life has sought to project idealized images of himself—and had also to worry about shielding contradictions to this idealized version of himself from public view. In this sense (though not in many others), Clinton was a bit like Nixon, who saw negative coverage not as an irritant to be overcome but as an almost violent assault on his own sense of self. "The people don't get it that the press runs the government," Clinton once raged to Morris. "They love to destroy people. That's how they get their rocks off" (Morris 1999a, 99).

Early in his term, Clinton imagined that it might be possible to leave this unhappy marriage altogether. Talk shows like *Larry King Live* would make it possible for him to reach the public directly, he boasted, avoiding the mainstream media's probing (Roberts 1993). But he learned in due course that his fantasized divorce from reporters was impossible. The proliferation of non-traditional news outlets did not mean that he could avoid traditional outlets. Instead, they must learn to communicate at multiple levels simultaneously. A modern White House must worry what is being said on *Larry King* and the *CBS Evening News,* on the front page of the *Washington Post,* and on the *Slate* magazine web site.

The open hostility between press and president that prevailed during the early years of the administration improved somewhat after the 1994 elections, roughly around the time I arrived on the beat. McCurry and White House senior adviser Douglas B. Sosnik were part of a new group of aides who, whatever their personal grievances, kept press relations on a civil (if sometimes sullen) level of professionalism. But these changes only helped minimize the consequences of negative news coverage. They did not solve the problem of presidential communication; that took something else, specifically about $100 million. This was the amount, in both Clinton-Gore reelection campaign money and White House–controlled Democratic National Committee "soft money," that was spent on polling and television advertising in the 1996 election cycle (Harris 1998a).

Clinton's reelection team began this advertising unprecedentedly early in the election cycle. Most of Clinton's White House staff, who thought advertising so far before election day was a waste of money, adamantly opposed this decision to spend. But Morris (who had a financial stake, given that, like most political consultants, he was compensated with a commission tied directly to ad spending) insisted on it. The deluge that followed was aimed squarely at the independent-minded swing voters who had grown disaffected with Clinton early in the first term and whose support he needed to revive for reelection. Morris believes that it is issues—rather than gauzy biographical portraits or slashing personal attacks on opponents—that drive swing voters in the modern climate (Morris 1999b, 31–40).

Clinton's team ran mostly issue-based ads, warning voters about the alleged extremism of Republicans' proposed budget cuts for Medicare, the environment, and education. They trumpeted Clinton's support for such things as the television "V-chip," which allows parents to block undesirable programming. At some level, political advertising challenges the very theory of democracy, since the appeals they make are almost by definition biased and designed to manipulate. What right-thinking citizen would make voting decisions based on an ad? But the Clinton ads deserve praise by faint damnation. Far more than many ads, they contained factual information, and their appeals were not—by the lamentably low standards of modern campaigns—particularly demagogic. These ads clearly did several things. They forced Clinton and Vice President Gore into a race for money, which clearly contributed to the lax standards in which the 1994 fundraising scandals blossomed. They also made the consultants rich, with a half dozen of them reaping profits of a million dollars or more from the 1996 presidential election (Harris 1998b).

But did the ads move votes? A 1998 study by the Pew Research Center found that Clinton's approval ratings generally moved in the same upward direction through 1995 and 1996, both in television markets where the ads ran and in those where they did not. Morris and his team say this finding directly contradicts their own polling, as well as common sense. "Corporations advertise because it works in getting information to consumers, and the same is true with candidates for office," said Tom Freedman, a 1996 Clinton campaign aide who had no financial stake in the advertising budget. "Clinton never could have furthered public understanding of his positions as dramatically as he needed to without advertising" (1999).

This view is shared by some leading Republican pollsters, such as Bill McInturff, who conducted his own study of the ads' impact. "I believed then, and do now, that the early ads created an additional marginal benefit that helped reshape the race and helped Clinton and the Democrats," he said (Edsall 1999).

In the end, the judgments of Freedman and McInturff are more compelling. Moreover, as one who arrived at the White House in 1995, when the president seemed at times an almost physically diminished man, I cannot discount another factor: Clinton's psychology. The ads, I am convinced, gave him the confidence that he was not merely responding passively to the Republican ascendancy and was in fact driving the public debate with his own message. In short, they were critical to solving Clinton's communication problem and to helping him climb out from a deep deficit to win reelection.

## The Future of the Clinton Political Style

Clinton's energetic polling and television advertising brought him survival. But what else did it bring him? This is the question the historians will ask as they assess the lasting impact of his presidency. It is also the question other leaders will ask as they determine which aspects of his political style they wish to praise through the sincerest way possible—imitation.

Was the Clinton style a success? This simple question invites labyrinthine answers. Yes, Clinton's improvisational political style worked, because it produced survival in the face of recurrent crises. But most of these personal and policy crises were self-inflicted, encouraged by the same improvisational approach to life that was Clinton's signature. Yes, Clinton's political manner helped him attain a measure of policy success. But it required him to yield more ground, both rhetorically and substantively, and to spend more time on the defensive than most ambitious presidents would wish to. On the whole, Clinton's style was so emphatically a reflection of his own circumstances and personality that it is not likely to be a lasting model for others.

This does not mean that the Clinton years will not echo. There no doubt will be substantial adaptation of some of Clinton's technical innovations. One notable borrower has been Hillary Rodham Clinton; though correctly viewed as a more doctrinaire liberal than her husband, she is using Mark Penn, her husband's expert on public opinion, as a polling and issues adviser. As polling has grown more sophisticated in its ability to identify swing voters and the policies that move them—as opposed to merely gauging simple approval ratings—all sensible politicians will want to avail themselves of these techniques.

So, too, will Clinton's philosophy of public persuasion reverberate. Advertising of all sorts, not just political advertising, is going through a transformation, with an uncertain destination, in the age of the Internet. But surely one lesson of Clinton's experience will remain valid: the distinction between seasons of campaigning and seasons of governing seems pretty much obsolete. Clinton, unlike the elder Bush he succeeded, understood that the battle for public opinion is a full-time endeavor, through every means possible: speeches, presidential travel, and advertising. Though the modalities of advertising may change, "the permanent campaign" is here to stay.

Some people see even more fundamental change imminently at hand. Dick Morris, with characteristic modesty, predicted that the poll- and advertising-based style he and Clinton inaugurated will soon enough turn all America into California, where public referendums often drive important policy changes more than politicians do (Morris 1998). I am deeply skeptical of this. Clinton's political style was in the end minimalist; it ensured survival. It never commanded a majority in a popular election, even against a comparatively weak opponent in the 1996 election. It did not build him the reservoir of public respect that allows presidents to consistently drive public opinion rather than follow it, nor the political influence to robustly advance a policy agenda.

Clinton's situation in the fall of 1999, with little more than a year left in his term, was sadly representative. A *Washington Post* survey showed some 60 percent of the electorate did not hold Clinton in high personal regard, even as a majority approved of his handling of the presidency (ABC News/Washington Post 1999), He was winning the political battle against congressional Republicans, but his policy agenda was anemic. At the start of the year, he had said that overhauling the nation's largest entitlement programs, Medicare and Social Security, was a top priority for him. Yet, wedded to the congressional Democrats who saved him during impeachment, Clinton did little to advance his supposed goals. He did not put forward detailed proposals of his own for entitlements, nor did he accept the political risks that would have been necessary for him to drive the debate. But this was not especially new. For all his boasting about fashioning a "New Democrat" agenda, Clinton's most important centrist policy victories were in the past: welfare reform in 1996, a bipartisan balanced budget deal in 1997. Clinton failed in 1997 to persuade his own party to give him the votes needed for fast-track authority to negotiate free-trade deals. He failed the next year to pass comprehensive anti-youth smoking legislation, when Senate Democrats would not back Clinton in saying that tobacco companies should be given some protection against lawsuits. Both these defeats called into question how much Clinton really had refashioned his party around a third way.

The vital center that Clinton claimed to have created in American politics with his 1996 reelection was starting to look like the dead center. Clinton managed to find politically safe ground on most issues. But the price was that someone who regarded himself as an activist president often showed a surprising degree of passivity toward the circumstances that greeted him. Arthur Schlesinger Jr., the man who in the late 1940s coined the phrase "Vital Center" to describe a brand of progressive politics considerably more robust than Clinton's, offers a suggestion of how this came to be. Clinton aspired to be a great national unifier; but the most consequential presidents, such as the Roosevelts, are usually leaders "who first divide . . . the nation before uniting it on a new level of understanding. Most great presidents are seen as unifiers only in retrospect" (Harris 1997b). Clinton's domestic policy was marked by what the writer Nicholas Lemann called his "flabby syncretism" (1998).

This criticism suggests the limits of his political style. Politics, at the end of the day, is about the search for substantive remedy to national problems. In other words, politics is fundamentally about policy more than it is about personality or image. Presidents with large aspirations will want to borrow some of Clinton's techniques but will be wary of his larger strategy that gave polling and advertising experts such a central place in the policymaking process.

Does any among the current crop of contenders have the potential to be this kind of president? Vice President Gore, though he helped orchestrate Clinton's political reinvention in 1996 and had borrowed some of the techniques in his own 2000 race, is in fact a vastly more ideological figure than Clinton. One needs only read his environmentalist tract, *Earth in the Balance,* with its call to eliminate internal combustion engines by 2020 and his denunciations of "finger-in-the-wind" politicians to appreciate this (Gore 1993, 15). In an October 1999 session with reporters and editors at the *Washington Post,* the vice president declined my invitation to defend Clinton's use of pollsters in the policymaking process. And Gore took pains to add that a campaign commercial he had shot earlier that month on the Nuclear Test Ban Treaty had been inspired by the candidate alone: "I did not poll it. I did not focus group it. I did not talk to a legion of advisers" (Gore 1999).

Texas governor George W. Bush, by contrast, is the kind of ideologically amorphous politician likely to borrow not merely Clinton's tactics but also his larger strategy. Already in 1999, journalists were writing of him in phrases that echoed those written about Clinton. My *Washington Post* colleague E. J. Dionne, in a mostly favorable magazine profile of Bush, asked: "Is Bush about political philosophy or political positioning? Pragmatism with a purpose or electoral calculation? Does he represent good-natured compromise or is he just looking for action?" (1999). He could not reach a conclusion.

And so Clinton's political legacy will depend, as it does for all presidents, in part on what comes after him. No doubt the debate about the impact of his policies will have a long echo as well. My own guess is that he will be seen as a plucky survivor, who helped Democrats and the country move into a new era of high-technology, post–Cold War politics. But he executed this transformation clumsily and incompletely—in part because he never found the confidence to lead public opinion more decisively. What the great columnist Walter Lippman said of DeGaulle will not be said of Clinton: "He gave his people not what they wanted but what they would in time learn to want."

CHAPTER 5

# COURTING THE PUBLIC

## Bill Clinton's Postmodern Education

BRUCE MIROFF

The paradoxes of Bill Clinton have bemused observers of his presidency ever since its oddly troubled beginning. Puzzling questions have piled up during Clinton's two terms: How can a president who is so bright make so many dumb moves? How can a president who is so beleaguered make so many bold comebacks? How can a president who is tainted by immorality succeed as the champion of middle-class values? Most important for the purposes of this chapter, how can a president who wins so little trust from the public gain such a strong standing in public evaluations of his presidential performance?

I do not aspire in this essay to resolve all of these paradoxes, but I do aim to provide a perspective on Clinton's ability to achieve popularity despite the low public regard for his character and morality. Bill Clinton has thrived as a public performer because he is a postmodern character attuned to a postmodern moment in American political history. By postmodern character, I mean a political actor who lacks a stable identity associated with ideological and partisan values and who is, thereby, free to move nimbly from one position to another as political fashion dictates. By postmodern moment, I mean an era where the organizing themes of modern American politics—the heroic presidency, the Cold War, the conflict between Democratic liberalism and Republican conservatism—are superseded by fleeting images and issues that do not produce any consistent or coherent political understanding.

The strengths and weaknesses of Clinton's postmodern character have both been on vivid display during his presidency. Narrowing the distance between president and public, Clinton has emphasized the democratic connection between the two through his rhetoric, gestures, and travels; even while doubting his honesty, the public has responded (as Diane Hollern Harvey notes in her chapter in this volume) by believing that the president cares about their problems. Highlighting the application of intelligence, free of ideology or dogma, to issues large and small, he has made substance rather than symbolics the core of his presidential politics. But Clinton's repeated postmodern reinventions of himself have cast a shadow over these appealing qualities. Substance, it often seems in the Clinton presidency, is less the alternative to symbolism than it is a cleverer form of symbolic appeal. And the democratic bond between president and people often seems manipulative and hollow, a product of polling rather than democratic purpose.

Clinton's biography provides several clues to his affinity with the postmodern political moment. His transformation from a McGovern organizer in the 1972 presidential campaign to a New Democrat in his own 1992 presidential campaign parallels the decline of liberal idealism that is one cause of the postmodern turn in American politics. The contemporary Republican Party employs postmodern media and campaign techniques, but its core leadership is still imbued with traditional conservative values. On the Democratic side, however, ideological enthusiasm faded after McGovern's catastrophic defeat, and subsequent crusades to revive it, such as the run for the presidential nomination by Senator Edward Kennedy in 1980, never recaptured the party. Although Democratic liberalism still contains adherents in the party's congressional contingent, its presidential standard bearers from 1976 through 1988 deemphasized the old liberal faith, setting the stage for Clinton to redefine his party as a postmodern collage no longer held together by its modern reconstruction in Franklin D. Roosevelt's New Deal.

Clinton's close ties with business interests during his five terms as governor of Arkansas point to a second source of his affinity with postmodern politics. The ascendancy of market values and a market vocabulary has led to the eclipse of distinctly political and social discourses. Emphasis on profitability and attention to the bottom line are supplanting alternative modes of thinking in many areas of American life—medicine is a notorious example—and politics is hardly immune from the same kind of postmodern mindset. Commitment to core values is burdensome to a politician who seeks to adapt to the fluctuating demands of the political marketplace; the postmodern politician, as Clinton has demonstrated, can escape the encumbrance of ideology to repackage himself in line with the most profitable political fashions.

Despite his preparation for postmodern politics in his Arkansas years, the national political terrain of the 1990s did not immediately yield its hidden postmodern contours even to such a flexible and adroit political character as Bill Clinton, who only found his way after two years of feckless wandering. But from his 1995 comeback in the battle with the Gingrich Republicans to his survival strategy in the Year of Lewinsky, he demonstrated that he had learned how to master the media politics of the postmodern moment. His two terms can thus be understood as the story of a postmodern political education.

Clinton's legacy for the public presidency depends on whether the postmodern moment proves to be our permanent condition or whether it is merely transitional to some new organizing framework for political conflict. It also depends on how Clinton's successors regard him. Whether Republican or Democratic, they are almost certain publicly to set themselves off from him when it comes to moral character in the White House. But will they, nonetheless, covertly copy Clinton's methods—for example, the constant opinion polling and media spinning—because they recognize that the shifting stances these methods generated, while failing to give the public a solid presidential character it respected, offered it the multiple presidential identities it desired?

## The Strengths and Weaknesses of Clinton's Public Presidency

It is possible to compile separate lists for the strengths and weaknesses of Bill Clinton's relationship with the American people. The problem is that the two lists turn out to look much alike, for Clinton's strengths and weaknesses are closely intertwined. Describing "the paradox of Bill Clinton," *New York Times* journalist Todd Purdum has written, "One of the biggest, most talented, articulate, intelligent, open, colorful characters ever to inhabit the Oval Office can also be an undisciplined, fumbling, obtuse, defensive, self-justifying rogue. His strengths and weaknesses not only spring from the same source but could also not exist without one another. In a real sense, his strengths are his weaknesses, his enthusiasms are his undoing, and most of the traits that make him appealing can make him appalling in the flash of an eye" (1996, 36).[1] Purdum is certainly on to something. Both the political insiders who have direct dealings with Clinton and the public that watches him from afar see the different sides of the president in frequent alternation. The "appealing" Clinton is exceptionally bright, energetic, optimistic, charming, and caring. The "appalling" Clinton is exceptionally cunning, manipulative, evasive, petulant, and self-indulgent.

Much of the time, Clinton comes across to the public as applying his outsized political talents to the nation's business with enthusiasm and skill. In these moments, he has the grace at presidential politics that marked his Democratic heroes, FDR and JFK. And the closer citizens come to him (in a town meeting or White House conference on some social issue), the more they are bathed in the glow of his concern for them; he is, Garry Wills observes, "a virtuoso empathizer (1997, 31). Clinton has never made the political mistake that cost George Bush so heavily in 1992: appearing distant from the anxieties and aspirations of ordinary American citizens. Running the opposite risk—seeming to lack the gravity and dignity appropriate to the nation's "First Citizen"—repeatedly Clinton has sought democratic connection to his mass public.[2]

But some of the time, Clinton's charms are exposed to the public as the wiles of a political seducer. As another *Times* reporter, Jacob Weisberg, has commented, Clinton cannot "escape his reputation for being slippery. He is not the first president to lie, or lie under oath. But he will surely be remembered as someone who habitually played games with the truth. . . . It will also be recalled that he was disloyal to friends and took advantage of people who worked for him" (1999, 35). Clinton's supporters generally like where he stands on the issues, and they find him an engaging public character (especially in comparison to his political enemies), but few can be said to believe in him. Many Americans have agreed in essence with what Clinton's adversaries say about his character even as they have reelected him and rallied to his defense against impeachment and removal from office.

These paradoxes that bewilder everyone else seem to nurture Clinton's public virtuosity: Take away the appalling traits and there might be little left of Clinton's appealing ones. Thus, a simpler and more honorable political figure would likely have been crushed by the defeats Clinton has suffered and constrained from pursuing the opportunistic and shape-shifting strategies that Clinton has followed to recover from them. Character, in the traditional sense of the word, would likely have made Bill Clinton into another Jimmy Carter. But Clinton lacks Carter's sense of shame. His former political lieutenant, George Stephanopoulos, observes: "I came to see how Clinton's shamelessness is a key to his political success, how his capacity for denial is tied to the optimism that is his greatest political strength" (1999, 5).

If presidents were still judged by the heroic imagery of the Cold War presidency or evaluated by the Founders' standard of republican dignity, Clinton's flaws would have spelled political doom for him (Miroff 1998;1999) But he has surmounted revelations of weak character that would have destroyed previous presidents because his public is prepared to accept a president as a larger-than-life version of Everyman. His is the archetypal story of the 1990s, with all the vital ingredients: self-absorption, ambition, sex, celebrity—and the promise of transcendence. As Weisberg has remarked: "To a public that consumes quantities of confessional entertainment and self-help advice, Clinton's turmoil seems not bizarre, but familiar. His cyclical progress through stages of sin, denial, contrition, and forgiveness has humanized him like no previous president" (1999, 52).

Acceptance by the majority of Americans of a protean president whose "good" and "bad" sides oscillate is not simply the mark of growing tolerance for moral imperfection or concern for the protection of privacy. It also reflects the ways in which the public has been saturated with postmodern media that emphasizes discontinuity and irony over consistency and conviction. In the era of the modern presidency, from Franklin Roosevelt through Ronald Reagan (George Bush may have been a transitional figure), presidents were expected to have stable identities and consistent political projects. In the postmodern presidency of Bill Clinton, both identity and political projects can be fluid and even reversible. The new political culture, like the new popular culture, is skeptical of certainties and fixities and welcoming of novelties so long as they provide the audience with the satisfactions it seeks at that moment. To posit just one analogy between the two cultures, if we associate *Father Knows Best* with the Eisenhower years, we should associate *Seinfeld* with the Clinton ones.

Comparing Clinton with Ronald Reagan, a predecessor who also excelled at the arts of the public presidency, should serve to clarify Clinton's postmodern public character. The Reagan White House was just as focused on courting the public as the Clinton White House was; its techniques for manufacturing attractive images and "spinning" the press indeed provided useful templates for a Clinton administration that initially came to power pledged to undo core elements of its policy legacy. But there are fundamental differences between the two administrations in the presentation of presidential character, the understanding of how to win public support, and the relationship between the press and the presidency.

Although he had undergone a profound political transformation of his own, from New Deal Democrat to Goldwater Republican, by the time Ronald Reagan entered the presidency he had the most clear-cut identity of any major American political figure. Reagan was the very definition of a conservative Republican (although his amiable persona softened his ideology's harsh edges). He appeared in political ads and tableaux as the living embodiment of traditional American verities. Rugged individualist, independent thinker, strong father—these roles may have been more characteristic of Reagan's movie parts than his real life, but the "Gipper" was presented by his media strategists as an icon of American virtues. In a 1984 campaign memo, Reagan aide Richard Darman proposed that the president's reelection strategy pivot on his mythic appeal: "Paint RR as the personification of all that is right with or heroized by America. Leave Mondale in a position where an attack on Reagan is tantamount to an attack on America's idealized image of itself" (quoted in Erickson 1985, 100).

No one would take Bill Clinton seriously as an exemplar of American virtues. Indeed, most observers would have difficulty getting a clear fix on Clinton's political convictions. Where Reagan was identified as a man of firm principles (and admired for pragmatic adaptations of them), Clinton has been a shape-shifter on many of the major public issues during his presidency. His political identity, associated with the lower arts of political maneuver ("Slick Willie") and not the higher purposes of public philosophy, lacks symbolic resonance. But it also frees Clinton of ideological baggage, allowing him to case the landscape of political issues and seize the more popular positions as measured by the polls. His Republican adversaries, assuming that he would pay a price for his inconsistency and opportunism in the 1996 elections, created a campaign ad in which Clinton's changing positions on the subject of a balanced budget followed in rapid succession. But they did not understand that in a postmodern environment consistency is largely irrelevant: what mattered was that Clinton wound up precisely attuned to the most popular stance on the budget (Morris 1999a, 289).

Deriving their approach to public opinion with television as the defining medium, Reagan's public-relations strategists perceived that in a television age the eye counts for more than the ear. Reagan's positions on issues were generally firm and frequently unpopular; a focus on the issues might alienate more citizens than it would attract. But appealing visual images on television could trump harsh words on the issues from journalistic or partisan critics. Writing about Michael Deaver, Reagan's top media adviser, John Anthony Maltese points out, "Deaver helped to create a counter-reality through his visuals. The idea was to divert people's attention away from substantive issues by creating a world of myths and symbols that made people feel good about themselves and their country" (1994, 199).

Clinton's public-relations strategists scarcely eschewed good pictures; they knew the Reagan method well. Instead of diverting the public from the issues so as to define the president through visuals, however, Clinton's advisers used issues to redefine the president in a more flattering light. Dick Morris, the strategist with the greatest influence over Clinton, writes, "for years Clinton and I had believed that issues are the paddle you use to power yourself through the political swamp. Others prefer images, photos, adjectives, and negatives. We believed it was through issues that the public learned who you really were" (1999a, 123). Who Clinton "really was," to be sure, did not rest on a stable character structure or set of convictions that undergirded his stance on the issues; instead, his political identity would be established, and could be changed, by the issues he and his advisers decided to highlight or to slight. Rather than replacing substance with symbolism, Morris and Clinton used substance *as* symbolism. Many of President Reagan's public-relations specialists were veterans of Richard Nixon's protracted war with the press. From the Nixon experience they drew the precedent of an administration speaking to the media in unison through a common "line of the day," thereby keeping control of the press's agenda. But while undertaking extensive efforts to manage the news, they avoided the Nixon administration's tendency to attack reporters every time the president and his aides disliked the tone of press coverage. A cordial president and a solicitous staff kept White House relations with the press on a friendly basis and generated coverage so favorable that Reagan media advisers were pleasantly surprised by how well their boss was treated (Hertsgaard 1989).

Bill Clinton has as much charm as Ronald Reagan, and he frequently bestows it on members of the public. But the press almost never receives the warm and fuzzy treatment from Clinton that it received from Reagan. From the opening day of his first term, when reporters were banned from areas of the White House where they had previously been able to seek information (Kumar 1995, 168), Clinton and the press have approached each other with suspicion and sometimes hostility (Kurtz 1998, 25). Some talented media handlers, particularly David Gergen and Michael McCurry, have made periodic attempts to alleviate the mutual animosity between Clinton and the press. But nothing has eliminated the underlying causes of the friction; and in press coverage of the campaign finance and Monica Lewinsky scandals during Clinton's second term, Howard Kurtz relates, reporters could not conceal their belief that "Clinton simply could not be trusted to provide an unvarnished version of the truth" (1998, 138). Nonetheless, while press coverage was kinder to President Reagan than to President Clinton, both achieved high levels of popularity. The appealing stances on issues that Clinton took impressed the public more than the critical judgments that journalists made about his character. Clinton's audience cared more about how his policies would affect their lives than about press charges of his duplicitous dealings (1998,105–6, 110, 241).

Perhaps the best indicator of the difference between Clinton's politics and Reagan's politics is that there is no issue that can pin Clinton down, no issue that he cannot escape. In his first term, Reagan earned the nickname of "the Teflon president." Nonetheless, a president who had sought a reputation for "standing tall" against America's global foes saw his public approval ratings tumble during his second term, when he was revealed to have cut a deal with a terrorist regime he had denounced. (Similarly, President Bush suffered politically when he was forced to reverse himself on *his* signature issue: "No new taxes!") But Clinton can dance away from defeats on issues that would have damaged previous presidents because no issue is allowed to define him for very long. Thus, the champion of a massive new social program to provide universal health-care coverage in 1993–1994 can become the prophet of the end of big government by 1996. For the postmodern president, the only real trap is to stick to a policy that has become unfashionable.

## A Postmodern Education

The political style that has characterized Bill Clinton's presidency was evident early in his life. Both the charm and the slickness in courting followers were on display in Clinton's races for office in high school, Boys Nation, and college (Maraniss 1995, 14–15, 52–69). Many of the specific media techniques employed in the Clinton presidency were honed in his five terms as governor of Arkansas (339–418). Clinton entered the presidency already marked by the chief sign of the postmodern character: a readiness to reinvent the self to match the moment. But he still had much to learn about his moment in political time. National politics in the post–Cold War, post-heroic period posed snares Clinton had not encountered before, along with opportunities he had not yet learned to exploit.

Clinton entered the presidency with a strategy for capturing public support that had been designed to build on the precedents of his predecessors while going them one better. Seeking to reach his public audience by circumventing a hostile press, he traveled extensively and favored alternatives to press conferences with the White House press corps, such as town meetings and appearances on *Larry King Live* and MTV. The White House employed (while the Democratic National Committee picked up the tab) most of the political consultants who had managed Clinton's 1992 campaign for advice on matters ranging from policy to appointments (Drew 1994, 124). Polling was conducted on a scale that dwarfed previous administrations in scale and cost (Edwards 1996, 234). Clinton thus approached the presidency as a "permanent campaign" (a term coined by Sidney Blumenthal, who served as a communications aide in Clinton's second term). But what was surprising about Clinton's initial forays into courting public opinion was not how elaborate they were but how poorly they worked. His popularity slumped as an alienated press played up embarrassing revelations of Travel Office firings and $200 haircuts. One small example can stand for the initial ineptitude of the Clinton White House at staging a spectacle of presidential leadership: at a reception for dignitaries attending the dedication of the Holocaust Museum in Washington, the Clinton White House served ham (Drew 1994, 134).

It was in the most dramatic political campaign of Clinton's first two years in office—the health-care-reform crusade—that the Clinton White House's weaknesses with the public were exposed. Yet the most disastrous defeat of the Clinton presidency proved its most important education in how to master postmodern politics. So many things went wrong with the Clinton health-care plan that its defeat seemed overdetermined. One crucial contributor to failure was the administration's clumsy approach in seeking public support for its plan. Clinton's political consultants came up with simple principles to sell the proposal—Quality, Responsibility, Choice, Savings, Simplicity, Security—but never crafted a message that explained the new government mechanisms at the core of the plan. As Theda Skocpol argues: "Vague and evasive explanations of how the reformed health-care system would work left Americans open to alternative descriptions purveyed by Health Security's fiercest opponents" (1996, 132).

Dominating the debate over health-care reform, these opponents taught Bill Clinton a lesson about the manipulative possibilities in postmodern politics. Interest groups steadfastly opposed to the Clinton plan—especially the Health Insurance Association of America (HIAA) and the National Federation of Independent Business (NFIB)—got the jump on the Clinton administration in the battle for public opinion and took away the definition of the issue from its initiators. Coordinating their efforts with Republican leaders in Congress, these interest groups turned Clinton's bid for grand accomplishment into a political boomerang (Skocpol 1996, p. 178).

Money was crucial in the battle for public opinion about health care, and the interest groups opposed to the Clinton plan raised far more of it than the Clinton White House did. HIAA, for example, raised about $50 million for the health-care war and spent about $15 million on television ads attacking the Clinton proposal (Johnson and Broder 1996, 212; Skocpol, 137). Its now classic attack ads, featuring the middle-class couple "Harry" and "Louise," trumped the Clinton promise of health-care security for the middle class with clever slogans that evoked the threat of rising costs and bureaucratic restrictions (Johnson and Broder 1996, 205). The Clintons and their supporters protested the distortions in these and other advertisements assailing the administration's health plan, but the doubts they planted were more potent than the hopes that the Clintons had initially inspired. Interest-group money paid not only for television advertising but also for a vast effort at grassroots mobilization. For example, NFIB directed a constant flow of faxes to its small-business constituents to send them into action, staged public forums in states where swing members of Congress had been targeted, and contacted scores of talk-radio shows across the nation to pillory the Clinton plan ( 213–24).

Through television advertising and grassroots mobilization, interest-group and Republican foes of the Clintons turned each of their health-care reform positives into negatives. Bill Clinton had made "change" the mantra of his race for the presidency, and his health-care reform delivered on the promise that he would propose fundamental change. The reform's foes bested him by instilling the fear of change. Clinton targeted middle-class insecurities with his health-care plan, making its symbol a health security card guaranteeing "health care that's always there, health care that can never be taken away" (Clinton quoted in Skocpol 1996, 1). Opponents successfully redefined the Clinton plan as a welfare-state scheme designed to benefit the uninsured in the working and lower classes at the expense of the already-insured middle class. Clinton presented his plan as a "managed care" system that was an innovative compromise between market-based and government-centered approaches. His adversaries overwhelmed this fuzzy presentation by depicting his plan as the latest and one of the largest incarnations of big government run amok (Skocpol 1996, 15–16, 168–72).

In the course of the battle over health-care reform, the opposition's negatives also became sharply personal. Since Bill Clinton had tied himself closely to the issue by putting his wife in charge of the task force creating the administration's plan, hoping to draw thereby on the respect Hillary had earned as a new kind of First Lady, his opponents set out to tarnish the president and his plan by trashing his wife's role. As Skocpol writes: "By using Hillary Rodham Clinton as a target, cartoonists and talk radio hosts could ridicule the Clinton plan for its alleged governmental overweeningness–and in the process subliminally remind people how much they resent strong women" (152–53).

Considering everything that was thrown against the Clinton health-care plan, it never really had a chance to maintain its initial public support and gain the momentum needed to pass Congress. After the administration proposal collapsed, one of the architects of its defeat commented to Haynes Johnson and David Broder that the Clintons had never realized what powerful forces and methods their opponents had mustered against them (1996, 196). But if Bill Clinton, for all of his supposed slickness, came across during the health-care campaign as something of the political innocent at postmodern politics on the national level, he lost that innocence with his defeat. In the next big battle with his foes, he would absorb the lessons they had taught him, and with perhaps the justification that the other side had victimized him first, he would outdo them in the techniques of political manipulation.

The health-care reform fiasco was a prime contributor to the drubbing that President Clinton and his party took in the historic off-year elections of 1994. As the architect of the Democrats' defeat, House Speaker Newt Gingrich, drove his Republican "revolution" through Congress in 1995, Clinton was thrown on the defensive. But Clinton not only played better on defense than Gingrich anticipated, he also took advantage of the power of negation that Gingrich himself had exploited in the past.

The vehicle for the Republican revolution was a balanced budget over seven years. Since Gingrich's Contract with America election platform had promised a major tax cut (eventually set at $245 billion), the Republicans had to find huge cuts in spending in order to balance the budget, and the biggest single source of savings appeared to be the Medicare program. Aware that the GOP had picked a risky target, party pollsters advised congressional leaders not to talk about the projected $270 billion in Medicare savings as a cut, but rather as a slowing down of anticipated increases in order to preserve a Medicare trust fund in jeopardy of insolvency (Drew 1996, 204–6).

Despite the care the Republicans took with their public-relations strategy, they had created a fat target for Bill Clinton and the political strategist he had summoned to mastermind his comeback, Dick Morris. (On the Clinton-Morris relationship, see the chapter by John F. Harris in this volume.) Clinton and Morris seized on Medicare as a handy issue to deflate the Republican revolution. One of the few journalists to detect what they were up to was the *New York Times*'s Alison Mitchell: "When the Clinton health-care proposal died in Congress last year, the administration belatedly realized that it had allowed opponents to define the terms of the debate, using television, lobbying, and grass-roots politicking to capitalize on the public's fear of change. Now, taking a lesson from that defeat, the White House is using the same tactics against the Republicans who control Congress" (Mitchell 1995, A1).[3]

Badly outspent in the public-relations battle over health-care reform, the Clinton team would not let money beat it again. To pay for the flurry of polls and political commercials that turned the tables on the Republicans, the White House engaged in frenzied fund-raising among fat cats that, among other things, provided Clinton with an insurmountable lead for 1996 and a campaign finance scandal in 1997. Some of the Clinton ads this fund-raising financed borrowed brazenly from "Harry and Louise"; this time, the middle-class couple worried not about government bureaucracy but rather: "What would your parents be reduced to if their health care collapsed?" (quoted in Johnson and Broder 1996, 585). While Republicans decried the scare tactics being used against them, the commercials, personally approved by the president, effectively pounded home the message that Gingrich and his followers were decimating Medicare for the elderly in order to pay for tax cuts for the rich (Fineman 1995, 39).

In the struggle over Medicare, a critical episode in the budget showdown of 1995–1996 that revitalized the president's political fortunes, the Clinton-Morris partnership was as adroit in its negative strategy as Clinton's opponents had been in 1993–1994. Clinton and Morris defined the issue: Republicans hurting seniors and jeopardizing the Medicare system in order to reward the party's rich supporters. They exploited the fear of change: instead of the party of big government threatening to expand the bureaucratic leviathan for the benefit of the disadvantaged, this time the danger was the party of the free market threatening to slash the social safety net for the parents of the middle class. They recast the characters: in place of Hillary Rodham Clinton as the emblem of feminist aggressiveness and government meddling, the demon figure in this drama would be Newt Gingrich, the emblem of white-male insensitivity and right-wing extremism.

The campaign to reposition the president in a more favorable light with the public was not restricted to the Medicare battle or the larger budget showdown. One of Dick Morris's postmodern insights was that with the right combination of issue stands (V-chips to screen out TV violence, curfews to keep adolescents home and studying, school uniforms to reduce gang battles and class resentments), Bill Clinton could become, improbably, the vessel of middle-class values. In fact, Morris had in mind an even more striking makeover for Clinton's political identity. If Clinton had campaigned as America's "buddy" in 1992, now he needed the air of maturity that would come from being "the nation's father" (Morris 1999a, 181). Morris even altered the president's wardrobe: the light-colored suits Clinton favored were replaced with the statesman's navy suit (Morris 1999a, p. 182). Clinton the baby boomer took a lesson too from the oldest president ever to occupy the White House, studying videotapes of Ronald Reagan in order to emulate "the Gipper's bearing, his aura of command" (Fineman and Turque 1996, 22). In postmodern politics, Clinton and Morris concurred, who the president "really" was had become largely insignificant; by a shrewd calibration of issues and images, identified by polls and propagated through the media, the president could be whatever the public wanted him to be at that moment.

The same methods that propelled Clinton's remarkable political comeback in 1995–1996 stood him in good stead when he faced the ultimate test of his political survival in the Monica Lewinsky affair of 1998–1999. For Clinton's opponents, frustrated heretofore that they could not convince the public that he was too untrustworthy and immoral to be president, the Lewinsky scandal seemed a golden opportunity to affix on the president labels that would have been ruinous for any previous chief executive: philanderer, liar, abuser of the highest public trust. But once again Clinton evaded Republican definition; he appeared in the Year of Lewinsky as a moral delinquent but not a malefactor guilty of "high crimes and misdemeanors."

When the first details of the Lewinsky affair exploded in the media in January 1998, many political observers and pundits thought that Clinton's presidency was doomed. How could Clinton survive the charges that he had had an affair with a twenty-one-year-old intern in the White House and then conspired to cover it up? After a few days of hesitation, when Clinton unconvincingly voiced denials of the charges, he and his advisers hit on the strategy that quelled the initial furor. First, the finger-wagging president indignantly repudiated reality: "I did not have sex with that woman." Second, he shifted the focus from his character to his stand on the issues: He was too busy doing the work for which the people had reelected him to be diverted by a sex scandal. Third, he refused to answer further questions while the investigation proceeded. Fourth, his supporters assailed the motives and methods of his pursuer, independent counsel Kenneth Starr (Bennet and Nagourney 1998, A13).

Ignoring advice to come clean and tell the public the whole story, Clinton, alerted of the risks in a poll taken by Dick Morris, put on the armor of his most successful past identities. Brushing off suggestions that he dare not appear before Congress for the scheduled State of the Union address, he turned this event, of which he was an acknowledged master, into a bravura reminder to the public of why they had reelected him. With a long string of popular, poll-tested proposals, presented with Clinton's trademark charm and good humor, he regained his political footing, soaring to over 70 percent in some opinion polls (Kernell 1999, 1–3).

Clinton's original strategy set him up for later humiliation when he had to confess to the truth of his liaison with Lewinsky. More important, however, it bought him time by allowing the public to get used to the idea that a president might be a reprobate in his private behavior yet talented and effective in his public performance. The drama that unfolded over the following months, endlessly fascinating to its aficionados but increasingly tedious to the majority of Americans, was characteristic of the postmodern moment. There were no heroes: the public had to choose between an untrustworthy president, a zealous and relentless prosecutor, polarized partisans, and a sensation-addicted press. There was little illumination: as the Starr Report vividly demonstrated, high-minded constitutional disputation seemed repeatedly to sink into sex talk. And there were Clinton's amazing poll ratings, which remained on an even keel despite repeated blows to his original defenses.

Characteristic of Clinton's survival strategy was his response to the release of the 445-page Starr Report in September 1998, which aimed to make an overwhelming factual and legal case for his impeachment and removal from office. In tested fashion, the Clinton team supplied the press and public with a rapid rebuttal. Starr's story, the White House said, was old news (in postmodern terms, what could be more boring?). The report, it charged, was replete with salacious details and was all about sex, not constitutional offenses (who was guilty of pandering to postmodern tastes?). Besides, the president had already confessed his moral (though not his legal) turpitude (Fournier 1998). A month earlier, forced to admit his liaison with Lewinsky in grand-jury testimony, Clinton had been insufficiently contrite in a televised address to the nation. But hours before the Starr Report was released to Congress, the president told a breakfast meeting of religious leaders: "I have sinned. I have repented" (quoted in Fournier 1998). Although Clinton's new identity as repentant sinner was not his most convincing one, it did recast him in softer tones just as his hunter fired his sharpest barbs at the president.

By the scandal's endgame, Clinton's impeachment by the House and his trial by the Senate, it had become fecund in postmodern ironies. Clinton had supposedly been stigmatized in the history books by impeachment, yet at the moment he was barely affected in his political identity, agenda, or popularity. Longtime critics in his party and among the liberal intelligentsia had been driven to become his passionate defenders. Two leaders of the opposition—a Speaker and a Speaker-elect of the House—had been driven into retirement. And the public was unhappier with his attackers than with Clinton.

The factors that contributed to Clinton's political salvation were many: a vibrant economy, a complacent public mood, scandal fatigue, conservative zealotry, and perhaps above all, the ideal foil for Clinton in Kenneth Starr. But Clinton's postmodern character and political moment should not be neglected in any list of explanations. Had Clinton had a stable character that the public had come to trust, revelations of his secret life in the White House would have come as more of a shock. But with a public that had already separated its appreciation for Clinton's talents and accomplishments from its skepticism about his honesty and integrity, it only took a short while for the majority to accept Clinton's compartmentalization as its own in the Lewinsky affair. Most Americans were content to see Clinton, already liberated from so many of his past political identities, escape this one as well.

## Clinton's Impact on the Public Presidency

In light of Bill Clinton's political successes in every venue since high school, it should hardly come as a surprise that he was a top student in postmodern politics while in the White House. Learning how to use the systematic combination of polling, advertising, and issue repositioning both from his adversaries in the health-care battle and from his adviser during the Republican revolution, Dick Morris, Clinton became increasingly adept at dominating the terms of political debate, demonizing his political enemies, and reinventing his own political personae. He was increasingly expert at pleasing the public with his shifting stances on issues large and small and at impressing the public with the skill of his performance on the job. Yet well before the Monica Lewinsky scandal the public had come to distrust Clinton's postmodern character and style. Multiple presidential identities may have allowed Clinton to shift with political fashions and to resurrect his political fortunes, but they also deprived him of the admiration and respect that his successful predecessors in the White House had garnered.

Since each of Bill Clinton's political identities has been ephemeral, perhaps his impact on the public presidency will be similarly short-lived. Although his presidency has been a story of growing sophistication in the courtship of public support, it will leave few political monuments when compared to the administration that set the contemporary standard for the public presidency. The Reagan administration could boast of bringing about powerful transformations in the party system, domestic and foreign policy, and public discourse with the aid of its public-relations strategies. The Clinton administration cannot claim nearly as much. Yet without disputing the conclusion that Reagan was a more successful president than Clinton, it is possible to argue that Clinton will be the more important model for future presidents in the arts of courting the public.

Clinton's attempt to rival Reagan by reshaping the agenda of American politics failed dramatically during his first two years in office, when he had Democratic majorities in the House and Senate. After the Republican takeover of Congress in the 1994 elections, he was pushed into the defensive posture that characterized most of his remaining six years in office. But if our only criterion of presidential success is grand legislative accomplishments, we underestimate the importance of Clinton's education after 1994 in how to win public support. The strategic context that confronted Clinton from the time he assumed office was never suited to policy breakthroughs (Rockman 1996, 325–62; 2000, 274–94; Skowronek 1997, 447–64). An intransigent Republican opposition, a badly divided Democratic following, a fearful and alienated public, above all a conservative rhetoric of politics that was probably Reagan's most profound legacy—all of these combined to block Clinton from the kind of reconstructive politics that we associate with presidential greatness (Skowronek 1997).

If we change the question from one of grand accomplishments and ask instead what Clinton's courtship of the public did gain for him, the list is impressive. It won him reelection in one of the most remarkable comebacks in the history of the presidency. What other president was so thoroughly repudiated in midterm elections after only two years in office and then reemerged to sail easily to electoral triumph? It shielded him during the tawdriest scandal in presidential history. What other president could have survived the taint of sexual impropriety and flagrant dishonesty with his popularity undiminished?

But Clinton's postmodern public talents were more than mere survival skills. The story of the 1990s might have been about a Republican, conservative realignment of American politics, with Newt Gingrich as its central figure. One reason why Clinton has so infuriated Republicans is that he subverted this story. By stealing Republican issues while excoriating conservative extremism, by hollowing out liberal Democratic ideas, by blurring rather than clarifying American political discourse, Clinton played a larger role than anyone else in forestalling a Republican revolution (Burnham 1997, 9–16; Wills 1997, 42). By the end of his second term, it was Clinton's brand of centrism that dominated most policy debates in Washington.

The Democratic Party was as deeply affected by Clinton's success with the public as the Republican was. Although congressional Democrats continued to mistrust Clinton, by his second term few could resist the majority of his postmodern issue stances. The party's center of gravity had shifted—to the right? the center? the poll-tested majority position?—as it followed Clinton's path away from its old identity (for a contrary view, see Shafer 2000, 1–32). In the race for the Democratic presidential nomination for 2000, both Vice President Al Gore and former senator Bill Bradley shared Clinton's reputation as being moderate (though both also appealed to liberal constituencies during the party's primaries), and there was a notable absence of candidates to their left who represented the party's liberal tradition.

Although it was Bill Clinton and not Newt Gingrich who left the larger mark on the American political system at century's end, few political figures were eager to claim him as their model or their inspiration. Just as presidential aspirants after Reagan stressed their competence, and presidential aspirants challenging Bush stressed their connectedness to the public, so candidates hoping to replace Clinton stressed their character. Deriding Clinton as immoral and inauthentic, Republicans seeking the presidency claimed to personify the traditional American virtues. Even Clinton's vice president, who had a closer relationship with his chief executive than any of his predecessors had, felt compelled to distance himself in his run for the White House by castigating the president's inexcusable behavior in the Lewinsky affair.

It is possible to imagine a return to a politics of character and conviction after Clinton leaves the White House. Many of the same Americans who have approved of Clinton's policies and performance have doubtless been unhappy with the slick but hollow postmodern style through which he has presented his changing political personae. "Virtue" is a resonant American theme, a reminder of our revolutionary and religious origins, and its appeal has only grown—among communitarian liberals as much as among Christian conservatives—during the Clinton presidency. Nonetheless, the postmodern mood threatens to subvert any reassertion of morals and principles by political leaders; a public schooled in postmodern skepticism by a distrustful press will look for the political payoff every time it hears professions of virtue. Perhaps only a dramatic economic or social issue that galvanizes the public and redraws the map of partisan cleavages will move Americans beyond postmodern detachment and irony.

Thus, while Clinton's approach to the public is unlikely to evoke open expressions of admiration in the short run, his long-run impact on the public presidency is likely to prove substantial. Ronald Reagan has been hard to emulate: What other American politicians possess his professional acting talents, his myth-making resonance, his iconic image? Furthermore, the heroic spectacle of the "Gipper" cannot easily be reenacted in cynical fin-de-siecle America. But Bill Clinton's postmodern techniques can be covertly copied and employed.

Credit (blame?) for developing these techniques should perhaps go to Dick Morris (Schell 1999, 30). But it is Bill Clinton who has shown how the shape-shifting politics that Morris prescribes can work. Clinton has repeatedly demonstrated how poll-tested repositioning on the issues can alter and enhance the president's image. Cultivating the appearance of rectitude, future presidents have to be careful to avoid accusations that they are as slick and slippery as Clinton. But especially when they run into difficulties, they will be able to turn to what will be the textbook case of the "Comeback Kid." That a president can reinvent himself to please the public will be the postmodern legacy of Bill Clinton.

CHAPTER 6

# THE PUBLIC'S VIEW OF CLINTON

DIANE HOLLERN HARVEY

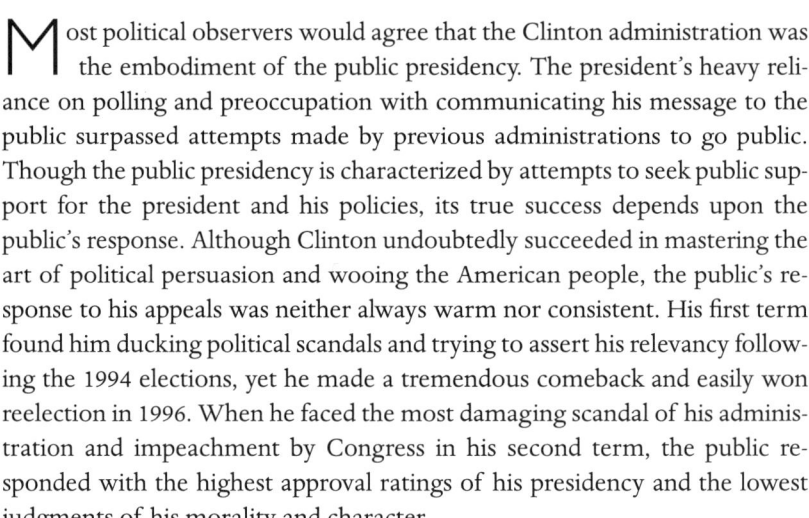

Most political observers would agree that the Clinton administration was the embodiment of the public presidency. The president's heavy reliance on polling and preoccupation with communicating his message to the public surpassed attempts made by previous administrations to go public. Though the public presidency is characterized by attempts to seek public support for the president and his policies, its true success depends upon the public's response. Although Clinton undoubtedly succeeded in mastering the art of political persuasion and wooing the American people, the public's response to his appeals was neither always warm nor consistent. His first term found him ducking political scandals and trying to assert his relevancy following the 1994 elections, yet he made a tremendous comeback and easily won reelection in 1996. When he faced the most damaging scandal of his administration and impeachment by Congress in his second term, the public responded with the highest approval ratings of his presidency and the lowest judgments of his morality and character.

To unravel these puzzling public responses, one must understand the unique relationship forged between Bill Clinton and the American people since his 1992 campaign. The public's reactions to his policies and leadership over his two terms carries both temporary and enduring implications for the future of American politics. The public's perceptions of his strengths and weaknesses as a president affected the pattern of demographic support received by Clinton, popular views of the political parties' capabilities, and the behavior and fate of the candidates competing to be Clinton's successor in 2000. Beyond these short-lived effects, the public's response to the Clinton presidency also tell us a great deal about the future role of morality and private behavior in presidential politics as well as the conditions governing the impact of presidential scandal.

## Evaluating the President

When placed in historical context, Bill Clinton's average approval ratings are not exceptionally high or low as compared with other post–World War II presidential averages (see Table 1). While he lacked the immense popularity of Eisenhower and Kennedy, he did not suffer from the continuous decline in ratings experienced by Truman and Carter. Perhaps the closest president to Clinton in popular approval is Ronald Reagan. They share a similar pattern in their approval ratings, as both presidents inherited economic difficulties, oversaw economic recoveries, and were hailed for their ability to communicate with the public. Their paths diverged, however, after the scandals that each experienced near the end of his presidency. Whereas Clinton's approval ratings remained quite high throughout the Lewinsky scandal, Reagan's approval levels dropped after the 1987 Iran-Contra affair, with a final rebound at the end. Of course, the public tended to rate Reagan much higher on personal qualities than job performance—even during the Iran-Contra scandal (Edwards 1990). In contrast, Bill Clinton's job performance ratings were higher than ratings of his honesty and trustworthiness after 1995, with a dramatic split between the two following the Lewinsky scandal (see Figure 1).

The overall trend in Clinton's popularity ratings does not vary greatly from the normal pattern predicted by scholars. They have long observed that presidential first terms begin with high approval ratings followed by decline

Table 1
Average Presidential Approval (in percentage)

| Kennedy | 70 | Reagan | 53 |
|---|---|---|---|
| Eisenhower | 65 | Nixon | 52 |
| Bush | 61 | Ford | 47 |
| Johnson | 55 | Carter | 46 |
| Clinton | 54 | Truman | 41 |

*Note:* Average derived from Clinton's approval ratings through June 1999.
*Sources:* Ragsdale, *Vital Statistics on the Presidency: Washington to Clinton;* Clinton average updated with data from *Gallup Poll Monthly,* 1993–1999.

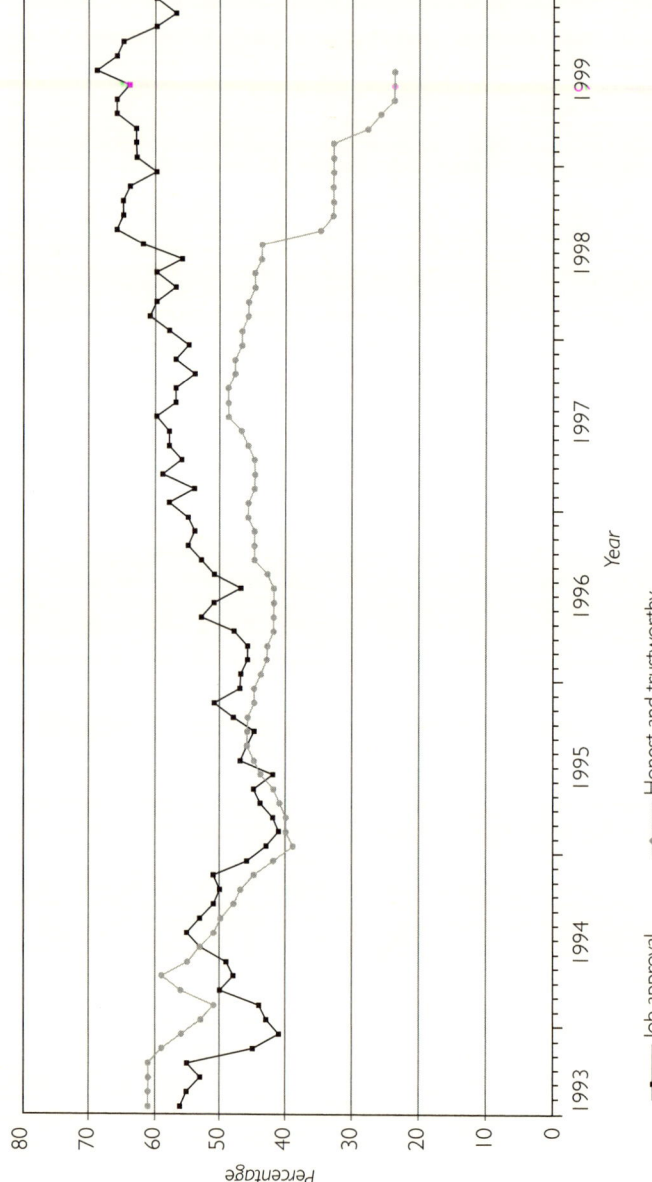

Fig. 1. Public evaluations of job performance and character

over the middle years, with a recovery in approval at the end of the term, when the public shows greater "forgiveness" to the president (Ragsdale 1996; Brace and Hinckley 1992; Stimson 1976). Clinton began his first term with 58 percent approval, which is lower than that of many other presidents, but comparable to the initial ratings of Nixon, Reagan, and Bush and higher than his popular vote total of 43 percent. The public failed to grant him a long inaugural honeymoon, however, as Clinton lost the approval of a majority of people after only three months in office. This was much shorter than most other presidential honeymoons, which last an average of anywhere from six months to one year (Ragsdale 1996). His ratings continued to decline until 1995, when they rebounded and carried him to reelection in 1996.

Whereas other two-term presidents enjoyed landslide victories followed by declines in approval in their second terms, Clinton enjoyed steadily increasing approval ratings that persisted despite the scandal in 1998 (Brace and Hinckley 1992). Many have examined the circumstances that kept Bill Clinton's popularity afloat in the midst of a sex scandal and impeachment in his second term; the explanations are found in popular perceptions of Clinton's strengths and weaknesses, the political conditions that governed the 1990s, and the factors that have traditionally influenced public support for presidents.

*The First Term: In Search of a New Democrat*

Bill Clinton's victory over Bush and Perot in the 1992 election occurred despite numerous controversies and public doubts regarding his character. His attraction of only 43 percent of the vote mirrored the Democratic Party's loss of ten seats in the House and failure to pick up seats in the Senate. Unfortunately, Bill Clinton seemed to ignore these troubling election results. In the early weeks of his administration, he began pursuing controversial policies that shortened the traditional honeymoon in approval ratings. By his own admission, he overestimated his capabilities in proposing sweeping policy changes in a political environment where he had earned less than a majority of votes (Mitchell 1996a).

The public wasted little time in making up its mind about Bill Clinton. By his second week in office, only 16 percent of the public had no opinion on the president's job performance—compared with the Reagan and Bush administrations, where approximately 40 percent of the American people withheld judgment on job performance at that early date (Newport and Saad 1993, 15). People's feelings of approval and disapproval of the president were primarily a function of Clinton's quick action on two controversial policies; he removed abortion restrictions and pursued acceptance of homosexuals into the military. His actions evoked disapproval from a sizable number of Americans and led to the perception that Clinton was paying attention to controversial social issues at the expense of economic concerns (Newport and Saad 1993, 15).

The abandonment of certain campaign promises, such as a middle-class tax cut, led many people to view him as a waffler who was incapable of keeping promises (Moore 1993b, 4). Clinton's public image was further damaged by the early gaffes and embarrassing missteps described by Bruce Miroff in the previous chapter. By the end of his first six months in office, Clinton had the lowest job approval rating of any modern president at that point in the first term (Moore 1993a, 6).

Despite his claims of being a New Democrat, citizens viewed Clinton as more liberal than themselves (Moore and Saad 1993, 15). Furthermore, the public failed to see any progress on reforming health care and improving the economy, two campaign planks that he had promised would receive quick action at the beginning of his term (Edwards 1998, 755). The public's regard for his foreign policy leadership also suffered blows with televised images of dead American soldiers in Somalia and U.S. troops being driven away from Haiti. Clinton's already low public approval on foreign affairs plummeted to 34 percent (Gallup poll, November 1993).

Although Clinton did achieve some notable legislative successes in 1993, such as NAFTA and the Family and Medical Leave Act, Americans did not give him sustained approval for these victories. The public could not discern a sense of priorities as he careened from one issue to another, trying to address too large an agenda and distracting the public from his successes (Pfiffner 1996; Edwards 1996). Although he started out well in the polls in 1994, his popular approval slowly eroded over the course of the year. The public's doubts about his character were being reinforced by Whitewater hearings and a sexual harassment suit. His approval on foreign affairs and image as an effective world leader declined, primarily owing to his handling of problems in Bosnia and North Korea (Saad and Newport 1994, 18). Furthermore, the public witnessed his highly prized health-care plan go up in flames (see Miroff's chapter, this volume). By summer, surveys were finding that a majority of Americans did not believe that Clinton was an effective world leader, was tough enough for the job, was honest and trustworthy, could get things done, or could keep his promises (Moore 1994, 19).

The Republican electoral victory in 1994 seemed to be the nail in the coffin of two frustrating years. In retrospect, it ended up being Clinton's political salvation, moving him closer to the public's vision of a New Democrat. The results of the 1994 election essentially echoed the nation's "simultaneously held aggregate preference for ideological conservatism and operational liberalism concerning government" (Burnham 1997, 9). As described in the previous chapter, the election forced Bill Clinton to move to the political center, where he co-opted some Republican ideas and took advantage of Republican missteps. Furthermore, he was able to demonstrate strong leadership and show empathy in the wake of the Oklahoma City bombing of a federal office building, which improved his public image (Keeter 1997, 117).

The 1996 State of the Union address unveiled a new Bill Clinton to the American public. As John Harris discusses in chapter 4, the president declared the era of big government to be over and outlined a Republican-sounding "values agenda." In the summer, he signed a conservative welfare reform bill and benefited from public perceptions of an improving economy. He also gained greater public respect in foreign affairs by committing troops to Bosnia and exercising more decisive leadership (Stanley 1997, 17).

By the time of the 1996 elections, the public was signaling that it had found the New Democrat promised it in 1992. As George Stephanopoulos observed, "He was saying yes and saying no at the same time. He was stealing the center, creating the center" (Mitchell 1996b, B5). This movement toward the center, combined with voter satisfaction with the economy and the progress of the nation, won him growing public approval (Keeter 1997, 120). While majorities did not see the president exemplifying certain personal qualities such as being honest and trustworthy and keeping promises, their perceptions of presidential empathy for their problems, popular proposals from the administration, and improving economic conditions helped propel Bill Clinton to a second term (122).

## *The Second Term: Peace, Prosperity, and Monica*

As the nation continued to prosper and remained at peace, Bill Clinton spent 1997 building his popularity ratings. He began his second term with a 62-percent approval rating—an all-time high for him at the time. Despite their solid approval, however, people remained skeptical of his ability to fulfill certain policy goals. In one survey, when asked for the greatest accomplishment from his first term, only half of the respondents could name one (Saad 1997, 6). At the same time, a majority of the public lacked confidence in Clinton's ability to significantly reduce the budget deficit, avoid raising taxes for middle income people, and reform the political system.

Although Bill Clinton and the Republican Congress arrived at a budget agreement that would erase the deficit by 2002, the public tended to give more credit for the agreement to Congress than the White House (Gallup poll, May

1997). Nevertheless, Clinton's approval ratings remained high, hovering around 60 percent, as a growing number of Americans sensed progress on national problems such as crime, the deficit, education, welfare, and AIDS (Pew Research Center Report, November 1997). This sense of progress, combined with the flourishing economy, kept Clinton's approval ratings much higher than usual for a second-term president (Connolly and Deane 1998).

The Lewinsky scandal in early 1998 seemed to be the pin that would burst the president's popularity balloon. The accusation that Clinton had engaged in a sexual relationship with a young White House intern and then proceeded to lie about it in a legal deposition in the Paula Jones case had all the earmarks of being a crisis that could sink his presidency. The scandal revived lingering public doubts regarding Clinton's character by bringing his personal morality and legal ethics into question. Instead of public support for the president being withdrawn, however, it actually increased in the weeks following the news of the scandal.

Despite Clinton's televised, finger-wagging denial of an improper relationship with Monica Lewinsky, growing majorities were concluding that the president did have sexual relations with the intern and lied about it under oath. The public's approval of Clinton held firm despite these conclusions and additional allegations by Kathleen Willey of sexual misconduct. His approval ratings remained unaffected by a televised confession of his misbehavior later in the summer, as most Americans had long believed in his guilt and majorities agreed with Clinton's assertion that it was a private matter of concern only to his family (Newport 1998a, 12).

As in the budget conflict of 1995, Republicans overplayed their hand in managing the Clinton scandal. After the release of the Starr Report and grand jury tapes for public viewing, Clinton's approval ratings actually increased, while support for impeachment fell. At the same time, the public's approval of Republican handling of the investigation dropped by 10 percent as many came to see it as merely partisan (Moore 1998, 12). By the fall, the public was expressing a desire for the whole thing to go away. Gallup surveys in August and September found majorities believing that the grand jury testimony and Clinton's public confession should end the matter. For a brief time in December, survey majorities believed Clinton should resign if impeached rather than drag the nation through a Senate trial (CBS/*New York Times* surveys, December 1998; ABC/*Washington Post* surveys, December 1998).

Although his approval ratings remained high in spite of the scandal, Clinton's personal evaluations declined throughout the year. By the fall of 1998, only 37 percent of Americans held a positive opinion of Bill Clinton as a person and only 30 percent believed that he provided strong moral leadership for the nation. These survey results did not seem to be consistent with his high job approval ratings, especially when 72 percent of the public believed it was important for the president to provide moral leadership to the country (Newport 1998b, 9–10). The apparent contradictions in these opinions can be explained by the relative emphasis the public places on moral values for effective leadership. A survey from earlier in the year had found that 55 percent of respondents believed that it was important but not critical to possess high moral values, while only 31 percent said the possession of high moral values was critical for effective leadership (Gallup poll, January/February 1998). As the majority of citizens did not regard moral values as being critical, it is not surprising that the public was willing to put aside their disapproval of Clinton's moral behavior in light of their satisfaction with his job performance.

Which charges against Clinton did the public believe to be true? By September, majorities believed that it was probably or definitely true that Clinton had lied to the American people, lied under oath, helped Lewinsky obtain a job, attempted to influence testimony, and lied to senior White House aides (Gallup poll, September 1998). At the same time, the public evinced little enthusiasm for impeachment for these offenses, despite their consideration of it earlier in the year. Surveys by the Pew Research Center found the percentage who believed Clinton should be impeached for lying under oath dropped from half the public in early February 1998 to only 29 percent by mid-August. Although it is possible that the public was persuaded that perjury was not serious enough for impeachment, it is also likely that this was an attempt to reduce cognitive dissonance on the part of the public. Americans had to reconcile their approval of Clinton's job performance and desire to retain him in office with their growing recognition and condemnation of his immoral personal actions. It is also possible that their declining support for impeachment was affected by White House accusations that the Starr investigation and the Republicans' handling of the scandal were driven by partisanship and politics.

In the end, the public failed to be persuaded that impeachment was the fitting punishment for Bill Clinton's actions. Almost one half of survey respondents in September favored some sort of congressional censure or reprimand of the president, while impeachment and no formal action each attracted a quarter of the public (Gallup poll, September 1998). Although a majority of Americans did not favor turning Clinton out of office, it is worth noting that approximately three-quarters of the public supported some sort of punishment for the president—an indication that they did not see his conduct as excusable or acceptable for a sitting president (Ladd 1998, 36).

There are four primary explanations that have been offered to account for Clinton's high job-approval ratings throughout the scandal and public resistance to calls for impeachment. The most persuasive theory is that the public bases its approval on accumulated impressions of a president's actual job performance (Keeter 1999; Pfiffner 1998; Brody 1991). It is possible for the public to evaluate performance alone, as people can compartmentalize their evaluations of the president by separating private and public performance (Kernell 1999; Zaller 1998; Edwards 1990). According to this explanation, people credited Clinton with a good economy, a nation at peace, budget surpluses, and progress on national issues. Their perceptions of Clinton's success in these areas kept his popularity ratings afloat despite personal scandal. Indeed, there is evidence that attitudes on public performance lay behind the approval ratings of Clinton and recent presidents, while ratings on character issues had little to no effect (Keeter 1999; Brody and Jackman 1999).

Another possibility is tied to the public's dislike of Starr and the Republicans' conduct of the investigation (Glassman 1999; Cronin and Genovese 1998; Jamieson and Aday 1998; Lyman 1998). Many in the public perceived Starr's investigation of Clinton to be partisan rather than impartial. Likewise, almost three-quarters of the public viewed the Republicans as going after Clinton for political motives (Pew Research Center Report, December 1998). A third explanation has attributed the public's approval of Clinton and opposition to impeachment to a moral decline in society (Bennett 1999; Wilson 1999). Despite disapproving of Clinton's actions, this explanation holds that the public looked at engaging in sexual relations with an intern and then lying about them under oath as inconsequential because the subject was sex rather than policy.

Finally, there is the popular perception that Clinton's behavior does not significantly differ from that of previous presidents (Jamieson and Aday 1998). Washington sex scandals are certainly nothing new to the public. Rumors of affairs by Kennedy, Johnson, and FDR have left the public with little doubt that presidents are capable of immoral behavior. In fact, 59 percent of the public believe that most presidents have had extramarital affairs while in office, and 75 percent believe that Clinton's faults are no worse than those of most other presidents (Gallup poll, January/February 1998). According to this explanation, the public was unwilling to punish Clinton for actions that his predecessors also committed.

When these potential explanations are tested in a regression model of presidential approval and support for impeachment, it is apparent that there is a bit of truth to at least three of them (see Table 2).[1] In the model, the public's evaluation of national conditions was measured by its judgments of the economy under Clinton, perceptions of the country as being on the right track, and evaluations of the U.S. position in the world. Clearly, a large component of the public's approval of Clinton was based on these evaluations, especially those of the economy. An equally powerful determinant was opinion of the Starr investigation, with those seeing it as partisan being more likely to approve of Clinton. Likewise, so were those who believed that moral standards should be adjusted to a changing society and that government officials should not be expected to display higher moral standards. The perception that most elected officials are crooked, however, surprisingly decreased approval of Clinton. Finally, the control variable of partisanship exerted the expected strong effect on approval.

Regarding impeachment, there was support for all four explanations, but the greatest determinants were attitudes toward Starr, the Republicans, and partisanship. The feeling that the investigation was partisan rather than impartial led people to oppose Clinton's impeachment. Opposition was also fueled by party identification, evaluations of national conditions, opinions on morality, and the perception of corruptness among public officials. In the end, however, the regression results demonstrate that the public's opposition to impeachment had more to do with feelings toward Starr and partisanship than attitudes toward morality.

After the conclusion of the Senate trial, Clinton's ratings continued to hover around the high-50 and low-60 percentage range in the spring of 1999, even with the mixed public reaction surrounding U.S. military intervention in Kosovo. Although such a conflict would be expected to increase his ratings, Clinton failed to get the normal rally that follows an international conflict, owing to doubts about whether the U.S. and NATO truly achieved their goals in the end (Broder 1999; Pew Research Center Report, June 1999). Nevertheless, he did succeed in ending the conflict before the public's doubts about intervention began to affect his approval ratings.

Although Clinton maintained public support throughout his second term and escaped removal from office, the scandal was costly to his presidency aside from the public embarrassment, wasted time, and legal fees. Despite his skills as a public president, there was not much desire on the part of the scandal-weary public to keep him around. Even several months after the conclusion

Table 2
Presidential Approval and Impeachment Opinion
(logistic regression with MLE coefficients)

| Variable | Presidential Approval | Effect on Approval | Impeachment | Effect on Impeachment |
|---|---|---|---|---|
| Evaluation of the economy | .80*** (.16) | .31 | .45*** (.16) | .18 |
| Perceived direction of the country | .68 (.14) | .11 | .68*** (.14) | .12 |
| Evaluation of U.S. position in the world | .60*** (.14) | .18 | .27** (.14) | .09 |
| Congressional handling of allegations | -.50*** (.21) | -.08 | -1.07*** (.20) | -.20 |
| View Starr investigation as partisan | 1.34*** (.21) | .23 | 1.46*** (.20) | .28 |
| Higher moral standards for officials | -.51*** (.22) | -.08 | -.74*** (.22) | -.12 |
| Adjust moral standards to societal changes | .21*** (.07) | .12 | .07 (.07) | .04 |
| View most politicians as crooked | -.27** (.14) | -.08 | -.36*** (.14) | -.11 |
| Party identification | .66*** (.13) | .20 | .73*** (.13) | .26 |
| Ideology | .17* (.13) | .05 | .15 .12 | .05 |
| Constant | -2.24 | | -.99 | |
| Predicted | 83.42% | | 81.79% | |
| Null | 71.90% | | 68.20% | |
| N | 953 | | 950 | |
| $X^2$ | 390.474 | | 400.167 | |
| DF | 10 | | 10 | |
| Probability | $p < .00001$ | | $p < .00001$ | |

Source: 1998 National Election Study.
Note: Standard errors in parentheses.

\* $p < .10$
\*\* $p < .05$
\*\*\* $p < .01$

of the impeachment hearings, 74 percent of the public reported being tired of all the problems associated with the Clinton scandal, and only 29 percent wished that he could run for a third term (Pew Research Center Report, March 1999). Furthermore, a Gallup survey in August 1998 found that almost three-quarters of Americans believed that Clinton would be remembered more for his involvement in personal scandal than his accomplishments—a very painful thing for a president who was so concerned with the legacy he would leave after his second term.

## The Public's Assessment of Success and Failure

By the end of his second term, the public had come to view Bill Clinton quite positively across numerous policy areas (See Table 3). His handling of race relations, education, and the environment were highly rated by the public in his first and second terms. Given the traditional emphasis on these issues by the Democratic Party, his attraction of majority approval by his handling of these matters is hardly surprising. He demonstrated his greatest public growth, however, in his management of the economy, foreign affairs, and crime policy. Although these were normally regarded as Republican-dominated issues, Clinton earned the approval of a growing majority on his handling of them over time. By far, the public regarded his economic management as his greatest governing strength in the end, with a jump in approval from 43 percent during his first two years to 76 percent in 1999. Ironically, health-care reform, the crown jewel of his 1992 campaign, was never regarded by the public as his strongest area of performance, given the failure of his plan in 1994 and his subsequent abandonment of the issue. It was not until the final years of his second term that he earned the approval of even a slim majority on this issue.

Although Clinton was perceived as increasing in strength across these issue areas, the public did not credit him with similar progress on matters of character (see Table 4). The public has always acknowledged Bill Clinton's weaknesses in morality and ethics. Being honest and trustworthy, keeping promises, and sharing the same values as the public appear to be his weakest

Table 3
Job Performance Strengths and Weaknesses (average percentages approving)

| Issue | 1993–1994 | 1995–1996 | 1997–1998 | 1999 |
|---|---|---|---|---|
| Economy | 43 | 48 | 64 | 76 |
| Foreign affairs | 45 | 47 | 54 | 56 |
| Education | 51 | 53 | 58 | 69 |
| Health care | 43 | 43 | 37 | 52 |
| Crime | 38 | 46 | 45 | 66 |
| Race relations | 57 | 55 | 61 | 76 |
| Environment | 57 | 62 | — | 69 |

*Source:* Gallup surveys, January 1993–September 1999.

Table 4
Public Perceptions of Character Strengths and Weaknesses (in percentages)

|  | 1993–1994 | 1995–1996 | 1997–1998 | 1999 |
| --- | --- | --- | --- | --- |
| Honest and trustworthy | 51 | 45 | 38 | 24 |
| Shares your values | 45 | 49 | 42 | 35 |
| Can get things done | 52 | 53 | 73 | 82 |
| Cares about the needs of people | 58 | 61 | 64 | 65 |
| Keeps his promises | 38 | 34 | 43 | 43 |
| Tough enough for the job | 53 | 51 | 69 | — |

*Source:* Gallup surveys, January 1993–September 1999.

character traits. The controversies that emerged during the 1992 election, his inability to follow through on certain campaign promises in his first term, and the various scandals that dogged his administration kept the public from ever fully trusting Clinton. The Lewinsky situation only confirmed the public's suspicions in these areas and pushed evaluations of his honesty and morality even lower.

Nonetheless, people admired certain aspects of Clinton's character. He experienced his greatest growth in personal characteristics that affected his job performance. As national conditions continued to improve during his second term, the public increasingly came to see him as someone who was tough enough for the job and could get things done. Clinton's greatest political strength, however, lay in the perception of him as a compassionate, empathetic person. Despite the American people's low regard for his performance during his first term and the damage to his character in the second, Bill Clinton always managed to maintain the image of someone who cares about people. Although he did earn strong approval of his policy-performance over time, it is this political strength that helped him to win the presidency twice and kept him afloat in the midst of scandal.

## The Public's Response to the Clinton Presidency

The public's relationship with Bill Clinton was unique. Never before has the nation been so torn between hailing a president's job performance and condemning his personal morality. In assessing the short-term impact of the Clinton presidency on public opinion, three areas should be considered: changes in demographic support for Clinton; perceptions of the Democratic and Republican Parties; and effects on Al Gore and the election of 2000.

*Demographic Support for Clinton*

Traditionally, Democratic presidents have attracted the support of the working class, blacks, liberals, and southerners (Edwards 1990). Yet a great deal has changed politically since the 1970s, when our last Democratic president was elected. Bill Clinton's presidency reflected these changes while it maintained loyalties from the traditional Democratic base (see Table 5). As with previous Democratic presidents, non-whites consistently gave higher approval ratings to the president than whites did, creating a gap as large as 28 percentage points in 1996. Clinton also easily maintained the support of liberals and Democrats who far exceeded national approval levels each year. The traditional class division between the parties was maintained, with Clinton attracting more support from the working class than from the wealthy. Regionally, Clinton's Arkansas roots failed to attract support from the South; in fact, he received the most support from easterners and the least support from southerners. Al-

Table 5
Group Differences in Clinton Approval, by Year

|  | 1994 | 1996 | 1998 |  | 1994 | 1996 | 1998 |
|---|---|---|---|---|---|---|---|
| Gender |  |  |  | Income |  |  |  |
|   Male | 46 | 53 | 62 |   Under $20,000 | 51 | 61 | 70 |
|   Female | 48 | 58 | 67 |   $20,000–29,999 | 48 | 53 | 63 |
| Age |  |  |  |   $30,000–49,999 | 43 | 53 | 61 |
|   Under 30 | 48 | 56 | 64 |   $50,000–74,999 | 48 | 57 | 69 |
|   30–49 | 47 | 55 | 65 |   Over $75,000 | 39 | 52 | 58 |
|   50–64 | 45 | 57 | 65 | Ideology |  |  |  |
|   Over 64 | 48 | 55 | 64 |   Liberal | 67 | 77 | 82 |
| Region |  |  |  |   Moderate | 55 | 63 | 70 |
|   East | 53 | 61 | 70 |   Conservative | 31 | 38 | 48 |
|   Midwest | 46 | 54 | 63 | Party identification |  |  |  |
|   South | 44 | 53 | 62 |   Democrat | 75 | 85 | 89 |
|   West | 45 | 54 | 64 |   Independent | 45 | 54 | 64 |
| Race |  |  |  |   Republican | 20 | 23 | 36 |
|   White | 44 | 52 | 61 | National approval | 47% | 56% | 65% |
|   Nonwhite | 67 | 80 | 87 |  |  |  |  |
| Education |  |  |  |  |  |  |  |
|   High school or less | 48 | 57 | 67 |  |  |  |  |
|   Some college | 44 | 53 | 63 |  |  |  |  |
|   College degree | 47 | 53 | 61 |  |  |  |  |
|   Postgrad degree | 50 | 57 | 64 |  |  |  |  |

*Note:* Average approval percentages for the survey year calculated from *Gallup Poll Monthly* demographic breakdowns.

though Democratic presidents had routinely been supported by the south, this region has experienced a realignment favoring the Republican party in recent years; it now appears that the more liberal east may be filling the shoes of the south regarding Democratic support.

Whereas previous Democratic presidents have attracted the support of the young, we find no such pronounced age division during the Clinton years, despite his attempt to court younger voters in his 1992 campaign. Furthermore, education appears to have only marginal effects on presidential approval. In 1994 and 1996, those with high school degrees or less and those with post-graduate degrees were slightly more approving of Clinton than those with some college or college degrees. In 1998, we still find these education differences, but those with the least education proved to be slightly more supportive of Clinton during the scandal that year than did the highly educated. This greater support may be tied to the working class's traditional Democratic support and the correlation between education and income. Finally, we can see a slight gender gap over Clinton's two terms, with women's approval of Clinton exceeding men's by as much as 5 percentage points in 1996. The gender gap proved much larger at certain points, however, as in early 1998, when the gap grew to 10 percent following news of the Lewinsky scandal. Despite Clinton's sexual misconduct, the 1980s-born gender gap persisted owing in part to his strong backing by women's organizations and his family-focused rhetoric.

## Clinton's Effect on the Public's Perceptions of the Parties

The Clinton presidency had very little effect on the public's views of the political parties and their perceived areas of expertise. When asked for party preference on handling certain problems, the Democrats came out ahead among the public in their traditional areas from the beginning of the Clinton administration. Gallup polls throughout Clinton's two terms favored the Democratic Party on education, Medicare, the environment, health-care policy, and Social Security. Republicans kept their traditional advantage in foreign affairs, crime, and moral values.

On matters related to the economy and taxes, Democrats did manage to edge out the Republicans during the Clinton administration. Since the recession in the early 1990s, Democrats have been perceived as the better party to handle the economy, with the exception of a brief period surrounding the 1994 election. Until 1997, when Democrats became the favorite, the public believed Republicans could best handle taxes. The party's success in capitalizing on these traditionally Republican areas can be attributed to public satisfaction with Clinton's economic performance and the achievement of a balanced budget agreement in 1997.

## The Election of 2000

The final area where the public's relationship with Bill Clinton may have a short-term effect is the election of 2000 and the reception of Al Gore. Although Gore has a more positive family image than Clinton, there is some indication that the public's weariness with the Clinton administration and its various scandals had an effect on Gore's campaign for the presidency (Pew Center Research Report, October 1999). In opinion polls, Americans blamed Clinton for the nation "losing its moral compass," and these negative perceptions depressed voter preferences for Gore (Balz and Connolly 1999). There is also evidence that Gore's favorability ratings were tied more closely to Clinton's troubled personal ratings than to his more positive job approval (Pew Center Research Report, March 1999). In response, Gore sought to distance himself from Clinton and emphasize his own morality and values, which caused some offense to the Clinton camp (Harris and Connolly 1999). Although Gore was not incapable of removing the taint of the Clinton scandal, his personal morality alone may not have been enough to overcome the public's desire for a change from the scandal-prone Clinton presidency.

We may also see the impact of the Clinton presidency in the nature of the candidates who were the most successful before entering the primary elections in 2000. Perhaps in response to the nearly perpetual existence of divided government and their experiences under the Clinton administration, voters appeared to prefer candidates who were more ideologically moderate and capable of working with their partisan rivals. If we consider the Republicans, the early favorites were political moderates rather than hard-line ideologues. The Republican frontrunner, George W. Bush, declared himself a compassionate conservative and was willing to abandon the party line in his open critique of the Republican Congress in the fall of 1999. His chief rival for the Republican nomination, John McCain, also earned a reputation as reaching for the political center and working with Democrats on issues normally opposed by Republicans, such as campaign finance reform. Before withdrawing from the race, McCain proved to be especially popular with independents and the general population, owing to his image as a political maverick. Polls from 1999 and early 2000 found these two candidates more popular with potential Republican primary voters and the general electorate than their more conservative Republican competitors, such as Steve Forbes. Popular support for these candidates is not surprising, however, if we consider that the public did not come to embrace Bill Clinton until he neared the political center following the 1994 election and began working with Republicans on issues such as a balanced-budget plan and welfare reform. Early preferences for the Republican candidates in 2000 is further indication that the public wanted to see in the next occupant of the White House a continuation of this cooperative policy-making and a focus on the political center.

## Public Approval of Future Presidents: Does Character Still Matter?

Predicting a president's long-term effect on the public is never easy, but the scandals and political conditions that governed the 1990s make Clinton's case particularly difficult to predict. Although he would rather be remembered for policy achievements, Clinton will likely be remembered by the public for both his personal charisma and the scandals that followed him throughout his presidency. The public's admiration for his ability to connect with people and understand their problems sets an important precedent for future presidents to follow. Likewise, the presidential candidates for 2000 have been analyzed for their comfort level with people; whereas Bush was praised from the beginning for connecting with people at campaign stops, Gore was judged repeatedly on his ability to shake his wooden and stiff image. It is possible that the public has come to expect more from a president in public displays of empathy and emotion after experiencing it so frequently in their eight years with Bill Clinton.

The long-term impact of the Clinton administration, however, will be found in the public's attitude toward presidential character and scandal. During the 2000 presidential race, there was some indication that the public would like a future president with a more upstanding moral character. Surveys in the months following the conclusion of the Lewinsky scandal found approximately three-quarters of the public claiming a candidate's personal moral character would be important to their vote in 2000 (Newsweek survey, April 1999; Fox News poll, March 1999). Almost two-thirds of survey respondents also believed that presidential candidates should be held to a higher moral standard than average citizens (U.S. News and World Report poll, February 1999). Finally, a majority of survey respondents claimed that they would prefer a president who sets a good moral example for the country over one who has political views they agree with (Gallup/CNN poll, February 1999).

Despite these claims, the public has occasionally selected the seemingly less moral candidate for office. Nixon's moral character was more questionable than Humphrey's in 1968, but the people elected Nixon on the basis of the issues (Zaller 1998). In 1992 and 1996, Bill Clinton's opposition was regarded as far more moral and ethical, but more people selected Clinton, with his flawed character but popular programs. This occurred even though a 1996 survey found almost two-thirds of respondents claiming that character and ethics were major reasons for their vote choice in 1996 (*Washington Post* survey, November 1996). These apparent contradictions indicate that, while Americans claim certain values, popular programs may win out over character in the end.

The American people certainly do not want a repeat of a Lewinsky-style scandal in the future, but their response to it does not echo their emphasis on seeking moral candidates. In a 1998 survey, almost two-thirds of the public believed the best way to avoid similar situations in the future was to make sure a president's life stays private, whereas only 34 percent said the solution was to elect a president with high moral character (Pew Research Center Survey, December 1998). Although some commentators believed that presidential character would be more closely scrutinized in future elections, others maintained that the public would be even less enthusiastic about probing into candidates' private lives after the Clinton scandal (Purdum 1999). Given the public's criticism, the latter argument seems to have more support (Holland 1998–1999); Pew Center Research Report, October 1999). There is evidence that the early presidential contenders for 2000 acted on this public desire to focus less on private behavior, as exhibited by Bush's unwillingness to discuss any past drug use or misconduct. Bill Bradley took this a step further by refusing to discuss his religious beliefs or church attendance, name his favorite books, or release medical records (Allen 2000).

Does the public's support of Bill Clinton throughout the Lewinsky scandal indicate that future presidents could survive public retribution for scandalous behavior? Some commentators claimed that Clinton's survival in public approval did not exactly establish precedent, given the political conditions and climate at the time. First, earlier analysis demonstrated that the public's dislike for the president's accusers and their favorable evaluations of national conditions tended to increase Clinton's job approval and decrease support for impeachment. This indicates that future presidents who are struggling with a bad economy and unpopular job performance may find their approval rates dropping even further under the weight of scandal. Second, Bill Clinton had suffered from public suspicion regarding his ethics and personal morality since the early days of his administration; some political commentators have questioned whether a Republican or a candidate holding a more ethical public image would have fared as well (Connolly and Edsall 1998).

In the end, certain political conditions may make a future president more vulnerable than Bill Clinton was to public scorn and disapproval. It is even possible that the public may say "no thanks" to future candidates possessing as many character flaws as Bill Clinton. It is more likely, however, that the Clinton scandal has somewhat desensitized the public to presidential scandals—especially sex scandals. As public doubts about the integrity of politicians have grown, there are fewer behaviors that shock or astonish citizens. This decline in expectations of elected officials' conduct was only reinforced by the various incidents that trailed Bill Clinton throughout both of his terms. As a result, it should come as no surprise that the public has adopted a "Machiavellian idea of political virtue," where morality is irrelevant to the achievement of political results (McWilliams 1997, 254). Until they come to believe that leaders can offer both personal virtue and successful governing or perceive that private behavior affects public performance, it is likely that future presidential scandals will be regarded by the public as business as usual.

# PART III

# Parties and Party Alignments

During his tenure in the White House, Clinton contributed several distinctive features to popular politics. The Clinton presidency helped to engender partisan change in a way that may well have large long-term implications for America's parties. John Coleman's essay argues that his presidency is one of the most consequential of the twentieth century for the future of the party system. According to Coleman, after 1992 the party system realigned, differences between the parties on economic policy grew, and Clinton provided the Democrats with "a way station to a possible new progressive identity." John Pitney and Nicol Rae find more modest legacies when examining Clinton's impact on the parties in the public and Congress. Both discuss how Clinton took control of traditionally Republican issues in ways that helped him politically but imposed costs upon both the Republican and Democratic parties. Republicans lost dominance over important issues with voters, and Democrats, when diverging from Clinton's agenda, at times found themselves marginalized at the left wing of American politics. Rae and Pitney also explain how Clinton unwittingly abetted the historic triumph of Republicans in the 1994 midterm elections, yet helped to strengthen the image of his party as populated by New Democrats.

CHAPTER 7

# CLINTON AND THE PARTY SYSTEM IN HISTORICAL PERSPECTIVE

JOHN J. COLEMAN

When leaving office, a president and his supporters tout his policy and partisan legacy. Political observers and political scientists are quick to reply that these claims strain credulity because most presidents leave only a modest mark on policy and the party system. Unlike the children in Garrison Keillor's Lake Woebegone, it seems, not every president can be above average.

Bill Clinton, however, might well challenge these standard interpretations. In policy, Clinton forged a centrist direction that had strong public appeal and erased the extremist label from his party. For the party system, one might also see the Clinton era as distinctive. In 1992, he reversed a long string of Republican domination of the presidency. At the same time, "change" was the word in Congress; newcomers won 25 percent of the seats in the House of Representatives, the highest percentage in over four decades. After the 1994 election, the Democrats controlled neither the House nor the Senate for the first time since 1954 and suffered massive losses in state and local elections. Defying predictions of his political demise, Clinton in 1996 became the first Democrat to win two presidential elections since Franklin Roosevelt. For the second time, he failed to receive 50 percent of the popular vote, joining Grover Cleveland (1884, 1892) and Woodrow Wilson (1912, 1916) as the only presidents to win twice with a minority of the popular vote. Then, for the first time since 1934, in 1998 the Democrats defied the "law" that the president's party loses House seats in the midterm election. Simply put, this was not a typical set of elections.

Certainly a president may affect his party's fortunes, but what about the condition of political parties in general? Scholars have shown that party organizations (the Democratic and Republican National Committees, the party campaign committees in the House and Senate, and state and local party committees) and congressional parties were more active in the 1980s and 1990s than their 1960s and 1970s counterparts (Cotter et al., 1989; Cox and McCubbins 1993; Crotty 1984; G. Pomper 1998; Rohde 1991; Wattenberg 1998). During the Clinton presidency, these trends accelerated, as the congressional parties took opposite stances on roll-call votes with a frequency not seen since the 1940s and party organizations raised unprecedented funds for electoral use. The extraordinary polarization Clinton inspired was a boon to congressional party cohesion and party organization fundraising. Even among the public, where parties were viewed skeptically, split-ticket voting was common, and voter turnout continued to decline (Mayer 1998), the Clinton presidency had a distinct impact. Public reaction to Clinton was sharply divided along party lines, with the response to Clinton's impeachment and trial—the first ever of an elected president—providing an extreme case in point.

More than for most presidents, then, with Clinton a case can be made for a legacy in policy and the party system. As the reader might suspect, itemizing the list of possible effects that a president might have had on specific parties or on the party system in general can be mind-boggling. So that history is not "just one damn thing after another," and with an eye to making comparisons across eras, scholars have developed models with which one can evaluate the party-system consequences of particular presidencies. I employ three of those frameworks in this chapter—partisan realignment, political time, and state-centered analysis—to consider the possible legacy of the Clinton presidency for the American party system.

I argue that the Clinton presidency was one of the most consequential of the past sixty-five years for political parties. Each of these frameworks suggests that the party system has changed dramatically compared to the recent past, and each suggests that these changes will have enduring consequences. Partisan realignment highlights the recent transformations in the coalitional composition of the parties and the shift toward a new and long-lasting balance of party competition. Political time points Bill Clinton's ability to forge a successful framework for his own success but leaves less certain whether he will have lasting consequences on his party and its policy priorities. I suggest that Clinton was better situated to have these lasting consequences than were other presidents who served in comparable political time. State-centered analysis indicates that the strength of political parties has much to do with the structural arrangement of government institutions and the dominant policy concerns processed by these institutions. Shifts in institutional power and policy concerns have contributed to greater party strength in the 1990s and opened up possibilities for future revitalization of the link between political parties and the general public. The obstacles to revitalization are significant, however, particularly in an era of economic transformation. To appeal to an electorate increasingly attuned to the individualistic ethos often thought associated with life in the age of new information technology, enduring relevance and strength for the parties may require the creation of innovative organizational strategies.

## Partisan Realignment

Partisan realignment theory examines the party system's transition from one type of competition to another. In effect, realignment theory takes "before and after" photographs of the party system. These images might be taken from a period in which one party is dominant and one in which another dominates, or from a time when a majority party has a particular coalition and one when that party has a different supporting coalition, or from an era in which one party dominates and one in which neither does. In either situation, significant policy changes accompany the party realignment.

### Secular Realignment

Our analytical eye is often drawn to the dramatic and disruptive, but V. O. Key (1959) reminded scholars that significant political change often results from secular realignment: the cumulation of small, incremental, gradual developments. As a social group becomes more affluent, for example, its members might find the policy appeals of a conservative political party more to their liking. As one particular social group becomes better represented within a political party, other groups might gradually pull out. Scholars have suggested that both these developments have occurred over the past few decades. For example, as Catholics moved steadily into the middle class, they became less reliably Democratic. As blacks gained a louder voice in the Democratic Party, whites, especially southern whites, increasingly supported Republicans. As religious and social conservatives played an increasing role in the Republican Party, Republican moderates found themselves increasingly likely to vote Democratic.

During the Clinton era, the two most common secular realignment claims concerned the death of the New Deal coalition and the dominance of cultural and religious values in the new party alliances. Each claim has some truth, but each has been overstated. Surely it is correct that the cluster of groups supporting Franklin Roosevelt and the Democrats in the 1930s and 1940s and the groups supporting Democrats in the 1990s have some differences. And it is also true that groups that were considered part of the New Deal coalition—organized labor, agricultural interests, urban ethnic groups, Catholics, Jews, southerners, industrial blue collar workers, liberals, individuals with moderate or low income, less educated individuals—tend to support Democrats less strongly in the 1990s than they had in the 1940s (Mayer 1998). Indeed, if these groups were still voting for Democrats at their traditional level, Democrats would not have lost control of Congress, state legislatures, and governorships in the 1990s.

But to assert that the New Deal coalition has disappeared is too strong. It is more accurate to say that this coalition is no longer enough. According to the National Election Study conducted by the University of Michigan's Survey Research Center, support for Bill Clinton in 1996 and House Democrats in 1998 was strongest among blacks, women, lower-income people, Catholics and Jews, union members, blue-collar workers, urban residents, those without college education, and Northeasterners. Aside from the presence of blacks and women, who were not major components of the New Deal coalition, and the absence of southern whites, who were, there is little in this constellation of groups that would surprise a late-1940s Democratic politician transported into the late 1990s.

Differences between the 1940s and 1990s are not inconsequential, however. By the 1990s a Democrat, particularly a Democratic presidential nominee, could no longer assume that simply rounding up the old coalitional suspects would be sufficient for victory. Even a candidate who did well with these traditional New Deal groups—and most Democratic candidates did do reasonably well with them—would need to reach outside this cluster to ensure victory (Abramowitz and Saunders 1998; Bartels 1998). For Bill Clinton, that meant gaining the votes of some moderates, conservatives; suburbanites; middle- and upper-middle-income whites; Midwesterners; Pacific Coast residents; and service-sector, high-tech, and research-based workers. In this sense, the Democratic coalition has been truly changed. Clinton demonstrated to fellow partisans that the core New Deal groups, an ever smaller proportion of the population, simply cannot reliably produce national Democratic victories.

Our hypothetical transported Democratic politician would recognize many of the groups supporting Democrats in the 1990s, but what about the issues? Have the party alignments gradually moved from an economic to a cultural basis? So far, the answer to this question is "no, but." It is certainly true that social, cultural, moral, and religious issues were playing a bigger role in politics in the 1990s than they had in previous decades. Beginning in the 1960s, "new liberals" in the Democratic Party pushed issues of social and racial justice onto the party platform alongside economic growth. Indeed, activists in both major parties were much more driven by this cluster of issues after the 1960s than before. During the Clinton presidency, there were heated conflicts over flag burning, gun control, homosexual rights, affirmative action, and "partial-birth" abortion.

For most voters, however, it really is "the economy, stupid." George Bush won in 1988 primarily because voters believed he would continue Reagan's successful management of the economy; his ability to paint Michael Dukakis as outside the cultural mainstream was the cherry on this electoral sundae. In 1992, Bush's similar attempts to cast Bill Clinton as a moral deviant were a resounding flop. Partly, this was because Clinton inoculated himself with conservative stands on social matters such as capital punishment and welfare reform, but Bush failed mostly because voters concentrated on the economy. The party most likely to push a broad-based social, cultural, and moral agenda, the Republicans, controlled Congress beginning in 1995 but advanced an agenda centered overwhelmingly on economic, financial, and regulatory matters. Clinton won reelection in 1996 despite widespread concerns about his moral and ethical behavior; his strengths on the fundamentally economic issues of employment, low inflation and interest rates, education, and protecting popular social insurance programs such as Social Security and Medicare trumped his weaknesses on moral and cultural issues. In 1998 the public overwhelmingly rallied around Clinton despite his admissions of marital infidelity and dishonest statements about this affair. Republicans supported the presidential candidacy of Texas governor George W. Bush in 1999 despite widespread rumors of his colorful past. The leading presidential candidates in early 2000—Democrats Bill Bradley and Al Gore, Republicans George Bush and John McCain—were not basing their campaigns primarily on cultural or moral issues. It is fair to say that the parties tailor appeals to specific social groups, and it is fair to say that voters care about social and moral issues—but Americans do not yet consistently elevate cultural and religious concerns above economic ones (Carmines and Layman 1997; Layman 1997).

In sum, secular realignment has changed the party system. Building over time, this transformation crested during the Clinton presidency: The old New

Deal coalition is not dead, but it is not sufficient for Democratic victories. Bill Clinton demonstrated to the party how to reach groups outside this traditional alliance. Clinton made these appeals primarily on economic grounds, but, aware of the problems cultural issues had caused Democratic candidates in the 1980s, he very skillfully staked out his conservative and moderate bona fides on a range of social issues. Even if these issues do not yet dominate party coalitions, Clinton helped cement the secular trend that successful candidates have to appear "safe" to the middle-of-the-road voter on at least some of them.

*Critical Realignment*

Critical realignment theory puts analytical teeth into the commonplace notion that some elections—critical elections—have more enduring consequences for the party system than do others (Burnham 1970; Key 1955). Rather than the gradual change that lies at the heart of secular realignment, critical realignment focuses on sharp, quick transformations of the political landscape that have effects lasting a generation or longer. Typically, critical realignments bring a new majority party to power and have effects at the local, state, and national level. Scholars generally agree that the 1800 (Jeffersonian Republicans), 1832 (Democrats), 1860 (Republicans), and 1932 (Democrats) elections fall into this category. Other realignments might keep the same majority party but create a new supporting coalition for that party, as in 1896 (Republicans).

Two points about these realigning elections stand out. First, they are spaced 28 to 36 years apart, suggesting to some writers that there might be some systematic regularity or predictability to realignment (Beck 1974; Burnham 1970). Second, none of them is recent. In the 1960s, scholars did their math—$1932 + 28 = 1960$, $1932 + 36 = 1968$—and awaited the next realignment. But none of the elections in the 1960s had the look of the classic realigning election in which a new majority party or coalition came to power, so political scientists began to wonder if the age of realigning elections had come to an end (Shafer 1991b).

Looking back, scholars such as John Aldrich (1995) and Walter Dean Burnham (1996) have argued that the 1968 election marked a critical realignment of a different type, one notable for its dealigning features: members of the public pulled away from their party loyalties, turnout dropped, and control over government was usually divided between the two major parties. Under this shared power, policy began to move in a more conservative direction. The key ingredients of critical realignment—a new pattern of party politics and significant changes in public policy—were thus in place after 1968. In this view, the dramatic victory of Republican Ronald Reagan in 1980 solidified the ongoing system rather than marking a realigning election in its own right. The Republican Party strengthened the conservative trend by gaining control of the Senate in the 1980 election, but Democrats controlled the House, so control of government in Washington remained divided. The Democrats also remained the majority party in the states and cities.

In 1994, twenty-six years after 1968, the election had all the hallmarks of a traditional critical realignment: issues were highly prominent; the political atmosphere seemed unusually energized; turnout, though not high by historical standards, was higher than in the recent midterm elections; the election results tilted almost universally toward one party; institutional reorganization (especially in the House) after the election was extensive; attempted policy changes were numerous and, for the most part, ideologically consistent (Burnham 1996). At last the Democratic era appeared over.

Unfortunately, history is hardly ever as neat and tidy as our models. In this new, supposedly Republican era, a Democrat won the presidency in 1996 and the Democrats pulled off the historical anomaly of gaining seats in the midterm election of 1998. Much of the conservative Republican agenda either failed or was watered down to ensure passage and the president's signature. Was there a realignment or wasn't there?

It is reasonable to describe the 1994 results as akin to those of 1896. The 1896 critical realignment did not create a new majority party, but it created a new supporting coalition for the existing Republican majority. Similarly, the 1994 realignment continued the likelihood of divided control of government that was typical of the 1968 shift, but it also changed the balance of power within that division. With 1994, the Republican Party achieved parity with the Democrats throughout the country and at all levels of government. Although a case could be made for the Republicans as the new majority party, it would be a shakier case than one could make, for example, for the Democrats after the realignment in 1932. The Republicans did not become the undisputed majority party following 1994 but it *was* a realignment with a clear partisan direction. The period from 1968 to 1994 featured divided government that leaned toward Democratic control at most levels and in most offices; the era after 1994 seems likely to continue the closely contested balance of party power but with the balance tilting more toward the Republicans. Pundits and commentators noted again and again in the years following the 1994 election how the Republicans had an amazing tendency to strip policy defeat from the jaws of victory. Yet, despite a seemingly endless string of strategic blunders on policy and repeated, unpopular attempts to knock Clinton off his perch, Republicans remained the majority party in Congress for three straight terms, something they had not accomplished in nearly 70 years. The party system had changed.

It would be inaccurate to state that Bill Clinton alone caused this realignment, because conditions for realignments brew over time—one can picture a water balloon being filled and becoming more expanded, stressed, and tense until it finally pops. The critical election is the pop that bursts the balloon. The water in the critical realignment balloon consists of the cumulative concerns, issues, and transformations in society and economy that place severe fissures in existing public policy paradigms. In the case of 1994, key stresses emerged from the transition to the information economy, a transition overlaid on broad social changes regarding women, minorities, and family structure. Combined with the gradual buildup of a pool of voters whose partisan allegiance was up for grabs, the conditions were ripe for political explosion.

Clinton's responsibility for the Democratic losses in 1994 was modest: 1994's outcome was predictable without any recourse to a unique "Clinton factor" in explanatory models (Campbell 1997; Coleman 1997b). Put differently, Clinton was no more or less responsible than other recent presidents for his party's fate in the midterm election. But critical realignments need triggering events to detonate the underlying stresses in the political system—pins to pop that expanding balloon—and Clinton's 1993–1994 tax hikes, health-care-reform debacle, crime legislation, gays-in-the-military support, and pro-choice advocacy may have served just this purpose among conservatives. More broadly, the mismatch between the public's economic expectations for a Democratic president who promised to focus on the economy "like a laser beam" and the relatively modest results of 1993–1994 may have served as a triggering "event." For his first two years, and more pertinently in the year prior to the election, Clinton presided over the slowest growing economy of any Democratic presidency in the postwar era. With these pins in hand, the public popped the balloon and restructured the American party system.

## The Prototypical Preemptive President

Critical realignment theory argues that not all elections are created equal; students of the presidency suggest the same about presidents. Just as political observers seek to discern patterns in election results, they also seek to find regularities in presidential behavior. Although this exercise risks forcing presidents into categories in which they fit uncomfortably, it has the benefit of highlighting that not every president faces the same obstacles and opportunities on entering office. Not every president can be Abraham Lincoln or Franklin Roosevelt.

One of the most useful ways to think about categories of presidents was developed by political scientist Stephen Skowronek (1993). Skowronek suggests that presidents take office in "political time," by which he means that presidents take office in a particular political context. Two components are especially important. First, is the ongoing policy regime, the dominant direction of public policy, strong, or does it appear to be weakening? If it is strong, citizens believe that it can still solve problems and is generally the right approach; if it is weak, there will be a widespread sense that policies are failing and that a new direction is needed. Second, is the president affiliated with this set of policies or is he seen as an opponent of these policies? Presidents connected to unpopular policies face very difficult leadership challenges, those unaffiliated with them have great opportunities to initiate bold change.

Using these two variables, four types of presidencies emerge. Disjunctive presidents are affiliated with a weak policy regime. Reconstructive presidents oppose these weak policies. Articulative presidents are associated with a strong set of policies. The final type, the preemptive president, serves during a strong ongoing policy regime but is not allied with it. As discussed elsewhere in this volume, the preemptive president seeks to find a "third way," combining features of the agendas of both major parties. Preemptive presidents such as Woodrow Wilson (1913–1920), Dwight Eisenhower (1953–1961), Richard Nixon (1969–1974), and Bill Clinton (1993–2001) are unlikely to reject the general policy direction in which the country is moving, but they will moderate that direction with some of the policy principles of their party.

The preemptive president seeks to occupy a middle ground largely defined by the priorities of his opponents, but with enough independence from these opponents and his own party to put a distinctive stamp on policy. Clinton, as a New Democrat, was eager to distance himself from some of liberalism's pet ideas and symbols. Although his conservative policy emphasis on personal responsibility may seem ironic in the extreme, it was an effective tool for separating himself from a liberalism that was perceived as blaming society first and holding individuals accountable for their behavior last. Throughout this volume, one can find a number of examples of Clinton seeking to forge a third way, one that blended conservative, liberal, and centrist approaches.

Frustrating opponents by "stealing" their issues, preemptive presidents frequently watch with amusement as these foes, determined to separate themselves from the preemptive interloper, drive themselves over the ideological cliff. Clinton's Republican opponents played their parts perfectly in episodes such as the government shutdown during the budget conflict of 1995–1996. The president's joy in watching his opponents play the fool, however, is offset by devastating attacks on his character and extraordinary political and personal distrust. It is no surprise that all four impeachment efforts in U.S. history—John Tyler, Andrew Johnson, Richard Nixon, Bill Clinton—were leveled against preemptive president.

As maddening as they have been to their opponents, third-way presidents have been successful electorally. Wilson, Eisenhower, Nixon, and Clinton all won second terms. But as Skowronek points out, the success of the preemptive president seems to be personal rather than partisan. Wilson and Clinton's Democrats and Eisenhower and Nixon's Republicans did not enjoy great success during these presidencies and, generally, came out no better and perhaps worse than they had been when the president started his term. Bill Clinton won two elections handily in the electoral college and raised astounding sums of money for his party, yet Democrats lost control of Congress and many governorships and state legislatures during his watch. Preemptive presidents have also been unsuccessful in passing the baton to their vice presidents. The party of each of the previous twentieth-century preemptive presidents lost the subsequent presidential election, and in two of those three cases it was the president's vice president who went down to defeat. Obviously, this pattern hung heavily over Vice President Al Gore in the 2000 presidential election. This personal success at the party's expense may seem surprising, but remember that the preemptive president makes his mark by portraying an image that straddles the two parties.

Unsuccessful in building a legacy of partisan election victories, preemptive presidents also have difficulty convincing their parties to continue on the third-way policy path. Republicans after Eisenhower and Nixon expressed discontent with the moderate, centrist, go-along-to-get-along strategy, especially because it did not appear to help the Republicans become the majority party. Only by staking out a distinctive ideological stance and nominating ideologically distinctive candidates—like Barry Goldwater in 1964 and Ronald Reagan in 1980—these critics argued, would the party make a credible claim for the voters' trust.

If party officials and politicians begin to believe that the Clintonian policy strategy will not build a solid majority for the party, one can certainly imagine a wave of such discontent sweeping through the Democratic Party. But there is a lesson in the conservative Republican response to Nixon that liberal Democrats should heed. Ronald Reagan expressed support and even some respect for the New Deal while acknowledging that some adjustments were necessary: less spending, less taxing, less regulation, a shift in power back to the states. Instead, Reagan and his fellow conservatives took aim more directly at the 1960s Great Society programs and policies and the disrespect for family, morality, and responsibility they believed was inherent in these. Even the more conservative Republicans of the 1990s did not withdraw the federal government from major areas of responsibility initiated in the 1930s and 1940s. They rearranged and restructured these areas and introduced new approaches but did not radically restrict federal responsibility in economy, society, and culture.

What this story suggests for Democrats is that an ideological approach that attempts to bring back the old liberal coalition will probably fail. A more promising scenario is for a "progressive" Democratic approach that emphasizes newer liberal themes, like environmentalism and quality of life, but even here with a nod to market-sensitive solutions rather than government dictates. More security in health care, while avoiding the connotations of "government takeover of the health-care system," might be another key. "Progressive" Democrats might be able to build support for regulatory reactions to negative side-effects of the ongoing information age economic transformation, but like Progressive regulations of the early twentieth century, these responses would need to be crafted in a manner that does not appear to repudiate economic progress and that would not scare off support from the middle class and the growing proportion of workers dependent on the information economy. In short, progressive Democratic policy will have to build on the transformations in economics and politics rather than repudiate them, and such an approach is not far removed from Clinton's third way.

If preemptive presidents do not transfer electoral success to their parties, does Clinton really matter? In two ways, the answer is yes. First, Democrats at the end of the 1990s were within striking distance of regaining Congress, while Republicans after Eisenhower and Nixon were in distinctly minority positions. Maintaining a Clintonian posture might keep Democrats close enough to gain control of Congress on occasion, and if enough Democrats concluded that "once in a while" is an acceptable and safe bet, that could blunt moves toward a more progressive posture. Being so close to majority status might steer Democrats from rolling the political dice on, say, income inequality as a political issue. Confronting this issue head-on would separate a new progressivism from the Clinton approach, but it would be a huge political gamble. Second, Clinton navigated the Democratic Party at least partway toward the progressive policies iterated in the previous paragraph. A necessary way-station, Clinton's presidency pulled its party away from the liberalism of the past toward a more centrist approach that accommodated the conservative drift in public policy. Clinton relieved Democrats from carrying much of the burden of the old liberal baggage—some of which had more to do with public perception than with actual policy failures—making it safer for future Democrats to pursue a new progressivism.

## Parties, the State, and Policy Feedback

Looking at the Clinton years through the lenses of realignment and political time highlights the implications of this presidency for the fortunes of particular political parties. Neither, however, provides much leverage to analyze the status of parties in general—that is, the strength of parties as political organizations and symbols of public attention and interest. If we want to consider the broader status of parties, we need to consider the context within which parties operate.

One way to think about this context is through the framework of the state (Coleman 1996). Parties are strong in the political system when they control important policy domains, when that policy divides the parties consistently across time, and when these policy domains are a key interest of elites and the mass public. The state provides a setting within which strong parties are more likely or less likely. By "the state," I mean a complex of institutions, dominant assumptions about the proper role of those institutions, and key policies that preoccupy these institutions and are compatible with the assumptions. The fiscal state established in the 1930s and 1940s consists of the economic policy-making *institutions* in the government; the free-market, limited-government, individual-liberty *assumptions* that guide the actions of actors in these institutions; and a *policy* set emphasizing macroeconomic regulation of the business cycle based on arm's-length transfers of cash from one social or economic sector to another.

The fiscal state, then, is characterized by its distinctive set of policy preoccupations and the manner in which policy was made. The impact of this state on political parties is a profound example of what political scientists refer to as policy feedback (Pierson 1993). The idea in policy-feedback models is that analysts need to consider not only how politics shapes policy making, but also how the content and process of policy-making can shape future politics. For example, the creation of Social Security and Medicare led to the development and growth of groups such as the American Association of Retired Persons (AARP), which would later prove to be significant protectors and shapers of these two programs.

Where do we see feedback effects in the fiscal state? First, economic policy in the fiscal state was centered in the executive branch and closely identified with the president—Nixonomics, Carternomics, Reaganomics, and so on—rather than the parties in general. Second, fiscal policy—changes in the size of budget deficits and surpluses to achieve specific economic goals—on autopilot weakened the link between parties and policy and removed issues from the partisan table. Such policy includes spending and taxing provisions that were implemented automatically because of changes in economic conditions rather than because of discretionary actions by politicians. Unemployment compensation, food stamps, and welfare are examples in which spending changes automatically when economic conditions change, even if politicians do nothing. Autopilot fiscal policy also includes spending that was "uncontrollable" because recipients had legal entitlements to receipt of the benefits regardless of the preferences of politicians at a particular point in time. Third, monetary policy—changes in interest rates and the ease of borrowing or investing money—was controlled by the independent Federal Reserve Board and outside the direct influence of political parties. Fourth, the public in this state tended to treat economic measures of growth, unemployment, and inflation as devices for plebiscitary evaluations of incumbent politicians, especially but not exclusively in presidential elections. In other words, policy discussion that focused on rates of growth, unemployment, and inflation encouraged voters to focus more on specific, objective economic outcomes than the philosophy and principles of party policy packages. Fifth, while parties portrayed themselves as keen combatants on economic policy, the reality was an overwhelming consensus around Keynesian fiscal policy philosophy (Schier 1992). Rather than assume that balanced budgets are always best, this philosophy employed budget deficits and surpluses to produce specific levels of growth, inflation, and unemployment.

These feedback effects significantly diminished the centrality of political parties in American politics, but the effects go even deeper. With economic leadership transferred to the president, candidates for Congress found that they could successfully campaign in a candidate-centered rather than party-centered mode and could to some degree detach themselves from the president's coattails. Voters who perceived leadership to be in the executive branch felt even less constrained to send a consistent team to Washington than they had in the past; divided government became the norm as split-ticket voting became not only more common but in a sense culturally enshrined as the "best" way to vote. Presidents won plebiscitary victories for solid economic performance, but voters felt no compunction to send fellow partisans to Congress to assist the president. As monetary policy grew in importance, a party team appeared even less significantly related to economic performance. And with automatic fiscal policy placing a significant proportion of economic policy on autopilot regardless of which party voters put in office, and a Keynesian consensus pushing the parties toward policy convergence, particularly during times of economic stress, it's no wonder the public thought less about the parties and less of the parties. The public did not reject political parties, but there was increased skepticism about exactly how it was that parties made much of a difference and, especially among the young, movement toward interest groups as the preferred way to express one's political preferences (Mayer 1998; Wattenberg 1998). With candidates able to fend for themselves, voters less attentive to parties when voting, and differences between the parties dissipating, party organizations also languished.

*Fractures in the Fiscal State*

Changes in the policy concerns or policy-making process of the fiscal state could have feedback effects that would help reverse the weakness of political parties. In the 1970s, changes began. Regarding institutions, Congress began to take a more aggressive role in fiscal policy formation through the passage of budgetary reforms (Sundquist 1981). With old Keynesian policies proving ineffective in addressing the economic woes of high inflation and high unemployment ("stagflation"), the arena was open for new ideas about economic management. Republican and Democratic assumptions about government's role in the economy and society, reflected in congressional roll-call votes, diverged modestly in the early to mid-1970s and much more notably in the late 1970s to early 1980s (Coleman 1997a; Poole and Rosenthal 1991; Rohde 1991).

As it became apparent that a fundamental struggle was underway to define economic policy for the next two to three decades, the party organizations became much more adept at raising substantial funds and improving the professionalism of their operations. New technologies helped the fundraising drive, but more important were large pools of individuals and groups in the population feeling threatened by economic and political disarray and eager to invest their money in the "right" message. Changes in the fiscal state had contributed to stronger, more unified congressional parties and stronger, more active party organizations.

The electorate, on the other hand, maintained its distance from the parties during the 1970s and 1980s: turnout dropped, split-ticket voting remained prominent, and skepticism and cynicism were the order of the day. Split-ticket voting peaked in the mid-1980s and held steady or declined slightly in the

1990s. Measures of public cynicism and trust demonstrated some modest improvement during the 1980s but increased sharply through the early years of the 1990s. In short, the kind of sustained resurgence seen in party organizations and in Congress did not surface (Aldrich 1995). More systemic unraveling of the fiscal state would be necessary before a fuller resurgence of political parties was possible.

Did the Clinton era introduce this unraveling? In some respects, the answer is clearly "no," and the constraints of the fiscal state remain. The public still seems to view national elections, especially the presidential election, as a plebiscite on macroeconomic performance. Even more important, the institutional role of the Federal Reserve has grown ever stronger in the 1990s. Policy adjustments to meet changing economic conditions are limited almost entirely to Fed monetary actions. Even more than in the past, the prime tool of economic management is outside the realm of serious partisan contestation. It will be harder for voters—and nonvoters—to take the party stances on economic policy terribly seriously as long as the Fed continues as the economic wizard behind the curtain.

In other respects, however, the fiscal state has been seriously revised. Institutionally, economic policy during the Clinton presidency resulted from presidential-congressional give-and-take rather than congressional concessions to a presidential framework. With his veto power, the president remains the senior partner in this negotiation, but the partners are more nearly equal in the late 1990s than previously.

Even more profound than shifts in institutional power have been the shifts in policy. Republicans were not as successful as they wished in converting "uncontrollable" entitlement spending into block grants, but they did enjoy some success. This partial victory means automatic stabilizers still operate, but, with welfare no longer an entitlement, that significant element of autopilot fiscal policy has been erased. More important, Keynesianism, the guiding fiscal philosophy after the 1930s, is largely defunct at the national level. There is little serious argument in Washington that Keynesian fiscal policy can fine-tune the economy. Across the spectrum, politicians tout the advantages of balanced budgets rather than the deliberate use of deficits or surpluses. Attempts to send a balanced budget amendment to the states failed during Clinton's presidency, but only by the narrowest of margins.

In the tax cut debate in the summer of 1999, each party asserted that its plan—ranging from a $300-billion cut supported by the president to a $792-billion cut supported by House and Senate Republicans—would preserve balanced budgets as far as the eye could see. Neither party emphasized Keynesian notions about "managing" the economy. Democrats complained that pumping more money into a robust economy via tax cuts would accelerate inflation—a Keynesian notion about the tradeoff between growth and inflation—but this was a transparent political tactic. At the same time as they lamented the infusion of tax cut dollars into the economy, a majority of Democrats wanted to increase the minimum wage and prod corporations to boost worker wages. Moreover, Democrats themselves were supporting sizable tax cuts during a time of solid economic growth and very low unemployment, an odd notion if one is guided by Keynesian precepts that tax cuts are a tool to stimulate the economy. For Republicans, making extravagant claims about the amount of taxes that could be cut without igniting inflation served their non-Keynesian goal of retrenching the scope of government. The Republican script was clearly "Reagan: The Sequel." Pinching the flow of funds into government would necessitate further spending cuts in later years if economic projections proved overly optimistic in estimating government revenues. Indeed, the essence of the non-Keynesian nature of the competing tax plans is that they were ten-year plans rather than plans sensitive to changing economic conditions over time.

This discussion about the proposed tax cuts in 1999 reveals something else about economic policy at the end of the 1990s: growth was no longer the key measuring stick. The Clinton administration came to office promising economic growth, but it also made clear that growth rates were only one measure of economic performance and not necessarily the most important one. Indeed, if one looked at growth rates alone, it would be hard to understand the deep economic unease and anger in the early 1990s; even the recession of 1990–1991 looks mild and brief by the traditional yardstick of economic growth rates. But this is the wrong yardstick. Growth matters—no president wants a major economic downturn during his term—but the growth rate no longer adequately captures the public's concerns with the economy. Educational quality and opportunities, technological innovation, high-paying and skill-intensive middle-class jobs, international competitiveness, flexibility in production and in worker skills, lifelong learning and retraining—these are the kinds of economic concerns that the Clinton team put central on its economic agenda. These items are perhaps best thought of as an economic-quality rather than economic growth agenda. Unlike the old Keynesian concerns about how to increase or decrease growth, the options available to achieve these economic quality goals stretch far beyond increasing or decreasing federal budget deficits or surpluses.

The demise of the Keynesian consensus as the central element in U.S.

economic policy is a boon to political parties. The collapse of this agenda suggests that the electorate will be presented with more policy options, particularly during times of economic stress. The near universal embrace of balanced budgets reduces the wiggle room available to the parties. Assuming that the size of government will not expand significantly—a safe assumption—the parties will need to make hard and specific choices about the proper role of government. During the 1980s, the parties could punt on this question simply by running large deficits: the Republicans got the tax cuts and defense spending they preferred, while Democrats got the social spending they preferred. With balanced budgets, this dodge is no longer available, or at least the parties will have to be more artful dodgers than before.

The consensus about the sanctity of balanced budgets opens up promising alternatives. For one thing, the parties may disagree about *how* to balance the budget, and they no longer have the option to shirk as they did in the 1980s and the early 1990s. For another, party competition may move beyond the kinds of growth discussions favored by the old economic management consensus and into new areas, such as the economic quality agenda. These areas would be less likely than the economic growth agenda to see the parties converge on appropriate priorities, goals, and policy options.

What do these changes in institutions, dominant assumptions, and policy mean for parties in the public? For stronger political parties, they are moves in the right direction. As the public perceives the congressional parties to be increasingly critical in the policy-making process, and as they appear to be contesting genuinely important policy areas, party may be elevated as a component of citizen decision-making. Signs of this resurgence are evident in the slightly declining proportion of split-ticket voters and voters identifying themselves as independents in the 1990s and, in 1992 and 1996, the lowest percentages of "split districts"—districts that support one party's candidate in the House election and another party's candidate in the presidential election—since 1952. Interest in third parties grew in the 1990s—Ross Perot did better in 1992 than any independent or third-party presidential candidate since Theodore Roosevelt ran in 1912—and, at about 70 percent, the number of House districts in which voters could vote for an alternative to the two major parties was higher by the mid-1990s than it had been for many decades. Although third-party strength may disconcert the major parties, it suggests that citizens still see some usefulness in political parties and believe that these minor parties introduce important policy perspectives.

These signs are modest, to be sure, and substantial skepticism about the parties remains (Grunwald 1999). It is best to think of these changes in the state as necessary but perhaps not sufficient for a resurgence of political parties in the public. Parties were discredited for decades by feedback effects from the fiscal state as well as by such effects from policy failures, petty political tactics, and shrill political rhetoric. Where earlier generations were socialized in an atmosphere supportive of strong partisanship, recent generations have grown up in an environment awash with negative messages about politics in general and party politics in particular. These are difficult but not impossible mindsets to overcome, as recent history shows. It was only two decades ago that many Americans wondered whether the presidency remained a viable institution, but Ronald Reagan reassured many Americans, even those who opposed his policies, that the presidency could still be a vital force for leadership and change.

Looking through a wider lens reaffirms that a transformation of the party system is not without obstacles. Unlike past party upheavals in the twentieth century, the most recent episode occurred during a simultaneous revolution in the economy. This revolution and its attendant technology and ethos appear to have privileged individualistic, libertarian principles at the expense of the kind of group and communal principles that have been important to the success of parties historically. The constant drumbeat that young Americans should be prepared to be "flexible" in their career choices, and that long-term employment with a single employer is debilitating rather than desirable, is but one example of this thinking. Political parties will need new methods to attract citizens increasingly skeptical of centralized authority and knowledge and to mobilize a population increasingly living in single-person households. This is particularly true for the major parties; third parties and independent candidates may stand to benefit from an electorate that is driven more by individualistic impulses. Parties failing to produce these new methods may well encounter an even more withdrawn, skeptical citizenry than they now face.

If the Internet and new information technologies do indeed promote the "horizontalization" of society—the breaking down of hierarchical communication, knowledge, and expertise structures—political parties will need to organize consonant with that sensibility, with approaches that appear individually empowering for the intended recipients of the parties' appeals. In an era in which "community" and "group" may be increasingly defined by electronic connections across the country or around the globe than by personal connections over the backyard fence or across town, and in which economic globalization may spark renewed interest in "local control" and small-scale local political action, new mobilizing strategies will be necessary.

All these pressures pushing toward individualism will not erode the basic human impulse for joining and togetherness. Humans are social, not solitary, beings. The question now, just as it was a hundred years ago, is whether parties have the means, motives, and opportunities to bring individuals and groups together in a changed society (Clemens 1997; Ware 2000). For years, younger Americans have been favoring interest groups over political parties, perhaps because these groups are tailored to individualistic interests and thinking. The information revolution and its technology might well be expected to reinforce this trend.

## The Party System in Flux—Again

As parties move beyond the old economic debates, it is impossible to say for certain what the new major concern of party competition will be, or if indeed any single concern will be dominant. Cultural and moral issues? The economic-quality issues mentioned above? Either of these issue sets would be more conducive to strong, vibrant parties that attract significant public interest and support than would a continuation of the old debates about economic management. Neither would be as likely to produce convergence between the parties as was macroeconomic management in the fiscal state.

Social and cultural issues are not new aspects of party competition. Significant and contentious social and cultural issues helped define the party coalitions in the nineteenth century. "New liberals" in the 1960s and 1970s forced a range of social and cultural concerns, such as civil rights, women's rights, and abortion, onto the Democratic Party agenda, and social and religious conservatives forged an array of such issues on the Republican agenda in the 1970s and 1980s. President Clinton demonstrated that the Democrats could build a winning formula, though one with little margin for error, based on a broadly traditional posture toward many social issues while remaining liberal on specific concerns such as child care, minority rights, gun control, and abortion. But while these issues were critically important for party activists, economic performance was the make-or-break issue for presidents and parties. The question for the future is whether these issues can be the *central*, sustaining issues dividing the parties or if, as analysts have noted about the late-nineteenth century, the parties will talk about culture but govern on economics (Gerring 1999; McCormick 1986).

If cultural and social issues promise party coalitions forged along the lines of religious, cultural, and ethnic identity, economic-quality issues promise a politics that is likely to be significantly more class-based. Keynesianism operated on the premise that economic growth could be a salve for nearly all social wounds. Growth, Keynesians might say, does not inherently discriminate by class. This proposition was never entirely right, but it was a linchpin uniting Democrats and Republicans throughout the fiscal-state era.

Economic quality issues, by contrast, starkly raise some basic tradeoffs between economic classes. For example, if education is vital to individual success in the new economy, what amount of expropriation from the wealthy is justifiable in order to create a more equal distribution of high-quality education? States have already faced this issue, and the politics have been bitter and polarizing. States as disparate as Texas and Vermont have considered plans to "equalize" education spending across districts and erupted in political turmoil. The issue need not only roil state politics. Education, long the province of local and state government, is becoming increasingly nationalized as an issue, so the question of taking resources from wealthier states to improve educational quality in poorer states might become a divisive one. International competitiveness is likewise an issue area that pits Americans with few economic advantages, vulnerable jobs, and modest incomes against well-paid service- and research-sector beneficiaries of global economic integration. Other economic-quality issues portend similar class-based conflicts. Some would fear what this development might mean for social and political stability, but both parties joining together on the side of the "haves" and attempting to keep these issues out of partisan competition would be a greater threat to stability. The inability or, worse, unwillingness to mobilize broad swaths of the electorate is already a great failing of the party system; continuing down that path imperils political and social peace. Whether destabilizing or not, from the perspective of the party system, a conflict organized along these lines could revitalize party organizations, parties in government, *and* the party in the public.

## Political Parties at the Dawn of a New Century

Viewing the Clinton era through the lens of realignment, political time, and the state suggests that the Clinton presidency was one of the three most significant presidencies for the fortunes of political parties in the past sixty-five years. Only the presidencies of Franklin Roosevelt and Ronald Reagan have had similarly profound effects on the party system.

Why do the Clinton years merit such status? The answer is straightforward. During the Clinton presidency, we witnessed a critical realignment of the party system; long-term secular realignment approaching or reaching its endpoint; a preemptive president redefining his party and providing a way-station toward a possible new progressive identity; and the erosion of some of the party-constraining pillars of the fiscal state in the midst of rapid economic change. Each of these developments, as discussed above, has already produced substantial change. Critical realignment has created a new balance of party power and secular realignment a shift in the coalitional bases of the parties. Political time and the preemptive presidency proved a great success for Bill Clinton and a less certain one for his party, but Clinton's potential to have lasting impact on his party appears greater than that of other preemptive presidents. And institutional and policy changes in the state have helped strengthen parties. Significant individually in producing recent party-system change, together these developments promise enduring implications for each major party and for the party system. That system is at a historical branching point.

The ongoing transformation of the party system will not necessarily follow any neat, preordained path, but there will be opportunities along the way to shape the parties and the system's connection to the American public. Too often, we assume in retrospect that parties had to adapt the way they did or that the chosen adaptation was the best available path. There is some merit to this assumption: once on a particular organizational or institutional path it may indeed be difficult to exit. Branching points, however, open up alternative routes with differing types of costs, benefits, and difficulties. At century's dawn there are several possible paths for party development, but it is not obvious which is the most likely to enhance the long-term status of political parties, particularly in the context of economic and societal transformations that complicate the selection of the best organizational strategies. Will old methods and old procedures work? Or do the parties need to develop new methods and principles of organization and mobilization? Political risk abounds.

I have suggested there is reason to be more optimistic about the relevance of political parties now than there was during the heyday of the fiscal state. Optimism about the party system, however, does not mean painless politics; both the cultural and economic quality dimensions of party competition portend bitter conflict. And, as discussed above, this optimism is tempered by the recognition that parties must reconnect with a public that became deeply skeptical toward all things political over the final thirty-five years of the twentieth century. It is an open question whether the parties wish to travel down this path or are content to compete for the affections of the more limited universe of political activists, financial contributors, and narrowly targeted swing voters. The latter strategy, which will be all too tempting, might serve short-term needs but does promise long-term disaster. To date, building these public connections has been a distinctly secondary or tertiary concern; in this, the parties remained distressingly unchanged, or changed for the worse, during the Clinton era.

If we wish to be analytically bold, we can look back at the political transformation of the 1890s and see echoes in the 1990s. Scholars see this earlier decade as a turning point in American political and economic development, a simultaneous revolution of society, economy, and polity that fundamentally changed how people lived their lives. Parallels in the 1990s suggest similarly profound transformations. More modestly, though, we can say with greater confidence than after most presidencies that we are entering a new era for political parties.

CHAPTER 8

# CLINTON AND THE REPUBLICAN PARTY

JOHN J. PITNEY JR.

"I equate this, our . . . Republican relationship with President Clinton, with that of the Wile E. Coyote and the Road Runner," said Senator John McCain (R-Ariz.) in 1999. "Republicans are always just about to get President Clinton and we've almost got our arms around him—and then the dynamite goes off or we run over the cliff or the train runs over us" (*Online Newshour* 1999). President Clinton frustrated the Republicans—just as President Nixon had frustrated the Democrats in the early 1970s. Not coincidentally, Republicans lashed back with the same technique Democrats had used against Nixon: revelation, investigation, and prosecution, or "RIP" for short (Ginsberg and Shefter 1990, 26). As in the Nixon case, the investigations led to impeachment proceedings. Clinton survived, in part because the Lewinsky affair was obviously less momentous than Watergate. Although even his staunchest defenders called his behavior "reprehensible," serious people could argue that the case against him fell short of the constitutional standard for removal from office.

Legalities were only part of the story. The 1992 campaign had revealed Clinton's political aggressiveness and verbal agility, but these qualities went into eclipse during the unsteady early years of his presidency, only to reemerge when the GOP won Congress. Clinton out-maneuvered his foes by turning their attacks against them and portraying them as the true villains. In this fight, he benefited from his own talents, his opponents' mistakes, and the lessons he drew from Nixon. Watergate loomed large in Clinton's political memory, since it had been the central issue of his first political campaign, a 1974 House race in Arkansas. Hillary Rodham Clinton was even more of a Watergate buff, for she had served on the impeachment inquiry staff of the House Judiciary Committee.

Through his talent for defense and counterattack, Clinton stayed on his feet. In doing so, he diminished his chances for historic achievements. Every day he spent trying to trip up his opponents or talk his way out of a jam was a day he could not spend on substantive policy issues. By demonizing and humiliating the Republicans, he made them resent him even more. They would deal with him when politics demanded, but they would not voluntarily help him build his legacy.

These dark overtones came as a surprise. A vague aura of tragedy always accompanied Nixon, but Clinton seemed different. When he began his bid for the White House in 1992, he would remind audiences that he grew up in a place called Hope.

## The Coming of Clinton

"I can't figure out a way to run against him from the right," said a Bush campaign official (quoted in Goldman et. al 1994, 527). Clinton campaigned as a New Democrat, avoiding the liberal orthodoxy that had hurt the party. On the economy, he promised a middle-class tax cut, made possible by "asking the very wealthy to pay their fair share" (Clinton and Gore 1992, 15). On poverty, he said: "We can provide opportunity, demand responsibility, and end welfare as we know it" (Clinton and Gore 1992, 164–65). On crime, he pledged to strengthen the police and fill the prisons. He embraced capital punishment, even using his authority as governor of Arkansas to permit the execution of a brain-damaged black man. Had Clinton spared the prisoner, says George Stephanopoulos, "I would have been proud, but the devil on my shoulder would have whispered that we were handing the Republicans a huge issue" (1999, 63).

Determined not to hand any issues to the GOP, the Clinton campaign set up a high-tech center—which Hillary Clinton dubbed the "War Room"—for monitoring and parrying Republican attacks (Matalin and Carville 1994, 243). A favorite War Room tactic was to make an issue of the attack itself, throwing Republicans on the defensive. When Bush questioned Clinton's youthful antiwar activities, Clinton noted the "extreme right-wingers" advising Bush. "He turned the Republican convention over to the far right for a few days; now he's apparently going to turn his campaign to that. It's very sad" (quoted in Matalin and Carville 1994, 380).

Clinton's cleverness could backfire. He became the butt of jokes when he stopped denying he had ever broken Arkansas drug laws, admitting that he had tried marijuana—in England—but had not inhaled. By the fall, voters were noticing that he fudged important policy issues. Several publications quoted his ambiguous 1991 "endorsement" of the congressional resolution authorizing the Persian Gulf War: "I guess I would have voted for the majority if it was a close vote. But I agree with the arguments the minority made" (quoted in Kelly 1992). Good timing buffered the damage from this "Slick Willie" persona; during the Cold War, character issues could have raised questions about his ability to handle military crises, but such concerns faded after the Soviet Union dissolved. When Gallup asked Americans to name most important national problem, 3 percent mentioned "the international situation," compared with 37 percent who cited the economy (1993, 160). Bad times were directing attention away from the Bush's national-security issues and toward Clinton's domestic issues.

Clinton benefited from GOP weakness. Bush had never been a sparkling candidate, and in 1992, thyroid medication was sapping his physical and mental energy (Woodward 1999, 197). By agreeing to tax increases, he had forsaken a standard GOP weapon, the portrayal of Democrats as tax-and-spend liberals. The tax hike worsened Bush's own character questions from the Iran-Contra scandal. (As vice president, Bush claimed that he was "out of the loop" on the arms-for-hostages deal. Few believed him.) Some 60 percent of poll respondents voiced doubt about Clinton's trustworthiness, but 47 percent said the same of Bush (Frankovic 1993, 122). "Clinton is a pathological liar," said a Bush aide. "Unfortunately, George Bush is the only politician in America who can immunize him against that tag" (quoted in Goldman et al. 1994, 527).

For Clinton, the 1992 campaign extended a long pattern of poor Republican opposition. In his 1974 House campaign, he came close to upsetting the low-key incumbent. He did lose the governorship of Arkansas in 1980, but mainly because of his own mistakes and the Reagan surge. The Republican who beat him proved an inept governor, crumbling under Clinton's 1982 comeback. In his three subsequent reelections, the Republicans never made an effective fight. That failure reflected the state GOP's parched grassroots: though Arkansas had supported Republican presidential candidates, the party seldom won down-ticket races. During Clinton's last year in the governorship, Republicans accounted for only a dozen of the state's legislators.

Clinton had never fought a long battle against tough Republican adversaries. On election night of 1992, however, his supporters overlooked this gap in his experience. And their cheers of "landslide, landslide" obscured something else: in a three-way race, he had won only 43 percent of the popular vote. By coincidence, the same had been true of Richard M. Nixon in 1968.

## Republicans Rising

Clinton entered the White House with a simple plan for dealing with Republicans: he would largely ignore them (Cohen 1994, 144). To get GOP congressional votes for his economic plan, however, he would have had to make concessions repellent to liberal Democrats. Such seemed unnecessary in light of large Democratic majorities, yet many Democrats backed away, nervous about tax increases. In the end, the crucial budget reconciliation bill passed both chambers by a single vote, with no Republican support. That result should have set off warnings, since each Democrat who backed the plan might now face the charge of "casting the deciding vote" for such unpopular provisions as raising taxes on social security recipients.

As his first year wore on, Clinton learned he would need GOP support for the North American Free Trade Agreement (NAFTA). White House aides reluctantly worked with congressional Republicans to pass the measure, but this cooperation was fleeting. Most administration staffers and officials came from the liberal wing of the Democratic Party, and few knew much about the GOP (Balz and Brownstein 1996, 83–84). Even David Gergen, who had worked for Republican presidents, was a self-identified independent with scant ties to the rising generation of Republicans.

The Clinton circle was slow to grasp how much the GOP leadership was changing. The befuddled Bush crew had left the scene; free at last to choose its own chair without presidential directive, the Republican National Committee turned to Haley Barbour, a veteran Washington operative who would prove a masterful organizer and spokesman (Klinkner 1994, 192–96). Barbour revived RNC fundraising, putting some of the money into issue ads attacking the Clinton agenda. Yet he knew that a purely negative approach would not work, so he set up the National Policy Forum, a group that held issue conferences and produced publications highlighting GOP ideas. The Forum supplied a national showcase for Republican governors who were carrying out well-regarded initiatives on welfare and education (Barbour 1996).

The GOP had a new look on Capitol Hill. Bob Dole (R-Kans.), now in his seventies, was still heading the Senate Republicans, but the real energy in his conference was coming from younger, more assertive members who had served in the House. And it was in the House that the biggest change was under way. Late in 1993, when long-serving Republican leader Bob Michel (R-Ill.) announced that he would retire at the end of the 103d Congress, Republican whip Newt Gingrich (R-Ga.) quickly rounded up enough votes to succeed him. At that point, Gingrich became the de facto leader of the House GOP.

Like Barbour, Gingrich knew that Republicans had to stand for something other than Democrat-bashing. During the 1980 campaign, he had organized Governing Team Day, an event where Ronald Reagan and GOP congressional candidates pledged themselves to a simple (if hazy) policy agenda. Building on that experience, he now led the House Republicans in drafting the Contract with America, a set of proposals that they would bring to a vote if they won a majority. The Contract consisted of items on which the GOP enjoyed consensus, such as a line-item veto, while sidestepping abortion and other divisive issues. Although most Americans never heard of the Contract per se, it did supply GOP candidates with common themes. "Before the contract, they [the Democrats] had an agenda," said Dick Armey (R-Tex.), who would become House majority leader. "We were the naysayers. After the contract, we had an agenda and they were the naysayers" (quoted in Barnes 1995, 22).

Republicans have overstated the Contract's electoral significance, overlooking other forces that contributed to GOP victory. First, the end of divided government put the majority party at risk. During the Reagan and Bush years, many Americans did not know who ran Congress, but now that one party controlled both political branches, "Congress" meant "Democrats." Scandals and policy failures had strengthened the "throw the rascals out" sentiment, and voters saw Democrats as the rascals (Greenberg 1996, 266–70). Second, demographic shifts and favorable redistricting had put many seats within the GOP's grasp. Bush's defeat held down GOP gains in 1992, but as some observers foresaw at the time (Benenson 1992), the Republicans were due for "time-release" pickups two years later. Third, Clinton was an issue; knowing that the next presidential election was years away and over-confident about Democratic congressional majorities, he made careless missteps ranging from national health insurance to gays in the military. His appointment of Joycelyn Elders as surgeon general offended not only the Christian right, but also mainstream Catholics, who resented her attacks on their "celibate, male-dominated church" (quoted in Hedges 1994). Discontent was high, especially among the 57 percent of the electorate who had voted against Clinton in 1992. By the fall of 1994, Republicans were grateful for Clinton. "We have what they call in the military," said Haley Barbour, "'a target-rich environment'" (quoted in Grove 1994).

## The Culminating Point

During his first year as speaker, Gingrich often spoke of "the permanent offense"—always staying on the march. But if he had reviewed the military literature, he would have read about "the culminating point," where a military force can no longer sustain the offensive and must revert to defense. A U.S. Marine Corps handbook explains: "We advance at a cost—lives, fuel, ammunition, physical and sometimes moral strength—and so the attack becomes weaker over time. Eventually the superiority that allowed us to attack and forced our enemy to defend in the first place dissipates and the balance tips in favor of the enemy" (1995, 33). In politics, likewise, an offensive can only continue for so long before the advancing party must consolidate its position and watch for counterattack.

For the House Republicans, that point came on April 5, 1995, when they fulfilled their campaign promise of voting on all Contract bills within the first hundred days of the session. Except for a constitutional amendment to limit congressional terms, which failed to get the necessary two-thirds vote, each measure passed the House. Though some have dismissed the Contract as gimmickry, it did lead Congress to consider proposals that had never gotten a full legislative hearing (Gimpel 1996, 128). And in the longer run, much of it became law. The 104th Congress saw enactment of the Congressional Accountability Act (applying workplace regulations to Capitol Hill), the item veto (overturned by the Supreme Court), and a far-reaching welfare reform bill. In the next Congress, the 1997 budget agreement included other Contract items such as a $500-per-child tax cut and tax reductions on capital gains.

The Republicans were trying to follow the example of Republican governors who had carried out domestic reforms. As Gingrich acknowledged, some of the party's wiser heads pointed out that governors' four-year terms give them time to recover from attacks. "Every member of the House faces reelection every two years. That is a very short time to take a pasting from your opponents and regain your ground." In short, they erred by acting "on what is actually an executive rather than a legislative sense of reality" (Gingrich 1998, 11). And as Gingrich later admitted, they had underrated the president's major institutional power. "I am speaking of the power of the veto. Even if you pass something through both the House and the Senate, there is that presidential pen. How could we have forgotten that?" (10).

Quick House action to the Contract left the misleading impression that congressional Republicans were marching in lockstep. But the Contract only included items on which they already agreed, so sooner or later, conflicts would surface. Social conservatives, believing that their issues had been decisive in 1994, wanted to curb abortion and ease gun controls. Suburban Republicans either opposed such measures on principle or feared the political risks. Tax-cutters fought with those who placed higher value on cutting spending and the national debt. And, as always, members took care of their own constituencies.

Republican senators had played no role in drafting the Contract, so they were in no hurry to pass it. Three of them—Dole, Phil Gramm (R-Tex.), and Richard Lugar (R-Ind.)—were running for president, and the competition among them and their allies created its own peculiar friction. On both sides of the Hill, Republicans were not just divided, they were also conflicted. Take the issue of federalism. They spoke of devolving power to states and localities, yet they also backed measures to expand the federal government's jurisdiction over crime (Meese and DeHart 1996) and to make it easier for property owners to fight local zoning decisions in federal court. Rep. Christopher Shays (R-Conn.) told reporter Elizabeth Drew: "One problem we have as a party is we have some conflicting interests and we want block granting and freedom for local and state governments when it fits our agenda and we want restriction when that fits our agenda. We make contradictory arguments" (quoted in Drew 1996, 101–2). Far from being a monolithic force, Republicans were of many minds. Often split and sometimes confused, they made an inviting target for a tough-minded political warrior . . . like Bill Clinton.

## Trigonometry and Nixon

"In war," wrote military theorist Carl von Clausewitz, "the will is directed against an animate object that reacts" (1984, 149). During the early months of 1995, Republicans neglected this dictum and forgot how Clinton had gained the nickname "the Comeback Kid."

Right after the GOP takeover, political consultant Dick Morris warned Clinton that he had drifted from the centrist course of 1992. What now? As we have seen elsewhere in this volume, Morris proposed a "triangulation" strategy to position Clinton between old-line Democrats and "revolutionary" Republicans. The administration would "work to eliminate the deficit, require work for welfare, cut taxes, and reduce the federal bureaucracy" while fighting GOP efforts "to cut Medicare benefits, eliminate Medicaid guarantees, weaken environmental protection laws, and reduce federal aid to schools" (Morris 1999a, 93).

Morris did not invent triangulation: the strategy had succeeded more than two decades earlier, for Richard Nixon. Contrary to myth, there was more to his 1968 campaign than "law and order" and a "secret plan to end the Vietnam War" (a phrase he never used). Nixon gave detailed speeches on social policy, quoting "new liberals," who he said were rejecting bureaucracy and embracing private-sector initiatives. "In that context, liberals and conservatives will find themselves coming closer together, rather than splitting apart" (Nixon 1968, 22). Advocating welfare policies to encourage work and aid the needy, Nixon spoke of "bridges to human dignity," a choice of words that anticipated Clinton's "bridge to the twenty-first century."

In office, Nixon followed a "third-way" domestic policy. "Tory men and Liberal policies," he explained, "are what have changed the world" (quoted in Moynihan 1973, 215). He retained Daniel Patrick Moynihan, a domestic policy expert from Democratic administrations, to work on a bold proposal for a federally guaranteed annual income. For liberals, the plan would have increased welfare benefits in many states while cutting them in none. For conservatives, it contained a work requirement. Though it failed to get through Congress, it preempted the usual Democratic attacks against "heartless" GOP policies. In 1996, likewise, Clinton snatched a major issue from Bob Dole when he reached an agreement with the GOP Congress on comprehensive welfare reform. But by promising to seek future changes to make the law more generous, the president also appeased liberals.

Triangulation worked in other issues as well. Clinton outflanked the Republicans with proposals to streamline government, just as Nixon had stayed ahead of the Democrats by establishing bureaucracies such as the Environmental Protection Agency. Herbert Stein, who chaired Nixon's Council of Economic Advisers, acknowledged that the administration had imposed more new regulations than had any administration since the New Deal ( 1984, 190).

In 1970, Nixon domestic adviser John Ehrlichman wrote a memo that prefigured Morris's advice to Clinton. Ehrlichman described Nixon policy strategy as "non-conservative initiatives deliberately designed to furnish some zigs to go with our conservative zags.... We will try to co-opt the opposition's issues (e.g., Muskie's environment) if the political cost is not too great" (1982, 217).

## Them and Us

According to speechwriter William Safire, the Nixon administration liked to frame political conflicts as fights between "us"—Middle America—and "them"—the student protesters and their liberal allies. "'They' could be useful to 'us,' as the villain, the object against which all of our supporters, as well as those who might become our supporters, could be rallied" (1977, 396). In a 1970 speech, Nixon approvingly quoted a newspaper editorial linking antiwar politicians to a recent fatal bombing: "It isn't just the radicals that set the bomb in the lighted, occupied building who were guilty. The blood is on the hands of anyone who encouraged them, anyone who talked recklessly of revolution, anyone who has chided with mild disparagement the violence of extremism, while hinting that the cause was right all the time" (Nixon 1970).

Through the first two years of his presidency, Clinton sometimes used similar rhetoric. In 1994, he said: "The interests—the violent, extremist interests in this country that are trying to keep health care out of the reach of ordinary American working people are a disgrace to the American Dream" (1994). He did not follow up this line of attack by identifying the "violent" and "extremist" groups.

In 1995, Clinton started crystallizing his "them-versus-us" approach. According to Morris, the terror bombing of a federal office building in Oklahoma City "afforded an important political opportunity" (1999, 418). Morris and other political consultants saw political gain in the "Extremist Issue versus Republicans." They urged Clinton to use "cultural differences with the radical right to separate it from the norms of American culture" just as "Nixon stressed patriotism and mainstream values against the culture of demonstrators" (1999a, 419–22). Clinton needed little prompting. In the spring of 1994, when the GOP won an upset in a special House election, he told Stephanopoulos: "It's Nazi time out there. We've got to hit them back" (Stephanopoulos 1999, 275).

In an interview shortly after the Oklahoma bombing, Clinton denounced those who "keep everybody torn up and upset all the time, purveying hate and implying at least with words that violence is all right" (Clinton 1995a). A few weeks later, he compared the radicals of the 1990s to those of the 1960s, saying "they were wrong then, and this crowd is wrong now." He then edged closer to implicating the GOP: "And it's very interesting to me to see that there are some public officials in our country who are only too happy to criticize the culture of violence being promoted by the media . . . but are stone-cold silent when these other folks are talking and making violence seem like it's okay" (Clinton 1995d).

Clinton frequently tagged Republicans as "extremists," again taking a cue from the Nixon era. In 1972, White House aide Ken Khachigian wrote "that the word to tar McGovern is 'extremist' and not 'radical,'" explaining, "It has become somewhat fashionable to be 'radical.'" McGovern had recently said that he would "plead guilty" to being a radical friend of the poor. The "extremist" label, however, was no asset. "Barry [Goldwater] tried to reverse the extremism thing, but it got him further into the quicksand. The same will happen to McGovern—to deny the 'extremist' label is to give it credibility" (1972). In the 1990s, Republicans relearned that lesson whenever they tried to rebut Clinton's charges.

The attacks made the Republicans skittish about certain issues, especially affirmative action. Polls showed widespread opposition to racial preferences, and a California ballot proposition to ban such preferences would win by a large margin in November 1996. Yet Republicans hesitated to adopt the issue, fearing the label of "extremist" or "racist." Clinton gave them reason to be wary. In a 1996 speech, he voiced concern about "church burnings or synagogues or Islamic centers being defaced—any of this is wrong." He hinted that opponents of racial preference were to blame. "And I saw where one of our friends in the other party the other day was saying, boy, we really need to jump on this affirmative action out in California; we can take the President down on this, this is one of those wedge issues. Well, let me tell you something, folks, those wedge issues nearly did us in. We have had about all the wedge issues we need." He closed by inverting the "love it or leave it" line that conservatives had once used against student protesters. "And I'd like them to take their wedges and go someplace else and let those of us who believe in unity get on with the business of making America a great place for every American to live in" (Clinton 1996).

Clinton reinforced verbal tactics with political action. Implementing what Morris (1999, 418), called "the ricochet theory," Clinton proposed measures to regulate firearms and counter hate groups. When Republicans opposed him, they inadvertently linked themselves to the extremists. In the same vein, Clinton took a hard line in budget talks, so that he could accuse the GOP of "extreme cuts and other unacceptable changes in Medicare and Medicaid" and emphasize his "profound differences with the extreme approach that the Republican majority has adopted" (Clinton 1995b). Again, Clinton was not merely playing for effect: he truly believed that conservatives like to hurt people. During subsequent negotiations on welfare, he said of Senator Trent

Lott (R-Miss.): "He loved cutting off children. You should have seen his face. He was delighted that he could savage them, delighted" (quoted in Morris 1999a, 300).

Clinton made effective use of the veto, as Gingrich would note. When his vetoes of fiscal legislation triggered partial government shutdowns, the public sided with him and blamed the GOP. Gingrich started to see the political damage, but newly elected Republicans did not. "The freshmen had become Newt's Frankenstein monster—and my new best friends," says Stephanopoulos (1999, 406). "The more they dug in, the better off we were." The shutdowns also deepened Gingrich's unpopularity. Democrats would link the "extremist" speaker with every Republican politician in their sights.

The shutdowns opened the curtain on a presidential election in which Republicans had little chance to beat Clinton. With neither a clear agenda nor an effective organization, Bob Dole was taking on an incumbent who was presiding over peace and prosperity. What is more, he had to exhaust his resources to secure his party nomination, while the Democrats were free to mount a yearlong advertising effort. Despite his admirable personal qualities, the Democrats attacked his association with the GOP leadership. Nearly all their ads referred to him as "Dolegingrich."

## Impeachment Politics

Both Nixon and Clinton enraged their political opponents by simultaneously demonizing them and poaching on their issues. Both raised concerns in Congress about usurpation of power. Nixon waged secret military operations and impounded funds, while Clinton bypassed congressional authority through far-reaching executive orders (Simendinger 1998). And in both cases, the resulting anger and distrust created the climate for impeachment.

Some might object to this comparison. It goes without saying that Watergate involved grave legal issues, yet we sometimes forget how partisanship fueled the investigations. Senator Edward Kennedy (D-Mass.) probed the break-in, and the subsequent report supplied guidance to the Ervin committee. He threatened to block the confirmation of Elliot Richardson as attorney general unless he agreed to name an acceptable special prosecutor. Richardson appointed Archibald Cox, whose name Kennedy had suggested. Cox had run research operations for JFK's 1960 presidential campaign and had served as a delegate to the 1972 Democratic convention (Matthews 1997, 324–27).

Nixon and his defenders complained about Cox much as Clinton's side would complain about Kenneth Starr. Cox was "deliberately delaying and dragging out" the probe, wrote Nixon. "The Grand Jury has been meeting for months. Instead of following up on the Watergate investigation and either bringing indictments or indicating that there is no ground for indictment, he is deliberately going into extraneous issues" (quoted in Oudes 1989, 591–92).

On the House side, John Doar led the impeachment staff. According to writer Renata Adler, then Doar's aide, "There was never any doubt among Doar and his small group that, unless there was overwhelming evidence of Nixon's innocence . . . the object of the process was that the President must be impeached" (1976, 79) In 1998, Democrats charged that the House Judiciary Committee's probe of the Lewinsky affair had a similarly preordained conclusion. They also accused the majority of attempting a "coup" that would reverse the presidential election. During Watergate, some Democrats entertained that very possibility. In June 1973, Rep. Henry Reuss (D-Wisc.) wrote that Nixon and Vice President Agnew should both resign so that House speaker Carl Albert (D-Okla.), "a man of unquestioned integrity," could become president (Reuss 1973). (Agnew's own scandal had not yet come to light.) Rep. Bella Abzug (D-N.Y.) told Albert to pursue such options: "Get off your goddamned ass, and we can take this presidency" (quoted in Gup 1982). When Gerald Ford succeeded Agnew, such talk faded.

Back to the main question, then: how did Clinton survive the kind of battle that had destroyed Nixon? As suggested at the beginning, the legal differences between the two cases constitute one important answer. But there are others. To start with, Clinton applied a Nixon maxim more skillfully than Nixon did. "Politics is battle," wrote Nixon, "and the best way to fire up your troops is to rally them against a visible opponent on the other side of the field. If a loyal supporter will fight hard for you, he will fight twice as hard against your enemies" (1991, 285). During Watergate, Nixon could never rally people against his accusers. Prior to the controversy, the relevant congressional leaders and committee chairs were unknown to the public and largely well-liked by their colleagues. (Kennedy wisely stayed behind the scenes.) Not so in the 1990s. Ordinary voters disliked Gingrich, and congressional Democrats hated him. "If you ask House Democrats how they feel about Bill Clinton, you'll get a wide range of answers," said one White House official in the fall of 1998. "But they all feel the same way about Newt Gingrich and what he's done to them. He's a great unifying factor" (quoted in Serrano and Lacey 1998, A1). By depicting the controversy as a fight between the Clinton White House and the Gingrich Congress, Clinton held Democrats on his side. During Watergate, GOP defections had lent an air of bipartisanship to the proceedings. During the Lewinsky affair, Democrats bemoaned a "partisan" impeachment.

Clinton remembered how Nixon erred by ordering the removal of Archibald Cox: instead of turning opinion against the prosecutor, he made himself look guilty. Clinton knew better than to seek the dismissal of Kenneth Starr, whose tactics eventually became the focus of debate. In the public's mind, Starr was not a martyr but a demon—a perception that the administration encouraged long before the Lewinsky story. Reporter Howard Kurtz wrote: "The White House war against Kenneth Starr was a curious and covert operation . . . through whispered conversations and strategic use of surrogates, White House aides assailed the former judge they viewed as their persecutor" (1998, 130).

From Nixon, Clinton aides also learned that stonewalling suggests guilt. Therefore they perfected the "document dump," the practice of overwhelming the press with information, confident that time-pressed reporters could not effectively sort through all the material (Walsh 1999). When some question reappeared, they could point to their previous disclosures and dismiss the new concern as "old news."

"Cast not the first stone" can also be an effective defense. Claiming that the Watergate affair was hardly the first or worst such scandal, Nixon wanted to highlight his predecessors' misconduct. Congressional investigations later would show that Kennedy and Johnson did indulge in shady practices, but these revelations would take years to emerge. In the Lewinsky affair, the "first stone" argument was easier to make. Though Republicans said the debate was about perjury, Democrats said it was about sex—and the press soon wrote of sexual misdeeds by top congressional Republicans.

Finally, whereas Nixon's Watergate opponents had long held power, Clinton was facing relative newcomers, particularly in the House. Republicans had shown ingenuity in gaining power, but after decades in the minority, they were still learning to govern. During the impeachment inquiry, they made mistakes that helped Clinton. For instance, early release of the "salacious" portions of the Starr Report unified Democrats over the issue of unfairness and led the general public to see the Republicans as dirty old men. And to put it bluntly, the GOP had some weak links. As chair of the Government Reform and Oversight Committee, Dan Burton (R-Ind.) bungled investigations of Clinton's campaign finances and embarrassed his party with questionable ethics and the disclosure that he had fathered a child out of wedlock.

As early as 1994, when the Democratic Senate was considering a special panel to look into Whitewater, Nixon worried about who would serve on the GOP side. As he told aide Monica Crowley, "We can't have a bunch of dumbos asking the questions" (Crowley 1998, 312).

## The Long Run

Bill Clinton liked to muse about his place in history, but the aftermath of impeachment put his historical legacy very much in doubt. Bitter congressional Republicans did not want to help him any more than they had to. In the fall of 1999, the Senate voted on a measure that could have been part of a Clinton legacy, a comprehensive nuclear test-ban treaty. With voters registering little interest and conservative critics raising plausible questions, the treaty's fate hinged on the president's personal capital with the Republican majority. He had none, and the treaty went down. "He will look you in the face and lie and that hinders any sort of true negotiations," one GOP congressional aide charged. "There's no trust there." Marshall Wittman of the conservative Heritage Foundation said: "We have reached an all-time low in relations between the executive and legislative branches. You'd probably have to go back to 1974 in the dark hours of the Nixon administration to find something comparable" (quoted in Mathis 1999, A1).

Clinton, like Nixon, sought a hybrid alternative to existing political ideologies. These examples suggest that while third-way politics can work in the short run, it may expose a president to charges of expediency (Skowronek 1997, 462). The opposition party may fear that the president is fooling them, while his own partisans worry that he is selling them out.

This pattern is not inevitable. Although Eisenhower was also a "preemptive" president, he never faced the same level of abuse. Why did no one speak of "Tricky Dwight" or "Slick Ike"? At least part of the answer is that Eisenhower kept his distance from attack politics, carefully tending the image of being "above the battle." Ironically, that was the trick. Behind the scenes, he was talented political operator who sent Vice President Nixon and other surrogates after the Democrats. While other Republicans were taking the heat for harsh tactics, his military background and friendly demeanor painted a picture of nonpartisanship. As a professional warrior, he understood aggressiveness but he also knew the value of stealth.

Nixon and Clinton did not accomplish the same feat. Both came to office with reputations as crafty professional politicians. Both attacked "extremists" on the other side, and even when they used surrogates to carry on the fight, everyone could see their fingerprints on the weaponry. By combining "mongrel" policies with "attack-dog" politics, they invited rabid opposition. Here is the moral: if you are going to run in the middle of the road, do not antagonize the oncoming traffic.

So what can future presidents make of Clinton's survival? Revelation, investigation, and prosecution—RIP—need not be lethal, if a president responds with tenacity and agility. By turning their own passions against them, Clinton made his foes pay a high price. He and his allies exploited the Republicans' mistakes and magnified their least attractive features, making them appear grotesque and hateful. One may stretch the highway metaphor into a second moral: if road-rage drivers do try to run you down, you might be able to maneuver them into the ditch. Of course, that advice applies only in desperate situations. Living dangerously is not the best revenge, since a prudent president will avoid such duels in the first place.

Despite the differences in the outcomes, Clinton's survival had a Nixonian ring. After resigning, Nixon commenced a two-decade campaign to rehabilitate his name, and he had some success. A year before his death, Nixon told campaign consultant Roger Stone that he sensed an affinity: "You know, he came from dirt and I came from dirt. He lost a gubernatorial race and came back to win the Presidency, and I lost a gubernatorial race and came back to win the Presidency. He overcame a scandal in his first campaign for national office and I overcame a scandal in my first national campaign. We both just gutted it out" (quoted in Stone 1994, A23).

The multiple comebacks of Nixon and Clinton suggest a further lesson: never underestimate an opponent or regard current conditions as fixed. For a while, Clinton lost track of this idea. In 1993 and 1994, he saw the congressional Republicans as a "permanent minority" who could be an irritant but not a threat. Had he defused the tax issue by bringing Republicans on board his economic plan, the GOP might not have gained such a strong electoral position. As it was, his world changed on Election Day 1994. Republicans then made a similar mistake, believing that they had vanquished the Democrats once and for all. Their hubris laid the basis for the events of the following years.

In the wake of the 1998 election, some observers thought that the Republicans had suffered mortal wounds. Mortal or not, the harm was real, and it seemed plausible that more setbacks were in store. Yet there were also signs of change, as some Republicans donned a kinder, gentler face and preached the third-way politics of "compassionate conservatism." As always, it was wise to remember that losers may learn from defeat and eventually become winners, or as Clausewitz wrote: "Even the ultimate outcome of a war is not always to be regarded as final" (1984, 80).

That observation should sober those who hoped that outcome of the impeachment trial would stop "the politics of personal destruction." Granted, just as the First World War taught that poison gas might blow back on the attacker, the Lewinsky scandal showed that politicians risk trouble when they exploit incidents involving consensual sex. But the horrors of gas warfare did not turn warriors into pacifists: it just prompted them to develop weapons that were both deadlier and more reliable. In the early days of the 2000 campaign, politicians routinely pledged to avoid personal attacks; and in fact, frontal assaults appeared less frequently than in the past. Yet throughout the political community, opposition researchers remained as busy as ever, looking for ammunition that would not backfire. When Texas governor George Bush began running for president, his foes were ready, or as one Austin journalist put it: "There are so many researchers in this town, they're stumbling over each other" (Baldauf 1999, 1).

The politics of the future might not be quite as salacious as in the Clinton years, but it will probably be just as tough.

CHAPTER 9

# CLINTON AND THE DEMOCRATS

## The President as Party Leader

NICOL C. RAE

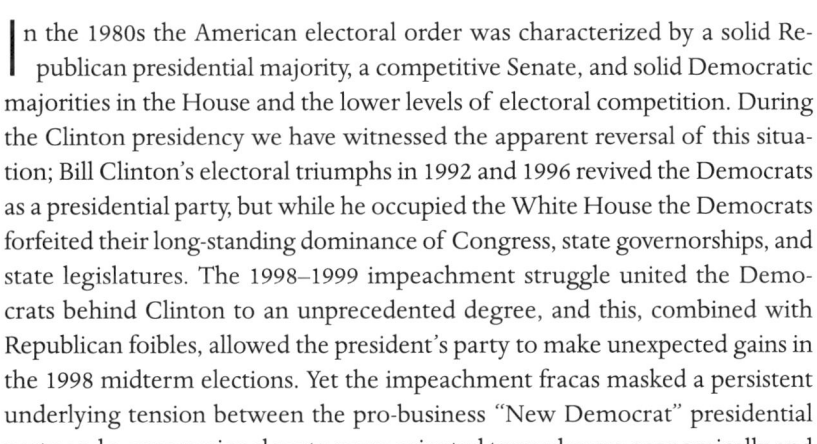

In the 1980s the American electoral order was characterized by a solid Republican presidential majority, a competitive Senate, and solid Democratic majorities in the House and the lower levels of electoral competition. During the Clinton presidency we have witnessed the apparent reversal of this situation; Bill Clinton's electoral triumphs in 1992 and 1996 revived the Democrats as a presidential party, but while he occupied the White House the Democrats forfeited their long-standing dominance of Congress, state governorships, and state legislatures. The 1998–1999 impeachment struggle united the Democrats behind Clinton to an unprecedented degree, and this, combined with Republican foibles, allowed the president's party to make unexpected gains in the 1998 midterm elections. Yet the impeachment fracas masked a persistent underlying tension between the pro-business "New Democrat" presidential party and a congressional party more oriented toward more economically and culturally liberal Democratic activists.

This chapter will assess Clinton's impact on the Democrats' electoral fortunes and the national party organization, and his tense relationship with congressional Democrats. One underlying theme will be that Clinton achieved his electoral triumphs at the expense of the other components of his party and that the contemporary dynamics of American electoral politics left him with little alternative. Clinton's grasp of 1990s electoral realities rebounded to the benefit of the Democrats as a presidential party in 1992 and 1996, but his presidency coincided with the heaviest Democratic losses at the sub-presidential level in decades.

James Coleman's chapter in this volume accurately notes that American parties have been strengthened in several aspects during the Clinton years, but at the mass level the response of the electorate to intensified partisanship in Washington is to continue splitting tickets, thereby denying both the Democratic and the Republican coalitions of ideologues and single-issue activists complete control of the federal government for any extended period of time. Clinton's grasp of this fact was the key to his own electoral success and to the electoral failure of his party elsewhere during his administration. Bill Clinton did not change the American electoral order of the 1990s; he merely accommodated himself to it, so he leaves the Democratic electoral coalition nearly as he found it (albeit in an electorally weaker position beneath the presidential level). His presidency thus gives us little indication of the potential evolution of the Democratic Party in the early decades of the twenty-first century.

## Minority Party? Democratic Electoral Performance under Bill Clinton

On every electoral dimension except for the presidency, the Democrats are significantly weaker than they were when Clinton took office in 1993. In the 1994 midterm election debacle their U.S. Senate majority was lost; a seemingly impregnable forty-year grip on the U.S. House evaporated; Republicans secured an overwhelming majority of state governorships, including almost all the major states, and achieved virtual parity in the most overwhelming Democratic bastion of all—state legislatures. While the Democrats recovered some ground in the 1996 and 1998, their electoral position is markedly weaker than it was in 1993 (see Table 1).

Table 1
Democratic Losses below the Presidential Level, 1992–1998

|  | 1992 | 1994 | 1996 | 1998 | Change, 1992–1998 | Percentage Change, 1992–1998 |
|---|---|---|---|---|---|---|
| U.S. House | 258 | 204 | 207 | 211 | -47 | -18 |
| U.S. Senate | 57 | 48 | 45 | 45 | -12 | -21 |
| Governors | 30 | 19 | 17 | 17 | -13 | -43 |
| State legislative chambers | 66 | 49 | 50 | 53 | -13 | -20 |

Source: *Congressional Quarterly Almanac* (1992, 1994, 1996, and 1998).

At the presidential level Bill Clinton certainly succeeded in breaking the Republican "lock" on the Electoral College that had seemed so impregnable during the 1980s. He did so by wiping out the Republicans in the Northeast and Great Lakes regions, securing a strong Democratic presidential foothold in California and the Pacific Coast, and even being competitive in the GOP's base region—the South. This guaranteed the Democrats overwhelming Electoral College majorities in 1992 and 1996. In neither of these presidential election triumphs, however, did Clinton achieve a popular majority, winning pluralities of 43 percent in 1992 and 49 percent in 1996. The relatively strong third-party candidacies of Ross Perot in both years meant that Clinton's overall percentages of the popular vote were either lower than or only marginally higher than those attained by the losing Democratic presidential candidates of the 1980s. Of course had Perot not been an option, it is likely that Clinton would have gotten popular vote totals of 50 to 55 percent in both elections, but given Clinton's moderate profile and his outstanding qualities as a candidate and campaigner, his failure to breach 50 percent when faced by weak Republican candidates and a highly controversial third-party nominee demonstrates the tenuous nature of the new-found Democratic presidential majority of the 1990s.

Party identification data during the Clinton years indicated no realigning advantage for the Democrats. Yet public opinion surveys did indicate that Clinton had succeeded in eradicating long-standing Republican advantages on issues such as law and order and neutralizing the GOP on economic issues. Moreover, with the ending of the Cold War, the traditional Republican advantage on foreign policy became far less electorally important. The most important issues to voters in the 1992 and 1996 presidential contests were Democratic issues—the economy, health, education, the environment (Abramson, Aldrich, and Rohde 1999).

Yet while these helped elect and reelect Clinton, they did not enable the Democratic Party as a whole to eradicate the electoral disaster of 1994. The reason for the upset remains something of a puzzle: Clinton had received plaudits from Wall Street and the economic establishment (represented by Federal Reserve Chairman Alan Greenspan, and inside the administration by Clinton's Treasury Secretaries Lloyd Bentsen and Robert Rubin) for his 1993 deficit-reduction package, and (despite the sluggish growth noted by Coleman in this volume) the economy was already giving indications of recovery by the fall of 1994. In such circumstances, what could possibly explain a fifty-two-seat turnover in the House of Representatives and equally catastrophic Democratic losses in state legislative elections?

The most accurate answer is that the voters reacted violently against the previous two years of unrestricted Democratic control of the federal government. The initial phase of the Clinton presidency failed to deliver on the 1992 promises of Democratic "moderation" and appeared to mainstream voters more like traditional post-1960s Democratic liberalism. The fact that the Clinton presidency commenced with a furious Washington row between the president and the chairman of the Joint Chiefs of Staff (and national icon) Gen. Colin Powell over gays in the military identified Clinton as a liberal after all, a perception reinforced by the president's unsuccessful national healthcare plan. The failure of the latter even to get out of committee in the Democratic controlled House also seemed to confirm that Congress was not working well and that the seemingly entrenched Democratic majority was part of the problem. As a party the Democrats managed to get on the wrong side of the reform issue whose potency is evinced by the successes of the term-limitations movement and Perot's 19 percent of the popular vote in 1992. Perot voters who voted in 1994 went overwhelmingly Republican (Rae 1998a, 60).

The Republican Congress, in a militant mood after forty years in the political wilderness, was, however, to provide the president with the perfect opportunity to reinvent himself as a pragmatic centrist resisting GOP "extremism." Congressional Democrats aided and abetted this strategy, but while it worked brilliantly for the president—ensuring his comfortable reelection in 1996—it brought little reward to the Democratic Party, which failed to recoup its 1994 losses at the other levels of electoral competition. In a consummate example of what Caeser and Busch have referred to as Losing to Win, the GOP was able to turn the certain defeat of its presidential nominee, Bob Dole, into an advantage elsewhere on the ballot, urging voters to reelect a Republican Congress to restrain the ambitions of a reelected Bill Clinton (1997). This enabled the Republicans to cling onto the House despite their less-than-stellar record in implementing the Contract with America, and the opprobrium of the late-1995 government shutdown.

In the 1998 midterm elections, the status quo of 1996 was largely maintained. Of course, given the Monica Lewinsky scandal hanging over the president and a history of generally poor performance for the party holding the White House in the second midterm election of a two-term presidency (witness 1938, 1958, 1966, and 1974), the Democrats' gain of five U.S. House seats, along with small gains or insignificant losses elsewhere, was impressive. But from a longer-term perspective, it was evident that the ground lost by the Democratic Party since Clinton came to office had not been recovered. The 1998 results seemed to be more a repudiation of the investigation of the president by Independent Counsel Kenneth Starr and the impeachment inquiry opened by the congressional Republicans than an endorsement of a Clinton-led national Democratic majority (see Diane Hollern Harvey's chapter in this volume).

Of course the failure of an incumbent president to lead his party to majority status in Congress and in the states only appears to be unusual if we adopt the traditional realignment and party-identification perspectives of American electoral behavior (Burnham 1970; Campbell et al. 1960; Sundquist 1983). These assume that successful presidents can shift voters toward their party by proven policy successes and that party loyalties invariably lead these voters to vote a "straight" partisan ticket for several subsequent elections. More recent scholarship has demonstrated that this model no longer reflects American political reality as split tickets, voter disaffection from parties, and divided government have become commonplace in American politics (Silbey 1991). Various explanations have been adduced for this change from theories of dealignment to more sophisticated reformulations of realignment theory in the concept of "electoral orders" (Nie, Verba, and Petrocik 1979; Shafer 1991a). Indeed, the example of Clinton and the Democrats appears to demonstrate that gaining the White House for its presidential candidate is the very *worst* thing that could happen for a national party at the other levels of electoral competition and that presidential policy success or popularity will likely rub off on the president's party only to a very limited extent. The dynamics of modern American electoral politics virtually compel successful presidents to distance themselves from their party even if, like President Clinton, they are solid partisans and avid fund-raisers for the cause. These issues will be further explored as we examine in turn President Clinton's impact on the national Democratic Party organization and his relations with congressional Democrats.

## Clinton as a National Party Leader

The roles of the national party committee and the national party chair vary greatly according to whether the party in question controls the presidency. When this is not the case, the national chairman serves as a highly visible spokesman for the party. In the opposite case, the national party organization and its chair (who is appointed by the incumbent president) generally function as extensions of the White House staff. The Clinton administration has not been exceptional in this regard with each of its four national party chairmen: David Wilhelm, Donald Fowler, Steve Grossman, and Joe Andrew, functioning essentially as spokespersons for the administration position and reflecting the values of Clinton's predominant New Democrat or neo-liberal faction within the party.

Clinton was also the first Democratic president to emerge, since national party committees began to play an unprecedented role in national party campaigns. During the 1980s, the Republicans were trailblazers in this regard, but under Clinton the Democrats caught up dramatically by raising vast sums of campaign money through the controversial soft-money loophole in the federal campaign-financing laws. As we shall see, Clinton took his role as a national party fund-raiser extremely seriously throughout his presidency, to the point where his fundraising zeal for the 1996 campaign damaged his party electorally. The political IOUs earned by his extensive fundraising, however, probably contributed to the high degree of Democratic Party unity that helped rescue his presidency from the mortal threat of the Monica Lewinsky debacle.

Bill Clinton's election gave the Democratic National Committee and its new chair—Clinton 1992 campaign manager David Wilhelm—the chance to push for the programs of a Democratic White House, after a dozen years of being compelled to react to a Republican policy agenda. Initially the Clinton administration envisaged a division of labor in which the White House would primarily engage in lobbying members of Congress while the DNC concentrated on mobilizing public opinion behind the president's proposals (Berkowitz and Lilienthal, 1996). As a result the DNC spent heavily on television and other promotional activities on behalf of the president's major policy initiative of his first term—national health care. After the failure of the health-care initiative and the disastrous election results of 1994, however, the DNC leadership team was dramatically overhauled, with Wilhelm being replaced as national chair by the two-person team of Senator Christopher Dodd (Conn.) as general chair (and major public spokesman for the party in the national media) and South Carolinian Donald Fowler as DNC chair, responsible for more mundane organizational activity. The same model was retained for the remainder of the Clinton administration: Colorado governor Roy Romer and Massachusetts Democratic chair Steve Grossman respectively replaced Dodd and Fowler (who had been implicated in the 1996 fundraising scandals) in early 1997 and were succeeded in turn by former Philadelphia mayor Ed Rendell and Indiana state chair Joseph Andrew in 1999.

After Wilhlem's departure the DNC dropped much of its focus on issues and reverted to the more usual role of an in-party national organization, as a component of the campaign apparatus to reelect the president. In fact the national committee proved to be a particularly convenient vehicle for the 1996 Clinton reelection effort, due to a loophole in the federal campaign financing laws. While these laws strictly limit the amounts that can be spent directly on the election of a presidential candidate by national party committees, as a result of the 1976 *Buckley v. Valeo* Supreme Court decision they do not restrict such party spending if it is on advertising advocating issue positions rather than expressly urging voters to vote for a candidate. The Clinton White House and the DNC quickly recognized the potential of this so-called advocacy loophole, and from July 1995 until June 1996 the DNC, in coordination with state Democratic parties, spent $34 million on TV ads extolling Clinton's issue positions while attacking the new GOP Congress in key 1996 electoral battlegrounds (Corrado 1997). Of this total, about $22 million (65 percent) was raised by the DNC in unregulated soft-money donations. This decisive early spending by the Democrats undoubtedly gave a distinct advantage to the Clinton reelection campaign, while Republican frontrunner Senate majority leader Bob Dole was still trying to fend off his GOP challengers.

"Soft money" refers to another loophole in the campaign finance laws that allows national, state, and local parties to raise funds for vaguely defined party-building activities without any restrictions on the size of individual donations or the total sums raised. The Republican National Committee had pioneered the use of soft money as an additional financial resource for presidential campaigns during the 1980s and continued to maintain an advantage ($141 million raised in 1995–1996, compared to $122 million for the Democrats) in the 1996 campaign. However, with President Clinton directing the effort from the White House the Democrats had caught up dramatically. Their soft money fundraising increased by 237 percent from 1992 (Corrado 1997).

Fundraising became a major priority for the president; after the 1994 election debacle it was imperative to avoid any intra-party nomination challenge and regalvanize enthusiasm at the party's dejected grassroots. Clinton was thus intensely involved in party fundraising throughout 1995 and 1996, playing a major role in enabling Democrats to significantly close the soft-money gap with the GOP (Drew 1997). In so doing, however, he dragged the party into a scandal when it was revealed that foreign corporations with ties to the Indonesian and Chinese governments had illegally contributed large sums in soft money to the Democrats. Even more embarrassing were the revelations of the degree to which the president and the vice-president had solicited soft money donations inside the White House itself. The stories broke near the end of the 1996 campaign and provided fodder for strong attacks on the president by his opponents, Republican Bob Dole and Reform Party candidate Ross Perot.

Even after the 1996 campaign finance scandals and the subsequent senatorial investigation led by Republican senator Fred Thompson (Tenn.), the president remained unrepentant about his fundraising prowess, refusing to "unilaterally disarm" and financially disadvantage his party as long as the soft-money loophole existed (Hager 1997). In the 1998 congressional campaign, with the survival of his presidency at stake, Clinton's fundraising efforts for the party were as strenuous as ever and even continued into 1999–2000, as the president strove to cement his legacy by electing his loyal vice president Al Gore and a Democratic Congress in the year 2000. Yet, for all his efforts, the party remained barely out of debt and still lagged behind the Republicans in funds raised (Van Natta 1999).

Overall then, beyond an extraordinary capacity to raise soft money and enhance the solvency of the national party committees, Clinton has not left much of a legacy to his party in terms of national organization; the president's national party and national chair reverted to their usual roles as adjuncts of the White House staff, and there were no bold new initiatives or major innovations in policy or organization. Clinton made the national party organization a captive of the prevailing party faction—his own neo-liberal or New Democrat section—and there was little room in its councils for the dwindling number of genuinely conservative Democrats or the highly skeptical New Left/Minority segment of the party.

## Factional Antagonists:
## Clinton and the Congressional Democrats

In 1992, thanks to good fortune, weak opponents, and an ability to be all things to all Democrats, Bill Clinton easily captured the nomination of a party out of power for twelve years and hungry for an attractive presidential candidate (Rae 1994). His combination of southern roots and neo-liberal themes proved irresistible as the increased frontloading of the primary season after 1988 worked to the advantage of more nationally known and heavily financed centrist candidates. This contrasts with the prolonged primary marathon of the 1972–1984 period, which tended to advantage outsider or ideological candidates who could translate isolated victories in low-overhead early primary and caucus battles into national momentum.

During the 1970s and 1980s the congressional Democratic Party encompassed southern and regular Democratic elements that had become all but extinct as factors in the presidential party. However, redistricting and long-term electoral realignment were slowly eroding the numbers of white southern conservative and regular "machine" Democrats in Congress, while enhancing the numbers of minority representatives and northern and western suburban liberals. This contributed to increased ideological homogeneity and partisan unity on the part of House Democrats, which brought an even stronger partisan counterreaction from the frustrated and infuriated Republican minority (Rohde 1991). In short, by the early 1990s the institutional bases of the two major Democratic party factions—Clintonian neo-liberals and the New Left/Minority group that clung to the liberal faith of the McGovern era—were changing, as the neo-liberals were better adapted to succeed in the new frontloaded nominating process, while their intra-party antagonists were becoming more prevalent in the traditionally more centrist congressional party (Rae 1998b).

The difficulty of getting the new Democratic president and Congress to work in harmony was exacerbated by the results of the 1992 elections, when the Republicans were able to pick up ten House seats while losing the presidency. Most of this was due to the decennial redistricting where Republicans (particularly in the South) worked with minorities to the disadvantage of white conservative Democrats (Hill 1995). The overall effect on the congressional party was to push the ideological median further to the Left and make it difficult for the New Democrat president to pursue a New Democrat governing strategy.

Of course this assumed that the president was a genuine New Democrat, whose governmental activism would be tempered by a dose of economic and social conservatism (see Pitney chapter). In his first two years, however, Clinton appeared to have neglected his New Democratic roots and returned to the party's traditional liberal government activism: a stance that should have pleased the Democrats on Capitol Hill. In fact, Clinton ended up getting the worst of both worlds: he was perceived by the public as insupportably liberal, while he was unable to rally the votes for his bold new government initiatives in a strongly Democratic Congress.

The main initiatives of Clinton's first two years demonstrated the administration's dilemma. Neo-liberals were impressed by the fiscal conservatism of Clinton's 1993 deficit-reduction package, while the party's Left liked Clinton's national health-care plan: a massive new extension of federal government activity. Yet the budget package passed the Democratic House by only a single vote and the Senate thanks to the tie-breaking vote of presiding officer Vice President Albert Gore. Given the comfortable Democratic majorities in each, this hardly indicated a rallying behind the New Democratic president. Worse was to follow with the National Health Care Initiative, a complex proposal easily depicted as "impersonal" big government by its conservative and Republican adversaries (Skocpol 1997). The proposal was given in toto to three House committees, none of which succeeded in reporting a bill to the floor. In the Senate the Clinton plan fared no better. The final indignity occurred when the 1994 crime bill (including the popular "assault weapons ban") was almost lost in a House procedural vote and could only be rescued by making significant concessions to the bill's conservative critics (Balz and Brownstein 1996, 91–94). Clinton's most significant achievement during the 103d Congress—the North American Free Trade Agreement (NAFTA) Treaty—certainly demonstrated his pro-business, pro–free trade, neo-liberal credentials, but a majority of his own party in both chambers voted against it, and it only passed due to heavy Republican support (Sinclair 1996, 109–11).

In short, Clinton's first two years were an absolute disaster for the Democratic Party. The president succeeded neither in leading his party in a new direction nor in advancing its traditional liberal political agenda. Caught between two stools, he was unable to assert his authority over the congressional Democratic Party and ran into a policy impasse. He got his budget through by the most meager of margins after he put the entire reputation of his young presidency on the line, and his other signal achievement—NAFTA—was opposed by most congressional Democrats. Fortunately for Clinton, it was the congressional Democrats, not he, on the ballot in November 1994, and they paid the price for the blunders and confusion of his first years as president and party leader. Ironically, it took the elimination of the Democrats' congressional majority in 1994 and the excesses of the new Republican majority for Clinton to assert his authority over the congressional Democrats and become a true national party leader.

## 1994–1996: The President as Party Leader and "Triangulation"

The 1994 election results and the Democratic Party's loss of its forty-year grip on the House ultimately strengthened President Clinton's control over the congressional Democratic Party. This was not immediately apparent, as many congressional Democrats blamed the Clinton administration for the heavy Democratic losses. Yet the presidency remained the sole branch of the federal government under Democratic control, and thus any Democratic revival from the depths of November 1994 was contingent on an improvement in the president's political fortunes. In fact, the highly ideological rhetoric emanating from the new Republican Congress and the exceptionally high public profile of its combative leader, House Speaker Newt Gingrich, were to provide the ideal context for a Clinton recovery.

The loss of Congress meant that Clinton no longer needed to placate more liberal Democratic congressional leaders and committee chairs and could thus now revert to the centrist themes that had been crucial to his election in 1992. As the key strategist for his 1996 reelection campaign, Clinton turned to a Republican political consultant, Dick Morris, who advocated a strategy of triangulation that would simultaneously preclude any potential Democratic primary challengers while also allowing the president to regain the political initiative from the Republican Congress (Drew 1997). The strategy was simple: first, do just enough to keep the congressional Democrats in line and preempt intra-party nomination challenges; second, take advantage of the rhetorical excesses and ideological zeal of the new Republican Congressional majority; and third, also reach out to conservative and moderate voters by adopting some modified versions of Republican stands on several carefully selected social/cultural issues.

As Clinton was now their last line of defense against the implementation of the GOP's Contract with America, which promised to dismantle many cherished federal programs and agencies, the congressional Democrats had little choice but to rally behind him. They hoped that Clinton's vetoes would show the new GOP Congress to be extreme and ineffectual and guarantee a quick Democratic return to power as had occurred after the brief post–New Deal Republican interludes of the 80th (1947–1948) and 83d (1953–1954) Congresses. The Clinton White House, the DNC, and the new congressional Democratic leaders, House Minority Leader Richard Gephardt (Mo.) and Senate Minority Leader Thomas Daschle (S.Dak.) now coordinated all their activities and policy positions in response to Republican initiatives (Koszczuk 1996). And while the White House began to adopt conservative-sounding rhetoric in several carefully selected areas—crime, welfare, family—as part of Morris's triangulation strategy, the reconstituted New Democrat stayed on the liberal side of issues such as affirmative action, which were most dear to the vast majority of congressional and grassroots Democrats in the nation.

As Pitney's chapter in this volume demonstrates, the new Republican House majority made Clinton's task easier by adopting a highly confrontational strategy. With the congressional Democrats united behind him, the president faced down the Republican Congress during the budget battle and highly unpopular shutdown of the federal government in late 1995, securing a massive political victory (Rae 1998a; Drew 1996). Two legs of the triangle had been completed: the Democratic base and the congressional minority had rallied behind the president, and Clinton had demonstrated his continuing relevance as a curb on Republican excesses in Washington.

This left the president free to pick out a few issues in which he could neutralize the Republicans' traditional appeal as the party of the conservative cultural values shared by the suburban swing voters necessary to seal his reelection. So in the summer of 1996 Clinton signed a tough new immigration law, a modified version of the Republican welfare bill, and the Defense of Marriage Act (a hastily constructed Republican measure to prohibit states from recognizing gay and lesbian unions). While several liberal stalwarts and intellectuals groaned, they could not now afford to desert the president, for fear of much worse to come on all policy fronts from a total Republican capture of the federal government.

Given the remarkable success of the Clinton-Morris reelection strategy, it initially appears odd that it was not translatable into bigger Democratic gains at other levels, particularly in the House, where the Democrats had been highly confident of regaining control in early 1996. In the congressional races, however, the new dynamics of the American electoral order worked to damage the Democrats.

During the period from 1952 to 1992, the American political system essentially operated on the basis of "Two Majorities": a Republican presidential advantage based on foreign policy and cultural issues and a Democratic congressional majority based on federal government protections for the disadvantaged (Shafer and Claggett 1995). The erosion of party ties and technological developments since World War II have encouraged more sophisticated, two-tier political alignments as opposed to the single-tier partisan alignments of previous electoral eras (Silbey 1991). The movement of the parties toward more polarized ideological positions over the past thirty years reinforced this tendency toward split partisan control by giving voters an additional motivation to split their tickets. With both parties appearing too ideological to be trusted with total control of the federal government, an electorate generally skeptical of ideological solutions to political problems invariably found a means to divide control of the federal government between the parties. In this context, a party's apparent success at one electoral level can be positively detrimental to its prospects at other levels, as the electorate's natural "restraining" instincts come into play.

The recent fortunes of the Democrats provide a perfect illustration of these dynamics. Electoral outcomes during the 1990s indicate that the partisan majorities at each of the electoral levels may be changing or at least becoming far more fluid than was the case in the 1952–1992 period. With the end of the Cold War and the increasing dominance of the more socially and culturally liberal baby-boom generation among the electorate, the Republican presidential majority based on national security and cultural issues appears to have badly eroded. In a time of concern over budget deficits, however, voters became more skeptical of big-government solutions to political problems and more impatient with the excesses and unresponsiveness of the forty-year Democratic Congress.

As a consequence the Democrats appear to have had a tenuous presidential majority and the Republicans an equally tenuous congressional margin. Experience of two years of unified Democratic control was sufficient to give the Republicans control of the U.S. House for the first time in forty years. Experience of the Republican revolution in the House was sufficient to ensure the reelection of President Clinton, as a necessary restraint.

The congressional Democrats were thus caught in an electoral bind in 1996 as it became clear that the president would be comfortably reelected. It was inevitable in these circumstances that the congressional Republicans would utilize the "need to restrain Clinton" argument as a fundamental reason for continued Republican control on Capitol Hill. Clinton could have conducted a Truman-style all-out partisan war to regain total Democratic control of the federal government, but that would have conflicted with the triangulation strategy for his own reelection as president. The latter demanded that he display his "New Democrat" credentials by signing onto compromise legislation, such as the 1996 welfare bill, thereby securing his own reelection but simultaneously assisting the reelection of the Republican Congress, which had gained a new respectability by cooperating with the president.

In short, Clinton sacrificed the risky prospect of total Democratic control of the federal government to the certainty of his own reelection as president. The alternative of wrapping himself in the colors of a Democratic Party still perceived as too liberal for the American political mainstream in an era of weak partisanship and habitual ticket-splitting was simply unacceptable for such a cautious political strategist. Thus the president set up the congressional Democrats for the blank-check TV ads that the national GOP ran continually through the last three weeks of the 1996 campaign (Drew 1997). And the massive national media attention on Democratic fundraising excesses in the final days sealed the congressional Democrats' fate; they lost two additional Senate seats and failed to make sufficient gains to take back the House. For Clinton and the Democrats, the 1996 elections provided the perfect illustration of "losing to win."

## Post-1996: Rallying around the President

Apart from raising large amounts of "soft money" (which ultimately backfired politically) President Clinton did little to help build a national Democratic governing majority. However, in the wake of the Monica Lewinsky scandal, the solid support of the congressional Democrats ensured the president's political survival. This was due less to sentimental reasons than the electoral reality that collaborating in the downfall of their own president would likely do nothing but exacerbate long-term damage to Democrats at all levels of government. The lesson of Watergate—which retarded Republican prospects of retaking the U.S. House for at least a decade—was not lost on the Democratic congressional leadership during the Clinton impeachment battles of 1998–1999.

While tensions between Clinton and the congressional Democrats surfaced again on trade issues during 1997, unwavering support from Democrats (working in close collaboration with the White House in their media strategy) ensured that investigations by Senator Fred Thompson (Tenn.) and Congressman Dan Burton (Ind.) into the 1996 Clinton fundraising scandals were largely dismissed by press and public as just another instance of GOP partisanship (Carr 1997).

The Monica Lewinsky affair and the Starr report's evidence of perjury and obstruction of justice on the part of the president, might have doomed many a politician less adroit than Clinton. But the White House's fortitude in the face of adversity, the continuing economic boom, and the shortcomings (both moral and otherwise) of his opponents enabled the president to maintain his public approval and survive (see Pitney's chapter in this volume).

The solid unity of congressional and other national Democratic officeholders behind the president was also critical to his survival. The congressional Democrats' bottom line was that the president was "a poor thing but our own" and that both the politically repulsive nature of those trying to defeat him and the likely electoral fallout justified rallying behind Clinton. Moreover, the fact that the Starr report and the impeachment inquiry were debated in the House Judiciary Committee—perhaps the most partisan committee in the House—also greatly assisted the Democratic cause. The Democratic leaders knew that if they could keep the public convinced that impeachment was just a partisan matter the president would avoid removal from office. Of course their own unity behind the president helped to ensure that this perception remained, and the Republicans' determination to proceed with impeachment even after their losses in the 1998 congressional elections only benefited the Democrats. On the crucial impeachment votes, only five House Democrats voted in favor, and no Democratic Senators did. Clinton, whose presidential success had been premised on not being a partisan Democrat, survived as president in part because of Democratic partisanship.

## 2000 and Beyond

On the surface, the battle for the Democratic nomination to succeed Clinton in 2000 indicated the triumph of the neo-liberal/New Democrat wing of the party, since both major contenders—Vice President Albert Gore and former New Jersey senator Bill Bradley—had their political roots in this faction. Possible contenders from the New Left/Minority faction, such as Minnesota senator Paul Wellstone and the Reverend Jesse Jackson were successfully pressured by the Clinton White House to stand aside for Gore. The even greater frontloading of the 2000 primary election schedule, which placed most major state primaries in early March and put a premium on name-recognition and fundraising prowess also helped Gore. His eventual nomination thus reconfirmed the 1990s advantage for more established and "centrist" presidential candidates in both major parties.

Despite the exertions of the White House, the Bradley campaign demonstrated a capacity to raise funds and thus remained competitive with the vice president through the fall of 1999. Bradley's neo-liberal background, however, precluded him from capitalizing fully on the widespread discontent with the Clinton-Gore administration on the New Left/Minority section of the party.

After their 1998 success in gaining House seats against the midterm trend, Democrats entertained high hopes of regaining control in 2000. In fact, Democratic prospects appeared so good during the Clinton impeachment and Senate trial that Dick Gephardt abandoned his presidential aspirations to concentrate on regaining the House and becoming speaker. The fact that New Left influence is much stronger in Democratic House ranks, however, exposes the Democrats to the classic GOP scare tactic should Al Gore appear to be a runaway winner in the presidential race—a particularly effective strategy at a time in which ticket-splitting has become commonplace and voters have come to distrust unified partisan (or, more accurately, ideological) control of the federal government. Perversely, the Democrats might have a better chance of winning the House if Republican nominee George W. Bush is in the driver's seat in the presidential race. In 1992 Bill Clinton won the presidency while his party *lost* ten House seats; this would prove more than enough to change partisan control in 2000. Given the dynamics of American electoral politics in the

1990s, the party's best prospect of recapturing unified control of the federal government might be a down-to-the-wire contest for both the presidency and the House, with the outcome uncertain right up to election day.

The initial stages of the 2000 campaign appeared to confirm the conclusion that structural changes in the presidential campaign calendar—specifically frontloading of primaries—and the homogenization of congressional districts following the 1990 census, have had a decisive impact on the institutional power bases of the party factions in both major parties. For the Democrats, the emphasis on name recognition and fund-raising prowess has helped insider candidates, reflecting the neo-liberal tendencies of the Clinton presidency. In Congress the New Left/Minority section of the party gained enhanced influence from redistricting and southern white realignment, although this may be arrested if the post-2000 redistricting process is less amenable to the creation of "majority-minority" districts. Enhanced Republican influence over the process, due to the GOP's gubernatorial and state legislative advances in the 1990s, and the Democrats' disinclination to offend their most loyal electoral constituency, will tend to militate against such a development, however.

A possible new phenomenon in the first decade of the new millennium may be an increasing tendency for candidates representing "disadvantaged" factions in the new "frontloaded" presidential politics—Republican religious conservatives and the Democratic left —to launch third- or even fourth-party bids for the presidency. For the 2000 election, Republican cultural conservative Patrick Buchanan abandoned the GOP to run for the Reform party label, while Hollywood legend and longtime liberal activist Warren Beatty also toyed with the idea of entering the presidential race as a third- (or fourth-) party candidate (Beatty 1999). Such a development would indicate the final confirmation of the predominance of ideology over party loyalty for many contemporary party activists and the arrival of multiparty politics in America, despite the plurality electoral system that militates against it. The first decade of the millennium will demonstrate whether these are likely to be long- or short-term phenomena.

## Conclusion

The 1990s appear to have been a period of transition in American electoral politics, bringing with it major changes in the party and electoral systems. Traditional partisan advantages at different levels of electoral competition have eroded, while new apparent Democratic advantages in presidential politics and Republican advantages in congressional politics appear highly vulnerable. Total control of the federal government remains possible for one party, but the odds against maintaining that control for more than a two-year span appear formidable. The fact that divided government coincided with unprecedented national prosperity during the 1990s only further legitimated the phenomenon among voters.

For political parties and party leaders, this presents a paradoxical situation—since a partisan advantage in one area of competition may actually jeopardize the party's prospects in other areas. During his eight years in office, Bill Clinton proved to be a master of this situation; with the help of Dick Morris, he was the national political figure who best understood what was going on. Thus the president used Republican partisanship and unremitting attacks on Republicans as "extremists" to solidify support from the now-minority congressional Democrats while doing deals with Republicans on selected issues to prove his conservative credentials to centrist voters. The congressional Democrats were left in a highly frustrating situation as their efforts to wipe out the narrow GOP House majority in 1996, and to some extent in 1998, were mitigated by the bipartisan deals between the GOP Congress and the Democratic White House that legitimated the Washington status quo. In 1998, Gary Jacobson has pointed out, correctly, that given the public hostility to the Republican impeachment inquiry against Clinton, the remarkable thing is that the Republicans did not lose more seats in Congress in the November poll (Jacobson 1999).

Yet the successful pursuit of triangulation has meant that Clinton leaves no significant legacy to his party in electoral or policy terms, beyond showing how to win two presidential elections and how to survive politically as a minority president for a full two terms. While it is true that his success has legitimated the political success of the neo-liberal or New Democrat faction of the party that he represented, Clinton has not converted the national Democrats into a "New Democratic" party. At the grassroots the Democratic Party is dominated by the New Left/Minority faction that also still predominates within the congressional Democratic ranks. The appearance of representatives of organized labor, environmentalists, and other elements of the Democrats' activist coalition at the late-1999 Seattle protests against the World Trade Organization (WTO), and by association the Clinton administration's avid free-trade position, demonstrates Clinton's failure to build a new "neo-liberal grassroots Democratic Party." Absent a series of leaders possessed of Clinton's political skills and tactical acumen, the party's prospects of becoming a majority governing coalition in the United States in the following decades appear marginal at best.

Moreover, American electoral politics as currently constituted militates against the kind of unified national party alignments beloved by political scientists and party scholars. As the public has become less motivated by partisanship, the parties have drifted into ideological realms that bear little relation to the concerns of most voters. Each development appears to sustain the other in a vicious cycle of partisan dealignment and polarization. Yet no one has devised a way to make American democracy function without political parties, and the parties have strengthened in some respects recently, as they have become more ideologically homogeneous, and in Congress more receptive to centralized leadership and direction. The electorate resolves the situation by invariably dividing its loyalties at the ballot box rather than entrusting control of national government policy to a national partisan majority. The economic success of the United States since 1994 appears to justify the voters' choice, and unless and until that prosperity erodes, the electoral order and partisan alignments of the 1990s will likely persist.

PART IV

# Cultural, Race, and Gender Politics

The domestic focus of the Clinton presidency produced an unusual salience of cultural, racial, and gender issues in American politics. James Guth reveals though survey analysis how the new culture wars of the 1990s found no resolution, and instead much exacerbation, during the Clinton presidency—culminating in the battle over impeachment. The Lewinsky affair made the president a uniquely controversial target for Christian conservatives. Unending culture wars became a major aspect of Clinton's legacy. Clinton focused unusual, if perhaps only symbolic, attention on racial issues in his second term. His initiative on race raised the figurative importance of the issue, according to Sharon Wright, but also received criticism from left and right about its substance or lack of it, leaving an ambiguous legacy for racial politics. Gender issues, however, received a more sustained focus. Barbara Burrell reveals how the administration consistently emphasized "women's issues" for both political and policy reasons. This approach aided Clinton's reelection, providing a lesson for future presidents.

CHAPTER 10

# CLINTON, IMPEACHMENT, AND THE CULTURE WARS

JAMES L. GUTH

As a New Democrat, Bill Clinton might have been expected to dampen the cultural conflicts agitating American politics. Moving the Democratic Party toward the center involved not only rejecting the excesses of the welfare state but also fostering traditional cultural norms. Clinton's admirers saw this project as an expression of his own values, while critics perceived a clever attempt to preempt Republican appeals to social conservatives. Nevertheless, by the end of the Clinton administration, divisions over abortion, gay rights, and the role of religion in public life seemed as sharp as ever, if obscured by satisfaction with his economic stewardship. Indeed, critics contend that the cultural cleavages underlying political conflict actually widened during the Clinton years.

If Bill Clinton could not tame the religious storms in American politics, his successors may have an even more difficult time. No recent president has had Clinton's potential for reducing the carnage in the culture wars. He grew up in a Southern evangelical environment, to which he returned as an adult, becoming an active member of a Southern Baptist church in Little Rock. He attended Catholic Georgetown University and by all accounts was personally close to several priests on the faculty and showed much interest in religion. His graduate education took place in the highly secularized atmosphere of two world-class universities. His wife, Hillary, was raised in the United Methodist Church and had been deeply immersed in the religious ethos of liberal mainline Protestantism, with its historic emphasis on the Social Gospel. Throughout his career, Clinton had cultivated a wide circle of religious acquaintances, especially in the Jewish and Black Protestant communities. But neither his broad understanding of American religion nor his personal charm could help him bridge the expanding religious gaps characterizing American politics.

Of course Clinton's impressive resources for dealing with the social and cultural issues confronting his administration were offset by other factors. His very facility in dealing with different religious traditions often occasioned distrust from all. On the other hand, Hillary Rodham Clinton's strong association with liberal Protestantism produced an instinctive aversion in many evangelicals and other religious conservatives. In the end, however, it was the president's personal behavior that convinced religious traditionalists to reject both Clinton's religious self-presentation and his efforts to bridge cultural divisions with policies designed to appeal to a broad spectrum of American believers.

In this chapter, I review Clinton's record on key social issues and examine the reactions of religious constituencies. First, I sketch the scholarly debate over the advent of "culture wars" in America and consider how they have shaped the religious underpinnings of electoral politics. I then outline Clinton's strategy for minimizing such divisions, reviewing his rhetoric and policy, especially during his first administration. Next, I examine religious group evaluations of Clinton and how social issues affected those evaluations. Finally, I address the role religious and cultural divisions played in structuring attitudes toward Clinton's impeachment and take a look at the future of cultural politics in America.

## Culture Wars in American Politics

Perhaps the first time many Americans heard about "culture wars" was in Pat Buchanan's prime-time speech to the 1992 Republican convention (Heineman 1998, 201). Although journalists seemed puzzled by the notion, Buchanan was echoing an academic debate set off by sociologist James Davison Hunter's *Culture Wars: The Struggle to Define America* (1991). Hunter argued that American politics were being reshaped by a new sort of religious conflict. Instead of the old *ethnocultural* struggles, pitting Democratic Catholics, Jews, and evangelical Protestants against mainline Protestant Republicans (Kleppner 1979), Hunter saw bitter divisions *within* traditions, between "the orthodox" and "the progressives." Orthodox believers are committed to "an external, definable, and transcendent authority," while progressives "resymbolize historic faiths according to the prevailing assumptions of contemporary life," making personal experience or scientific rationality the basis of morality (Hunter 1991, 44). The growing numbers of secular Americans, naturally, favored the "progressive" side.

Although Hunter's thesis quickly caught the attention of scholars, other social scientists argued that his bifurcation of the electorate was too simplistic, that battle lines shifted much more from issue to issue than he implied, and that most citizens were noncombatants (Williams 1997). Furthermore, the old markers of ethnicity, religious tradition, and social class proved quite robust, retaining a good bit of electoral influence. Nevertheless, many analysts have confirmed, at least in part, the political cleavages Hunter envisioned (Guth and Green 1991; Shafer and Claggett 1995; Green et al. 1996; Layman 1999).

## Bill Clinton and the Culture Wars

Although economic issues dominated the 1992 campaign, Clinton had to address many contentious social issues, a task complicated by a personal history that raised questions that intersected with public concerns. His avoidance of the draft, experimentation with marijuana (but "not inhaling"), participation in the 1960s counterculture, and rumored marital infidelities elicited close scrutiny from traditionalists. Indeed, Clinton's unexpected 1980 defeat for reelection as governor of Arkansas had been preceded by attacks from conservative clergy who objected to both his policies and his lifestyle. After that episode, he had moved toward the cultural right, joining Little Rock's Immanuel Baptist Church, singing in the choir, attending Pentecostal revivals, and appointing new staff with ties to religious conservatives. And, of course, Ms. Rodham became Mrs. Clinton, eliminating another irritant to traditionalists (Maraniss 1995, 405–6; Baptist Press 1992).

Clinton's approach to social issues in 1992 paralleled his New Democratic economic strategy. He rejected close ties to the left, but remained liberal enough to win its support in the general election contest with a socially conservative Republican Party. Thus, Clinton often sought to demonstrate his centrist position: "dissing" rap singer Sister Souljah before a black audience; pledging to make abortion "safe, legal, and rare"; promising gays the right to serve in the military, but not endorsing more advanced proposals; and reiterating support for capital punishment and welfare reform. Above all, he issued fervent appeals to "family values," "personal responsibility," and other traditionalist themes, wrapped in a biblical call for a "new covenant" between Americans and their government.

Clinton's strategy was successful: he won the election. But his tactics failed to convert his strongest critics, evangelical Protestants, who actually gave him less support in November than they had in early summer. Still, social moderation seemed to help Clinton among mainline Protestants, many Catholics, and seculars, who moved substantially in his direction during the campaign, though motivated in large part by economic concerns (Kellstedt et al. 1995). President Bush, on the other hand, used moral issues to counteract his disadvantage on economics; as a result, the presidential contest probably enhanced rather than reduced religious polarization.

Once in office, Clinton persistently wooed religious groups. Indeed, his first activity on inauguration day was an ecumenical prayer service attended by an army of religious leaders (Steinfels 1993). Even Clinton's personal religious routine was shaped by political imperatives. Invited by several Baptist pastors to join their flocks, Clinton chose instead the Foundry United Methodist Church, Hillary's congregation, and was often pictured in the TV news leaving church, Bible in hand (Steinfels 1992). Although he declined to appoint a White House liaison for religious issues, he often played that role himself. During his first weeks in office, he met with mainline Protestant leaders from the liberal National Council of Churches, who responded with grateful elation to the end of their twelve-year exile from the corridors of executive power (Wall 1993). Similarly, Clinton called on many personal ties with Catholic clergy and familiarity with Catholic social teaching to propitiate the American bishops, emphasizing common interests in social welfare policy, while minimizing differences over abortion (Toner 1993). Finally, the President did his best to reinforce his rapport with the Jewish and African American Protestant communities, always vital in Democratic politics.

As Gustav Niebuhr astutely observed, Clinton had a talent for appealing simultaneously to different religious traditions, leaving all listeners hearing the language of *their* faith (1994). And indeed the president and Mrs. Clinton publicly framed their agenda in universal religious terms. The president applauded Stephen Carter's *The Culture of Disbelief* to buttress his own assertion that religious values should infuse politics, while Hillary Clinton lauded the "politics of meaning" espoused by Jewish publicist Michael Lerner, combining his insights with lessons taught in her own Methodist heritage (Kelly 1993). This projection of a broad, progressive religious perspective attracted many mainline Protestants, Catholics, and Jews, who—to be sure—were easy to convince (Schaeffer 1996). And throughout the Clinton years, "mainstream" religious organizations, dominated by cultural progressives, vocally endorsed administration policy (Guth et al. 1997; Fowler and Hertzke 1995).

Much more daunting, however, was the task of achieving détente with the increasingly politicized evangelical Protestant community, now the core of the GOP. Southern Baptists Clinton and Gore did only slightly better among evangelicals than Greek Orthodox Michael Dukakis had done four years earlier, but if Clinton could win back a significant minority, he would enhance prospects for both reelection and legislative success. As a first step, Clinton ostentatiously invited prominent moderate and liberal evangelicals to the White House for prayers and policy briefings. The overture paid off with a cautious rapprochement between some evangelical leaders and the president (Yancey 1994). Clinton's help in passing the Religious Freedom Restoration Act of 1993 not only pleased mainline church leaders, but it also built some credit with many evangelicals (Tapp 1993).

And that was not all: Clinton held weekly phone conversations with his Baptist pastor in Little Rock and recruited prominent evangelical clergy as "spiritual mentors," most notably Bill Hybels, founder of the gigantic Willow Creek Community Church in suburban Chicago, and Tony Campolo, an American Baptist preacher, teacher, and author. Clinton's monthly Bible study and prayer sessions with Hybels were "off-the-record" but nevertheless well publicized, despite the stir they created among Willow Creek's conservative members. The president also continued to meet regularly with politically moderate evangelical clergy, although there was always some tension in these relations (Niebuhr 1997; Nash 1996).

Nevertheless, Clinton's early decisions frustrated his personal diplomacy. Although his personnel choices were to make government "look more like America," they provided little symbolic reassurance to some religious constituencies. Evangelicals were mostly ignored, a fact noted quickly by even Clinton's religious allies. More surprising, Catholics failed to receive appointments proportional to their presence in the Democratic electorate (Edsall 1993). Traditionalists soon complained that the Clinton regime was dominated by the cultural left, including even a few gays, or by ethnic and religious minorities. Some hotly contested nominations, such as that of Surgeon General Joycelyn Elders, especially raised conservative hackles. Her vocal stances on abortion, sex education, decriminalization of drugs, and a seemingly endless array of social topics instantly elicited criticism. Nor was Clinton's image helped by the First Family's hobnobbing with the Hollywood elite, anathema in conservative religious circles.

Clinton's first major policy moves also escalated the culture wars, especially on abortion and gay rights. He quickly rescinded Reagan-Bush executive orders restricting scientific research on fetal tissue, imposing gag rules on federally funded clinics, and otherwise restricting abortion. Clinton lobbied for legislation preventing pro-lifers from blocking access to abortion clinics and endorsed the proposed Freedom of Choice Act (O'Brien 1995). His appointment of Jewish jurist Ruth Bader Ginsburg to the Supreme Court was viewed critically by social conservatives, despite the moderation of her feminist and pro-choice views; selection of another Jewish moderate, Stephen Breyer, to fill the next vacancy failed to reassure them. But if abortion created problems for Clinton, his plan to allow homosexuals to serve in the armed forces elicited a firestorm of protest from conservative religious groups, one that was not squelched by the final "don't ask, don't tell" compromise. Although Clinton's initiatives on abortion and gay rights generally pleased the progressive wing of American religion, along with secular liberals, they reanimated the culture wars with evangelical Protestants and mainline Protestant and Catholic traditionalists. Thus, his dream of an all-inclusive supporting religious coalition evaporated, as personal diplomacy failed to overcome serious policy differences.

In any event, Clinton's overtures to evangelicals were soon buried by their powerful conservative wing, never open to détente. By early 1994, Jerry Falwell, the Christian Coalition, Focus on the Family, the Traditional Values Coalition, and the American Family Association had declared war. Clinton's own Southern Baptist Convention produced special prayers for members, designed to effect his repentance (Chambers 1993), and several evangelical organizations declined to issue customary invitations to address their conventions (Kennedy 1994). Abortion also proved a continuing irritant to the Catholic bishops, unhappy about Joycelyn Elder's criticism of their church from her post as surgeon general (Price and Witham 1994). And the string of scandals and ethical lapses endemic to the administration bothered traditionalists. By mid-1994 the religious alignment in Washington clearly mimicked Hunter's description: "progressives" and seculars aligned with Clinton, with "the orthodox" arrayed on the other side.

Frustrated by this onslaught, Clinton worried about the 1994 congressional elections, as polls hinted that his weak standing among religious conservatives might hurt Democrats, especially in the south. In June 1994 a Washington meeting arranged by presidential pollster Stan Greenberg considered Clinton's quandary. Attended by officials of the three Democratic national committees, polling experts, White House consultants, and several political scientists, the session canvassed possible options. James Carville argued that Democrats should ignore social issues and revert to their 1992 stress on the economy and health-care reform (Clinton's health plan was then dying in Congress). Carville also urged Democrats to tie Clinton's religious foes to their unpopular leaders by attacking the Christian Coalition and Pat Robertson by name, but others feared that such tactics would be perceived as a Democratic assault on all conservative Christians. In the end, no consensus was achieved (Guth 1994).[1] Democratic National Congressional Committee chair Vic Fazio soon broke the impasse, attacking the Christian Coalition directly, an action quickly followed by other Democrats.

The sweeping Republican victory in 1994, bolstered by a strong Christian conservative vote (Green et al. 1995), clearly called for a course adjustment. Clinton summoned his old adviser Dick Morris, who advocated a strategy of "triangulation," in which the president would position himself between contending political forces, in effect reassuming a New Democratic posture (Drew 1996; Harris, this volume). Whatever Morris's influence elsewhere, Clinton did try to triangulate on social issues, reverting occasionally to liberal stands to mollify vital Democratic constituencies. By January 1995 Clinton had produced both symbolic and policy appeals to religious conservatives and moderates. Although this approach risked antagonizing progressives, he perceived little choice if he hoped to win reelection in 1996.

The president first renewed his symbolic appeal by frequent public references to his own spirituality. In February 1995 he spoke on TV about his "deep" and "humble" faith, musing on recent devotional readings in the Psalms (Niebuhr 1995). At the same time he announced an initiative on religious activities in the public schools, noting that students' right to pray and engage in voluntary religious activities had often been violated by school authorities. Drawing on a document drafted by the Department of Education with the help of religious groups, Clinton declared that schools were not required to be religion-free (Novak and Frisby 1995), even hinting that he might accept a carefully drawn school prayer bill. Beyond that, he renewed a call for "school choice," although only among public schools, rejecting anything resembling vouchers for religious schools. He eventually signed a drastic welfare reform law that had strong support from religious conservatives but had been opposed by virtually all liberal religious organizations. He talked up the "V-chip," which would permit parents to control television viewing by their children. And just before the election he signed the Defense of Marriage Act, pushed through Congress by religious conservatives fearing legalized homosexual unions.

On some things, however, Clinton refused to budge. He continued to protect affirmative action, refused to back massive reductions in immigration, and rejected media censorship. But none of these issues had the political potential of "partial-birth" abortion. Pro-life groups had hit upon prohibiting this late-term procedure as an effective appeal to the agonized center of American opinion. Indeed, the ban had overwhelming support in both houses of Congress, almost enough to override a veto. The American Catholic bishops, including all the cardinals, publicly appealed to Clinton to sign the bill (Prendergast 1999, 210). His subsequent veto was attacked by conservatives from all the major religious traditions, but was supported by the mainline Protestant and Jewish lobbies. Despite the fervor it aroused, however, the issue did not prove an obstacle to Clinton's impressive 1996 reelection victory. Upon his return to office, Clinton determined to follow the same "mixed" strategy on social issues that had proven so successful in 1995 and 1996 (Mitchell 1997).

## The Clinton Impact: Presidential Evaluations

How did Clinton's social-issue gyrations intersect with emerging religious divisions? In Table 1 we look at how religious groups evaluated Clinton's performance as president, as revealed by the 1994, 1996, and 1998 National Election Studies. The religious categories incorporate followers of the old religious *traditions*, including evangelical Protestants, mainline Protestants, white Catholics, African American Protestants, and Jews (along with several smaller groups), but also recognize culture-war divisions *within* major traditions.[2] To isolate the impact of religious factors, we included statistical controls for income and education, along with gender and age. The results we see are thus the effects of religious membership, not the product of social class or other traits. The first line shows Clinton's job ratings in each election year from 1994 to 1998. The rest of the table reveals how each religious group deviated from the national mean, in either a negative (-) or positive (+) direction.

As Table 1 shows, Clinton received better evaluations as his tenure wore on. On a five-point scale, he was rated slightly below the midpoint in 1994, but improved substantially by the 1996 election, and had made further gains before impeachment proceedings began in late 1998. By that time a substantial majority of all Americans approved his performance. Those higher approval ratings ran across all the religious groups. (To confirm this, simply add each deviation to the national mean and compare results across the period.)

Although Clinton's job approval rose among all religious groups, his poli-

Table 1
Religious Traditions and Presidential Evaluation, 1994–1998

|  | 1994 | 1996 | 1998 | Change in Deviation, 1994–1998 |
|---|---|---|---|---|
| National mean* | 2.93 | 3.46 | 3.77 |  |
| Deviations from national mean:** |  |  |  |  |
| Evangelical Protestants*** |  |  |  |  |
| High commitment | -.68 | -.86 | -.77 | (-.09) |
| Low commitment | -.15 | -.07 | -.39 | (-.24) |
| Mainline Protestants |  |  |  |  |
| High commitment | -.59 | -.40 | -.13 | (+.46) |
| Low commitment | -.19 | -.09 | +.09 | (+.28) |
| Hispanic Protestants |  |  |  |  |
| High commitment | -.43 | -.38 | -.21 | (+.22) |
| Low commitment | -.06 | +.35 | +.92 | (+.98) |
| Roman Catholics |  |  |  |  |
| High commitment | -.15 | -.22 | -.31 | (-.16) |
| Low commitment | +.21 | +.11 | -.04 | (-.25) |
| Hispanic Catholics |  |  |  |  |
| High commitment | +.66 | +.60 | +.64 | (-.02) |
| Low commitment | +.92 | +.57 | +.66 | (-.26) |
| Black Protestants | +1.05 | +.84 | +.99 | (-.06) |
| Jewish | +.88 | +.92 | +.83 | (-.05) |
| Secular | +.06 | +.09 | +.14 | (+.08) |
| All other religions | -.10 | +.44 | -.14 | (-.04) |

Source: 1994, 1996, and 1998 National Election Studies

*Mean scores based on survey responses to the question: "Do you approve or disapprove of the way Bill Clinton is handling his job as president?" The response options as recorded were: 1, "Disapprove Strongly"; 2, "Disapprove"; 3, Neutral; 4, "Approve"; and 5, "Strongly Approve." Thus, high scores are more approving.

**The table entries represent the "deviation" by each religious group from the national mean. In 1994, for example, committed evangelicals had a score of 2.25 or .68 below the national mean, a substantially less favorable evaluation of Clinton. Similarly, positive scores indicate that the group had more favorable evaluations of the president than the national public. All scores are adjusted for the impact of family income, education level, gender, and age.

***The number of respondents in each religious tradition varies slightly by year of survey and with the amount of missing data. For example, in 1994 the Ns were: Evangelical (381), Mainline (238), Hispanic Protestant (36), white Catholic (313), Hispanic Catholic (60), Black Protestant (144), Jewish (28), Secular (247), all other religions (74).

cies failed to *reduce the gaps* created by the culture wars, with few exceptions. First, his rating among evangelicals seriously lagged his overall scores. In fact, committed evangelicals were actually farther below the national mean in 1998 than they had been in 1994, and less committed evangelicals were also relatively negative, although not as critical as their traditionalist brethren. Clinton did make clear progress elsewhere, however. Committed mainline Protestants—who had almost matched their evangelical counterparts in hostility toward Clinton in 1994—had moved much closer to the national mean by 1998, joined by their less devout brethren, who by 1998 were slightly *more* approving of Clinton than the general public. Something very similar happened among Hispanic Protestants (mostly evangelical), who in 1994 were quite critical of Clinton's work, especially if they were religiously active. By 1998 active Hispanic Protestants had gravitated toward the mean and the less devout had actually become strongly supportive of the president.

White Roman Catholics confirmed their recent reputation as a "swing" group by never deviating far from the national mean, but they did shift in relative position. In 1994 Catholics exhibited the same split between active and less-active adherents found among Protestants, but by 1998 both Catholic groups had become *relatively* more critical of the president. Hispanic Catholics, however, were different: whether religiously active or not, they were some of Clinton's most ardent admirers. Thus, we see increasing polarization among Catholics, as the growing number of Hispanics and their Anglo counterparts drift apart politically. Meanwhile, African American Protestants and Jews vied for position as the most pro-Clinton constituency, and seculars moved slightly toward Clinton but were not nearly as Democratic in *evaluating* him as in *voting* for him.

All in all, Clinton's posture as a New Democrat, his moderate positions on tough social issues, and his cultivation of religious traditionalists had mixed success. Evangelicals evidently credited him with good economic management but remained on the periphery of any national cheering section. Devout white Catholics were less skeptical than Evangelicals to begin with but became relatively more critical over time. Clinton's efforts had some real success among mainline Protestants, softening the judgment of traditionalists and actually attracting the less devout to his side of the mean. And he solidified support among usually Democratic religious minorities such as Black Protestants and Jews, while making some inroads among Republican-leaning committed Hispanic Protestants.

## Cultural Issues and Clinton Ratings

How did Clinton's policies affect religious group assessments? If his effort to neutralize cultural issues succeeded, we should find that "hot button" social issues had less impact on the president's job evaluations in 1996 than in 1994. As our theoretical orientation suggests, the clear differences we have seen in religious-group evaluation of Clinton should be the artifact of their particular attitudes on issues. Thus, committed believers in all three white Christian traditions should be more critical because their views on abortion, gay rights, feminism, and other aspects of moral traditionalism are more conservative. (For a full demonstration of the different attitudes among religious groups, see Green et al. 1996.)

Did Clinton's improving job ratings reflect the neutralization of social issues, or did he merely overcome them with successful economic management? Table 2 confirms that attitudes on social issues, along with partisanship, stances on economic issues, and economic assessments shaped presidential evaluations. Model 1 has the president's thermometer rating as the dependent variable and incorporates only social issues, religious variables, and the demographic controls.[3] In both 1994 and 1996, Clinton benefits from support of those who have a strong feminist orientation, back government assistance to blacks, have favorable attitudes towards gays and, in 1994, toward immigrants. Surprisingly, attitudes toward school prayer and abortion have minimal effect in 1994, but the abortion coefficient rises and becomes statistically significant in 1996, perhaps because of the partial-birth abortion controversy. In addition, Clinton gets warmer responses from those with more modest levels of education and income, as well as from older citizens. As we predicted, religious location makes little difference once the attitudes associated with religious groups are in the equation. The only clear exception is for African American Protestants, whose warmth toward Clinton exceeds what might be expected, based on their political views and demographic traits.

What happens when we add partisanship, economic assessments, and views on social welfare policies? Not surprisingly, Democratic identification is by far the best predictor in Model 2 for both years, followed by assessments of the economy. Both measures have greater impact in 1996 than in 1994. A preference for bigger government providing more services did not influence assessments of Clinton in 1994, but it became significant two years later. In 1994, when the ill-fated Clinton health plan was still fresh in voters' minds, attitudes toward a federal health plan influenced perceptions of Clinton much more than in 1996.

Party identification and the other political variables in Model 2 might be expected to overwhelm the social issues, but they do not. Although some of the impact of cultural questions is undoubtedly captured by partisanship, several key issues of Clinton's first administration retain an independent impact, especially pro-feminist orientations and favorable attitudes toward gays. Given the controversies over immigration that dogged the 1996 campaign, it is surprising that pro-immigration sentiments positively influenced Clinton's rat-

Table 2

Religion, Social Issues, Political Factors, and Presidential Evaluation, 1994–1996
(OLS regression analysis, standardized coefficients)

|  | 1994 | | 1996 | |
| --- | --- | --- | --- | --- |
|  | Model 1 | Model 2 | Model 1 | Model 2 |
| Social and cultural issues | | | | |
|   Feminist orientations | .26*** | .15*** | .29*** | .15*** |
|   Assistance to blacks | .13*** | .00 | .15*** | .04 |
|   Policy toward gays | .13*** | .06* | .18*** | .10** |
|   Immigration | .10*** | .09*** | .00 | -.01 |
|   School prayer | .07** | .03 | .04 | .01 |
|   Abortion | .05 | .00 | .10** | .02 |
| Religious variables | | | | |
|   Evangelical commitment | .01 | .00 | .01 | .02 |
|   Mainline commitment | -.01 | .04 | -.06* | -.01 |
|   Catholic commitment | .05 | .03 | .03 | -.02 |
|   Black Protestant | .11*** | .08*** | .07* | .04 |
| Status and demographic controls | | | | |
|   Education level | -.12*** | -.11*** | -.07* | -.03 |
|   Income | -.08** | -.01 | -.10*** | -.04 |
|   Age | .09*** | .04* | .09*** | .03 |
|   Gender (female) | .03 | .00 | .04 | .03 |
| Partisanship, economic, and "New Deal" issues | | | | |
|   Party identification | — | .41*** | — | .46*** |
|   Economic assessment | — | .16*** | — | .20*** |
|   Services vs. spending | — | .02 | — | .07** |
|   Federal health plan | — | .13*** | — | .06* |
| Adjusted $R^2$ | .29 | .50 | .35 | .61 |

*Source: 1994 and 1996 National Election Studies.*
*Note:* Entries are standardized regression coefficients, indicating the relative power of each factor in predicting presidential approval scores. The number of asterisks indicates the statistical significance of each coefficient, that is the probability that the result could have occurred by chance. The adjusted $R^2$ measures the proportion of the variance in approval scores that is accounted for by the variables in each equation.

*** $p < .001$
** $p < .01$
* $p < .05$

ings in 1994 but not in 1996. Note also that *all* the status and demographic measures disappear from Model 2 in 1996. As with the religious variables, their influence is channeled through citizens' attitudes.

Although religious membership does not directly influence Clinton's evaluations once the characteristic attitudes of believers are included, different issues seemed to matter to individual religious communities. If we confine our analysis to each religious tradition and run the same regressions used in Table 2, we find some interesting deviations from the national results. For evangelicals, social issues influence their feelings about the president a good bit more than does their perception of the economy or their views on "New Deal" policy issues, especially in 1994. In addition, their evaluations are influenced less by partisanship, perhaps reflecting their recent move from Democratic to Republican status. For mainline Protestants, the best predictors are partisanship, economic assessment, and the government-services issue, although feminism has an impact in both years, and stance on immigration influences Clinton's 1994 rating. The only social issue stance that affects white Catholics' evaluation of Clinton is feminism, joined by partisanship and economic assessments in both years, the Clinton health plan in 1994, and the government services issue in 1996. Surprisingly, abortion does not influence Catholics' evaluation of Clinton in either year, reinforcing findings that Catholics are especially responsive to economic conditions and economic policy (Prendergast 1999).

Clinton's job ratings, then, are best explained by the usual suspects: he was evaluated on partisan grounds, on the basis of the nation's economic performance, and in response to his administration's policy initiatives. The public's increasingly positive sentiment about the economy lifted his political standing among all religious groups, and his record on social issues brought him an added boost from proponents of liberal policies on gender, racial, and gay-rights issues. But by the same token, his administration had only moderate success in reducing the cultural-issue divide. Indeed, the very policies that buttressed his support among religious liberals and seculars contributed to continuing disaffection among traditionalists, especially evangelicals.

## Cultural Alignments and Impeachment

Although Clinton continued to enjoy public approval after his reelection, the Lewinsky scandal and subsequent impeachment battle dominated his second administration. No controversy was better calculated to reinforce the new cultural divisions in American politics, given the centrality of sexual issues to social conservatives. Indeed, more than a few combatants and professional observers alike saw the issue eliciting fundamental moral divisions among both political elites and the mass public (Sullivan 1998; Broadway 1999). Here we look at the public reaction through the lens of the 1998 National Election Study, which asked questions about the scandal and also included queries about the role of religious faith in politics. Thus, the data is especially suited for testing the claim that the impeachment drive represented what jurist Richard Posner has called a conservative *Kulturkampf* (Posner 1999).

How did religious constituencies react to the scandal? Table 3 shows that less than 40 percent of the public wanted either Clinton's resignation or his impeachment, but that response varied by religion. Devout evangelicals overwhelmingly favored Clinton's departure, but casual evangelicals were not so insistent. Mainline Protestants and white Catholics were less favorable toward removal than evangelicals, but the highly committed were more supportive than were the less devout. Religious minorities generally opposed Clinton's removal: African American Protestants were most hostile, followed by Jews and Hispanic Catholics, and less than a third of seculars wanted Clinton to depart. Thus we find the familiar pattern: committed evangelicals were the vanguard of the anti-Clinton army, followed by their mainline Protestant and Catholic cohorts at some distance. A larger alignment of less-committed mainliners and Catholics, most religious minorities, and the bulk of secular voters opposed this conservative coalition.

Other perceptions shaped popular reactions. Judgments that Special Prosecutor Kenneth Starr was engaged in a partisan vendetta played a role: fewer respondents were convinced that Starr had conducted an "impartial" investigation than actually wanted the president to leave office! Even committed evangelicals felt that way, despite Starr's visibility as a prominent evangelical Christian (Abramson 1998). Still, the same basic pattern among religious groups obtains, with evangelicals most supportive of Starr and committed members of all religious groups more positive than their less-active counterparts. Once again, religious minorities and seculars were very hostile to the special prosecutor. The same religious patterns held, by the way, on popular assessments of the fairness of the congressional impeachment inquiry and the media's handling of the issue (data not shown).

Some analysts explained Clinton's strength by arguing that citizens do not expect politicians to be moral exemplars. As the table shows, however, two-thirds of the public wanted greater morality from public servants. Committed believers were more demanding than the less committed, although church-going evangelicals actually rank a little lower than their mainline and Catholic counterparts do. Religious minorities and secular citizens have a considerably lower estimate of the importance of official morality than do members of the larger traditions. In any event, very few Americans saw Clinton as a moral exemplar. Although the president got the benefit of the doubt from a large minority of black Protestants and over a third of Hispanic Catholics,

Table 3
Religious Traditions and Presidential Impeachment, 1998

| | Resign/ Impeach | Starr Fair | Need Moral Leaders | Clinton Not Moral | Public Issue (Agree) | Economic Disapproval of Clinton |
|---|---|---|---|---|---|---|
| National mean* | 37% | 31% | 67% | 83% | 37% | 21% |
| Evangelical Protestants | | | | | | |
| Traditionalist | +.29 | +.20 | +.05 | +.11 | +.25 | +.17 |
| Modernist | +.01 | +.03 | +.02 | -.02 | +.04 | +.07 |
| Mainline Protestants | | | | | | |
| Traditionalist | +.11 | +.08 | +.12 | +.11 | +.03 | -.10 |
| Modernist | -.07 | -.08 | -.02 | +.08 | -.09 | -.04 |
| Hispanic Protestants | | | | | | |
| Traditionalist | +.15 | +.09 | +.01 | +.16 | +.03 | +.17 |
| Modernist | -.32 | -.23 | -.16 | -.08 | -.30 | +.02 |
| White Roman Catholics | | | | | | |
| Traditionalist | +.09 | +.15 | +.09 | +.06 | +.12 | -.04 |
| Modernist | +.01 | +.07 | +.02 | +.04 | +.04 | -.03 |
| Hispanic Catholics | | | | | | |
| Traditionalist | -.10 | -.03 | -.10 | -.16 | -.09 | -.19 |
| Modernist | -.15 | -.05 | -.08 | -.12 | -.18 | -.07 |
| Secular | -.10 | -.07 | -.08 | -.04 | -.07 | +.01 |
| Jewish | -.09 | -.20 | -.15 | -.09 | -.03 | -.15 |
| Black Protestants | -.26 | -.19 | -.11 | -.23 | -.18 | -.17 |
| All Other Religious | +.16 | -.04 | +.13 | -.06 | +.05 | +.10 |

*Source: 1998 National Election Study.*

*Except for the national means in the first line, all other scores are deviations of each group from the national means. All variables are coded so that a positive (+) score represents higher disapproval of Clinton and a minus (-) score represents greater support for the President. All scores are adjusted for the effects of family income, education level, gender, and age and thus represent the net effects of membership in the particular religious group.

public perception of his morality was certainly not an effective defense. And his ratings on "honesty" were almost as bad (data not shown).

If Clinton did not suffer politically from his low ratings for morality and honesty, it may be because many did not perceive these traits as relevant to impeachment. Only 37 percent thought the Lewinsky affair was a public issue, as opposed to a purely private one, thus agreeing with Clinton's own argument. Once again, religious groups differed strikingly: 62 percent of committed evangelicals said the affair was a public concern, compared with only 40 percent of their inactive co-religionists. Although fewer mainliners and Catholics thought the issue was a public one, a significantly larger proportion of the active did. On the other hand, large majorities of Jews, Hispanic Catholics, Black Protestants, and seculars agreed with the president's definition.

For many Americans, of course, reaction to Clinton's behavior required far more than judging his moral status. As pundits repeated endlessly, Clinton retained his office because of the public's favorable assessment of his job performance, especially on the economy. As the last column shows, few citizens disapproved of Clinton's economic job performance, even among active evangelicals. Although the usual differences appear among the religious groups, the conventional wisdom was clearly correct: proponents of impeachment faced a towering barrier in such public sentiments.

What ultimately determined the public's judgment about removal? In Table 4 we report the results of several logistic regressions that test the most important factors influencing such judgments.[4] Religious location tells us something about public attitudes toward removal (Model 1). As we might expect, evangelical commitment produces significant sentiment for Clinton's departure. Active mainline Protestants and Catholics are also slightly more likely to favor the president's political demise, while African American Protestants were dramatically warmer toward Clinton. None of the other religious groups had distinctive attitudes. Interestingly, gender, income, and education had no statistically significant effects (data not shown), but older citizens were more likely to *oppose* Clinton's removal. Together these factors allow us to classify over 61 percent of respondents correctly, a considerable improvement on chance.

These results suggest a clear cultural element in the drive to remove Clinton. Another way to look at that component is to consider what might be called "traditionalist politics" (Model 2). First, we used a standard moral traditionalism scale, tapping respondents' willingness to tolerate other moralities (Conover and Feldman 1985). We also calculated the gap between citizens' desire for more moral politicians and their personal assessment of Clinton's morality. In addition, we included a scale assessing whether voters felt religion should be involved in public life (Wald et al. 1998). The final variable was whether the respondent had been contacted by a religious group during the 1998 campaign. Although each provides some insight, the best predictor is the gap between the felt need for greater official morality and assessment of Clinton's personal morality. Those perceiving the largest gap were most likely to favor removal; those who saw official morality as unimportant or who rated Clinton highly on moral grounds were less prone to favor removal. Moral traditionalism is the next best predictor, followed by a preference for more religious influence over political life and, finally, contacts by religious groups. In-

Table 4
Religion, Social Issues, Political Factors, and Presidential Impeachment, 1998
(logistic regression analysis)

|  | Model 1 | Model 2 | Model 3 | Model 4 | Model 5 |
|---|---|---|---|---|---|
| Religious variables | | | | | |
|   Evangelical commitment | .19*** | | | | |
|   Mainline commitment | .07** | | | | |
|   Catholic commitment | .07** | | | | |
|   Black Protestant | -.09** | | | | |
| Demographic controls | | | | | |
|   Age | -.11*** | | | | |
| Traditionalist politics | | | | | |
|   Moral assessment | | .16*** | | | .07** |
|   Moral traditionalism | | .14*** | | | |
|   Religious politics | | .11*** | | | .14*** |
|   Religious group contact | | .07* | | | |
| Political variables | | | | | |
|   Democratic identification | | | -.32*** | | .13*** |
|   More government services | | | -.12*** | | .07** |
|   Oppose school vouchers | | | -.10*** | | |
|   Environmental protection | | | -.04* | | |
|   Pro-choice | | | -.07** | | |
|   Oppose school prayer | | | -.07** | | |
| Personal assessments | | | | | |
|   Clinton job approval | | | | -.31*** | .24*** |
|   Warm toward Hillary | | | | -.18** | .07** |
| Percentage Correctly Classified | 61.4 | 64.6 | 73.4 | 80.2 | 81.5 |

*Source: 1998 National Election Study.*

Note: The dependent variable is dichotomous: whether or not the respondent wanted President Clinton to leave office, either by resignation or impeachment. All variables are coded so that positive scores on the variable indicate greater support for removal, negative scores mean that higher scores produce less sentiment for removal. The size of the logistic coefficient r indicates the relative explanatory power of each variable.

*** $p < .001$
** $p < .01$
* $p < .05$

terestingly, other religious cue-giving, such has having political information available in the church, or receiving clergy guidance about politics seems to have no impact (data not shown). Traditionalist politics variables do slightly better in predicting than the religious measures, correctly classifying almost 65 percent of the respondents.

To what extent were opinions on removal shaped by political variables? As we might expect from the bitter partisan divisions in Congress, voters' party identification is a very strong guide to attitudes, but a few other issues also had a role, even when partisanship was in the equation (Model 3). A liberal stance on government services and pro-environmental views worked in the president's favor, while conservatism on these issues moved citizens in the other direction. Attitudes on school vouchers, school prayer, and abortion also influenced feelings about removal. On the other hand, guaranteed jobs, gay rights, women's equality, immigration, affirmative action, and other social issues had no independent effect once partisanship was in the equation (data not shown). These political indicators are quite useful in predicting support for Clinton's removal, producing 73 percent accuracy.

Not surprisingly, attitudes toward Clinton's removal are best predicted by public sentiment toward the president and his wife (Model 4), especially voters' assessment of Clinton's overall performance in office. Interestingly, a specific item on his economic management provided no additional predictive power. As some speculated during the crisis, the president also benefited from positive public response to Hillary Clinton. Those who gave her high ratings were less likely to support her husband's removal, even when approval of his own job performance is taken into account. The public's response on just these two measures allows us to predict attitudes toward removal with over 80 percent accuracy. When variables from all the models are incorporated in a single regression in Model 5, only six survive. Clinton's job rating retains the strongest influence, followed by the public's willingness to bring religious influence and people into public life. Democratic partisanship follows close behind, with approval of Hillary Clinton, moral assessment of the president, and liberal attitudes on government services also providing some help. These factors allow us to classify more than 81 percent of the respondents correctly.

Clearly, religious groups reacted quite differently to Clinton's impeachment, in ways shaped by their characteristic moral preoccupations and larger worldview. Traditionalists, especially evangelicals, were most critical of the president and evaluated his behavior through a substantially different lens than did religious progressives and secular citizens. Although it is impossible to disentangle completely these partisan, ideological, and religious influences, there is no question that the struggle elicited fundamental moral and religious differences, differences evident in Congress as well. In the House, for example, evangelical Republicans voted for an average of 3.75 of the 4 impeachment counts, mainline Republicans, 3.36, and Catholic Republicans, 3.23. And the House team for the Senate trial included a large number of evangelicals, as well as some of its most religious members.

## Conclusion

Did Bill Clinton produce what his predecessor once referred to as a "kinder, gentler" America, reducing polarization over social issues? Our preliminary answer must be "no." Although the president often avoided or minimized the political impact of cultural and religious conflict, especially through the good fortune of sustained economic growth, he did not bring all the contending forces in the culture wars behind his administration's policies. Indeed, religious constituencies evaluated his stewardship quite differently, depending on their attitudes toward feminism, gay rights, and other social issues. Personal charm and religious sophistication were not enough to overcome the continuing ideological and theological divides within the American public. Indeed, his own behavior ultimately served to reinforce these divisions among America's religious—and secular—citizens.

Thus, the Clinton administration produced no fundamental transformation in the religious structure of American electoral and presidential politics. Although his handling of some cultural issues resulted in temporary increases in Democratic vote totals, the underlying structure of cultural issues persisted. While some moderate mainline Protestants, Catholics, and Hispanic Protestants moved toward the Democrats as a result of the president's careful triangulation, most evangelical Protestants—the new core of the GOP—actually moved farther away. And this is not surprising: the fundamental cultural positions of the Clinton administration did little to appease the strong concerns of this constituency over abortion, gay rights, school choice, and similar issues. The administration's moderate positions on personal responsibility, school violence, and V-chips appealed to some religious traditionalists, but not to most evangelicals. On the other end, the strong approval Clinton received from religious minorities and secular citizens often reflected support for the same policies that evangelical traditionalists found so distasteful. At the end of his administration these fundamental divisions were just as visible as they had been in 1993—if not more so.

All this suggests that the current religious alignment in American politics has been some time in the making and has achieved a considerable resilience. Of course, constant changes in the world of American religion make it impossible for either party to rest on its laurels. The declining number of mainline Protestants continues to undermine one ancient GOP constituency, while the defection of traditionalist Catholics to the Republican Party reduces an ancient Democratic stronghold. In addition, the political emergence of "new" religious groups, such as Hispanic Catholics and Protestants, Muslims, and Hindus, as well as the growing contingent of seculars, forces both parties to develop strategies for expanding their religious coalitions. Nevertheless, any president will have to build an administration and formulate policies within the electoral and legislative parameters created by these cultural alignments.

Although Clinton's presidency failed to alter the structure of religious politics in the United States, his open discussion of religious faith, endorsement of the application of religious values to public policy, and frequent consultation with religious leaders certainly encouraged public discussion of religion's role in politics. Perhaps as a result, some surveys show that Americans are increasingly inclined to think that religious values are relevant to political choices. And many political leaders seem to think so. Almost all of the candidates for the Democratic and Republican nominations for president in the 2000 race either "volunteered" their religious beliefs in public debate (including Al Gore and all the Republicans) or, in the case of Bill Bradley, were forced to explain a refusal to do so. Although GOP candidates had a special electoral incentive to appeal to the strong traditionalist constituency within their party, there can be little doubt that eight years of public religiosity on Clinton's part had served to legitimize such discussions, just as his behavior raised the importance of candidates' personal moralities.

In a related vein, Clinton's posture also helped raise important public-policy issues on the role of religious institutions in addressing national problems. Although the whole notion of "charitable choice" had more initial support on the Republican side of the aisle, Clinton's willingness to consider expanded roles for religious organizations in providing social welfare and other government services opened a whole new arena for religious involvement—and public discussion. Vice President Gore expanded this opening during his campaign for the Democratic nomination in 2000, and the Republican candidates were even more eager to help religious institutions play a larger role in addressing social problems. Evidence that the public had grown more favorable toward such involvement, of course, raised cries of alarm from church-state separationists and civil libertarians. In any case, the Clinton presidency may ultimately be remembered not only as a period in which new cultural divisions in American politics solidified, but also as a time when religious people and institutions began to play new roles in the formulation and execution of public policy.

CHAPTER 11

# CLINTON AND RACIAL POLITICS

SHARON D. WRIGHT

This chapter assesses the consequences of the Clinton presidency for American racial politics. More specifically, it attempts to provide explanations for Clinton's high rate of approval among African Americans. The majority of blacks voted for him in 1992 and in 1996 because of his Democratic partisan affiliation, and primarily supported the actions of Clinton's administration during both of his terms in office. Many analysts have accused black Americans as having a "blind allegiance" or "blind loyalty" to President Clinton especially during the most difficult moments of his presidency. In analyzing the immediate and future consequences of the Clinton presidency for racial politics in America, this chapter will outline its major accomplishments and dilemmas, the significance of the "President's Initiative on Race," and the attempts of the Clinton presidency to respond to the needs of African Americans and other minority groups.

President Clinton emerged as a populist candidate with the ability to establish a broad-based coalition transcending racial and class lines. Many scholars of the presidency would argue that he has demonstrated an aggressive leadership style. Others would highlight his errors and numerous problems as indicative of a "weak" style of leadership. Clinton appointed a number of minority federal judges, cabinet, and sub-cabinet members. Nevertheless, his closest and most influential advisors are white males. Also, his foreign policy agenda, race initiative, and failure to support controversial nominees were disappointments to many people of color.

## The New Democratic Agenda in Racial Politics

In 1992 President William Jefferson Clinton's centrist-mainstream campaign strategy was successful enough for him to defeat a once seemingly invincible incumbent. When he entered the race in 1992, Bill Clinton lacked widespread recognition outside of his native Arkansas and was running against an incumbent who in 1991 had the highest approval rating among Americans (78 percent) of any president in the post–World War II era (Barker, Jones, and Tate 1998). Before his veto of the Civil Rights Act of 1990, George Bush had earned a higher approval rating from blacks (56 percent) than any other Republican president since Dwight D. Eisenhower.

The Clinton campaign focused on the politics of the economy rather than the politics of race. In *Putting People First: How We Can All Change America*, the Clinton-Gore team stated its intention to reduce the nation's deficit, create jobs, improve public schools, provide universal health care, reform the welfare system, and revitalize the central cities (1992, 3–4). Bill Clinton was able to mobilize an electoral coalition that consisted of African Americans, Asian Americans, gays and lesbians, Latinos, liberal and moderate whites, Native Americans, and women. After winning the Democratic nomination, Clinton entered the race a strategy for reaching out to groups that felt neglected during twelve years of Republican presidential rule.

In order to gain the trust of black Democrats, he pointed out that he was a New South politician and a New Democrat who would not take them for granted. While an undergraduate at Georgetown University, Clinton had participated in many civil-rights protests (Marable 1993, 81). Moreover, he had frequently visited black churches as a child in Hope, Arkansas, had many black friends throughout his lifetime, had lived in racially mixed neighborhoods as an adult, and had appointed a larger number of blacks to his administration as governor of Arkansas than all of the state's previous governors combined. On many occasions, however, Bill Clinton has had a questionable record concerning African Americans. While he served as governor of Arkansas, the state was one of only two in the nation that failed to pass a civil rights law. Also, blacks in Arkansas had one of the highest poverty rates in America (43 percent) during the Clinton administration (Marable 1993, 78).

Although his critics have accused him of "playing the race card" in order to maintain and increase his base of support from minority voters, President

Clinton's racial politics have not been as blatant as those of former presidents Bush, Reagan, Carter, and Nixon. He offended many of his liberal and black supporters, such as Rev. Jesse Jackson, the National Coalition to Abolish the Death Penalty, and the NAACP Legal Defense Fund in 1992, however, when he left the campaign trail to oversee the execution of Ricky Ray Rector, a forty-year-old black man, in Arkansas (Edsall 1992, A14). It was indisputable that in March 1981 Rector killed a white police officer and suffered permanent brain damage after shooting himself in the forehead immediately after the murder. In the arduous appeals process, Rector's attorney argued that his self-inflicted injury rendered him mentally incompetent to stand trial. In 1992, Clinton traveled to Arkansas to thwart efforts to further delay Rector's execution. By doing so, he enhanced his reputation with conservative voters as a law-and-order candidate. Despite his involvement in the Rector execution, Clinton received approximately 82 percent of the black vote, 78 percent of the Jewish vote, 62 percent of the Latino vote, 58 percent of the vote from women who lacked a high school education, 50 percent of the vote from Americans over the age of 60, and 59 percent of the vote from low-income Americans (incomes of $15,000 of less) in 1992 (Marable 1993, 78). His narrow victories over Bush in the states of Georgia, Louisiana, New Jersey, Ohio, and Tennessee resulted from his success in garnering the black vote.

After taking office, Clinton's symbolic actions won him even greater levels of admiration from the majority of African Americans. During his presidential campaigns, he frequently appeared in black churches, professional organization meetings, and neighborhoods. The racially mixed Central High School choir of Little Rock, Arkansas, and Reverend Jesse Jackson's daughter Santita sang at his 1992 inauguration ceremony; and African American poet Maya Angelou wrote an original poem for the event. Clinton's other symbolic actions included apologizing for slavery during a trip to Africa, apologizing to the victims of the Tuskegee syphilis experiment, creating "One America in the Twenty-first Century: The President's Initiative on Race," and publicly stating his commitment to "mend" not "end" affirmative action (Sapiro and Canon 2000, 225).

In addition to his effective campaigning and his symbolic political actions, President Clinton attempted to "achieve excellence in diversity." Early in his political career, Clinton realized that blacks would vote for Democratic candidates in large numbers but would have a lower turnout at the polls if they sensed that their needs were being neglected. In order to ensure a large black voter turnout rate during his reelection campaign, the president appointed a record number of African Americans to administrative, cabinet, and federal judicial posts. Shortly after his 1992 victory, Clinton promised to appoint a multiracial cabinet that "looks like America." To this end, he successfully nominated ten minorities as cabinet members, including in the not-traditionally black positions of secretary of agriculture, commerce, energy, and veterans' affairs. Blacks also received key appointments in the sub-cabinet positions of solicitor general, assistant secretary of the treasury for enforcement, surgeon general, and deputy secretary of state (Sirgo 1995, 94). Moreover, Clinton appointed more minority and female federal judges than any other president in U.S. history. During his first two years in office, 58 percent of the federal judges he appointed were women and minorities (O'Brien 2000, 114).

President Clinton also assembled a seven-member race-initiative advisory board, which consisted of one Republican, former New Jersey governor Thomas H. Kean; two other whites, Robert Thomas and William Winter; one Asian American, Angela E. Oh; one Latina, Linda Chavez-Thompson; and two African Americans, Chairman John Hope Franklin and the Reverend Dr. Suzan D. Johnson Cook. When he announced its formation in June 1997, he promised not that the advisory board would solve the nation's racial divisions but that "a national dialogue on race" would take place. Eventually, Clinton and the advisory board hoped, race relations would improve and economic and educational disparities among whites and minorities would decrease. After fifteen months of approximately 300 meetings, the board issued a 229-page report, which recommended that efforts be undertaken to improve educational achievement among Latinos, increased investment take place in inner-city and rural communities, money be allocated to reduce class sizes in schools, the minimum wage be increased, television shows portray minorities in a more positive light, and more federal funds be devoted toward school construction and improvement. In addition, conferences, forums, roundtable discussions, and town meetings were held in many cities and on many college campuses on a variety of topics concerning race and inequality.

President Clinton's effective campaigning, symbolic politics, and commitment to diversity attracted minorities as his greatest supporters during his 1996 reelection campaign and later during the impeachment hearings. Despite the Whitewater, travelgate, and filegate scandals, minorities enthusiastically supported Bill Clinton's reelection in 1996 by again voting for him in large numbers and having a high turnout rate (Knight Ridder Newspapers 1998, A10). Clinton received 80 percent of the black vote, 65 percent of the Latino vote, and 47 percent of the Asian vote in 1996. Democratic candidates have garnered approximately 70 to 80 percent of the black vote since the early 1960s; however, President Clinton received higher percentages of the Latino and Asian vote in 1996 than had any other Democratic or Republican presidential candidate in U.S. history. After he took office, minorities were more likely than whites to attribute to the Clinton administration the stable economy, a decrease in the nation's crime rates, a decrease in poverty and unemployment rates, efforts for improved race relations, and increases in median incomes, the minimum wage, and homeownership rates (Johnson 1998, A12). Because many low- and middle-income minority communities experienced economic recovery and greater levels of prosperity during the Clinton administration than during previous administrations, most were generally pleased with his performance in office. For example, a 1993 *USA Today*/CNN/Gallup poll found that 57 percent of blacks and 31 percent of whites approved of Clinton's economic agenda, while 55 percent of blacks and 44 percent of whites commended Clinton's efforts to improve race relations (Nichols 1993, 6A). Also, many minorities believed that Clinton had been the victim of a right-wing conspiracy since the earliest days of his presidency mainly because of his commitment to diversity.

## Minority Discontent with the Clinton White House

From 1992 to 1994, a Democratic president governed with the benefit of a Democratic majority in Congress. As a result, Clinton should have been able to secure a greater level of congressional support for his proposals than had Reagan or Bush. However, he failed to capitalize on this opportunity and others during his first two years in office.

In 1992 President Clinton had the ability to fill 109 federal judicial posts. Although he appointed a record number of minorities and women as federal judges, he had not filled most of these vacancies by the end of his first year in office. In addition, he was plagued by low approval ratings and the Whitewater scandal, and his attempt at health-care reform failed during his first two years in office. David O'Brien described Clinton's difficult first two years in office: "In his first two years as President, Clinton failed to communicate a clear and convincing political vision as a 'New Democrat' as well as to move quickly to secure a strong staff to carry out that vision. Nowhere was Clinton's failure to fill crucial positions to carry out policies more evident than in his dealing with the Department of Justice (DoJ). Opportunities to forge a new legal policy in his first two years were forfeited and lost irretrievably. Mistakes and mismanagement were only part of the story, however, though they tell much about the importance of a President's first two years in office and how they constrain later opportunities" (O'Brien 2000, 111).

During the last two years of President Clinton's first term, partisan divisions were more apparent after Clinton was forced to compromise with the Republican majority in Congress. When the White House and Congress are in the hands of different parties, ideological, partisan, and other divisions result in a system of divided government (Rose 1993, 462). From 1968 to 1992, Republican candidates won five of six presidential elections and had to govern along with majority Democratic Congresses. During the 1994 midterm elections, the Democrats lost their majorities in both Houses of Congress for the first time in 40 years. The Republicans won a majority in the U.S. House of Representatives for the first time since 1954 and elected the most members since 1946 (230 Republicans, compared with 204 Democrats and 1 independent) (Burnham 1996, 365). Republicans reelected all 157 of their incumbents who sought reelection in Congress and won 24 of 36 gubernatorial races (Democrats won 11; independents, 1) (Jones 1996, 44). In the elections for the U.S. House of Representatives, Democrats lost 35 of 225 races that had incumbents running for reelection and 21 of 31 open seats vacated by Democrats (Burnham 1996, 365). The backlash occurred primarily among white male voters: "The angry white male was said to feel left out and left behind, especially by the president's emphasis on such issues as gays in the military; affirmative action, which might help blacks and women; the North American Free Trade Agreement (NAFTA), which was widely seen as hurting the bulk of traditional blue-collar working men; his large number of controversial appointments, especially of women and minorities; his failure on the health care plan, spearheaded by the dreaded Hillary Rodham Clinton; and his inability to follow through on promises to cut taxes and 'end welfare as we know it'" (Sapiro and Canon 2000, 207–8).

Because of divided government and other constraints, President Clinton failed to support controversial judicial nominees and cabinet members in an effort to avoid conflicts with Republicans and more readily compromised his stances on issues of concern to liberals, minorities, and the poor—key members of his electoral coalition. Many African American and liberal white members of Congress were outraged when he signed the Personal Responsibility and Work Opportunity Reconciliation Act in July 1996. These lawmakers agreed that the welfare system needed to be reformed but believed that the denial of food stamps to some single and unemployed adults, elimination of Aid to Families with Dependent Children (AFDC), five-year lifetime limit for welfare recipients, state work requirements, and other state restrictions would place an undue hardship on poor women and children (Polakow 1999, 171-

172). Senator Edward M. Kennedy (D-Mass.) called an earlier version of the law "legislative child abuse" (Case 1997, 36). Peter Edelman, who resigned from the Department of Health and Human Services in protest, described the welfare law as "the worst thing Bill Clinton has done" (Case 1997, 36). Only two of the thirty-nine black members of Congress voted for the welfare-reform legislation, despite poll showings that 58 percent of black voters and 66 percent of white voters supported it (Neal 1998, C2). On the issue of crime, President Clinton supported the controversial "three strikes you're out" provision of a crime bill requiring that persons receive sentences of imprisonment without parole after committing three violent federal crimes. Most of the black members of Congress opposed this provision, although 73 percent of black citizens supported it (1998, C2).

The Clinton administration was also accused of practicing a double standard in the award of foreign aid to black and white countries during times of conflict and in the granting of asylum to black and white refugees. In 1994 the U.S. provided very little assistance to the African country of Rwanda during its ethnic civil war in which several hundred thousand people were murdered within months; children were left orphaned; and citizens lacked food, clean water, and adequate medical care. Yet the United States sent clean water, doctors, food, NATO troops, and refugee flights to Kosovo during its ethnic war. During his 1992 presidential campaign, Clinton criticized George Bush for returning Haitian refugees back to their homeland and asserted, "I wouldn't be shipping those poor people back" (Drew 1994, 417). However, the Clinton administration later began the practice of repatriating Haitian refugees, while allowing white refugees to remain in the United States. He ended this practice eventually, after receiving criticism from the Congressional Black Caucus and from Randall Robinson, the head of the TransAfrica Forum.

Even before the Republican victories in 1994, Clinton had failed to support controversial minority nominees. During the summer of 1993, he angered members of the Congressional Black Caucus, led by its chairman Kweisi Mfume (D.-Md.), NAACP Executive Director Benjamin Chavis, Rev. Jesse Jackson, and other African Americans when he withdrew the nomination of Lani Guinier, an African American civil-rights lawyer and University of Pennsylvania law professor, for the position of assistant attorney general for civil rights. Conservative organizations, Jewish groups, and some members of the Senate Judiciary Committee opposed Guinier's nomination because of her controversial views on minority voting rights. The president eventually withdrew her nomination, saying that he had only read some of her writings shortly before the withdrawal (Drew 1994, 332). Soon thereafter, a *USA Today/ CNN/Gallup* poll indicated that Clinton's approval rating among blacks had fallen from 75 percent to 61 percent. Fifty-five percent of blacks and 31 percent of whites disapproved of Clinton's position on the Guinier nomination (Nichols 1993, 6A).

The Clinton administration experienced a high rate of turnover of cabinet members, many of whom were minorities, who either resigned voluntarily or at Clinton's request. From 1994 to 1998, U.S. Attorney General Janet Reno appointed seven independent counsels to investigate allegations of corruption by some of President Clinton's cabinet members, including African Americans Ron Brown (Secretary of Commerce), Joycelyn Elders (U.S. Surgeon General), Mike Espy (Secretary of Agriculture), and Alexis Herman (Secretary of Labor), and Latino Secretary of Housing and Urban Development Henry Cisneros (Novak 1998, 36). Clinton asked for the resignation of Espy in October 1994 and of Elders in December 1995. Cisneros resigned in 1996, and Hazel O'Leary chose not to return as Secretary of Energy during Clinton's second term.

Finally, Clinton failed to reach out to other minority groups, especially to the growing Latino electorate. The next section of the chapter discusses the consequences of this neglect of Latino voters for future Democratic presidential candidates. Although he appointed Latinos, Asian Americans, and Native Americans in key administrative, cabinet, and judicial posts, he selected a much larger number of African Americans. In addition, Clinton's race initiative emphasized the conflicts among blacks and whites. Only one Asian American, one Latina, no Native Americans, and no white females served on the seven-member committee.

At other times, Clinton's measures and proposals failed to benefit Latinos as expected. The North American Free Trade Agreement (NAFTA), for example, resulted in a loss of jobs in some trade-related industries and environmental problems near the U.S.–Mexican border. Although the Clinton administration assured Latino communities that government programs would alleviate these problems, such did not occur, to the dismay of the Congressional Hispanic Caucus. In November 1997, sixteen Hispanic Democrats drafted a letter of protest to the president because of his failure to aid workers and communities disadvantaged by NAFTA. This action provided evidence that Latinos and other minorities at times were disappointed with Clinton's actions.

## The Legacy and Implications of the Clinton Presidency

Richard E. Neustadt defined the concept of presidential leadership in *Presidential Power*: "In the U.S. we like to rate a President. We measure him as 'weak' or 'strong' and call what we are measuring his 'leadership'" (1960, 69). Several factors must be considered when evaluating whether a president has exhibited strong leadership during his two terms in office. Neustadt defined a successful president as one who had "taken charge" in Washington. In "Evaluating Presidents" Richard Rose stated that a successful president managed to find the right "fit between intentions and political conditions" (Rose 1993, 477). In other words, these presidents had the ability to fulfill campaign promises and secure congressional support for their legislation despite the constraints they faced.

In order to evaluate whether President Clinton will be perceived as a success or a failure in the area of racial politics, one must define what constitutes success in this area. In other words, what do minorities want from the president of the United States? It is difficult to answer this question; the interests of various minority groups are very distinct. The interests of "fourth-wave immigrants"—Hispanics and Asians—differ from those of African Americans. The former are more focused on issues such as bilingualism and immigration, which little concern most African Americans. In addition, because of the diversity within each group, generalizations are risky about African Americans, Asian Americans, Latinos, and Native Americans. The policy preferences of low- and middle-income blacks and of Mexican, Puerto Rican, and Cuban Americans differ, as do those of Chinese, Japanese, and Vietnamese Americans.

Despite these differences, the literature in racial politics has illustrated that minorities have some common desires of the president. First, they want to believe that he has a commitment to alleviating social problems such as crime, poverty, and unemployment (Harrigan 1993; Perry and Parent 1995). If the president has a concern about these and other societal problems, other political figures and members of the federal government will as well. Lucius Barker, Mack Jones, and Katherine L. Tate described the president's ability to influence others: "The powers at the president's disposal are indeed impressive, and so blacks tend to focus on the person and the office in their struggle for social justice. In part, this concentration can be seen as an attempt to use the symbolism of the presidency to capture broad public attention and support" (1998, 307).

Minorities cast their most substantial bloc votes for Presidents Lyndon B. Johnson, Jimmy Carter, and Bill Clinton because these presidents addressed social ills that disproportionately affected people of color. The Johnson administration waged a "war on poverty" and strongly supported civil-rights legislation such as the Civil Rights Act of 1964 and the Voting Rights Act of 1965. The Carter administration addressed the fiscal crisis in New York and other Northeastern and Midwestern cities by developing a National Urban Policy proposal, which devoted federal funds to and encouraged industries to invest in these cities (Harrigan 1993, 10). President Clinton sponsored crime, healthcare, and welfare reform legislation and created an empowerment-zone program during his two terms in office. Also, the goals of his 'New Market Initiatives' were to reduce poverty, bring about economic development in areas such as Appalachia; East St. Louis, Illinois; Indian reservations; the Mississippi Delta; and Watts, California (Chen 1999, A15).

In addition, scholars in racial politics have found that minorities desire political power and inclusion in the governing process (Barker, Jones, and Tate 1999, 303–39; Browning, Marshall, and Tabb 1997, 3–14). John J. Harrigan, in *Political Change in the Metropolis,* defines political power as "the extent that a given group or individual has influence on what a government does or does not do" (1993, 12). As stated earlier, Bill Clinton has devoted many efforts toward African American inclusion throughout his presidency, but has made fewer efforts for the inclusion of Latinos, Asian Americans, and Native Americans. Clinton appointed two Latinos to his fourteen-member cabinet in 1992, Secretary of Transportation Federico Peña and Secretary of Housing and Urban Development Henry Cisneros, and in 1996 one Latino, Secretary of Energy Bill Richardson (Barabak 1998, A1). He has also supported issues of concern to minority communities—such as affirmative action, bilingual education, and self-determination for Puerto Ricans.

President Clinton's failure to encourage the mobilization and naturalization of Latino immigrants, however, will have major implications for Democratic presidential candidates in the future. Louis DeSipio, in *Counting on the Latino Vote: Latinos as a New Electorate,* recommended that President Clinton and other Democratic political figures place more of an emphasis on the naturalization and voter registration of Latino immigrants as a long-term strategy to enhance the political power of both Latinos and of the Democratic Party (1998). In 1990, approximately 21 million Latinos resided in the United States. (Harrigan 1993, 147); DeSipio's research found that approximately 4.2 million Latinos voted in the 1992 presidential election. Because he garnered a substantial vote from Latinos, Bill Clinton carried the states of Arizona, Colorado,

Florida, Illinois, New Jersey, New Mexico, New York, and Texas (de la Garza and DeSipio 1996; DeSipio 1998). However, 10.5 million Latino adults failed to participate in the 1992 election. Many had a lack of interest in voting; others were unable to vote because of a lack of citizenship.

According to DeSipio and Rodolfo de la Garza, President Clinton did not specifically direct any aspect of his campaign to Latino voters but addressed economic issues that concerned them generally. During his 1996 campaign, Clinton courted white suburban swing votes rather than Latino votes. The failure of Democratic candidates, state Democratic parties, and the national party to increase and mobilize the Latino electorate has been described as a "missed opportunity" that must be taken advantage of in the future (Avalos 1996, 95).

The next Democratic presidential candidate will benefit from the balanced budget and economic surplus of Bill Clinton's two terms and the fact that both minorities and whites believed themselves better off economically under President Clinton than they had been under former president Bush. A 1995 report from the U.S. Department of Commerce revealed that the national poverty rate fell in 1994 for the first time in five years, from 15.1 percent in 1993 to 14.5 percent in 1994. The incomes of female-headed households increased from $19,020 in 1993 to $19,872 in 1994. Although minor, this marked the first income gain for female-headed households since 1987. The poverty rate among whites fell from 12.2 percent in 1993 to 11.7 percent in 1994, and among blacks it decreased from 33.1 percent in 1993 to 30.6 percent in 1994. However, in the same time period poverty rates remained unchanged for Latinos—30.7 percent—as well as for Asians and Pacific Islanders —4.6 percent. Finally, the report found African Americans the only racial group to experience gains in median household incomes, which rose from $20,032 in 1993 to $21,027 in 1994 (Peterson 1995, A4).

The next Democratic presidential candidate will also benefit from Clinton's ability to assemble a multiracial electoral coalition among voters of all classes. Clinton has been a shrewd campaigner, so successfully overcoming his personal shortcomings that he has often been called "Slick Willie." In the future, presidential candidates will have to develop similar kinds of coalitions in their efforts to win office and to remain there during times of potential disgrace.

The numerous scandals during Clinton's two terms and his House impeachment may have a detrimental effect on the next Democratic presidential contender. A 1999 survey by the Pew Research Center found that Vice President Al Gore's popularity declined because of his campaign finance problems.

Also, many Americans had grown tired of the Clinton administration's controversies and associated Gore with Clinton. Fifty-eight percent of the survey's participants had viewed Gore favorably in December 1998, but that percentage fell to 47 percent in April 1999. Polls indicated that women preferred Republican Governor George W. Bush of Texas over Gore by a margin of 52 percent to 42 percent, while Latinos favored Bush by a margin of 51 percent, compared to 38 percent for Gore (Connolly 1999, A11; Simon 2000, A5).

The next Democratic presidential candidate may also be harmed by President Clinton's failure to appoint a large number of liberal judges (O'Brien 2000, 130). The legacy of former Presidents Reagan and Bush lay in their judicial appointees, who, after their appointers had left office, continued to provide a conservative interpretation of the law. Clinton, on the other hand, appointed moderate and conservative judges so that he could avoid Republican opposition and lengthy confirmation battles. Moreover, many described Clinton's Initiative on Race as a disappointment, partly because the president was unable to lead the initiative, due to his preoccupation with his personal problems. Numerous ideological conflicts existed among the advisory board members, who disagreed about ways to mitigate conflicts among blacks and whites without ignoring the plight of the nation's rapidly growing Latino and Asian populations. The white members of the advisory board desired to focus on the civil rights gains which have occurred since the 1960s while the African American members preferred to highlight the educational, housing, income, and social inequities which still exist largely along racial lines. These disagreements have resulted in numerous delays for the publication of a planned book on the race initiative's observations. Because of these shortcomings, President Clinton's administration and legacy have been weakened—as has the institution of the presidency.

## Racial Politics and the Impeachment Hearings

Americans' opinions on the Clinton impeachment hearings depended largely on whether they were pleased with his performance as president. His supporters viewed the hearings and House impeachment as evidence of a mean-spirited attempt to overturn the election of a relatively popular president. They believed that U.S. Representatives Henry Hyde (R.-Ill.), Bob Livingston (R.-La.), and other Congress members seeking Clinton's impeachment and removal from office had always been resentful about his 1992 victory and 1996 reelection, jealous of his popularity during the latter half of his first term and the earliest years of his second term, and determined to ruin his political career (Lewis 1998, 5). Supporters also viewed it as ironic that many of the individuals who had demanded that Clinton resign from office were also guilty of personal indiscretions. Clinton's critics perceived his imprudence in the Oval Office as a national embarrassment. They believed that he permanently damaged the institution of the presidency. Also, his military actions during the height of the impeachment debates were questioned as attempts to divert the nation's attention from his personal scandals.

William Jefferson Clinton's impeachment in the U.S. House of Representatives has major implications for racial politics in America, as shown by the almost universal support the president received from the African Americans, Asian Americans, Latinos (to a lesser extent Cuban Americans), and Native Americans in Congress. After the Republican members of Congress refused to censure rather than impeach President Clinton, the Democratic members walked out of the Capitol in protest. All of the black and Latino Democrats in the House of Representatives participated. The black House vote for impeachment then split along party lines, with all the black Democrats in the House voting "no" on all four articles of impeachment. U.S. Representative J. C. Watts (R.-Okla.), the only black Republican in Congress, voted "yes" on all four. Latino Congress members showed the same level of solidarity in support of President Clinton; only one voted "yes" on any of the articles of impeachment. No Asian American or Native American House representative favored the impeachment of President Clinton.

The members of the Congressional Black Caucus supported Clinton because of the symbolic and substantive benefits black America had received during his two administrations. Also, because most of their constituents had been pleased with the president's performance, its members could not withhold their support. Despite their differences with President Clinton on the issues of crime, foreign policy, welfare reform, and the Lani Guinier nomination, all of the members of the Caucus opposed his impeachment. Their backing was so unwavering that at their 1998 annual dinner, Clinton thanked them "for standing up for me and understanding the true meaning of repentance and atonement" (*St. Louis Post-Dispatch* 1998, A12).

President Clinton earned high approval ratings among all Americans, but polls indicated that his support was higher among blacks than among whites. A poll by the Pew Research Center for the People and the Press, taken just before Kenneth Starr's report was released in September 1998, showed Clinton with an 88-percent job-approval rating among African Americans, considerably higher than the 61 percent approval rating he received from whites. The poll did not provide the rating among Latinos; however, political analysts have claimed that two of every three Hispanic Americans approved of Clinton's job performance in 1998 (Shepard 1998, A16).

The impeachment of the president who arguably had done more for minorities than any recent predecessor confirmed the beliefs of many people of color that conservatives will destroy political figures who encourage diversity in any way. In "Bill Clinton As Honorary Black," black columnist Ida E. Lewis gave one explanation as to why the majority of African Americans did not support the removal of President Clinton: "Black people know that men's (and women's) lying about sex is an ancient practice. They know that the Starr investigation is much less about sex than about overturning an election. . . . The right wing powers-that-be are working overtime to write the final chapter of The Niggerization of Bill Clinton. . . . The right wing has not rested in its shameless resolve to drag Clinton, his wife, and, unforgivably, their daughter, through the electronic gutters of America. In the process they are decapitating the office he holds, and the constituencies whose will he embodies, as surely as the good ole boys down in Jasper, Texas, last June reduced decency, humanity, and compassion to bloody clumps of torn flesh littering a county road" (1998, 5). Although the House impeachment will probably not change the views of minorities and others who admire the president, it will affect his legacy.

## Conclusion

This chapter explained the ways in which President Clinton used his presidency to place the interests of minorities on the national agenda but also pointed out his willingness to compromise and renege on issues of concern to minorities when it was politically expedient. In the future, blacks will remain loyal to the Democratic presidential contender. It is undisputable that they have supported Democratic candidates since the 1960s, but it is questionable whether the black voter turnout rate will be high enough to sway the election in favor of the Democratic nominee. In addition, it is unclear whether Latino voters in the future will provide the same level of loyalty to the Democratic party as blacks have traditionally. Latinos approved of President Clinton's job performance, but have also shown more willingness to vote for Republican candidates than African Americans have. During the twenty-first century, the Latino population will probably outnumber the black population. Thus, it will be imperative for the Democratic party to naturalize and mobilize Latinos. It will also be imperative for Latinos and Asians to naturalize and mobilize the members of their racial groups so that they can translate their growing population into a political base, as African Americans have.

Finally, when assessing the Clinton administration's impact on racial politics, one must question whether minorities, especially African Americans, gained influence in the political process as a result of the Clinton presidency. According to polls and surveys, they were very pleased with the president's attempts to include them in his governing coalition. Also, one must ask what the future is for African Americans, Asian Americans, and Latinos in American politics as a result of the Clinton presidency. Minorities will continue to demand that members of their groups be represented in administrative, cabinet, and judicial positions; that the president address issues of concern to their communities, especially to their more disadvantaged members; and that the president take a position on controversial issues in which Americans are divided along racial lines. Despite his mistakes and personal shortcomings, President Clinton made a significant and relatively positive impact on racial politics in America.

CHAPTER 12

# THE CLINTONS AND GENDER POLITICS

BARBARA BURRELL

Presidential gender politics is a multidimensional phenomenon involving the voting behavior and policy preferences of men and women and the context in which divisions between the sexes become a focal point of presidential campaigns. It also concerns the actions of the president while in office, notably the extent to which the president appoints women to leadership positions in the administration. A third area of presidential gender politics is the administration's policies aimed at maintaining women as a constituency and public relations efforts to make sure that message is heard.

This chapter examines how the Clinton administration acted toward constituencies in terms of women and of men, investigates the extent to which it attempted to exploit the contemporary phenomenon of gender politics, and considers what may be the long-term impact of the Clinton administration regarding both gender politics and women gaining greater representation in political leadership. The Clinton presidency has made women more visible in political leadership positions, most notably by appointing the first female secretary of state and the first female attorney general. This administration has also produced a stream of initiatives aimed at making this presidency appear as responsive as possible to the special concerns of women. Bill Clinton viewed women as a supportive constituency (especially after the 1994 election), and indeed women reelected him president in 1996, as discussed below.

His sexual escapades, however, weakened support for Democratic presidential candidates in the 2000 election. The sexual politics of his personal actions will tarnish his legacy as a president who advanced political, economic, and social equality for women.

## Gender Politics and the Clinton Presidency

In media characterizations Bill Clinton has been declared the first feminist president and America's first "woman" president (see Stark 1996; Kiefer 1999). The Clinton administration has been distinctive in its focus on gender politics as a major political theme. With the help of the First Lady, Bill Clinton made women's and children's issues a prime focus of his administration's policies and activities. The first piece of legislation President Clinton signed into law was the Family and Medical Leave Act, which enables workers to take up to twelve weeks of unpaid leave to care for a new baby or ailing family member without jeopardizing their job. (While in office, former president Bush had vetoed a family medical leave bill.) Throughout the years of the Clinton administration, following the passing of that law, a fairly steady stream of legislative initiatives, executive orders, and White House conferences occurred that focused on government as an agent for helping women and children.

Clinton also broke the barrier against the appointment of women to the inner cabinet and appointed the second woman to the Supreme Court. He substantially increased the number of women in appointive, administrative, and staff positions in the executive branch and the Office of the White House. Women, in turn, helped reelect Bill Clinton president in 1996. Through his focus on the government as an agent for helping families in ways particularly attractive to women, Bill Clinton attempted to blunt the "family values" message of conservative politicians. As he said during the 1992 campaign, "We don't need an administration that talks about family values, we need an administration that values families" (Mathis 1992; A1). He would then cite his potential plans for family-leave, health-care, welfare-reform, job-training, and other such legislative areas. Bill Clinton's rhetorical style and approach to communication, at least anecdotally, seemed to reinforce his policy connection to women. He presented "a listening, empathetic, some would say 'touchy-feely' approach that appeals to many women voters" (Kiefer 1999, 2). He made women feel that he identified with their problems and knew how to do something about them. The combination of Clinton's politics and open style created a rapport with women voters unique in the modern presidency

(1999). They then stood by him in the dark days of revelations concerning his sexual escapades. In the 1998 American National Election Study more women than men said Clinton made them feel hopeful (57 percent to 52 percent).[1]

In the town-hall meetings that were his preferred method of communicating with the people, Clinton developed a mediated conversational style that made folks think that they knew and understood him and that he knew and understood them. These meetings offered the president a unique opportunity to use a personal, intimate conversational style to connect with the public. He would often use the inclusive first person plural pronoun, "we," suggesting an "other-centered" discourse. Such usage created a relationship between the president and his audience, uniting them in common purpose. Clinton gave the impression that he and the public together would find solutions to problems or at least discuss possible ones (Denton and Holloway 1997). In the town-hall meeting settings "people told him their problems and he would bite his lip; occasionally a tear would appear. He would express his sympathy with their plight—and then spell out some program he had proposed that would deal with it. Clinton's empathy, actual or feigned, became one of his trademarks" (Drew 1994, 95).

To fully capture the gender politics aspects of the Clinton administration, we need to include in our assessment First Lady Hillary Rodham Clinton, a leader in advocating and promoting gender equality and women's rights policies during her husband's administration. She is linked to the women's rights community domestically and internationally and has been an important factor in the symbolic and substantive politics of the administration on issues of gender. She has also been a "lighting rod" for critics of the administration.

### The Clinton Administration and Public Policy

Bill Clinton emphasized his administration's support for using government to promote family concerns and women's issues. The Clinton White House championed many pieces of legislation aimed specifically at women, such as the Violence Against Women Act, and increased funding for women's health research. The Clinton administration also sought broader legislative actions that would use government to promote family concerns in areas such as education, pensions, health care, employment, and gun control—which would especially resonate with women. Further, Clinton took a strong pro-choice stance on the abortion issue, including such actions as reversing the "Gag Rule" that had limited the information federally funded family planning clinics could give to women and vetoing the so-called partial-birth abortion bans. (While men and women have not differed in their opinions regarding this issue— that is, it has not been a gender-gap matter—it has been a central concern for women's-rights groups and an area of difference among male and female Republican activists.)

The 1994 midterm election created a Republican majority in both houses of Congress for the first time in four decades. Men provided the Republicans with their victory. In that election men voted Republican by a margin of 57 percent to 43 percent.[2] They cost the Democrats control of Congress. Turnout among women was the lowest since 1974. Women represented 54 percent of the drop-off voters in 1994, that is, people who voted in 1992 but not in 1994. Those who were particularly likely to have dropped out were from the Democratic base of voters (48 percent were non-college-educated women). In a follow-up poll, among those women who voted in 1992 but not in 1994, Bill Clinton held a 33 point lead over Republican Bob Dole (Jacobs 1996). Winning those individuals back as voters was key to a Clinton reelection victory. Thus, in 1995 the Clinton administration intensified its public relations efforts aimed at women (Barnes 1995, 427).

White House events in 1995 included a ceremony in April announcing $26 million in grants to combat violence against women (part of a new program authorized under the Violence Against Women Act), an Early Child Development and Learning Conference, the White House Conference on Child Care, a roundtable on pay equity, a special announcement publicizing recommendations to "make work better for women," and an event in October to highlight domestic violence. At the latter affair, President Clinton called domestic violence an "American issue, not just a woman's issue. . . . This is a children's problem and it's a man's problem" (Devroy 1995, A8). He directed federal agencies to run programs that would raise awareness of domestic violence as a national problem. Both Clintons were very visible at these events.

In 1995 President Clinton created the White House Office for Women's Initiative and Outreach to showcase his administration as being "pro-woman" and "pro-family." The Office's website highlights eight areas in which the administration took initiatives aimed at increasing equality for women, promoting economic opportunities for them and helping them care for their families: expanding economic opportunities, caring for the country's children, investing in education and training, improving national health, making homes and communities safer, promoting reproductive-health services for women, strengthening equal-employment protections, and generating more business opportunities for women. In 1996, the Office held roundtables across the country on women's issues.

Among Clinton's legislative proposals have been bills that would ban workplace discrimination against parents, an equal-pay initiative—the paycheck fairness act—and a forty-eight–hour hospital stay for new mothers. Citing that women earned seventy-five cents for every dollar men did, Clinton in his equal pay initiative proposed that funds be included in the fiscal year 2000 budget for the Labor Department and the Equal Employment Opportunity Commission to identify wage discrimination, to educate employers about discrimination and train qualified women in sectors where few women traditionally work. He also called on Congress to pass legislation that would provide damages as remedies for equal-pay violations and put gender-based wage discrimination on an equal footing with wage discrimination based on race or ethnicity.

In 1999, he introduced legislation to expand the reach of the Family and Medical Leave Act. In July of that year, he once again "played the gender card" (to quote Tom Brokaw on the NBC's *Nightly News*) and "enlist[ed] women in the Medicare fight" (*Capital Times* 1999). He (and Hillary) held a White House event to argue that Republican tax cuts would jeopardize Medicare and consequently disproportionately hurt older women. They highlighted a study by the Older Women's League, which showed that women rely on Medicare more than men do. Thus, a central feature of the Clinton administration was its continuous and activist record on public policies aimed at women.

## Appointments in the Clinton Administration

Thirty percent of all judicial appointments in the Clinton administration went to women (compared with the Bush administration, in which 19 percent of the federal judgeship appointments were to women) (Idelson 1993, 318). As of 1997, sixty women had been appointed to federal district and appeals courts. Six women were named to the cabinet, including the first ever as secretary of state and as attorney general. In addition, other major policy positions in the Clinton administration went to women, and women were given cabinet status in positions such as the administrator of the Environmental Protection Agency, chair of the Council of Economic Advisors, and U.S. trade representative.

Kathryn Dunn Tenpas calculated that, in its early years, 39 percent of the Clinton White House staff were women; this figure compares with 25 percent in the Bush administration. In the first two years of the Clinton administration, twenty-five women were in midlevel positions and eight were in policy/managerial positions (1997).

Numbers and percentages are only one aspect of an evaluation of an administration's efforts to integrate women into leadership positions. The manner in which women are selected is also important for building confidence in their leadership and, once appointed, in the roles they play and their visibility. Here Bill Clinton faltered; the process of appointing more women to high level positions, especially to his cabinet, was far from a flawless process and did little to make men feel confident in the administration or encourage women that their skills were valued. The process by which President-elect Clinton attempted to make his cabinet "look like America" caused problems and made the substantive qualifications of those selected appear suspect. A national coalition of women's organizations had formed to lobby for greater numbers of women in high-level policymaking positions in the administration. They flooded the transition team with resumes and then openly criticized the team for not appointing more women to cabinet positions early in the selection process. They suggested that Clinton would do no better than Presidents Reagan and Bush had done. They wanted him to break what they considered to be the "glass ceiling" of three women in the cabinet. Their criticism led to the infamous Clinton remark at a press conference in December 1992 that they were bean counters concerned only with quotas, not with competence. There was a sense, however, that his outburst was calculated to show that the women's groups could not push him around, which had been a gender concern regarding the masculinity of the executive office.

Hillary Clinton was very much involved in the appointment process; she would interview candidates after the president-elect had done so. She was "vested by her husband with selecting an Attorney General... and it was understood that the Attorney General would be a woman" (Drew 1994, 24). But here, too, Clinton stumbled in his goal of appointing a woman attorney general when potential nominees were withdrawn because of issues concerning the hiring of illegal aliens to care for their children. The image of gender discrimination in the withdrawal of their nominations was strong, given the attention focused on child-care arrangements tripping them up, an issue never raised against male appointees.

Further, the increased numbers of women appointees did not seem to directly translate into equal power and influence in the White House for women. Tenpas noted that Clinton's "inner circle has yet to include a woman" (99). And female officials in the administration in 1995 publicly challenged the gender power structure within the White House. As reported in the news media, "High-level female officials in the Clinton administration sought to form a 'Kitchen Cabinet' . . . after some of them complained that their male colleagues just didn't get it." As one official reportedly put it, "It's very hard for women in the White House to be taken seriously politically" (Anderson 1995, 6). Thus, it would appear that while the Clinton administration advanced women in the executive branch, hurdles still remain regarding power and influence. Questions remain about the extent to which the Office of the President continues to be a masculine institution. The Clinton sex scandals, too, raised concerns about how women were treated in the White House.

But one can also find examples of how women in leadership positions in the Clinton administration acted in the interest of women. Madeleine Albright as ambassador to the United Nations and secretary of state stands out here for her *Vital Voices* initiative. *Vital Voices* is a Clinton administration public/private partnership effort aimed at exploring ways of strengthening the role of women in new democracies and free-market economies. The First Lady was actively involved in this program with the secretary of state. *Vital Voices,* located within the United States Information Agency (USIA), in its website describes itself as "an ongoing global initiative that implements U.S. Secretary of State Madeleine Albright's commitment to promote the advancement of women as a U.S. foreign policy objective." Its purpose is to create "unprecedented partnerships among governments, non-governmental organizations, and the private sector to support the full participation of women in the economic, social, and political progress of their countries." *Vital Voices* sponsored a number of international conferences to launch initiatives—at which Hillary Rodham Clinton usually gave the keynote address and Secretary Albright often spoke. Madeleine Albright was also instrumental in organizing women foreign ministers to lobby the United Nations regarding the addition of a prohibition on human trafficking to a convention on international organized crime (Crossette 1999, A12). In the domestic area, Donna Shalala, as secretary of Health and Human Services, worked on women's health-care issues and child-support concerns, among other issues of special importance to women.

## The Gender Gap and the Clinton Administration

According to the Voter News Service (VNS), the gender gap in the presidential vote in 1992 was 4 percent, as measured by the difference in men's and women's votes for the Democratic candidate. Forty-five percent of women, compared with 41 percent of men, voted for Bill Clinton for president in 1992.

However, in 1996, while men divided their votes quite evenly between the president and his opponent, former U.S. senator Bob Dole, a majority of women cast their votes for Bill Clinton. The gender gap was eleven percentage points; this election not only resulted in the largest gender gap in presidential history that we know about, but it was the first in which a majority of men and women voted for opposing candidates. Fifty-four percent of women, compared with 43 percent of men, voted for Bill Clinton's reelection. Had only men voted, according to exit polls, Bob Dole would be president; 44 percent of men voted for Bob Dole, compared with 43 percent of women.

A substantial percentage of women did not vote for Bill Clinton's reelection, however. The constituency of women who were the base of Clinton's support, according to Anna Greenberg's analysis of data from the EMILY's List Vote Monitor project, which surveyed women leading up to the 1996 election, tended to be economically vulnerable women and women with working-class sensibilities. Dole tended to attract socially and economically secure women. Clinton captured the support of 89 percent of African American women, 69 percent of single mothers, 61 percent of women from union households, and 62 percent of female residents of large cities. Clinton was much less likely to attract socially and economically secure women, such as suburban women (51 percent), married women (47 percent), married mothers (45 percent), regular churchgoers (44 percent), and homemakers (37 percent) (Greenberg 1998).

Hillary Rodham Clinton helped polarize men and women regarding the Clinton administration. Figure 1 shows the relative popularity of the Clintons as measured by Gallup Poll favorability ratings. As shown, favorable impressions of Bill and Hillary closely track in Gallup polls. They rise and fall together in 1993 and 1994. Then Hillary loses favor relative to Bill in August 1995, climbs back to parity in the October 1997 poll where she obtains a favorable rating of 61 percent and he achieves 62 percent. The average of three Gallup polls taken in January 1998 as the Lewinsky scandal begins to unfold shows Hillary gaining greater favor while Bill's favorability starts to shrink. In those January 1998 polls, Hillary had an average favorability rating of 61 percent to 56 percent for Bill. At the end of 1998, 67 percent said they had a favorable opinion of Hillary compared with Bill's 56 percent. Figure 2 and Table 1 show that the gender gap in the First Lady's favorability ratings was greater than the president's gap.

Hillary was a force in the election campaigns of the Clinton presidency, which raise the question of her effect on these elections. Interestingly, given her rather controversial role in the 1992 campaign, in which there was a me-

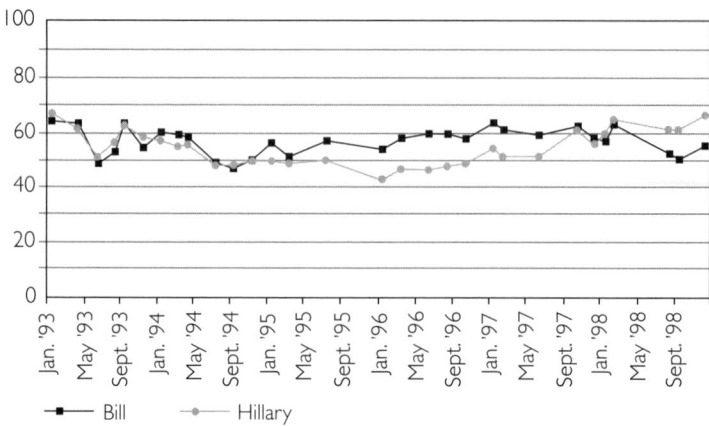

Fig. 1. Bill and Hillary: percentage favorable

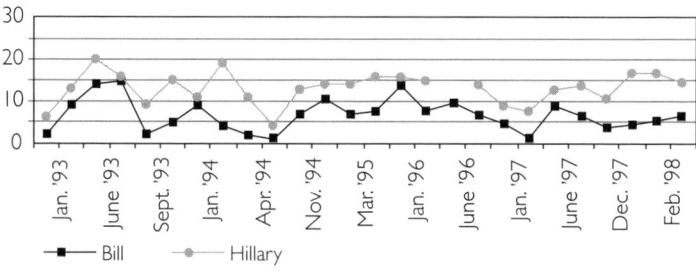

Fig. 2. Gender gap in favorability ratings (women minus men)

Table 1
Mean Favorability Scores by Sex, ANES Studies

|  | 1992 | | 1994 | | 1996 | | 1998 | |
|---|---|---|---|---|---|---|---|---|
|  | B.C. | H.C. | B.C. | H.C. | B.C. | H.C. | B.C. | H.C. |
| Men | 54.4 | 53.4 | 51.6 | 42.9 | 54.7 | 46.7 | 58.1 | 57.3 |
| Women | 57.6 | 55.7 | 56.9 | 52.4 | 62.6 | 57.4 | 58.9 | 62.2 |
| Gender gap | 3.2 | 2.3 | 5.3 | 9.5 | 7.9 | 10.7 | 0.8 | 4.9 |

*Note:* The gender gap is the difference between women's and men's mean thermometer scores.

dia reaction to the "co-presidency" (two-for-the-price-of-one) idea that Bill Clinton talked about early in the campaign and her outspokenness got her into trouble, a quantitative analysis of her effect on the vote for Bill Clinton was positive. Mughan and Burden showed that "Bill Clinton's share of the vote . . . benefited more from his wife than did George Bush's from his" (1995). Hillary's positive effect was determined through an analysis of affect for Hillary as measured in the American National Election Studies feeling-thermometer scores, controlling for other factors. In the 1996 election, Mughan and Burden concluded, Hillary was even more influential in shaping the outcome of the presidential election than she had been in 1992, even though she was less popular. Hillary Rodham Clinton "had a greater impact on the vote than either Barbara Bush or Elizabeth Dole despite attracting lower thermometer ratings on average than either of them . . .[and her] impact increased marginally in 1996" (1997). The 1996 vote analysis of Tien et al. concurs with this assessment. They showed that "first wives play an important role in the election. First wives, especially Hillary Clinton, had a strong impact on the public popularity of their husbands, and they also influenced the vote. The results suggest that first wives are important players in national politics. . . . The popularity of first wives does influence the popularity of the presidential candidates" (1999, 165).

The conclusions of each of these studies are based on the size of regression coefficients of wives' feeling-thermometer scores on the vote for their spouses, controlling for other factors considered important predictors of the vote. What this means is that the more people like a wife, the more likely they are to vote for her husband—all other things being equal. But to disentangle the causal effect here is difficult: To what extent are people voting for the man because of the woman behind him? Focusing on the strategic role they have played in presidential campaigning more meaningfully captures the effect of wives.

Wives can play a more qualitatively important or strategic role in campaigns, and Hillary Clinton was particularly effective in this regard. The importance of wives in campaigns comes principally from their role in shoring up support for their husbands in particular quarters. As Mughan and Burden have summarized the role of wives, "The trick is less to have them appeal outside their husband's partisan fold and more to have them shore up loyal support within it" (1997, 13). Hillary played that role powerfully in each election of her husband's administration.[3]

Hillary had an effect in 1996 because of her popularity with the left wing of the Democratic Party. She was used to reinforce the support Bill Clinton had jeopardized by moving to the center. As described by journalist Elizabeth Bumiller, during the 1996 campaign Rodham Clinton served as his "administration's official, oratorical liberal . . . overwhelmingly popular among the core Democratic constituencies that Mr. Clinton wants to rally for the fall [1996]." She kept a relatively low profile during the campaign but had an extensive schedule of raising money for Democratic candidates and rallying the faithful. She did the party work, building the base and campaigning for women candidates, while the President went after swing voters.

In 1998, Hillary was again a formidable force in the Democratic campaign strategy of that midterm election. She was much more visible than she had been in 1996, because of the dramatic positive change in her popularity. In that election year, she offered to attend fundraisers for House and Senate Democratic candidates, many of them challengers against incumbents, as part of the Democratic congressional and senate campaign committees' efforts. In June and July of 1998 she attended six such fundraisers. After the August debacle regarding President Clinton's relationship with Monica Lewinsky, the First Lady emerged as an energetic and popular campaigner while the president was unwelcome on the campaign trail. During the fall campaign she made a nineteen-state tour on behalf of Democratic candidates. She made more than a hundred radio and television spots for Democratic candidates and raised millions of dollars for Democratic campaigns. (In the 1996 presidential campaign she had appeared in only one commercial.) EMILY's List, in conjunction with the coordinated campaign of the Democratic National Committee, targeted women in key states who tended to vote in presidential elections and then drop out during midterm elections. Hillary Rodham Clinton signed a letter to those women, with the theme that "children's issues are bigger than politics." She was clearly seen as one who could connect with women and stimulate them to turn out to vote. The aim was not to have a repeat of 1994, when women had disproportionately dropped out of voting.

Hillary stumped especially hard for Democratic women, particularly embattled senators Barbara Boxer and Carol Moseley-Braun, in addition to visiting New York on several occasions to campaign for U.S. House member Charles Schumer against Senator Alfonse D'Amato. She visited Illinois three times, appeared in a thirty-second television advertisement, and wrote a personal fundraising letter that brought in $145,000 in the first ten days following its posting. Her efforts to shore up Democratic women candidates and energize women voters contributed to the further identification of the Clinton presidency with women and women's issues. Hillary emerged from that election as a potential candidate for national office herself.

## The Lewinsky Scandal and Gender Politics in the Clinton Administration

An initial reaction would be to view President Clinton's relationship with Monica Lewinsky and the resulting situation as part of the constellation of elements comprising gender politics in the Clinton administration. However, it is important to make a distinction between gender politics and sexual politics. For the Lewinsky affair to be a gender-related issue, it would have had to have affected at least one of the three elements discussed here as comprising gender politics—policy, appointments, and men's and women's distinctive perspectives on the President and his administration. Men and women responded similarly to the scandal, and women's support for the President did not disproportionately decline during this time period. In the 1998 American National Election Study, 75 percent of women and 72 percent of men said they approved of the job Bill Clinton was doing as president. Table 2 compares the responses of men and women to a set of questions in the 1998 ANES about how well certain character traits described Bill Clinton. Differences between the sexes were minimal.

The Lewinsky scandal may have played a role in the President's attempts to shore up his support among women—by continuing policy initiatives directed at concerns of particular interest to them in the final months of his administration. This debacle also affected gender politics, putting the President's supporters in women's rights organizations on the defensive. Among other things, conservatives framed the scandal as sexual harassment issue.

Further, and perhaps most importantly, the scandal seems, at least it did in the early stages of the 2000 presidential election, to have negatively affected the Democratic Party's advantage among women voters. Media attention on

Table 2
Men's and Women's Views of President Clinton's Character Traits, 1998 ANES
(percentage saying trait extremely or very well describes him)

|  | Men | Women |
|---|---|---|
| Strong leader | 59 | 63 |
| Honest | 21 | 19 |
| Really cares | 51 | 58 |
| Moral | 17 | 17 |

women in the 2000 election stressed their support for George W. Bush in terms of their being tired with the sexual scandals of the Clinton administration. Vice President Al Gore's campaign for the presidency, at least in its early stages, suffered from the residual effects of this affair.

This early media emphasis is well illustrated by an NBC *Nightly News* story headlined "George W. Bush appeals to women voters." According to the report, "for the first time in a long while, a Republican front-runner appeals to *women*. . . . For years, women have voted disproportionately for Democrats. But when it comes to Bush, the so-called 'gender gap' may be dead. . . . In a sweeping survey of female voters . . . 54 percent of Republican women back Bush. John McCain is second at 8 percent. And in a hypothetical match-up, Bush beats Vice President Gore among all women by 7 percentage points, and Bill Bradley by 15 points" (emphasis in original; 1999) George W. Bush then said, "Well, it's because I've got a heart that people can see and sense. I've got an agenda that's positive and optimistic." Among other things, the piece went on to quote a spokesperson for the Independent Women's forum, suggesting that women "believe him when he says. 'I want to be compassionate.' George loves his wife, obviously, and loves his mother. I think that those are things that resonate, especially with women voters, as a change from Bill Clinton" (NBC Nightly News 1999).

This last statement may be degrading to women, by suggesting that their political support for a candidate would be based on the fact that he obviously loves his mother and his wife, but its point is more the contrast made to Bill Clinton's image, which hurt the Democrats in 2000. It also shows the contextual nature in which the gender gap in American politics must be considered.

## Gender Gap in Elections

Men and women have historically diverged in their opinions on a number of public policy issues, but perhaps their views on the role of government captures most broadly the distinctive perspectives that affect their voting behavior and contribute to the gender gap of the Clinton years. Women believe in government more than men do; they are more likely to think they need assistance in carrying out the competing responsibilities for which they are held accountable. "Women are disproportionately charged with the burdens of stretching family budgets, caring for children and aging parents. So their concerns as voters are with economic stability, health care and family security" (Basu 1996, 3). The following example illustrates this gap; the American National Elections Study asked respondents the following, about the role of government in several elections: "Some people think the government should provide fewer services even in areas such as health and education in order to reduce spending. Suppose these people are at one end of the scale, at point 1. Other people feel it is important for the government to provide many more services even if it means an increase in spending. Suppose these people are at the other end, at point 7.... Where would you place yourself on this scale, or haven't you thought much about this?" (Center for Political Studies).

In 1994 and 1998, women were 11 percent more likely to opt for more governmental services than men, In 1994, 32.2 percent of women compared with 21.1 percent of men placed themselves at the high end of the scale (points 5 through 7), and in 1998, 46.7 percent of women, compared with 35.4 percent of men, placed themselves at the high end of the scale.

In the 1996 election, the Clinton campaign highlighted images and rhetoric that would identify with women and their concerns. According to the analysis of Kathleen Hall Jamieson, Erika Falk, and Susan Sherr, families and children appeared repeatedly throughout the Clinton campaign's advertisements, which used a rhetoric that cast government as the protector of women's rights, health, and families. As Jamieson and her colleagues conclude, "This rhetoric not only blunts traditional Republican attacks but also explicitly defines government as a means of empowering women" (1999, 16). Clinton's speeches more prominently featured women, children and families than did Senator Dole's, and Clinton spoke more to the empowerment of women, while Dole stressed their victimization.

## The Clinton Administration and Gender Politics

The concepts of strengths and weaknesses may not best capture the legacy of the Clinton presidency in the area of gender politics. We first have to ask, "What does it mean to be strong in the area of gender politics? The term suggests divisiveness. A strategy that focuses on gender implies a division between men and women; if you appeal to the interests of one, you appear to dismiss the concerns of the other. Bill Clinton, for instance, heightened the idea of a divide between men and women in American politics. Thus, his policies and rhetoric that played to women's interests, concerns, and emotions contributed to men feeling alienated. The 1994 election was interpreted as the "revolt of the angry white male voter," a term that was coined after the election. And as noted above, it was the votes of women that returned Bill Clinton to the White House in 1996. The problem, then, from a strength-and-weakness perspective, is that President Clinton's strategy to develop and sustain his strength among women contributed to a weakness in his support among men.

Bill Clinton's relationship with men was not totally negative; in fact, the figures and tables presented in this article show him being perceived more positively then negatively by men for the most part during his term in office. Exit-poll data from the 1998 midterm congressional election indicated that while a gender gap still existed, it had closed considerably, not so much because women moved away from voting for Democratic candidates, however, but because men moved toward them (Neal and Morin 1998). In the 1994 congressional elections, there was a ten percentage-point gender gap in the vote for Republican candidates for the U.S House of Representatives, according to the 1994 Voter News Service exit polls; 57 percent of men, compared with 47 percent of women, voted Republican. In 1998, 52 percent of men, compared with 46 percent of women, voted Republican, a six point gap (Roper Center 1999).

Differences between men and women on public policy issues were minimal in the 1998 election. On eight items asked in that year's ANES study, women were only slightly more liberal than men on seven of the issues and slightly more conservative on one issue—abortion (Table 3).[4]

Further, while Bill Clinton has certainly had a problem with building a base of support among men, he lost the male vote to Bob Dole by only one percentage point, whereas House Democrats lost the male vote by eight points. Clinton's New Democratic formula, which has stressed such themes as welfare reform, won male voters "who have eluded other Democrats" (Starobin 1997). In order to appeal to both men and women and minimize a gender gap in voting behavior, the key for future presidents is to be able to combine the image of government as helping people while at the same time helping

Table 3
Male-Female Differences on Public Policy Issues, 1998 ANES (in percentages)

|  | Percentage Liberal | |
|---|---|---|
|  | Men | Women |
| Pushing equal rights | 44.6 | 45.2 |
| Government see to a job | 32.5 | 39.0 |
| Government help blacks | 26.5 | 29.5 |
| Preferential hiring | 16.5 | 18.4 |
| School voucher system | 48.1 | 50.2 |
| Willing to use military force | 15.7 | 18.3 |
| Environmental regulation | 56.8 | 60.3 |
| Abortion | 43.6 | 40.2 |

people to help themselves. The degree of the gap has varied across elections, depending on contextual factors surrounding vote choices. The scandals of the Clinton administration have given the Republicans an opportunity to appeal to women (and men) in ways not available previously when the emphasis was more on issues than on character. It should be noted, however, that more definitive empirical accounting of people's perspectives and ultimate voice choice in the 2000 election remains to be conducted.

The actions of the Republican Party helped Bill Clinton to maintain a base of support among women. In the aftermath of the 1994 election, Republican Party leaders seemed harsh and uncaring; the public perceived the Republican Congress as being responsible for the shutdown of the federal government, which hurt people dependent on government programs, disproportionately women. There were large gender gaps in ratings of the Republican Congress and Speaker Newt Gingrich; "women disapproved of House Speaker Gingrich and his Congress, 2-1" (Basu 1996, 3). Columnist Jane Ely captured that negativity and Clinton's benefit from it in a report from one of the White House Initiative Office's roundtables in 1996: "Interestingly, and consistent with the usual gender-gap politics, a fair number of those at that roundtable were less inclined to be swayed by Clinton's tune than they were eager to get out of earshot of the awfully sour notes they think the GOPers are producing these days" (1996).

Presidential nominee Bob Dole did not deliver an appealing message to women in the 1996 election, as noted above. The long-term impact of gender politics is dependent on the politics of both parties. George W. Bush's "compassionate conservatism" was certainly an attempt to lessen the gender gap, and in the early days of the 2000 election campaign he was successful according to national polls.

In the area of gender politics, as president, Bill Clinton raised to a central place in presidential policymaking the visibility and articulation of issues of special concern to women. His administration made women more visible in advisory and policymaking roles in the executive branch; future presidents would be foolish not to recognize that change in American politics. The real legacy of the Clinton years regarding gender issues, however, is that as a result of his administration, women in leadership positions is a given, and approaches to policymaking are more naturally women-friendly. Gender politics in the future, then, may decrease as a force in American presidential politics.

We can expect women to continue to expand their numbers in political leadership positions. As of this writing, we already have had one woman win a major party's nomination for vice president (Geraldine Ferraro in 1984 on the Democratic ticket). In the early days of the 2000 presidential race, the possibility of both parties nominating a woman for vice-president was very real; women were seen as viable candidates and the presence of a woman on the ticket was a major plus for the party.

Although she withdrew from the race early in the primary season, Republican Elizabeth Dole ran a more viable campaign for a presidential nomination than had any woman previously. She withdrew not because of the difficulties of being a female candidate, but primarily because of her inability to raise money anywhere near the amount frontrunner Governor George W. Bush was garnering. (He was breaking all records and had caused other candidates to withdraw even earlier.) In some polls she was second behind Governor Bush, and she did well in an Iowa straw poll. Dole's presence and campaign was a major breakthrough for women, helping them make it through the ultimate glass ceiling of the U.S. presidency. Her viability and credibility as a candidate were important; stories of her candidacy focused not on her ability to serve as president because of her gender. Instead they were, much like tales about other candidates, traditional articles discussing her internal campaign problems and her ability to articulate a message. There were, however, also articles about her strength among women voters. This focus, although not without aspects of a gender lens in some of the reporting, was a result of the tremendous focus of the previous eight years of presidential politics and policy on women and women's issues, added to women's own efforts to increase their presence in the pipeline of political leadership.

Thus, while some elements of gender politics may lessen as a result of the Clinton years, the idea and numbers of women in political leadership will continue to grow. Clinton's legacy looms large regarding women in political leadership positions and policies to assist women in the work force, in addition to governmental attention to the fact that women are the main caregivers both for elderly parents and for children. Women's issues will not disappear from the political landscape. Further, it would be very difficult for future administrations to decrease the numbers of women, both white and ethnic minorities, appointed to leadership positions.

CONCLUSION

# AMERICAN POLITICS AFTER CLINTON

STEVEN E. SCHIER

This book's premise is that Bill Clinton's actions while president have consequences for the politics of the early twenty-first century. His legacy, while limited, is highly important. Indeed, the limits of Clinton's legacy may be the largest lesson of all about his presidency; Clinton had the misfortune to govern during a time when "institutional thickening" (Skowronek 1997, 31) was far advanced in American national government, particularly in the conduct of domestic policy. Power is now scattered across Congress, the courts, and bureaucracy in a fashion that makes its coordinated exercise by the president more difficult. Also, the influence of thousands of organized interests has reduced government's ability to make bold departures from the status quo. Any contemporary presidency is inevitably "preemptive," in Skowronek's terms, requiring presidents to "build new, personal bases of political support outside of regular political alliances and often outside of institutional politics altogether" (44).

Bill Clinton is perhaps the first president of this preemptive era. The absence of a stable, supportive political establishment throughout his presidency taxed his impressive political agility and produced an innovative postmodern style, well described by Bruce Miroff in this volume. Clinton's constantly changing personal identity seemed well suited to satisfying a public primarily focused on the pleasures of the moment. His success in overcoming scandals and impeachment produced lessons that will not be lost on his successors. Yet despite his remarkable gyrations, Clinton produced only a limited set of policy accomplishments. His modest policy legacy reflects the difficulties of governing in a preemptive era, one characterized largely by policy stasis resulting from a stable political establishment that lacked consensus on policy direction. In this conclusion, I explain the attributes of that establishment and the reasons for its existence. Later, I examine the underlying pillars of that establishment and other current national political arrangements—American prosperity at home and geopolitical hegemony abroad.

## A Permanent Establishment?

Stephen Skowronek writes of the presidency as a "battering ram" (1997, 28) that can break through established political arrangements and create new patterns of political and institutional authority. The 1990s proved a time when that ram hit an impregnable wall. In the past, "reconstructive" presidents have successfully repudiated "preestablished commitments of ideology and interest" in American politics (36). The last president to have even partial reconstructive success, according to Skowronek, was Reagan. Since then, "institutional thickening" has proceeded apace. Clinton lacked the institutional and political authority to reconstruct Washington arrangements, as much as he did try. Unlike Franklin Roosevelt, who created a strong new establishment based on party, patronage, bureaucracy, and policy, modern presidents face a Washington designed to continue business as usual regardless of the White House occupant. It is simply harder now for a President to bend Washington to his will. Instead, future presidents will have to exercise personal leadership aimed adversarially at rival, established Washington institutions, as did Clinton during most of his term.

The decline of party power contributed greatly to the institutional thickening of national governance. Electoral victories are more personal than they are party victories, and probably will remain so into the future. This allows candidates for the presidency or Congress to build their own electoral coalitions and maintain office based on a customized, individualized appeal. Voters split tickets more, as John Coleman notes in this volume, and have declining attraction to political parties as institutions (Wattenberg 1998). As a result, few officeholders see a need to renovate institutions or policies at the behest of a new president.

Another strong inducement to stasis lies in the partisan balance and behavior of Congress. Neither party has a firm grip on majority status, making coalition-building difficult because today's minority dreams of majority status just after the next election. The Congressional parties are ever more ideologically homogeneous and distinct from each other (Burden and Clausen 1998). Legislators rely on the support of party activists back home, and those activists have become more ideologically extreme in recent years (King 1997). Congressional Democrats and Republicans prefer ever more distinct agendas and constantly seek partisan advantage in lawmaking. Such a legislature is certain to frustrate many presidential initiatives in the future, just as it has in the 1990s. Clinton's health-care debacle, well assessed here by Arnold and Miroff, is the signal example of this. When deals were made, such as in the presidential-congressional compromises on budget issues in the late 1990s, neither party received much satisfaction (Harris 1999c, 10).

The proliferation of interest groups in Washington is an another aspect of "institutional thickening" that weakens the power of parties and president to direct national government (Rauch 1994; Schier 2000). At least 20,000 lobbyists ply their trade in Washington, more than ever before. Jonathan Rauch defines this as "hyperpluralism"—"an escalating spiral where groups breed more groups, and the system gradually chokes" (1994, 59). Groups provide money, voters, and policy arguments to legislators receptive to their agendas. The result is a blizzard of specific policy demands that individualistic congressional politicians frequently accommodate at the expense of broader policy departures, including those promoted by presidents with reconstructive aspirations. The presence of thousands of narrow agendas in competition for governmental attention creates a pervasive incrementalism that frustrated Clinton and will vex his successors. Proliferating interests in combat with each other, combined with divided partisan control of government, produces a policymaking "establishment" of unprecedented staying power in Washington. Though taking on the "establishment" is often popular with a cynical electorate, it has never been a tougher presidential task.

Ultimately, a president cannot oust an "old establishment" without the sustained support of the voters. In the past, firm and lasting changes in party identification produced the reconstructive presidencies of Abraham Lincoln and Franklin Roosevelt. Today, a less partisan populace is pretty much evenly split on the major issues confronting the nation (Keeter 1997). Closely contested presidential and legislative elections result, with any form of electoral volatility magnified, as in the 1994 Republican sweep of the congressional elections. The remarkable electoral turbulence of the 1990s, portrayed in my introductory chapter, produced no consistent partisan verdict, and thus no party-based assault on "old establishment" of Washington.

Elections are less conclusive for government than ever before. Instead of "new establishments" succeeding in Washington based on partisan election results, each of the major parties has established great influence over particular Washington institutions. In 1990, Republicans dominated the Presidency and the military, Democrats the Congress and bureaucracy, with the courts a continuing battleground. In 2000, the Democrats hold the presidency and bureaucracy, while Republicans hold sway in the Congress and military (Ginsberg and Shefter 1999). Future elections are unlikely to produce one-party dominance of all such institutions. Instead, Washington is apt to witness more of the same: interminable combat between institutions dominated by rival partisan/interest-group coalitions.

Permanent changes in our electoral politics make this new establishment difficult for any future president to dislodge. As partisan messages wither in effectiveness, campaigns center on the personalities and programs of particular candidates. Modern campaigns now command expensive new technologies by which they identify the crucial swing voters in elections. Polls, focus groups, and carefully composed ads aim at persuading a small but crucial set of undecided voters for each campaign. These technologies have produced two major effects: first, they have displaced partisan messages and party organizations in the electoral process; and second, they have allowed candidates to frame campaign messages that ignore increasingly large numbers of citizens (Schier 2000). Elections feature televised advertising without broad appeal, and each of the major parties relies on individualistic candidates—supported by ideological activists, interest group cash, and votes—to win office. This does not link government to major swings in public opinion as effectively as did the old partisan verdicts earlier in American history (Schier, 2000). Those verdicts made reconstructive presidencies possible, based on new "establishments" resulting from the electoral triumph of an insurgent, newly dominant party—as in the cases of Lincoln and FDR.

Elections are unlikely to dislodge the interest-saturated, split-partisan Washington establishment now in place. Given this, how is a president to lead? Future presidents will have little alternative but to employ a plebiscitary politics that uses "their public standing to compel that establishment into following their lead" (Skowronek 1997, 54). That means creating a permanent campaign to build personal support for the president. Bill Clinton's most lasting governing legacy to his successors in the early twenty-first century is surely this. As John Harris, James Guth, and Diane Harvey note in their chapters, what began as a useful reelection strategy eventually became a vital survival strategy during the impeachment controversy. Given the need to target issues carefully to keep the approval of swing voters, Clinton learned quickly, moving from the risky terrain of heath care to symbolically safe school uniforms. Partisan rule promising big policy change went in the ashcan, replaced with a governing strategy likely to be the presidential prototype for the early twenty-first century. Governing as campaigning, employing modern communication and polling technologies, can save a president from lasting defeat in the institutional combat of Washington. In return, however, the president must restrict his agenda to keep the poll ratings up. Hence the Clinton-inspired formula for future presidents: public popularity and reelection through agenda construction aimed at targeted swing voters, informed by polling and focus groups and ensured by sophisticated use of campaign technologies. We might, following Bruce Miroff, call this the postmodern political style.

## Postmodern Style and Multicultural Focus

To succeed in the often-frustrating politics of preemption, a president must above all be ideologically and tactically flexible. New coalitions and messages must be constantly improvised in the White House to keep the president popular, because popularity is essential to success in an era of plebiscitary politics. With popularity, presidential success at challenging the Washington establishment becomes more possible. In a culture in which "a cynical public is skeptical of certainties and welcoming of novelties that satisfy the satisfactions of the moment" (Miroff), new campaign and communication technologies can identify what the public wants and give the president the means to communicate it to them. This conflation of direction and facilitation, described in my introductory chapter, is the signature Clinton governing style.

How can a president get away with such a variable identity? From Washington to Reagan, the public seemed particularly to value presidents with fixed personal identities exemplifying admirable personal qualities and clear-cut partisan and programmatic visions. Clinton has none of this, yet he enjoyed great popularity. His variable identity has proved a great advantage because of the very nature of the Washington political establishment that he confronts. That establishment had no clear partisan or ideological profile but instead a muddle of conflicting power centers with a cumulative bias toward stasis. Without great political and personal flexibility, a president is likely to crash into the many barriers erected by an establishment in which power is fragmented and no partisan or programmatic governing coalition consistently prevails. A variable identity also helps in courting the public, as Harris, Pitney, and Miroff demonstrate here. An increasingly post-partisan public that is evenly divided on major issues provides no clear formula for presidential success based on a fixed program and personal identity. Without presidential transformation and improvisation, failure is more likely. A dynamic, postmodern political identity, Clinton demonstrates, can be a recipe for political success his successors can copy.

Besides presidential flexibility, a successful governing style requires a president to determine carefully the preferences of those persuadable voters in the middle who dictate election outcomes and are essential to poll popularity. Women disproportionately populate this group, possessing lower levels of political information and weaker partisan affiliations than men do. This explains much of the Clinton administration's focus on women's issues explained by Barbara Burrell in her chapter. The vital "swing faction" will increasingly include Latinos and Asians in the twenty-first century. As Sharon Wright notes in her chapter, these ethnic groups are less reliably partisan voters than are African Americans, who overwhelmingly vote Democratic and probably will continue to do so. Successful presidential politics in our era of permanent preemption will have to be not only increasingly postmodern in personal style but also increasingly multicultural in strategic focus.

## Continuing Policy Stasis?

The portrait sketched thus far gives little hint of any great possibilities for sweeping presidential leadership in the early twenty-first century. Clinton in 1997 supposedly bemoaned his inability to break into the ranks of the greatest presidents because he had not had to lead the nation through a great national crisis. Our period of peace and prosperity helps to maintain a divided and intractable Washington establishment that curbs presidential leadership abilities and ambitions. Out of this has come a policy stasis that blunts the most extreme agendas evident among the activists of either major party. As Clinton, inspired by Dick Morris, triangulated after 1994, limited, centrist compromises became the common policy output in Washington. Tatalovich and Frendreis note here that Clinton departed from the agendas of previous Democratic presidents and many Democratic activists in deemphasizing redistribution as a major domestic policy goal. This abandonment flowed naturally from the aversion of swing voters to such initiatives and from Clinton's postmodern malleability. As a result, as Peri Arnold notes, the big expansions of government called for in the 1993–1994 health-care plan vanished from the presidential and national agenda. The health-care defeat marked the end of reconstructive attempts by Clinton and a resignation to the tactical politics of preemption. Future presidents will likely face similar choices early in their terms, and Clinton provides a recipe for political success at the expense of agenda constriction.

Divided public opinion and a muddled and conflictual Washington establishment will probably prevent major domestic reconstruction by Clinton's successors. The domestic agenda in the near future will likely continue to concern a variety of regulatory issues (health care, environment, trade) of at most a middling scale, and the nagging question of managing future entitlement burdens. Despite the surging economy, Medicare is likely to face bankruptcy in the early twenty-first century. Recent upticks in health-care cost inflation make that likely. Lengthening life-spans promise to make the bankruptcy of Social Security, now scheduled for the mid-2030s, draw nearer (Pear 1999). Clinton's unwillingness to cross important interests in his own party to create long-term solutions for Medicare and Social Security marks the limits of his postmodern flexibility. On these issues, challenging the core interests of one's party coalition remains a great political risk, even for postmodern, preemptive presidents like Clinton. A lasting solution remains postponed, perhaps awaiting a crisis that will force an innovative, bipartisan way out.

If an absence of policy consensus constricts possibilities for domestic change, it also inhibits the coherence of America's foreign policy. James McCormick in this volume notes the absence of foreign policy consensus in Washington, most strikingly evident in 1999, when the Senate voted down the Comprehensive Test Ban Treaty Clinton had negotiated and the House failed to muster majority support for the administration's military action in Kosovo. But even in 1993, Congress quickly voted to withdraw troops from Somalia, after eighteen servicemen died there. Partisan hostility between President and Congress over foreign policy boiled over as it had not in previous decades. Several reasons account for this. As McCormick notes, strategic consensus in Washington over America's role in the world did not develop during Clinton's presidency. Much of the blame, he argues, lies with the administration for failing to define threats to America's security and how to address them. Also, divided government encouraged a Republican Congress to defer less to the president, particularly in the wake of the impeachment crisis.

Broader characteristics of the foreign-policy-making environment also explain Clinton's problems. With the end of the Cold War, the costs of partisanship to America's national interests are far lower. The incentives for institutional combat, ever strong in Washington, carried the day increasingly in foreign policy as the national costs of disagreement declined. The rising number of players in foreign policy, also noted by McCormick, further obstructed consensus. As the president paid uneven attention to foreign policy, officials in his administration quarreled over strategies and tactics. Proliferating interest groups pressed Congress and the administration in all sorts of disparate directions. Clinton's obsession with poll results produced yet another tug on foreign policy direction, to the point where he managed the military intervention in Kosovo with reference to overnight poll results. Many of Clinton's difficulties are likely to confront his successors because the reasons for them seem rooted in the very structure of Washington governance.

One major foreign-policy innovation for which Clinton must be credited is the focus on foreign economic policy. International trade received far more attention in the 1990s than it had in prior decades. The president's emphasis on free trade brought him bipartisan success in the congressional approval of the North American Free Trade Agreement in 1993 and of permanent normal trade relations with China in 2000. In between these events, though, the administration suffered a series of reversals on trade policy, failing to secure from Congress an expansion of NAFTA to Latin America and an extension of fast-track negotiating authority and making scant progress at the Seattle WTO trade talks in 1999. Because of his string of reversals, Clinton's legacy on trade policy remains uncertain. He has not convinced major interests within his own party—notably labor unions and environmentalists—to follow his agenda. Many entrenched Washington interests will fight future trade liberalization. Instead of creating a new consensus on trade, then, Clinton's emphasis may have politicized the issue more than ever. The large demonstrations surrounding the Seattle WTO negotiations suggest that trade liberalization still faces strong opposition, much of it from within Clinton's own party.

## Clinton and the Future

The mixed picture sketched above suggests a limited policy legacy for Clinton. John Coleman, writing in this volume, disagrees. He argues that Clinton has moved the domestic agenda toward new issues of "economic quality," involving an emphasis on environmentalism, workplace equity, wage fairness, and health-care coverage that may constitute a "new progressivism." Further, according to Coleman, parties may become more important in policy making, due to the decline of the bipartisan Keynesian consensus and the rise of economic quality issues over which the parties differ. Parties now offer contrasting views of economic issues important to many Americans, setting the stage for a possible resurgence of their importance in American politics. Reconstructive presidents whose power rests in innovative party-based governing coalitions may well reappear.

Coleman's view contrasts with those of John Pitney and Nicol Rae. Pitney views Clinton primarily as an astute preemptive tactician like Richard Nixon and sees limited reconstructive possibilities from his tenure in office. Rae finds little sign of an end to the ongoing cycle of partisan dealignment and activist extremism in the political parties. Clinton, he argues, "leaves no significant legacy to his party in electoral or policy terms."

Though Rae's assessment may be a bit too minimalist, the analysis here sides more with his and Pitney's than with Coleman's. Coleman admits that the current economic prosperity makes a public return to partisanship unlikely. Only during economic stress is this likely to happen, as it did in the 1928–1932 period, creating the lasting Democratic New Deal coalition. But the public today is far less interested in parties as the vehicles for their political allegiances. Even if economic stress occurs, it may not manifest itself in lasting new allegiance to one of the two major parties. The relatively mild economic stress of 1992 produced the largest support for a third-party candidate for President in twentieth-century history. The year 1992 seems a more instructive example in this regard than does 1932.

Coleman also raises the possibility that the established parties may not attempt to connect more broadly with a skeptical public but instead may "compete for the affections of the more limited universe of activists and financial contributors." The experience of 1998 suggests that the emphasis on the "limited universe" will prevail in the future. Both parties focused narrowly on turning out their voting base—rounding up the usual suspects—and helped to produce the lowest midterm turnout since 1942. As I demonstrate in my recent book, *By Invitation Only: The Rise of Exclusive Politics in the United States* (2000), candidates, parties, and interests have little incentive to reach beyond those already participating in the political system. The costs of inducing such people to participate are large and the benefits at best uncertain. New targeting technologies make it possible to identify the swing voters and persuade them of one's message. That is what American campaigns and, increasingly, governance are now about.

The party system, in short, will not revive—given how elections are currently practiced. Individual candidates target swing voters carefully and build personal coalitions for office. Multitudinous interests provide resources to candidates and elected officials, producing fragmentation of the governmental agenda. A postpartisan electorate chooses divided governments in which institutional combat is the norm. In the 1990s, this produced a conflictual policy stasis that seems unlikely to end soon. Future presidents may attempt reconstruction, but pervasive institutional thickening remains very much in their way.

## Tilting the Pillars

Unless, of course, the underlying pillars of the current governing system collapse. Coleman himself notes that economic stress may be necessary to make partisan government and reconstructive presidencies possible again. Bruce Miroff similarly argues that "perhaps only a dramatic economic or social issue that galvanizes the public and redraws the map of partisan cleavages will move Americans beyond postmodern detachment and irony." An economic or social trauma is indeed necessary to create more partisan politics, but it may no longer be sufficient—recall Perot in 1992. It may well be that economic stress instead will produce an improvised coalition, led by a charismatic personality, that gains control of part of the Washington political system. One-party control of both the presidency and Congress seems unlikely unless such a movement takes a durable and popular partisan form. Partisan forms do exist at present, but they do not command much attention or affection from most of the public. Instead, as Rae notes, the parties have decayed into aggregations of narrow, particular interests and strongly ideological activists. It is difficult to see the future of politics in such vehicles.

The future may produce victories more similar to Jesse Ventura's election to the Minnesota governorship in 1998 than FDR's triumph in 1932. Ventura led a personality-based repudiation of politics-as-usual and has worked in uneasy coalition with the established parties to govern the state. His reform party remains a negligible organization within Minnesota, while the two major parties retain the support of many interests and activists. Likewise, nationally it will be hard to replace the two major parties through an election, but it may be possible to displace them temporarily with a president arising from a post-partisan popular movement. Such a presidency would by definition be preemptive. Indeed, as Skowronek notes, it is difficult to see any other governing approach available to ambitious future presidents.

Another pillar that might collapse is that of American geopolitical hegemony. Such an eclipse is unlikely to occur dramatically and climactically, though. Many scholars of international relations hold that "when one state becomes too powerful, other states become fearful and unite to balance against it. That is, they build up their own military power and, if necessary, form alliances to create a strategic counterweight" (Layne 1999, 22). This may already be happening—not militarily, but economically. The failure of the Seattle WTO round came as Europe refused to drop farm trade barriers protecting its farmers, the Japanese objected to trade-dumping rules aggressively enforced by the United States, and developing nations refused to accede to American demands for international environmental and workplace standards. America's many opponents at the talks viewed the U.S. demands as attempts to perpetuate its global economic hegemony (Kahn and Sanger 1999). The politics of trade are apt to remain rocky in the twenty-first century and to produce immediate tests of America's international hegemony. This challenge, while troublesome, is unlikely to demolish the pillar of hegemony that maintains our current national governmental system.

Similarly, one seeks in vain for a rival nation likely to put together a coalition to counterbalance American military power in the early twenty-first century. China may eventually pursue such a strategy, but the present threat from any quarter seems minimal. More likely sources of international disruption may come from international terrorism or the erratic behavior of "rogue states." It is difficult to find a major and lasting shift in American politics and governance in such possibilities.

## Conclusion

America's political future will probably resemble its recent past. The early twenty-first century should witness the persistence of a post-partisan public, institutional thickening in Washington, institutional conflict in governance, and an electoral politics of narrow targeting. Bill Clinton's presidency helped to maintain these trends. Clinton proved that popular success as president can occur in a Washington that is increasingly difficult to govern, among a cynical public, and through campaigning and governing that narrowly targets swing voters. Indeed, Clinton's success at present reveals the only way to negotiate successfully the multiple obstacles that current conditions place before new presidents. Narrow agendas, limited governmental possibilities, and flexible, postmodern personal styles seem likely to appear as frequent traits among Clinton's successors. The times seem to demand it.

Then again, one or both of those pillars could collapse. Where, indeed, would we be then?

# NOTES

Chapter 3. Clinton and Foreign Policy: Some Legacies for a New Century

1. In nationwide poll results issued about the time of the Kosovo air campaign, in no instance did a majority of the public support the use of American troops in several hypothetical interventions, including one labeled "if Serbian forces killed large numbers of ethnic Albanians in Kosovo" (Rielly 1999b, 26).

2. Just as NATO authorized the air campaign in Kosovo, a divided U.S. Senate passed a resolution of support by a 58-41 margin. See "Senate Votes to Approve NATO Airstrikes over Kosovo," Mar. 23, 1999, at http://cnn.com/US/9903/23/us.ksoovo.06/. The House was supportive of American military involvement in Kosovo operations almost unanimously (424-1), but it did not address the merits of the air action at that time (Pomper 1999). See the discussion in the text below.

3. For another recent discussion of the strategy of enlargement and its implementation by the Clinton administration, see Goldman and Berman (1999, 268–82).

4. President Clinton received low ratings on foreign policy in late 1994, often lower than his overall approval rating, and he also was rated behind most post–World War II presidents in being "very successful" in foreign policy at that time (see Rielly 1999a, 98–99). Furthermore, in late 1994, only 31 percent of the public rated the Clinton administration's conduct of foreign policy as "good" or "excellent" (Rielly 1995, 16).

5. For another assessment of the foreign policy legacies of the Clinton administration, also see Goldman and Berman (1999).

6. Interestingly, on the one occasion in 1993 when the third-ranking official at the State Department raised the possibility of a reduced global role for the United States, he was quickly rebuked by Secretary of State Warren Christopher (McCormick 1998a, 220).

7. On the problem of defining a foreign policy "doctrine," especially in the new environment and some judgments on the "Clinton Doctrine" in foreign affairs, see Goldman and Berman (1999, 268–74).

8. On the key economic officials attending National Security Council meetings under the Clinton administration, see Goldman and Berman (1999, 280).

9. For an analyst's doubts about significant foreign policy restrictions, except in extraordinary circumstances, see Mueller (1999).

## Chapter 4. A Clouded Mirror: Bill Clinton, Polls, and the Politics of Survival

1. As an illustration of Clinton's problems, note that in the September 9, 1999 survey, 38 percent of those polled said they had a "favorable impression of Bill Clinton as a person," compared with 59 percent who had an unfavorable impression—even though 58 percent approved "of the way Bill Clinton is handling his job as president."

## Chapter 5. Courting the Public: Bill Clinton's Postmodern Education

My thanks to Jeffrey Hilmer for his research assistance on this article.

1. Many observers have commented on Clinton's paradoxical character and multiple personae. Clinton's postmodern strategist, Dick Morris, describes "Saturday-night Bill" and "Sunday-morning President Clinton" (1999a, xiv). His most caustic editorial observer, the *New York Times*'s Maureen Dowd, has called Clinton "the man of a thousand faces" (1997, E15).

2. These qualities distinguish Clinton from another president to whom he is increasingly compared: Richard Nixon. The most interesting psychobiographical treatment of Clinton, Stanley Renshon's *High Hopes: The Clinton Presidency and the Politics of Ambition,* pairs Nixon and Clinton, even suggesting that "'Tricky Dick' and 'Slick Willy' are characterological siblings" (1996, 118). But the dour Nixon had none of Clinton's public warmth and empathy, while the privately explosive Clinton does not appear to nurse the lasting grudges that spawned the paranoia of the Nixon White House.

3. In his memoir, Dick Morris claims that by running political ads in key swing states but not in New York City or Washington, D.C., the Clinton team flew under the media's radar: "One or two reporters—notably Alison Mitchell of the *New York Times*—realized in part what we were doing, but most had no idea" (1999a, 139). In *his* memoir, Clinton aide George Stephanopoulos confirms the Clinton/Morris strategy: "The insurance industry's 'Harry and Louise' campaign had demolished us during the health-care fight; this time we'd beat them to the punch. And Medicare was our best weapon—the only Democratic issue as potent as the Republicans' 'less government, lower taxes' mantra" (1999, 384).

## Chapter 6. The Public's View of Clinton

The author would like to thank Roger Davidson and Scott Keeter for their insightful comments and advice on this research.

1. Regression analysis examines the relationship between an independent and a dependent variable while controlling for the effects of other variables in the model. In the logistic regression results shown, effect refers to the change in probability of either approving of Clinton's job performance or believing he should not be impeached by moving the independent variable from its lowest to highest values with all other variables held constant at their means. The statistical significance of each relationship (as displayed by stars) is the probability that the relationship found in the sample is by chance and does not exist in the larger population. Coding for dependent variables—Clinton job approval: 0 = Disapprove, 1 = Approve; Impeach Clinton: 0 = Yes, 1 = No. Coding for independent variables—Economy under Clinton: 0 = Gotten worse, 1 = Stayed the same, 2 = Gotten better; Direction of country: 0 = Wrong track, 1 = Right track; U.S. position in world: 0 = Weaker, 1 = Same, 2 = Stronger; Congressional handling of allegations: 0 = Disapprove, 1 = Approve; Opinion on Starr investigation: 0 = Impartial investigation, 1 = Partisan investigation; Higher moral standards for officials: 0 = No, 1 = Yes; Adjust moral standards: 0 = Disagree strongly, 1 = Disagree somewhat, 2 = Neutral, 3 = Agree somewhat, 4 = Agree strongly; Crooked

government officials: 0 = Hardly any, 1 = Not very many, 2 = Quite a few; Party: 0 = Republican, 1 = Independent, 2 = Democrat; Ideology: 0 = Conservative, 1 = Moderate, 2 = Liberal.

Chapter 10. Clinton, Impeachment, and the Culture Wars

1. The following account is from notes made by the author, who was a participant in the day-long session. Attendees were enjoined from writing about the meeting for one year. To my knowledge, this is the only account in print of the discussions, which had little impact on campaign strategy, despite the presence of many leading Democratic campaign specialists.

2. Although the National Election Study religious items do not allow us to measure all the elements of Hunter's "orthodox" and "progressive" categories, we can develop an acceptable proxy. As there is a fairly strong tendency for "orthodox" believers to participate more in conventional religious practices than do progressives, we created a religious commitment measure comprising items on religious salience, attendance at services, frequency of private prayer, and frequency of Scripture reading. We then divided the major religious traditions into "high-commitment" and "low-commitment" groups. We have not split the African American Protestants or Jews, however. Theological divisions among black Protestants are still fairly minor; high commitment adherents do not differ consistently from those with weaker commitments. Although such religious divisions do appear among Jews, they are not as consistent or dramatic as in the larger Christian traditions, and the number of Jews in the surveys is too small for further division.

3. Unfortunately, the somewhat truncated National Election Study of 1998 does not permit us to conduct a fully comparable test of such perceptions, as it has different (and fewer) social-issue measures and a considerably smaller sample. Thus, the analysis in this section focuses on the 1994 and 1996 surveys. We have substituted the NES presidential thermometer rating for the job evaluation item used to this point. This rating is highly correlated with the job-performance item, and has the analytic advantage of a wider range. We have used only measures available in both years and run identical regressions for maximum comparability. We have also included questions tapping the historic New Deal economic issues, controlled for class and demographic variables, and included dummy variables for the major religious groups to determine if group membership has any residual impact, once *attitudes* shaped by that membership are entered directly.

4. Given the small sample in the 1998 National Election Study and the missing data on some variables, we used stepwise procedures to evaluate those measures that showed significant promise as predictors of respondents' attitudes toward removal. We examined in turn religious variables, moral traditionalism, political indicators, and personal evaluation, followed by a combined model. We report here only those variables that demonstrated significant predictive power. As the dependent variable here is dichotomous, we used logistic regression to analyze the impact of various influences on citizen attitudes. For description of this technique, see Menard 1995.

Chapter 12. The Clintons and Gender Politics

1. Women were also more likely to say that he made them angry (60 percent of the women polled, to 54 percent of the men) and had disgusted them (72 percent to 65 percent). This greater intensity of negative feelings expressed after the Monica Lewinsky affair had been revealed suggest a response to that affair rather than to policy or other leadership disagreements.

2. Female voters favored Democratic House candidates over Republicans 54 percent to 46 percent.

3. Similarly, Elizabeth Dole held meetings with conservative Christian groups to keep their support for her husband.

4. The wording of the questions was:

   a. We have gone too far in pushing equal rights in this country. (Do you agree strongly, agree somewhat, neither agree nor disagree, disagree somewhat, or disagree strongly with this statement?)

   b. Some people feel the government in Washington should see to it that every person has a job and a good standard of living. (Suppose these people are at one end of a scale, at point 1.) Others think the government should just let each person get ahead on their own. (Suppose these people are at the other end, at point 7.) And, of course, some other people have opinions somewhere in between, at points 2, 3, 4, 5, or 6. (Liberal position = points 1, 2 , 3 on scale.)

   c. Some people feel that the government in Washington should make every effort to improve the social and economic position of blacks. (Suppose these people are at one end of a scale, at point 1.) Others feel that the government should not make any special effort to help blacks because they should help themselves. (Suppose these people are at the other end, at point 7.) And, of course, some other people have opinions somewhere in between, at points 2, 3, 4, 5, or 6. (Liberal position = points 1, 2, 3 on scale.)

   d. Some people say that because of past discrimination: blacks should be given preference in hiring and promotion. Others say that such preference in hiring and promotion of blacks is wrong because it gives blacks advantages they haven't earned. What about your opinion—are you for or against preferential hiring and promotion of blacks? (Liberal position = for.)

   e. Do you favor or oppose a school voucher program that would allow parents to use tax funds to send their children to the school of their choice, even if it were a private school? (Liberal position = oppose.)

   f. In the future, how willing should the United States be to use military force to solve international problems—extremely willing, very willing, somewhat willing, not very willing, or never willing? (Liberal position = not very willing and never willing.)

   g. Some people think we need much tougher government regulations on business in order to protect the environment. (Suppose these people are at one end of a scale, at point 1.) Others think that current regulations to protect the environment are already too much of a burden on business. (Suppose these people are at the other end of the scale, a point number 7.) And, of course, some other people have opinions somewhere in between at points 2, 3, 4, 5, or 6. (Liberal position = points 1, 2, 3 on scale.)

   h. There has been some discussion about abortion during recent years. Which one of the opinions on this page best agrees with your view? 1. By law, abortion should never be permitted. 2. The law should permit abortion only in case of rape, incest or when the woman's life is in danger. 3. The law should permit abortion for reasons other than rape, incest or danger to the woman's life, but only after the need for the abortion has been clearly established. 4. By law, a woman should always been able to obtain an abortion as a matter of personal choice. (Liberal position = 4 on scale.)

# REFERENCES

Dates following URLs indicate day accessed.

ABC News/*Washington Post* poll. *Washington Post.* Sept. 8, 1999, A1.

Abramowitz, Alan I., and Kyle L. Saunders. "Ideological Realignment in the U.S. Electorate." *Journal of Politics* 60 (1998): 634–52.

Abramson, Jill. "Baby Boomers and There the Likeness Ceases." *New York Times.* Feb. 16, 1998, A11.

Abramson, Paul R., John H. Aldrich, and David W. Rohde. *Change and Continuity in the 1996 and 1998 Elections.* Washington, D.C.: *Congressional Quarterly* Press, 1999.

Adler, Renata. "Searching for the Real Nixon Scandal." *Atlantic Monthly* 238 (Dec. 1976): 76–95.

Advisory Board of the President's Initiative on Race. *One America in the Twenty-first Century Forging a New Future.* Online. Available: www.whitehouse.gov/Initiatives/OneAmerica/cevent.html. Sept. 18, 1998.

Albright, Madeleine. "Use of Force in a Post–Cold War World." *Dispatch* 4, no. 39 (Sept. 27, 1993): 665–68.

———. "Enlarging NATO: Why Bigger Is Better." In *The Future of American Foreign Policy.* 3d ed., edited by Eugene R. Wittkopf and Christopher M. Jones, 176–81. New York: Worth, 1999.

Aldrich, John H. *Why Parties? The Origins and Transformation of Party Politics in America.* Chicago: University of Chicago Press, 1995.

Allen, Mike. "Bradley Tries to Redefine the Privacy Zone." *Washington Post.* Jan. 2, 2000, A1, A12.

Anderson, Jack. "Some Clinton Administration Women Not Satisfied." *(Illinois) State Journal-Register.* Nov. 1, 1995, 6.

Arnold, Peri. "The Institutional Presidency and the American Regime." In *The Presidency Reconsidered,* edited by Richard Waterman, 215–45. Itasca, Ill.: F. E. Peacock, 1993.

———. *Making the Managerial Presidency.* 2d ed., rev. Lawrence: University Press of Kansas, 1998.

Arterton, F. Christopher. "Campaign '92: Strategies and Tactics of the Candidates" In *The Election of 1992,* edited by Gerald M. Pomper, 74–109. Chatham, N.J.: Chatham House, 1993.

Avalos, Manuel. "Promise and Missed Opportunity. The 1992 Vote in Arizona." In *Ethnic Ironies: Latino Politics in the 1992 Elections,* edited by Rodolfo de la Garza and Louis DeSipio, 95–110. Boulder, Colo.: Westview Press, 1996.

Baldauf, Scott, "Dirt-Diggers Descend on Bush Country." *Christian Science Monitor.* Aug. 23, 1999, 1.

Balz, Dan, and Ceci Connolly. "Bipartisan Poll Shows Bush Gains with Women, Hispanics." *Washington Post.* June 25, 1999, A7.

Balz, Dan, and Ronald Brownstein. *Storming the Gates: Protest Politics and the Republican Revival.* Boston: Little, Brown, 1996.

Baptist Press. "New President Is a Southern Baptist." *Baptist Courier.* Nov. 12, 1992, 4.

Barabak, Mark Z. "Latinos Struggle for Role in National Leadership; Politics: Uneven Population Distribution and Lure of the Private Sector Thin Ranks of Potential Candidates." *Los Angeles Times.* July 7, 1998, A1.

Barbour, Haley. *Agenda for America: A Republican Direction for the Future.* Washington, D.C.: Regnery, 1996.

Barker, Lucius, Mack H. Jones, and Katherine L. Tate. *African Americans and the American Political System.* 3d ed. Englewood Cliffs, N.J.: Prentice-Hall, 1998.

Barnes, Fred. "Contract Hit!" *American Spectator* (Jan. 1995): 20–22.

Barnes, James A. "Why the Gender Pitch Has Its Limits." *National Journal* 27 (Apr. 1, 1995): 827.

Barro, Robert J. "Reagan vs. Clinton: Who's The Economic Champ?" *Business Week* (Feb. 22, 1999): 22.

Bartels, Larry. "Where the Ducks Are: Voting Power in a Party System." In *Politicians and Party Politics,* edited by John Geer, 43–79. Baltimore: Johns Hopkins University Press, 1998.

Basu, Rekha. "Understanding the Gender Gap." *Des Moines Register.* Apr. 28, 1996, 3.

Beatty, Warren. "Why Not Now?" *New York Times,* National Edition. Aug. 22, 1999, sec. 4, p. 13.

Beck, Paul Allen. "A Socialization Theory of Partisan Realignment." In *The Politics of Future Citizens: New Dimensions in the Political Socialization of Children,* edited by Richard G. Niemi and Associates, 199–219. San Francisco: Jossey-Bass, 1974.

Benenson, Bob. "Arduous Ritual Of Redistricting Ensures More Racial Diversity." *Congressional Quarterly Weekly Report* 50 (1992). Online. Available: http://library.cq.com. July 29, 1999.

Bennet, James. "Impeachment: Beyond the Vote President Maps Out a Strategy for Governing While on Trial." *New York Times.* Dec. 20, 1998, A31.

———. "Again, Clinton Creates His Own Political Aura." *New York Times.* Jan. 27, 1999, A1.

Bennet, James, and Adam Nagourney. "The President Under Fire: The Strategy." *New York Times.* Jan. 30, 1998, A13.

Bennett, William J. "Clinton, the Country, and the Political Culture: A Symposium." *Commentary* 107 (Jan. 1999): 22–23.

Berger, Samuel R. "Remarks by Samuel R. Berger, Assistant to the President for National Security Affairs." Center for Strategic and International Studies, Washington, D.C., Mar. 27, 1997. Online. Available: http://www.pub.whitehouse.gov/uri-res/12R?urn:pdi://oma.eop.gov.us/1997/3/28/1.text1. July 12, 1999.

Berke, Richard. "After Hours at White House, Brain Trust Turns to Politics." *New York Times.* July 20, 1996, A1.

Berkowitz, Laura, and Steve Lilienthal. "A Tale of Two Parties: National Committee Policy Making, 1992 and 1994." In *The State of the Parties: The Changing Role of Contemporary American Parties—People, Passions, and Power,* edited by John C. Green and Daniel M. Shea, 273–88. 2d ed. Lanham, Md.: Rowman and Littlefield, 1996.

Brace, Paul, and Barbara Hinckley. *Follow the Leader: Opinion Polls and the Modern Presidents.* New York: Basic Books, 1992.

Brinkley, Douglas. "Democratic Enlargement: The Clinton Doctrine." *Foreign Policy* 106 (Spring 1997): 111–27.
Broadway, Bill. "Impeachment Raises Questions of Faith." *Washington Post*. Jan. 9, 1999, B10.
Broder, John M. "Laurels Elude President as Public Judges a War." *New York Times*. June 22, 1999, A24.
Brody, Richard A. *Assessing the President: The Media, Elite Opinion, and Public Support*. Stanford: Stanford University Press, 1991.
Brody, Richard A. and Simon Jackman. "The Lewinsky Affair and Popular Support for President Clinton." Paper presented at the 1999 Annual Meeting of the Midwest Political Science Association, Chicago, April 1999.
Browning, Rufus, Dale Rogers Marshall, and David Tabb. "Can People of Color Achieve Power in City Government? The Setting and the Issues." *Racial Politics in American Cities*, 3–14. New York: Longman, 1997.
Bumiller, Elizabeth. "Running Against Hillary." *New York Times Magazine* (Oct. 13, 1996): 13–20.
Burden, Barry C., and Aage R. Clausen. "The Unfolding Drama: Party and Ideology in the 104th House." In *Great Theatre: The American Congress in the 1990s*, edited by Herbert F. Weisberg and Samuel C. Patterson, 152–75. Cambridge: Cambridge University Press, 1998.
Burke, John. *The Institutionalized Presidency*. Baltimore: Johns Hopkins University Press, 1992.
Burke, John, and Fred I. Greenstein. *How Presidents Test Reality*. New York: Sage, 1991.
Burnham, Walter Dean. *Critical Elections and the Mainsprings of American Politics*. New York: W. W. Norton, 1970.
———. "Realignment Lives: The 1994 Earthquake and Its Implications." In *The Clinton Presidency: First Appraisals*, edited by Colin Campbell and Bert A. Rockman, 363–95. Chatham, N.J.: Chatham House, 1996.
———. "Bill Clinton: Riding the Tiger." In *The Election of 1996: Reports and Interpretations*, edited by Gerald M. Pomper, 1–20. Chatham, N.J.: Chatham House, 1997.
Burns, James MacGregor, and Georgia J. Sorenson. *Dead Center: Clinton-Gore Leadership and the Perils of Moderation*. New York: Scribners, 1999.
Cammisa, Anne Marie. *From Rhetoric to Reform*. Boulder, Colo.: Westview Press, 1998.
Campbell, Angus, Philip E. Converse, Warren E. Miller, and Donald E. Stokes. *The American Voter*. New York: Wiley, 1960.
Campbell, Colin. "Demotion? Has Clinton Turned the Bully Pulpit into a Lectern?" In *The Clinton Legacy*, edited by Colin Campbell and Bert A. Rockman, 48–69. New York: Chatham House, 2000.
Campbell, James E. "The Presidential Pulse and the 1994 Midterm Congressional Election." *Journal of Politics* 59, no. 3 (1997): 830–57.
*Capital Times*. "Clinton Enlists Women in Medicare Fight." July 27, 1999, 1.
Carmines, Edward G., and Geoffrey Layman. "Issue Evolution in Postwar American Politics: Old Certainties and Fresh Tensions." In *Present Discontents: American Politics in the Very Late Twentieth Century*. Chatham, N.J.: Chatham House, 1997.
Carr, Rebecca. "Republicans Find Hearings Off to a Shaky Start." *Congressional Quarterly Weekly Report* 55 (1997): 1601–4.
Carter, Stephen L. *The Culture of Disbelief: How American Law and Politics Trivialize Religious Devotion*. New York: Basic Books, 1993.
Case, Daniel. "Why Welfare Reform Is Working." *Commentary* 104, no. 3 (Sept. 1997): 36–43.
Ceaser, James W. "The Reagan Presidency and American Public Opinion." In *The Reagan Presidency: Promise and Performance*, edited by Charles O. Jones, 172–210. Chatham, N.J.: Chatham House, 1988.

Ceaser, James W., and Andrew E. Busch. *Losing to Win: The 1996 Elections and American Politics.* Lanham, MD: Rowman and Littlefield, 1997.

Center for Political Studies. American National Election Study. University of Michigan, Ann Arbor, Mich.

Chambers, Jack. "Baptists Pray for Prodigal President." *Wall Street Journal.* June 15, 1993, A18.

Chen, Edwin. "Clinton Tour Seeks to Tap 'New Markets': Economy: Four-Day Trip Begins in Kentucky, Ends in Watts. President's Plan Offers Businesses Loan Guarantees and Credits for Investing in Poor Areas." *Los Angeles Times,* July 5, 1999, A15.

Christopher, Warren. "Building Peace in the Middle East." *Dispatch* 4, no. 39 (Sept. 27, 1993[a]): 654–57.

———. "Statement of Warren Christopher before the Committee on Foreign Relations of the United States Senate." Jan. 13, 1993b. Online. Available: http://dosfan.lib.uic.edu/ERC/briefing/dossec/1993/9301/930113dossec.html. Aug. 2, 1999.

———. "Principles and Opportunities for American Foreign Policy." *Dispatch* 6, no. 4 (Jan. 23, 1995): 41–46.

Clausewitz, Carl von. *On War.* Edited and translated by Michael Howard and Peter Paret. Princeton: Princeton University Press, 1984.

Clemens, Elisabeth S. *The People's Lobby: Organizational Innovation and the Rise of Interest Group Politics in the United States, 1890–1925.* Chicago: University of Chicago Press, 1997.

Clinton, Bill. "A New Covenant for American Security." Address at Georgetown University. Dec. 12, 1991.

———. "Remarks of Bill Clinton." Address at the Los Angeles World Affairs Council, Aug. 13, 1992.

———. "Confronting the Challenges of a Broader World." *Dispatch* 4, no. 39 (Sept. 27, 1993): 649–53.

———. Remarks upon Arrival, Selfridge National Guard Base, Detroit, Michigan, Aug. 6, 1994. Online. Available: http://www.whitehouse.gov/uri-res/I2R?urn:pdi://oma.eop.gov.us/1994/8/8/2.text.1. July 14, 1999.

———. Interview on *60 Minutes,* Apr. 23, 1995a. Online. Available: http://www.whitehouse.gov/uri-res/I2R?urn:pdi://oma.eop.gov.us/1995/4/24/7.text.1. July 30, 1999.

———. Message to Congress on Veto of HR 2491, Continuing Resolution, Dec. 6, 1995b. Online. Available: http://www.whitehouse/uri-res/I2R?urn:pdi://oma.eop.gov.us/1995/12/7/14.text.1. July 31, 1999.

———. "President's Veto Message." *Congressional Quarterly Weekly* 53 (1995c): 3763.

———. Remarks at Town Hall Meeting, Billings, Montana, June 1, 1995d. Online. Available: http://www.whitehouse.gov/uri-res/I2R?urn:pdi://oma.eop.gov.us/1995/6/2/3.text.1. July 30, 1999.

———. Remarks at 26th Annual Congressional Black Caucus Foundation Dinner, Sept. 14, 1996. Online. Available: http://www.whitehouse.gov. July 30, 1999.

———. *Economic Report of the President.* Washington, D.C.: U.S. Government Printing Office, 1998.

———. "Remarks by the President on Foreign Policy." Grand Hyatt Hotel, San Francisco, California, Feb. 26, 1999a. Online. Available: http://library.whitehouse.gov/uri-res/I2R?urn:pdi://oma.eop.goveb. June 28, 1999.

———. "Statement by the President to the Nation." The Oval Office, Washington, D.C., Mar. 24, 1999b. Online. Available: http://www.pub.whitehouse.gov/uri-res/I2R?urn:pdi://oma.eop.gov.us/1999/3/25/1.text1. June 27, 1999.

Clinton, Bill, and Al Gore. *Putting People First: How We Can All Change America.* New York: Random House, Times Books, 1992.

Cohen, Jeffrey E. *Politics and Economic Policy in the United States.* Boston: Houghton Mifflin, 1997.

Cohen, Richard E. *Changing Course in Washington: Clinton and the New Congress.* New York: Macmillan, 1994.

Cohn, Roger. "Memory Goes to War." *New Republic* 221, no. 2 (July 12, 1999): 29–35.

Coleman, John J. *Party Decline in America: Policy, Politics, and the Fiscal State.* Princeton: Princeton University Press, 1996.

———. "The Decline and Resurgence of Congressional Party Conflict." *Journal of Politics* 59, no. 1 (1997a): 165–84.

———. "The Importance of Being Republican: Forecasting Party Fortunes in House Midterm Elections." *Journal of Politics* 59, no. 2 (1997b): 497.

*Congressional Quarterly Almanac, 1993.* "Clinton Outlines His Plan to Spur Economy," 7D–12D. Washington, D.C.: *Congressional Quarterly* Press, 1994a.

———. "Evolution of Tax Proposals," 120. Washington, D.C.: *Congressional Quarterly* Press, 1994b.

*Congressional Quarterly Almanac, 1995.* "No Winners in Budget Showdown," 2-59, 2-63. Washington, D.C.: *Congressional Quarterly* Press, 1995a.

———. "President Counters Republican Blueprint . . . Offers 10-Year Balanced Budget Plan," 2-29.Washington, D.C.: *Congressional Quarterly* Press, 1995b.

*Congressional Quarterly Almanac, 1996.* "Clinton Sends Fiscal '97 Budget to Hill," 2-4. Washington, D.C.: *Congressional Quarterly* Press, 1997.

Connolly, Ceci. Voters' Residual Anger at Clinton Could Hurt Gore Bid, Poll Finds; Popularity Has Dropped Sharply; Support from Women Is Weak. *Washington Post.* Apr. 18, 1999, A11.

Connolly, Ceci and Claudia Deane. "Clinton Ratings Trend Up." *Washington Post.* Dec. 16, 1998, A5.

Connolly, Ceci and Thomas B. Edsall. "Political Pros Looking for Explanations." *Washington Post.* Feb. 9, 1998, A6.

Conover, Pamela Johnston, and Stanley Feldman. "Morality Items on the 1985 Pilot Study." *A Report to the 1985 NES Pilot Study Committee.*

Cook, Charles. "Behind Clinton's Approval Ratings." *National Journal* 31 (1999): 1614–15.

———. "Puzzling Through the Demographics Of The Nov. 3 Vote." *National Journal's Cloakroom.* Internet edition. (Nov. 17, 1998): 1. Online. Available: http://www.cloakroom.com. July 5, 1999.

Corrado, Anthony. "Financing the 1996 Election." In *The Election of 1996: Reports and Interpretations,* edited by Gerald M. Pomper, 135–71. Chatham, N.J.: Chatham House, 1997.

Cotter, Cornelius P., James L. Gibson, John F. Bibby, and Robert J. Huckshorn. *Party Organizations in American Politics.* 1984. Pittsburgh: University of Pittsburgh Press, 1989.

Council of Economic Advisers. *Economic Report of the President, 2000.* Washington, D.C.: Government Printing Office, 1999.

Cox, Gary W., and Mathew D. McCubbins. *Legislative Leviathan: Party Government in the House.* Berkeley: University of California Press, 1993.

Cronin, Thomas E., and Michael A. Genovese. "President Clinton and Character Questions." *Presidential Studies Quarterly* 28 (Fall 1998): 892–97.

Crossette, Barbara. "Albright Gathers Top Women to Address Women's Issues." *New York Times.* Sept. 26, 1999, A12.

Crotty, William. *American Parties in Decline.* 2d ed. Boston: Little, Brown, 1984.

Crowley, Monica. *Nixon in Winter.* London: I. B. Tauris, 1998.
Daynes, Byron W., Raymond Tatalovich, and Dennis L. Soden. *To Govern a Nation: Presidential Power and Politics.* New York: St. Martin's Press, 1998.
de la Garza, Rodolfo and Louis DeSipio, eds. *Ethnic Ironies: Latino Politics in the 1992 Elections.* Boulder, Colo.: Westview Press, 1996.
Denton, Robert, and Rachel Holloway. "Clinton and the Town Hall Meetings: Mediated Conversation and the Risk of Being 'In Touch'." In *The Clinton Presidency: Images, Issues, and Communication Strategies,* edited by Robert E. Denton Jr. and Rachel L. Holloway, 17–42.Westport, Conn.: Praeger, 1996.
DeSipio, Louis. *Counting on the Latino Vote: Latinos as a New Electorate.* Charlottesville: University Press of Virginia, 1998.
Destler, I. M. *The National Economic Council: A Work in Progress.* Washington, D.C.: Institute for International Economics, 1996.
Devroy, Ann. "Clinton Friends Cited in Travel Staff Purge; Report Says First Lady Monitored Actions." *Washington Post.* July 3, 1993, A1.
———. "Clinton Shines Spotlight on Family Violence; Agencies Urged to Run Programs About Issue." *Washington Post.* Oct. 3, 1995, A8.
Devroy Ann, and John F. Harris, "Clinton Says Record Shows 'Remarkable Consistency.'" *Washington Post.* Jan. 31, 1996, A1.
Devroy, Ann, and Al Kamen. "Longtime Travel Staff Giving Walking Papers." *Washington Post.* May 20, 1993, A1.
Dionne, E. J. "In Search of George W." *Washington Post Sunday Magazine* (Sept. 19, 1999): W18.
Dodd, Lawrence C. "The New American Politics: Reflections on the 1990s." In *The New American Politics: Reflections on Political Change and the Clinton Administration,* edited by Bryan D. Jones, 257–74. Boulder, Colo.: Westview Press, 1995.
Doherty, Carroll J. "Clinton's Big Comeback Shown in Vote Score." *Congressional Quarterly Weekly Report* 54 (1996): 3427–29.
Dowd, Maureen. "Bubba Don't Preach." *New York Times.* Feb. 9, 1997, E15.
Drew, Elizabeth. *On the Edge: The Clinton Presidency.* New York: Simon and Schuster, 1994.
Drew, Elizabeth. *Showdown: The Struggle Between the Gingrich Congress and the Clinton White House.* New York: Simon and Schuster, 1996.
Drew, Elizabeth. *Whatever It Takes: The Real Struggle for Political Power in America.* New York: Viking, 1997.
*Economist.* "In Bob We Trust." (Dec. 10, 1994): 28.
———. "Calling Dr. Kissinger." (Jan. 14, 1995): 23.
———. "Department of Debunkery: Economic Policy Advice." (Jan. 18, 1997): 71.
Edelman, Peter. "Clinton's Cosmetic Poverty Tour." *New York Times.* July 8, 1999, A25.
Edsall, Thomas B. "Three Democrats Now Willing to Support Death Penalty; Candidates Abandon Traditional Liberal Tenets." *Washington Post.* Jan. 23, 1992, A14.
———. "A Chance for the Democrats to Start Fresh." *Washington Post,* National Weekly Edition. Jan. 25–31, 1993, 11.
———. "Study Disputes Clinton 1996 Campaign Strategy." *Washington Post.* May 22, 1999, A4.
Edwards, George C., III. *Presidential Approval: A Sourcebook.* Baltimore: Johns Hopkins University Press, 1990.
———. Frustration and Folly: Bill Clinton and the Public Presidency." In *The Clinton Presidency: First Appraisals,* ed. Colin Campbell and Bert A. Rockman. Chatham, N.J.: Chatham House Publishers, 1996. 234–61.
———. "Bill Clinton and His Crisis of Governance." *Presidential Studies Quarterly* 28 (Fall 1998): 754–60.

———. "Campaigning Is Not Governing: Bill Clinton's Rhetorical Presidency." In *The Reagan Legacy*, edited by Colin Campbell and Bert A. Rockman, 33–47. New York: Chatham House, 2000.

Edwards, George C., III, and Stephen Wayne. *Presidential Leadership: Politics and Policy Making.* New York: Saint Martin's Press, 1994.

Ehrlichman, John. *Witness to Power: The Nixon Years.* New York: Simon and Schuster, 1982.

Ely, Jane. "A Glance over the Political Gender Gap." *Houston Chronicle.* Apr. 28, 1996, 2.

Erickson, Paul D. *Reagan Speaks: The Making of an American Myth.* New York: New York University Press, 1985.

Fineman, Howard. "MediScare." *Newsweek* (Sept. 18, 1995): 38–40.

Fineman, Howard, and Bill Turque. "How He Got His Groove." *Newsweek* (Sept. 2, 1996): 21–25.

Fisher, Louis. *Constitutional Conflicts Between Congress and the President.* 4th. ed., Lawrence: University Press of Kansas, 1997.

Fournier, Ron. "Clinton Strategy: Express Sorrow, Hit Hard." Associated Press. Sept. 11, 1998. Online. Available: http://www.canoe.ca/CNEWSClinton/sep11_strategy.html. May 1, 2000.

Fowler, Robert Booth, and Allen D. Hertzke. *Religion and Politics in America.* Boulder, Colo.: Westview Press, 1995.

Fraley, Colette, and A. Rubin. "Opponents Solidify Stand on Health Care Proposal." *Congressional Quarterly Weekly* 53 (1995): 2995–99.

Francis, David R. "Despite Growth, Families Struggle to Prosper in U.S." *Christian Science Monitor.* Aug. 7, 1996, 1.

Frankovic, Kathleen "Public Opinion in the 1992 Campaign." In *The Election of 1992,* edited by Gerald M. Pomper, 110–31. Chatham, N.J.: Chatham House, 1993.

Freedman, Thomas L. Interview with John F. Harris, Sept. 20, 1999.

Frendreis, John P., and Raymond Tatalovich. *The Modern Presidency and Economic Policy.* Itasca, Ill.: F. E. Peacock, 1994.

Friedman, Thomas. "Bosnia Reconsidered." *New York Times.* Apr. 8, 1995, A5.

Galbraith, James K. "The Clinton Administration's Vision." *Challenge* 40 (July–Aug. 1997): 45.

———. "The Economic Report of the President for 1998: A Review." *Challenge* 41 (Sept.–Oct., 1998): 87.

———. "The Economy Doesn't Need the Third Way." *New York Times.* Nov. 24, 1999, A25.

Gallup, George. *The Gallup Poll: Public Opinion 1992.* Wilmington, Del.: Scholarly Resources, 1993.

Geertz, Clifford. "Centers, Kings, and Charisma: Reflections on the Symbolics of Power." In *Local Knowledge, Further Essays in Interpretive Anthropology,* edited by Clifford Geertz, 121–46. New York: Basic Books, 1983.

Gerring, John. "Culture versus Economics: An American Dilemma." *Social Science History* 23 (1999): 129–72.

Gimpel, James G. *Fulfilling the Contract: The First Hundred Days.* Boston: Allyn and Bacon, 1996.

Gingrich, Newt. *Lessons Learned the Hard Way: A Personal Report.* New York: HarperCollins, 1998.

Ginsberg, Benjamin, and Martin Shefter. *Politics by Other Means: The Declining Importance of Elections in America.* New York: Basic Books, 1990.

———. *Politics by Other Means: Politicians, Prosecutors and the Press from Watergate to Whitewater.* 2d ed. New York: W. W. Norton, 1999.

Glassman, James K. "Clinton, the Country, and the Political Culture: A Symposium" *Commentary* 107 (Jan. 1999): 30–32.

Goldgeier, James. "NATO Expansion: The Anatomy of a Decision." In *Domestic Sources of American Foreign Policy: Insights and Evidence*. 3d ed., edited by Eugene R.Wittkopf and James M. McCormick, 317–32. Lanham, Md.: Rowman and Littlefield, 1999.

Goldman, Emily O., and Larry Berman. "Engaging the World: First Impressions of the Clinton Foreign Policy Legacy." In *The Clinton Legacy*, edited by Colin Campbell and Bert A. Rockman, 226–53. New York: Chatham House, 2000.

Goldman Peter, et al. *Quest for the Presidency 1992*. College Station: Texas A&M University Press, 1994.

Goley, Michael. *Where America Stands*. New York: John Wiley and Sons, 1997.

Gore, Albert, Jr. *Earth in the Balance: Ecology and the Human Spirit*. New York: Plume, 1993.

———. Interview comments made to reporters and editors at the *Washington Post*. Oct. 15, 1999.

Gosselin, Peter G. "Economy Still the Key to Clinton Presidency: Issue Proves Both an Asset, Liability." *Boston Globe*. Sept. 15, 1996, A1.

Green, John, James Guth, Lyman Kellstedt, and Corwin Smidt. "Evangelical Realignment." *Christian Century* (July 5–12, 1995): 676–79.

———. *Religion and the Culture Wars*. Lanham, Md.: Rowman and Littlefield, 1996.

Greenberg, Anna. "Deconstructing the Gender Gap." Paper presented at the Midwest Political Science Association Annual Meeting, Chicago, Apr. 1998.

Greenberg, Stanley B. *Middle Class Dreams: The Politics and Power of the New American Majority*. Rev. ed. New Haven: Yale University Press, 1996.

Greenhouse, Steven. "Seattle Protest Could Have Lasting Influence on Trade." *New York Times*. Dec. 6, 1999, A1.

Greenstein, Fred I. "Nine Presidents in Search of a Modern Presidency." *Leadership in the Modern Presidency*, ed. Fred Greenstein, 296–352. Cambridge: Harvard University Press, 1988.

———. "The Political Leadership Style of Bill Clinton: An Early Appraisal." *Political Science Quarterly* 108 (1993–1994): 589–601.

Greider, William. "The Education of David Stockman." *Atlantic Monthly* (Dec. 1981): 27–54.

Grove, Lloyd. "Drawing Power: GOP Chairman Haley Barbour Is Cautiously Counting His Chickens." *Washington Post*. Aug. 11, 1994, B1.

Grunwald, Michael. "Voters Hesitant to Choose Sides." *Washington Post*. Jan. 3, 1999, A1.

Gup, Ted. "Speaker Albert Was Ready to Be President." *Washington Post*. Nov. 28, 1982, A1.

Guth, James. "Notes on Washington Conference." June 1994.

Guth, James, and John Green, ed. *The Bible and the Ballot Box*. Boulder, Colo.: Westview Press, 1991.

Guth, James, John Green, Lyman Kellstedt, Corwin Smidt, and Margaret Poloma. *The Bully Pulpit: The Politics of Protestant Clergy*. Lawrence: University Press of Kansas, 1997.

Hacker, Jacob. *The Road to Nowhere*. Princeton: Princeton University Press, 1997.

Hager, George. "Budget Battle Came Sooner Than Either Side Expected." *Congressional Quarterly Weekly Report* 53 (1995): 3503–9.

———. "Republicans Throw in Towel on Seven-Year Deal." *Congressional Quarterly Weekly Report* 54 (1996): 213–16.

———. "Amid Cries for Reform, Parties and Politicians Pack Coffers." *Congressional Quarterly Weekly Report* 55 (1997): 1911–12.

Hargrove, Erwin. *The President as Leader: Appealing to the Better Angels of Our Nature*. Lawrence: University Press of Kansas, 1998.

Harrigan, John J. *Political Change in the Metropolis*. 5th ed. New York: HarperCollins College Publishers, 1993.

Harris, John F. "Clinton Had Ingredients for Victory a Year Ago." *Washington Post.* Nov. 4, 1996, A1.
———. "Morris's Tactics Still Hold Sway at the White House." *Washington Post.* Jan. 27, 1997a, A1.
———. "Winning a Second Term; Waiting for a Second Chance." *Washington Post.* Jan. 20, 1997b, E10.
———. "Clinton's Consultants Reaped Millions from TV Ads." *Washington Post.* Jan. 4, 1998a, A4.
———. "On the Road, Away from Crisis." *Washington Post.* Aug. 11, 1998b , A1.
———. "In Handling of Crisis, a Different President." *Washington Post.* June 8, 1999b, A1.
———. "Victory Comes with a Price." *Washington Post,* National Weekly Edition. Nov. 22, 1999c, A10.
———. Telephone interview with Steven Schier. May 7, 1999d.
Harris, John F., and Peter Baker. "A Swing From Partisan to Presidential; Clinton's Speech To Try to Reach The Unaligned." *Washington Post.* Aug. 28, 1996, A27.
Harris, John F., and Ceci Connolly. "Rivalry Between Clinton and Gore Camps Gets Heated." *Washington Post.* June 27, 1999, A2.
Hart, Gary Warren. *Right from the Start: A Chronicle of the McGovern Campaign.* New York: Quadrangle, *New York Times* Books, 1973.
Hart, John. *The Presidential Branch.* 2d ed. Chatham, N.J.: Chatham House, 1995.
Heclo, Hugh. "The Changing Presidential Office." *The Managerial Presidency,* 2d ed., edited by James Pfiffner, 22–36, College Station: Texas A&M University Press, 1999.
Hedges, Michael. "White House Finally Moves to Put Out Liberal Fire; Elders Created Constant Uproar." *Washington Times.* Dec. 10, 1994, A13.
Heineman, Kenneth J. *God Is a Conservative: Religion, Politics, and Morality in Contemporary America.* New York: New York University Press, 1998.
Henriksen, Thomas. *Clinton's Foreign Policy in Somalia, Bosnia, Haiti, and North Korea.* Stanford: Hoover Institution Essays in Public Policy, 1996.
Hertsgaard, Mark. *On Bended Knee: The Press and the Reagan Presidency.* New York: Schocken Books, 1989.
Hill, Kevin A. "Does the Creation of Majority Black Districts Aid Republicans? An Analysis of the 1992 Congressional Elections in Eight Southern States." *Journal of Politics* 57, no. 2 (1995): 384–401.
Hoffmann, Stanley. "Requiem." *Foreign Policy* 42 (Spring 1981): 3–26.
Holland, Keating. "Sex Scandals Are Survivable." *The Public Perspective* 10 (Dec. 1998–Jan. 1999): 38–39.
Hunter, James D. *Culture Wars: The Struggle to Define America.* New York: Basic Books, 1991.
Huntington, Samuel. "The Erosion of American National Interests." *Foreign Affairs* 76, no. 5 (Sept.–Oct. 1997): 28–49.
Ickes, Harold. Interview with John F. Harris, Aug. 29, 1999.
Idelson, Holly. "Clinton's Unexpected Bequest: Judgeships Bush Did Not Fill." *Congressional Quarterly Weekly Report* 51 (1993): 317–20.
Jacobs, John. "Return of the Gender Gap." *Sacramento Bee.* Apr. 14, 1996, F4.
Jacobson, Gary C. "Congress: Unusual Year, Unusual Election." In *The Elections of 1992,* edited by Michael Nelson, 153–82. Washington, D.C.: *Congressional Quarterly* Press, 1993.
———. "Impeachment Politics in the 1998 Congressional Elections." *Political Science Quarterly* 114 (Spring 1999): 31–51.
James, Frank, and Carol Kleiman. "Economy is Rich with Disparities." *Chicago Tribune.* Sept. 30, 1997, sec. 1, p. 11.

Jamieson, Kathleen Hall, and Sean Aday. "When Is Presidential Behavior Public and When Is It Private?" *Presidential Studies Quarterly* 28 (Fall 1998): 856–60.

Jamieson, Kathleen Hall, Erika Falk, and Susan Sherr. "The Enthymeme Gap in the 1996 Presidential Campaign." *PS: Political Science and Politics* 32, no. 1, (Mar. 1999): 13–17.

Jentleson, Bruce W. "The Pretty Prudent Public: Post Post-Vietnam American Opinion on the Use of Force." *International Studies Quarterly* 36, no. 1 (Mar. 1992): 49–74.

Jentleson, Bruce W., and Rebecca L. Britton. "Still Pretty Prudent." *Journal of Conflict Resolution* 42, no. 4 (Aug. 1998): 395–418.

Johnson, Bill. "Black Support for Bill Clinton Understandable, But Incorrect." *Detroit News*. Oct. 23, 1998, A12.

Johnson, Haynes, and David S. Broder. *The System: The American Way of Politics at the Breaking Point*. Boston: Little, Brown, 1996.

Johnston, David Cay. "Gap between Rich and Poor Found Substantially Wider." *New York Times*. Sept. 5, 1999, 14.

Jones, Charles O. "Campaigning to Govern: The Clinton Style." In *The Clinton Presidency: First Appraisals,* edited by Colin Campbell and Bert A. Rockman, 15–50. Chatham, N.J.: Chatham House, 1996.

———. *Separate but Equal Branches: Congress and the Presidency*. 2d ed. Chappaqua, N.Y.: Chatham House, 1999.

Judah, Tim. *The Serbs: History, Myth, and the Destruction of Yugoslavia*. New Haven: Yale University Press, 1999.

Judis, John B. "Old Master: Robert Rubin's Artful Role." *New Republic* (Dec. 13, 1993): 21.

Kahn, Joseph, and David E. Sanger. "Seattle Talks on Trade End with Stinging Blow to U.S." *New York Times*. Dec. 5, 1999, A1.

Keeter, Scott. "Public Opinion and the Election." In *The Election of 1996: Reports and Interpretations,* edited by Gerald M. Pomper, 107–33. Chatham, N.J.: Chatham House, 1997.

———. "The Perplexing Case of Public Opinion about the Clinton Scandal." Paper presented at the 1999 Annual Meeting of the American Association for Public Opinion Research, St. Petersburg Beach, Florida, May 13–16, 1999.

Kellstedt, Lyman, John Green, Janes Guth, and Corwin Smidt. "Religious Voting Blocs in the 1992 Election." In *The Rapture of Politics: The Christian Right as the United States*, edited by Steve Bruce, Peter Kivisto, and William H. Swatos Jr., 85–104. New Brunswick, N.J.: Transaction Publishers, 1995.

Kelly, Michael. "Clinton Defends Position on Iraqi War." *New York Times*. July 31, 1992, 3.

———. "Saint Hillary." *New York Times Magazine* (May 23, 1993): 22–25, 63–66.

Kennedy, John F., Jr. "Interview with Mike McCurry." *George Magazine* 4, no. 3 (Mar. 1999): 74.

Kennedy, John W. "NRB Shuns Clinton." *Christianity Today*. Mar. 7, 1994, 48.

Kernell, Samuel. *Going Public: New Strategies of Presidential Leadership*. 2d ed. Washington, D.C.: Congressional Quarterly Press, 1993.

———. "The Challenge Ahead for Explaining President Clinton's Public Support." *PRG Report* 21 (Spring 1999): 1–3.

Key, V. O. "A Theory of Critical Elections." *Journal of Politics* 17 (1955): 3–18.

———. "Secular Realignment and the Party System." *Journal of Politics* 21 (1959): 198–210.

Khachigian, Ken. "Memorandum for Patrick J. Buchanan, June 9, 1972." White House Staff Files, Nixon Presidential Material Staff, National Archives, College Park, Md.

Kiefer, Francine. "The Clinton Presidency's Feminine Mystique." *Christian Science Monitor*. June 7, 1999, 2.

King, David C. "The Polarization of Political Parties and the Mistrust of Government." In *Why People Don't Trust Government,* edited by Joseph S. Nye, Philip D. Zelikow, and David C. King, 155–78. Cambridge: Harvard University Press, 1997.

Kissinger, Henry. "How to Achieve the New World Order." *Time* 143, no. 11 (Mar. 14, 1994): 73–77.

Kitfield, James. "Kosovo: This One Just Feels Messy." *National Journal* 31 (1999): 836.

Kleppner, Paul. *The Third Electoral System, 1853–1892: Parties, Voters, and Political Cultures.* Chapel Hill: University of North Carolina Press, 1979.

Klinkner, Philip A. *The Losing Parties: Out-Party National Committees, 1956–1993.* New Haven: Yale University Press, 1994.

Knight Ridder Newspapers, "What about Whitewater, Foster Case, Travelgate, Filegate? Investigations Fail to Implicate Clinton, But Some Continue." *St. Louis Post-Dispatch.* Sept. 13, 1998, A10.

Koszczuk, Jackie. "Democrats' Resurgence Fueled by Pragmatism." *Congressional Quarterly Weekly Report* 54 (1996): 1205–10.

Kristol, William, and Robert Kagan. "Toward a Neo-Reaganite Foreign Policy." *Foreign Affairs* 75, no. 4 (July–Aug. 1996): 18–32.

Kumar, Martha Joynt. "President Clinton Meets the Media: Communications Shaped by Predictable Patterns." In *The Clinton Presidency: Campaigning, Governing, and the Psychology of Leadership,* edited by Stanley A. Renshon. Boulder, Colo.: Westview Press, 1995.

Kurtz, Howard. *Spin Cycle: Inside the Clinton Propaganda Machine.* New York: Free Press, 1998.

Kuttner, Robert. "The Economy: Clinton Has Played His Cards Well." *Business Week* (Feb. 1, 1999): 22.

Lacitis, Erik. "Images From an Impeachment." *Seattle Times.* Jan. 22, 1999, E1.

Ladd, Everett Carll. "Why Reporting of the Polls Has Consistently Understated the Drop in Clinton's Support." *Public Perspective* 9 (Oct.–Nov. 1998): 35–37.

Lake, Anthony. "From Containment to Enlargement." *Dispatch* 4, no. 39 (Sept. 27, 1993): 658–64.

Layman, Geoffrey C. "Religion and Political Behavior in the United States." *Public Opinion Quarterly* 61 (1997): 288–316.

———. "Culture Wars in the American Party System." *American Politics Quarterly* 27, no. 1 (Jan. 1999): 89–121.

Layne, Chrisopher. "The Problem with Being No. 1." *Washington Post* National Weekly Edition (Nov. 22, 1999): 22.

Lemann, Nicholas, "America Left and Right." *Atlantic Monthly* 281 (Apr. 1998): 103.

Lewis, George, Lisbeth Gronlund, and David Wright. "National Missile Defense: An Indefensible System." *Foreign Policy* 117 (Winter 1999–2000): 120–37.

Lewis, Ida E. "Bill Clinton as Honorary Black: To Those Who Fail to Understand Why the Majority of African-Americans Do Not Support the Removal of President Clinton." *Crisis* (Sept.–Oct. 1998): 5.

Lippman, Thomas. "Clinton, Albright Cite U.S. Interest in Kosovo." *Washington Post.* Feb. 5 1999, A27.

Lowi, Theodore. *The Personal President.* Ithaca, N.Y.: Cornell University Press, 1985.

Lyman, Rick. "As Opinions Harden, the Joking Subsides." *New York Times.* Dec. 16, 1998, A31.

McCormick, James M. *American Foreign Policy and Process.* 3d ed. Itasca, Ill.: F. E. Peacock, 1998a.

———. "Interest Groups and the Media in Post–Cold War U.S. Foreign Policy." In *After the End: Making U.S. Foreign Policy in the Post–Cold War World,* edited by James M. Scott, 170–98. Durham, N.C.: Duke University Press, 1998b.

McCormick, James M., Eugene R. Wittkopf, and David M. Danna. "Politics and Bipartisanship at the Water's Edge: A Note on Bush and Clinton." *Polity* 30, no. 1 (Fall 1997): 133–49.

McCormick, Richard L. *The Party Period and Public Policy: American Politics from the Age of Jackson to the Progressive Era.* New York: Oxford University Press, 1986.

McCutcheon, Chuck, and Lori Nitschke. "Clinton Will Have to Fight for Democratic Backing in Votes on China Trade Deal, Members Say." *Congressional Quarterly Weekly Report* 57 (1999), 2795.

McWilliams, Wilson Carey. "The Meaning of the Election." In *The Election of 1996: Reports and Interpretations*, edited by Gerald M. Pomper, 241–72. Chatham, N.J: Chatham House, 1997.

Maltese, John Anthony. *Spin Control: The White House Office of Communications and the Management of Presidential News.* Chapel Hill: University of North Carolina Press, 1994.

Mandelbaum, Michael. "Foreign Policy as Social Work." *Foreign Affairs* 75, no. 1 (Feb. 1996): 16–32.

Marable, Manning. "Race and Class in the U.S. Presidential Election." *Race and Class* 34, no. 3 (Jan.–Mar., 1993): 75–85.

Maraniss, David. *First in His Class: A Biography of Bill Clinton.* New York: Simon and Schuster, 1995.

Marcus, Ruth. "Clinton Allies Criticized in Travel Office Firings." *Washington Post.* May 3, 1994, A21.

Matalin, Mary, and James Carville. *All's Fair: Love, War, and Running for President.* New York: Random House, 1994.

Mathis, Nancy. "Clinton, Bush Clarify 'Family Values' Rhetoric." *Houston Chronicle.* Sept. 12, 1992, A1.

———. "Treaty Vote Draws Wrath of President." *Houston Chronicle.* Oct. 15, 1999, A1.

Matthews, Christopher. *Kennedy and Nixon: The Rivalry That Shaped Postwar America.* New York: Simon and Schuster, Touchstone Books, 1997.

Mayer, William G. "Mass Partisanship, 1946–1996." In *Partisan Approaches to Postwar American Politics*, edited by Byron E. Shafer, 186–219. Chatham, N.J.: Chatham House, 1998.

Meese, Edwin III and DeHart, Rhett. "How Washington Subverts Your Local Sheriff." *Policy Review* 75 (Jan.–Feb. 1996). Online. Available: http://www.policyreview.com/jan96/meese.html. July 21, 1999.

Menard, David. *Applied Logistic Regression Analysis.* Thousand Oaks, Calif.: Sage, 1995.

Milkis, Sidney. *The President and the Parties.* New York: Oxford University Press, 1993.

Milkis, Sidney M., and Michael Nelson. *The American Presidency: Origins and Development.* Washington, D.C.: *Congressional Quarterly* Press, 1999.

Miroff, Bruce. "From 'Midcentury' to Fin-de-Siecle: The Exhaustion of the Presidential Image." *Rhetoric and Public Affairs* 1, no. 2 (Summer 1998): 185–99.

Miroff, Bruce. "Moral Character in the White House: From Republican to Democratic." *Presidential Studies Quarterly* 29 (Sept. 1999): 707–11.

Mitchell, Alison. "Clinton Applies '94 Lesson to Fight G.O.P. on Budget." *New York Times.* Oct. 13, 1995: A1.

———. "Despite His Reversals, Clinton Stays Centered." *New York Times.* July 28, 1996a, 1, 28–30.

———. "Stung by Defeats in '94, Clinton Regrouped and Co-opted G.O.P. Strategies." *New York Times.* Nov. 7, 1996b, B1, B5.

———. "Clinton Seeks Help for the Nation's Spirit." *New York Times.* Jan. 7, 1997, A1.

Moore, David W. "Clinton's Job Ratings Fall, but Character Ratings Remain High." *Gallup Poll Monthly* 333 (June 1993a): 6–9.

———. "The First 100 Days: Clinton's Personal Popularity High." *Gallup Poll Monthly* 331 (Apr. 1993b): 4.

———. "President Clinton's Ratings Slide." *Gallup Poll Monthly* 346 (July 1994): 19.

———. "Clinton Support Strong after Release of Grand Jury Tapes." *Gallup Poll Monthly* 396 (Sept. 1998): 12–13.

Moore, David W. and Lydia Saad. "Clinton More Liberal than American Public." *Gallup Poll Monthly* 333 (June 1993): 15–16.

Morris, Dick. *Behind the Oval Office: Winning the Presidency in the Nineties*. New York: Random House, 1997.

———. "President Clinton's Accomplishments." A speech at Nassau Community College, recorded by *C-Span* and available for order at *C-Span* archives (www.c-span.org), ID Number 116089. Dec. 2, 1998.

———. *Behind the Oval Office: Getting Reelected Against All Odds*. Los Angeles: Renaissance Books, 1999a.

———. *The New Prince*. Los Angeles: Renaissance Books, 1999b.

Moynihan, Daniel Patrick. *The Politics of a Guaranteed Income: The Nixon Administration and the Family Assistance Plan*. New York: Random House, Vintage Books, 1973.

Mueller, John. "Public Opinion and Foreign Policy: The People's 'Common Sense.'" In *Domestic Sources of American Foreign Policy: Insights and Evidence*. 3d ed., edited by Eugene R.Wittkopf and James M. McCormick, 317–32. Lanham, Md.: Rowman and Littlefield, 1999.

Mughan, Anthony, and Barry C. Burden. "The Candidates' Wives." In *Democracy's Feast*, edited by Herbert F. Weisberg, 136–52. Chatham, N.J.: Chatham House, 1995.

———. "Hillary Clinton and the President's Reelection." Paper presented at the 1997 annual meeting of the American Political Science Association.

Naim, Moises. "Clinton's Foreign Policy: A Victim of Globalization?" *Foreign Policy* 109 (Winter 1997–1998): 34–45.

Nash, Ronald. *Why the Left Is Not Right: The Religious Left, Who They Are, and What They Believe*. Grand Rapids, Mich.: Zondervan, 1996.

NBC Nightly News. "George W. Bush Appeals to Women Voters." NBC News transcripts. Lexis-Nexis Academic Universe Internet Service. Sept. 13, 1999.

Neal, Terry M. "The Black Vote: A Turnout You Shouldn't Stereotype." *Washington Post*. Nov. 8, 1998, C2.

Neal, Terry, and Richard Morin. "For Voters, It's Back toward the Middle." *Washington Post*. Nov. 5, 1998, A33.

Neustadt, Richard E. *Presidential Power*. New York: Wiley, 1960.

———. *Presidential Power and the Modern Presidents: The Politics of Leadership from Roosevelt to Reagan*. New York: Free Press, 1990.

*New York Times*. "Clinton's Words: 'Open the Meetings.'" Dec. 2, 1999a, A15.

———. "Lott's View: 'It Was Not About Politics, It Was About the Substance.'" Oct. 15, 1999b, A13.

———. "Another Term for Mr. Greenspan." Jan. 5, 2000, A24.

Newport, Frank. "Clinton Maintains High Job Approval Ratings throughout Tumultuous Week." *Gallup Poll Monthly* 395 (Aug. 1998a): 12–13.

———. "Majority of Americans Still Feel Clinton Should Remain in Office." *Gallup Poll Monthly* 396 (Sept. 1998b): 9–10.

Newport, Frank, and Alec Gallup. "Clinton's Popularity Paradox." *Gallup Poll Monthly* 388 (Jan. 1998): 14–15.

Newport, Frank, and Lydia Saad. "The New President: Americans Making Up Their Minds Much Faster than Usual." *Gallup Poll Monthly* 329 (Feb. 1993): 15.

Nichols, Bill. "For Some Blacks, Guinier Case Part of a Pattern." *USA Today.* June 8, 1993, 6A.
Nie, Norman H., Sidney Verba, and John R. Petrocik. *The Changing American Voter.* Enl. ed. Cambridge, Mass: Harvard University Press, 1979.
Niebuhr, Gustav. "The Gospel according to Bill Clinton." *Washington Post,* National Weekly Edition. Mar. 21–27, 1994, 12.
———. "Clinton Says Psalms Bring Him Relief." *New York Times.* Feb. 3, 1995, A11.
———. "Not All Presidential Advisers Talk Politics." *New York Times.* Mar. 18, 1997, A1.
Nixon, Richard M. *Nixon Speaks Out: Major Speeches and Statements by Richard M. Nixon in the Presidential Campaign of 1968.* New York: Nixon-Agnew Committee, 1968.
———. Remarks in Anaheim, California, Oct. 30, 1970. American Freedom Library. Orem, Utah. Western Standard Publishing, 1997. [CD-ROM].
———. *In the Arena: A Memoir of Victory, Defeat and Renewal.* New York: Pocket Books, 1991.
Nordlinger, Eric A. *Isolationism Reconfigured: American Foreign Policy for a New Century.* Princeton: Princeton University Press, 1995.
Novak, Viveca. "Spending Spree?" *National Journal* 25 (1993): 509–11.
———. "Was This A Bad Idea? A Verdict Clearing Espy is the Latest Sign that the Independent-Counsel Statute is Likely to Perish." *Time* 152 (Dec. 14, 1998): 36.
Novak, Viveca, and Michael Frisby. "Clinton to Issue Initiative on School Prayer." *Wall Street Journal.* July 12, 1995, A16.
Nye. Joseph S., Jr. "Conflicts after the Cold War: Realism, Liberalism, and U.S. Interests." In *The Future of American Foreign Policy.* 3d ed., edited by Eugene R. Wittkopf and Christopher M. Jones, 68–82. New York: Worth Publishers, 1999a.
———. "Redefining the National Interest." *Foreign Affairs* 78, no. 4 (July/Aug. 1999b): 22–35.
O'Brien, David M. "Clinton Legal Policy and the Courts." In *The Clinton Presidency: First Appraisals,* edited by Colin Campbell and Bert A. Rockman, 126–62. Chatham, N.J.: Chatham House, 1995.
———. "Judicial Legacies: The Clinton Presidency and the Courts." In *The Clinton Legacy,* edited by Colin Campbell and Bert A. Rockman, 96–117. New York: Chatham House, 2000.
*Online Newshour with Jim Lehrer.* "Sen. McCain on the Trail." (Sept. 1, 1999). Online. Available: http://www.pbs.org/newshour/bb/election/july-dec99/mccain_9-1.html. Jan. 20, 2000.
Oudes, Bruce, ed. *The President: Richard Nixon's Secret Files.* New York: Harper and Row, 1989.
Palazzolo, Daniel. *Done Deal.* Chatham, N.J.: Chatham House, 1999.
Parks, Daniel J. "A Legacy of Budget Surpluses and Thriving Markets." *Congressional Quarterly Weekly Report* 58 (2000): 228–33.
Pear, Robert. "Panel Says Social Security Needs Are Underestimated." *New York Times.* Dec. 7, 1999, A7.
Penny, Timothy J. [Democratic U.S. Representative, 1984–1994.] Personal interview with Steven Schier. June 30, 1999.
Perry, Huey L., and Wayne Parent, eds. *Blacks and the American Political System.* Gainesville: University Press of Florida, 1995.
Peterson, Jonathan. "Number of Poor Americans Declines, U.S. Report Says." *Los Angeles Times.* Oct. 6, 1995, A4.
Pew Research Center for the People and the Press. "Early Ads and the Clinton Comeback." Poll Analysis, May 13, 1999.
Pew Research Center Report. "Progress Seen on AIDS, Crime, and Deficit." Nov. 1997.
———. "Public's Good Mood and Optimism Undeterred by Latest Developments." Dec. 1998.
———. "Clinton Fatigue Undermines Gore Poll Standing." Mar. 1999.
———. "Candidate Qualities May Trump Issues in 2000." Oct. 1999.

———. "Muted and Mixed Public Response to Peace in Kosovo." June 1999.
Pfiffner, James. *The Strategic Presidency*. 2d ed. Lawrence: University Press of Kansas, 1996.
———. "Sexual Probity and Presidential Character." *Presidential Studies Quarterly* 28 (Fall 1998): 881–86.
Pianin, Eric. "Turnabout on Defense Funds; Bipartisan Consensus Supporting Major Buildup." *Washington Post*. May 29, 1999, A1.
Pianin, Eric and John Harris. "Budget Surplus Forecast Grows by $1Trillion." *Washington Post*. June 29, 1999, A1.
Pierson, Paul. "When Effect Becomes Cause: Policy Feedback and Political Change." *World Politics* 45 (1993): 595–628.
Pins, Kenneth. "Military Ranks Thinning Out." *Des Moines Sunday Register*. July 18, 1999, 1B–2B.
Pious, Richard. *The Presidency*. New York: Allyn and Bacon, 1996.
Polakow, Valerie. "Savage Distributions: Welfare Myths and Daily Lives." In *A New Introduction to Poverty: The Role of Race, Power, and Politics*, edited by Louis Kushnick and James Jennings, 167–84. New York: New York University Press, 1999.
Pomper, Gerald M. "The Presidential Election." In *The Election of 1992*, edited by Gerald M. Pomper, 132–56. Chatham, N.J.: Chatham House, 1993.
———. "The Alleged Decline of American Parties." In *Politicians and Party Politics*, edited by John Geer. Baltimore: Johns Hopkins University Press, 1998.
Pomper, Miles A. "Deal Gives Clinton IMF Credit; GOP Wins Conditions on Loans," *Congressional Quarterly Weekly Report* 56 (1998): 2833–34.
———. "Members Rally around Kosovo Mission Despite Misgiving About Strategy." *Congressional Quarterly Weekly Report* 57 (1999): 763–65.
Poole, Keith, and Howard Rosenthal. "Patterns of Congressional Voting." *American Journal of Political Science* 35, no. 1 (1991): 228–78.
Posner, Richard. *An Affair of State: The Investigation, Impeachment, and Trial of President Clinton*. Cambridge, Mass.: Harvard University Press, 1999.
Prendergast, William B. *The Catholic Voter in American Politics*. Washington, D.C.: Georgetown University Press, 1999.
Price, Joyce, and Larry Witham. "Cardinal Attacks Elders on Gay Advocacy." *Washington Times*. Mar. 23, 1994, A1.
Purdum, Todd S. "Facets of Clinton." *New York Times Magazine* (May 19, 1996): 36–41.
———. "A Year of the Lewinsky Ordeal May Add Up to a Brief Memory." *New York Times*. Feb. 14, 1999, 26.
Putzel, Michael. "Clinton Weighs a Shuffle in Top White House Staff." *Boston Globe*. May 5 1993, 1.
Quirk, Paul J., and William Cunion. "Clinton's Domestic Policy: The Lessons of a New Democrat." In *The Reagan Legacy*, edited by Colin Campbell and Bert A. Rockman, 200–225. New York: Chatham House, 2000.
Rae, Nicol C. *Southern Democrats*. New York: Oxford University Press, 1994.
———. *Conservative Reformers: The Republican Freshmen and the Lessons of the 104th Congress*. Armonk, N.Y.: M. E. Sharpe, 1998a.
———. "Party Factionalism, 1946–1996." In *Partisan Approaches to Postwar American Politics*, edited by Byron E. Shafer, 41–74. Chatham, N.J.: Chatham House, 1998b.
Ragsdale, Lyn. *Vital Statistics on the Presidency: Washington to Clinton*. Washington, D.C.: Congressional Quarterly Press, 1996.
Rauch, Jonathan. *Demosclerosis: The Silent Killer of American Government*. New York: Times Books, 1994.

Reich, Robert. *Locked in the Cabinet.* New York: Knopf, 1997.
Renshon, Stanley A. *High Hopes: The Clinton Presidency and the Politics of Ambition.* New York: Routledge, 1998.
Reuss, Henry. "An Alternative." *New York Times.* June 1, 1973, 35.
Rielly, John E., ed. *American Public Opinion and U.S. Foreign Policy 1995.* Chicago: Chicago Council on Foreign Relations, 1995.
———. "Americans and the World: A Survey at Century's End," *Foreign Policy* 114 (Spring 1999a): 97–114.
———, ed., *American Public Opinion and U.S. Foreign Policy 1999.* Chicago: Chicago Council on Foreign Relations, 1999b.
Roberts, Roxanne, "Clinton and Co. Dish Scraps to Press." *Washington Post.* Mar. 19, 1993, A1.
Rockman, Bert A. "Leadership Style and the Clinton Presidency." In *The Clinton Presidency: First Appraisals,* edited by Colin Campbell and Bert A. Rockman, 325–62 Chatham, N.J.: Chatham House, 1996.
———. "Cutting with the Grain: Is There a Clinton Leadership Legacy?" In *The Clinton Legacy,* edited by Colin Campbell and Bert A. Rockman, 274–94. New York: Chatham House, 2000.
Rohde, David W. *Parties and Leaders in the Postreform House.* Chicago: University of Chicago Press, 1991.
Roper Center. *America at the Polls 1998.* Storrs, Conn.: Roper Center for Public Opinion Research, 1999.
Rosati, Jerel, and Stephen Twing. "The Presidency and U.S. Foreign Policy after the Cold War." In *After the End: Making U.S. Foreign Policy in the Post–Cold War World,* edited by James M. Scott, 29–56. Durham, N.C.: Duke University Press, 1998.
Rose, Richard. "Evaluating Presidents." In *Researching the Presidency: Vital Questions, New Approaches,* edited by George C. Edwards III, John H. Kessel, and Bert A. Rockman, 453–84. Pittsburgh: University of Pittsburgh Press, 1993.
Rosenbaum, David E. "In Balanced-Budget Deal, Bush Is off the Seesaw." *New York Times.* Aug. 8, 1997, A17.
Rosenbaum, David E., and Steve Lohr. "With a Stable Economy, Clinton Hopes for Credit." *New York Times.* Aug. 3, 1996, 38.
Rubin, Alissa. "Highlights of Clinton's Proposal." *Congressional Quarterly Weekly Report* 53 (1995): 3722–23.
Saad, Lydia. "Clinton Riding High as Second Term Begins." *Gallup Poll Monthly* 383 (Jan. 1997): 6–7.
Saad, Lydia, and Frank Newport. "Clinton's Foreign Policy Rating Tumbles." *Gallup Poll Monthly* 343 (Apr. 1994): 18.
Safire, William. *Before the Fall: An Inside View of the Pre-Watergate Nixon White House.* New York: Ballantine, 1977.
*St. Louis Post-Dispatch.* "Clinton Thanks Blacks for 'Standing Up for Me.'" Sept. 20, 1998, A12.
Sanger, David E. "Clinton Says 'New Isolationism' Imperils U.S. Security." *New York Times.* Oct. 15, 1999a, A1, A10.
———. "How Push by China and U.S. Business Won over Clinton." *New York Times.* Apr. 15, 1999b, 1, A6.
Sapiro, Virginia, and David Canon. "Race, Gender, and the Clinton Presidency." In *The Clinton Legacy,* edited by Colin Campbell and Bert A. Rockman, 169–99. New York: Chatham House, 2000.
Schaeffer, Pamela. "Is There a Left Left to Carry on the Fight?" *National Catholic Reporter.* May 17, 1996, 3.

Schell, Jonathan. "Master of All He Surveys." *Nation* (June 21, 1999): 25–30.
Schier, Steven E. *A Decade of Deficits: Congressional Thought and Fiscal Action.* Albany: State University of New York Press, 1992.
———. "Why Campaigns Are Now like Target Practice." *Washington Post.* Oct. 24, 1999, B2.
———. *By Invitation Only: The Rise of Exclusive Politics in the United States.* Pittsburgh: University of Pittsburgh Press, 2000.
Schlesinger, Arthur M. "Has Democracy a Future?" *Foreign Affairs* 76, no. 5 (Sept.–Oct.1997): 2–12.
Schmitt, Eric. "Senate G.O.P. to Allow Vote on Pact to Ban Nuclear Tests." *New York Times.* Oct. 1, 1999, A8.
Schneider, Bill. "After the Honeymoon, Reality Dawns." *National Journal* 25 (Apr. 17, 1993): 962.
Sciolino, Elaine, and Ethan Bronner. "How a President, Distracted by Scandal, Entered Balkan War." *New York Times.* Apr. 18, 1999, A1.
Serrano, Richard A., and Marc Lacey. "GOP Leaders Insist on Path of Impeachment." *Los Angeles Times.* Sept. 24, 1998, A1.
Shafer, Byron E. "The Notion of an Electoral Order: The Structure of Electoral Politics at the Accession of George Bush." In *The End of Realignment? Interpreting American Electoral Eras,* edited by Byron E. Shafer. Madison: University of Wisconsin Press, 1991a. 37–84.
———. "The Partisan Legacy: Are There Any New Democrats? (And By the Way, Was There a Republican Revolution?) In *The Clinton Legacy,* edited by Colin Campbell and Bert A. Rockman, 1–32. New York: Chatham House, 2000.
———, ed. *The End of Realignment? Interpreting American Electoral Eras.* Madison: University of Wisconsin Press, 1991[b].
Shafer, Byron E., and J. M. William Claggett. *The Two Majorities: The Issue Context of Modern American Politics.* Baltimore: Johns Hopkins University Press, 1995.
Shalala, Donna. Comments made by the Health and Human Services Secretary at an American Enterprise Institute panel. Jan. 5, 1999. Notes made by John F. Harris.
Shepard, Scott. "Blacks, Hispanics Rally behind Clinton; Minorities Wary of Law." *Austin-American Statesman.* Sept. 16, 1998, A16.
Shogan, Robert. *The Fate of the Union.* Boulder, Colo.: Westview Press, 1998.
Silbey, Joel H. "Beyond Realignment and Realignment Theory: American Political Eras, 1789–1989." In *The End of Realignment? Interpreting American Electoral Eras,* edited by Byron E. Shafer, 3–23. Madison: University of Wisconsin Press, 1991.
Simendinger, Alexis. "The Paper Wars." *National Journal* 30 (July 25, 1998): 1732–39.
Simon, Richard. "Bush Solidly Leads Gore in New National Poll Targeting Latinos." *Los Angeles Times.* Jan. 20, 2000, A5.
Sinclair, Barbara. "Trying to Govern Positively in a Negative Era: Clinton and the 103rd Congress." In *The Clinton Presidency: First Appraisals,* edited by Colin Campbell and Bert A. Rockman, 88–125. Chatham, N.J.: Chatham House, 1996.
Sirgo, Henry B. "Blacks and Presidential Politics." In *Blacks and the American Political System,* edited by Huey L. Perry and Wayne Parent, 75–104. Gainesville: University Press of Florida, 1995.
Skocpol, Theda. *Boomerang: Clinton's Health Security Effort and the Turn against Government in U.S. Politics.* New York: W. W. Norton, 1996.
———. *Boomerang: Health Care Reform and the Turn Against Government.* Rev. ed. New York: W. W. Norton, 1997.
Skowronek, Stephen. *The Politics Presidents Make: Leadership from John Adams to George Bush.* Cambridge, Mass.: Harvard University Press, 1993.

———. *The Politics Presidents Make: Leadership from John Adams to Bill Clinton.* Cambridge, Mass.: Belknap Press, 1997.

Sloan, John W. *The Reagan Effect: Economics and Presidential Leadership.* Lawrence: University Press of Kansas, 1999.

Solomon, Burt. "Scrimping on White House Staff Could Damage Clinton's Fortunes." *National Journal* 25 (1993): 2046.

Stanley, Harold W. "The Nominations: Republican Doldrums, Democratic Revival." In *The Elections of 1996*, edited by Michael Nelson, 14–43. Washington, D.C.: Congressional Quarterly Press, 1997.

Stark, Steven. "Gap Politics." *Atlantic Monthly* 274, no. 7 (July 1996): 71–80.

Starobin, Paul. "Man Trouble." *National Journal* 29 (Dec. 6, 1997): 2450–54.

Steel, Ronald. "The Domestic Core of Foreign Policy." *Atlantic Monthly* 275, no. 6 (June 1995): 85–92.

Stein, Herbert. *Presidential Economics: The Making of Economic Policy from Roosevelt to Reagan and Beyond.* New York: Simon and Schuster, 1984.

Steinfels, Peter. "The President's Church: Pastors Want Clinton in Their Flocks." *New York Times.* Dec. 7, 1992, A13.

———. "Beliefs: God at the Inauguration." *New York Times.* Jan. 23, 1993, 10.

Stengel, Richard and Eric Pooley. "Masters of the Message." *Time.* Internet edition (Nov. 6, 1996): 1–28. Online. Available: http://www.time.com. Nov. 20, 1996.

Stepanek, Marcia. "Clinton Drops Bid for Trade Deal Powers." *Albany (New York) Times Union.* Sept. 14, 1994, A2.

Stephanopoulos, George. *All too Human: A Political Education.* Boston: Little, Brown. 1999.

Stevenson, Richard W. "Greenspan Named to a Fourth Term as Fed Chairman." *New York Times.* Jan. 5, 2000, A1, C8.

Stiglitz, Joseph. "Defending the Clinton Administration." *Challenge* 40 (May–June 1997): 22.

Stimson, James A. "Public Support for American Presidents: A Cyclical Model." *Public Opinion Quarterly* 40 (Spring 1976): 1–21.

Stokes, Bruce. "Mexican Roulette." *National Journal* 25 (May 15, 1993): 1161.

Stone, Roger. "Nixon on Clinton" *New York Times.* Apr. 28, 1994, A23.

Sullivan, Andrew. "Going Down Screaming." *New York Times Magazine* (Oct. 11, 1998): 46–51, 88–91.

Sundquist, James L. *The Decline and Resurgence of Congress.* Washington, D.C.: Brookings Institution, 1981.

———. *Dynamics of the Party System: Alignments and Realignment of Political Parties in the United States.* Rev. ed. Washington, D.C.: Brookings Institution, 1983.

Szamuely, George. "Clinton's Clumsy Encounter with the World." *Orbis* 38, no. 3 (Summer 1994): 373–94.

Tapp, Michele. "RFRA Passage Inches Closer." *Christianity Today.* Oct. 4, 1993, 51.

Taylor, Andrew. "Clinton's Strength Portends a Tough Season for GOP." *Congressional Quarterly Weekly Report* (Feb. 6, 1999): 290–95.

Tenpas, Kathryn Dunn. "Women on the White House Staff: A Longitudinal Analysis, 1939–1994." In *The Other Elites: Women, Politics, and Power in the Executive Branch*, edited by MaryAnne Borrelli and Janet M. Martin. Boulder, Colo.: Lynne Rienner Publishers, 1997: 91–106.

Tien, Charles, Regan Checchio, and Arthur H. Miller. "The Impact of First Wives on Presidential Campaigns and Elections." In *Women and Politics: Outsiders or Insiders?* 3d ed., edited by Lois Duke Whitaker, 149–68. Upper Saddle River, N.J.: Prentice-Hall, 1999.

Toner, Robin. "The Catholic Hierarchy and Clinton: Already a Complicated Relationship." *New York Times.* Feb. 3, 1993, A10.
Towell, Pat. "Congress Set to Provide Money, but No Guidance, for Kosovo Mission." *Congressional Quarterly Weekly Report* 57 (1999): 1036–40.
Twentieth Century Fund Task Force on the Presidential Appointment Process. *Obstacle Course.* New York: Twentieth Century Fund Press, 1996.
United States. Executive Office of the President. *A National Security Strategy for a New Century.* National Security Council, Washington, D.C., May 1997. Online. Available: http://www.whitehouse.gov/WH/EOP/NSC/Strategy/#11-promoting. Aug. 4, 1999.
U.S. Marine Corps. *Warfighting.* New York: Doubleday, Currency, 1995.
Uchitelle, Louis. "Rising Incomes Lift 1.1 Million Out of Poverty." *New York Times.* Oct. 1, 1999. A1, A22.
Van Natta, Don, Jr. "Democrats Aim for Record in Unregulated Donations." *New York Times,* National Edition. July 25, 1999, A1.
*Vital Voices: Women in Democracy.* Online. Available: http://usinfo.state.gov/vitalvoices/. May 1, 2000.
Walcott, Charles and Karen Hult. *Governing the White House.* Lawrence: University Press of Kansas, 1995.
Wald, Kenneth, John Green, James Guth, Ted Jelen, Lyman Kellstedt, Corwin Smidt, and Clyde Wilcox. "Evaluation of the New Religious Items on the NES 1997 Pilot Study: A Report to the NES Board." Feb. 1998.
Wall, James M. "A Visit to the White House." *Christian Century,* Apr. 7, 1993, 355–56.
Walsh, Kenneth T. "The New State of the Art Spin." *U.S. News and World Report* (Apr. 26, 1999): 36.
Ware, Alan. "Anti-Partism and Party Control of Political Reform in the United States: The Case of the Australian Ballot." *British Journal of Political Science* 29, no. 3 (2000): 1–29.
Wattenberg, Martin P. *The Decline of American Political Parties, 1952–1996.* Cambridge, Mass.: Harvard University Press, 1998.
*Weekly Compilation of Presidential Documents.* "Executive Order 12835—Establishment of the National Economic Council." (Feb. 1, 1993): 95.
———. "The President's News Conference." (May 26, 1994): 1169.
———. "Remarks to the National League of Cities." (Mar. 13, 1995): 398–408.
———. "Remarks Announcing the Appointment of Laura D'Andrea Tyson as Chair of the National Economic Council and an Exchange with Reporters." (Feb. 27, 1995b): 282.
Weisberg, Jacob. "The Governor-President." *New York Times Magazine* (Jan. 17, 1999): 30–35, 41, 52, 65.
Will, George. "The Kerrey Difference: Detachment." *Washington Post.* Mar. 16, 1997, C7.
Williams, Rhys H., ed. *Cultural Wars in American Politics.* New York: Aldine de Gruyter, 1997.
Wills, Garry. "The Clinton Principle." *New York Times Magazine* (Jan. 19, 1997): 28–35.
Wilson, James Q. "Clinton, the Country, and the Political Culture: A Symposium." *Commentary* 107 (Jan. 1999): 41–42.
Woodward, Bob. *The Agenda.* New York: Simon and Schuster, 1994.
———. *The Agenda: Inside the White House.* New York: Pocket Books, 1995.
———. *The Choice: How Clinton Won.* New York: Simon and Schuster, 1996.
———. *Shadow: Five Presidents and the Legacy of Watergate.* New York: Simon and Schuster, 1999.
Yancey, Philip. "The Riddle of Bill Clinton's Faith." *Christianity Today* (Apr. 25, 1994): 24–29.
Zaller, John R. "Monica Lewinsky's Contribution to Political Science" *PS: Political Science and Politics* 31, no. 2 (June 1998): 182–89.

# CONTRIBUTORS

Peri E. Arnold is professor of government at the University of Notre Dame and director of the Hesburgh Program of Public Service, Notre Dame's Public Policy Program. He is the author of *Making the Managerial Presidency,* which won the Louis Brownlow Award of the National Academy of Public Administration.

Barbara Burrell is associate director of the Public Opinion Laboratory, Northern Illinois University. She is the author of *A Woman's Place is in the House: Campaigning for Congress in the Feminist Era,* and *Public Opinion, the First Ladyship and Hillary Rodham Clinton.*

John J. Coleman is associate professor of political science at the University of Wisconsin–Madison. He is the author of *Party Decline in America: Policy, Politics, and the Fiscal State.*

John Frendreis is professor of political science at Loyola University Chicago. His publications include articles in the *American Political Science Review,* the *American Journal of Political Science,* the *Journal of Politics, Social Science Quarterly, Comparative Political Studies,* and the *Journal of Urban Affairs;* and he is the author (with Raymond Tatalovich) of *The Modern Presidency and Economic Policy.*

James L. Guth is William Rand Kenan Professor of Political Science at Furman University. His most recent books are *The Bully Pulpit: The Politics of Protestant Clergy* and *Religion and the Culture Wars: Dispatches from the Front.*

John F. Harris graduated in 1985 from Carleton College with a degree in history and a concentration in political economy. He has been with the *Washington Post* since 1985, in a succession of news beats, including Virginia state politics, the Pentagon, and, since 1995, the Clinton White House.

Diane Hollern Harvey is an assistant professor in the Department of Public and International Affairs at George Mason University. Her teaching and research interests include electoral behavior, public opinion, the presidency, and Congress.

James M. McCormick is professor of political science at Iowa State University. He has published or edited five books, including the third edition of *American Foreign Policy and Process* and *The Domestic Sources of American Foreign Policy: Insights and Evidence*.

Bruce Miroff is professor and chair of political science at the State University of New York, Albany. He is the author of *Pragmatic Illusions: The Presidential Politics of John F. Kennedy* and *Icons of Democracy: American Leaders as Heroes, Aristocrats, Dissenters, and Democrats*—as well as numerous articles on the presidency, political leadership, and American political theory. He is also the co-author of *The Democratic Debate: An Introduction to American Politics* and coeditor of *Debating Democracy: A Reader in American Politics*.

John J. Pitney Jr. is associate professor of government at Claremont McKenna College in Claremont, California. He has published many academic studies on Congress, political parties, and the mass media. He has also written articles for the *New Republic*, the *Los Angeles Times*, the *Weekly Standard*, and the *Wall Street Journal*. He is a contributing editor to *Reason* magazine.

Nicol C. Rae is professor of political science at Florida International University. His publications include *The Decline and Fall of the Liberal Republicans, Southern Democrats*, and *Conservative Reformers: the Republican Freshman and the Lessons of the 104th Congress*, and *Governing America* (with Tim Hames). He is also co-editor (with Colin C. Campbell) of *New Majority or Old Minority: The Impact of Republicans on Congress*.

Steven E. Schier is the Dorothy H. and Edward C. Congdon Professor of Political Science at Carleton College. He is the author of five books and numerous scholarly articles. Schier has also contributed articles and opinion pieces to the *New York Times*, the *Washington Post*, and the *Chicago Tribune*, among other newspapers, and is political analyst for KSTP television in Minneapolis.

Raymond Tatalovich is professor of political science at Loyola University Chicago. He recently co-authored a presidency textbook, entitled *To Govern a Nation: Presidential Power and Politics* and has previously collaborated with John Frendreis on *The Modern Presidency and Economic Policy*.

Sharon D. Wright is an assistant professor of political science and black studies at the University of Missouri at Columbia. She is the author of *Race, Power, and Political Emergence in Memphis*.

# INDEX

abortion, 210; and approval ratings of Clinton, 127, 213, 215; Clinton's stance on, 205, 208, 240–41; conservatives' dissatisfaction over, 152, 173; differences between men and women on, 252

advisers, presidential: economic, 29, 42, 45–47, 49, 51, 53; foreign policy, 35; on national security, 32–33; political, 3, 28, 113–14; pollsters as, 9; on welfare reform, 28, 96. *See also* Morris, Dick

affirmative action: Clinton's support for, 90, 193, 210, 225; Republican nervousness about, 176

African Americans, 7, 229, 231; support for Clinton by, 226, 235; support for Democrats by, 236, 260

age, and approval ratings for Clinton, 138

agendas, 257; Clinton's, 10, 103–4, 128, 259, 260; economic, 160; narrowness of interest groups', 257; Republicans', 171, 177; Republican *vs.* Democratic, 149; *vs.* naysaying, 171

Agnew, Spiro, 178

Aid to Families with Dependent Children (AFDC), 13, 26, 229

Albright, Madeleine, 34–35, 244

alliances: in Clinton's foreign policy, 65–66; and intervention in Bosnia, 68. *See also* NATO

Andrew, Joe, 187–88

appointments, by Clinton, 227; of African Americans, 225–26, 230, 232; controversy over Lani Guinier's, 229–30; judicial, 226–27, 234, 242–44; religious background of, 207; in transition to presidency, 22–24, 36; of women, 4, 239, 242–44

approval ratings: of Bush, 224; of character *vs.* job performance, 19, 103, 119–20, 125, 131–32, 136; of Clinton, 9, 19–21, 70–71, 129–30, 210–15, 227, 252; of Clinton among minorities, 227, 230, 235; of Clinton during impeachment, 31–32, 146, 249; of Clinton's job performance, 19, 88; for economic programs, 42–43; honeymoon periods for new presidents, 127; patterns over two terms, 125–27, 130; of presidents, 110, 125. *See also* popularity

Arkansas: Clinton as governor of, 97–99, 113, 224–25; weakness of Republicans in, 169

Armey, Dick, 171

Asia, IMF crises in, 71

Asian Americans, 231, 260; dissatisfactions with Clinton of, 230, 232; support for Clinton by, 224, 227, 235

Asia-Pacific Economic Cooperation (APEC), 75

Barbour, Haley, 170, 172

Barro, Robert, 43

Barshefsky, Charlene, 51

Beatty, Warren, 198

Bennet, James, 31

Bentsen, Lloyd, 45–47, 48, 49, 185

Berger, Samuel "Sandy," 65, 95

Bernstein, Jared, 55–56

Blumenthal, Sidney, 114

Bosnia: Bush's policy on, 32; and Clinton's approval ratings, 128–29; Clinton's policy on, 33–35, 38, 67–68, 72

Boxer, Barbara, 248

Bradley, Bill, 51, 122, 141, 197; appeal to voters, 91–92; campaign based on economic issues, 59, 149

Breyer, Stephen, 208
Brown, Ron, 230
Buchanan, Pat, 198, 204
*Buckley v. Valeo,* 189
budgets: balanced, 57, 103, 159–61; Congress *vs.* Clinton on, 28–31, 191, 193–94; deficits, 26, 37–38, 47–48; influencing foreign policy through, 71; in Keynesian fiscal policy, 157; Republican pressure for balancing, 46, 51–53, 116; Republican *vs.* Democratic priorities in, 58; surpluses, 37–38, 57. *See also* deficit reductions
Burnham, Walter Dean, 6
Burns, James MacGregor, 56–57
Burton, Dan, 179, 196
Bush, George, 2, 224, 239, 242; campaigning by, 168, 169, 206; Clinton criticizing foreign policy of, 32–33, 50, 62–63, 229; effects of economy on presidency of, 42, 149; foreign policy of, 34, 67; legacy of, 234; noncommunicativeness of, 36, 109; and public opposition to raising taxes, 58; trade policy of, 48–49, 69
Bush, George W., 139, 197; campaigning by, 149, 182; personal information about, 141, 182; political style of, 90, 104–5, 140; popular support for, 149, 234, 250, 253
business, 58; Clinton's ties to, 107; and trade agreements with China, 50–51
cabinet, Clinton's: appointments to, 23, 226, 232, 239, 242–44; high turnover in, 230; involvement in foreign policy issues of, 32, 78–79, 82
campaign finance scandal, 11, 117, 189–90, 195–96; effects on Gore of, 233–34
campaigning, governing by, 9, 15, 103
campaigns, 23, 258; in 2000, 182, 197–98; Clinton's, 47–48, 98, 168–69, 224–25; national party organizations in, 188–89; permanent, 98–99, 103, 114, 258–59; role of Hillary Clinton in, 245–49. *See also* governing by campaigning
Campolo, Tony, 207
Carter, Jimmy, 109, 232
Carter, Stephen, 206
Carville, James, 209
Catholics: approval ratings of Clinton by, 212, 216–18; Clinton's relations with, 203, 206; dissatisfactions with Clinton of, 207–8
censorship, Clinton's opposition to, 210
centrism, 203; of Clinton, 89, 103, 121, 140, 156, 173, 193, 205; of Democrats, 156, 190–91; as effect of 1994 Republican victories, 129; public wanting more, 139–40
Chavez-Thompson, Linda, 226
Chavis, Benjamin, 229
Chemical Weapons Convention, 73, 80
child care, 57
children: Clinton's initiatives for, 239, 241, 251; in welfare reform, 26–28. *See also* families
China, 76; in campaign fundraising scandal, 50, 189; Clinton criticizing Bush's policy on, 32–33, 50; loss of nuclear secrets to, 11, 50; trade policy with, 50–51, 68–69
Christian Coalition, 208–9
Christopher, Warren, 32–33, 64–65
Cisneros, Henry, 230, 232
Civil Rights Act of 1964, 232
Civil Rights Act of 1990, 224
civil-rights legislation, under Johnson, 232
civil suits, claims of presidential immunity from, 39
class, social: and approval ratings for Clinton, 137–38; and Clinton's promised tax cuts, 168; and economic-quality issues, 163–64; in health-care reform battle, 115; and increasing income inequalities, 55–57; role in politics of, 41
Cleveland, Grover, 145
Clinton, Hillary Rodham, 96, 168; in appointments of women, 243; effects on gender gap of, 245; expansion of First Lady's role by, 3, 14; in health-care reform battle, 25–26, 115, 117; involvement in *Vital Voices* initiative of, 244; partnership with Bill of, 3–4; political style of, 102; religious background of, 203–4, 206; roles of, 3, 14, 240, 245–48; Senate campaign of, 3–4; support during impeachment for, 220
Clinton, William Jefferson, 10; background of, 97–98, 107; character of, 89, 100, 108–9, 118–19, 122, 128, 135–36, 140, 180, 216–17, 239–40; as "the Comeback Kid," 123, 173; concern about legacy of, 180; demographics of support for, 137–38; economic beliefs of, 46–47, 49; leadership by, 8–9, 129, 131, 223; Nixon comparing to self, 181; partnership with Hillary of, 3–4; personality of, 87, 90–91, 97–98, 102; political identity changes of, 15, 88, 110–13, 117–20, 259; political style of, 8–10, 102–5, 113, 120; religious background of, 203, 205, 209; as "Slick Willie," 89, 111, 169;

views on role of government, 87, 91, 260. *See also* Clinton presidency
Clinton presidency, 6, 13–14; economic philosophy of, 53; effects on culture wars of, 221; effects on Democrats of, 139, 154–56, 187–90; evolution of, 66–67, 94; extent of reliance on polls of, 96–97; firsts in, 3, 14–15; foreign policy of, 60–83; inconsistencies in, 2–3, 87–88; lack of legacies of, 120, 199, 255–56; legacies of, 35–40, 58, 74–81, 123, 140–42, 146–47, 251; limitations of, 26, 90, 121; passivity in, 103–4; and political parties, 146, 164–66; as preemptive, 2–3, 12, 39, 152–56, 164–65, 260, 263; as public presidency, 108–13, 120, 124; public response to, 132–33, 136–40; questionable legacies of, 108, 135, 236, 239; role of communication in, 99–102; trade policies of, 48–51; transition into, 22–24, 35–36, 99, 114–16, 227–28; uniqueness of, 1, 5–7, 93–94
*Clinton v. Jones,* 11–12
Cold War, effects of end of, 5, 32, 74–76
communicativeness: Clinton's style, 239–40; need for presidents', 36–37, 99–102; presidents judged by, 140; of Reagan and Clinton, 125
Comprehensive Test Ban Treaty, 71, 80, 261
Congress, 210; budgets in, 28–31, 54–55, 57, 129; Clinton's relations with, 10, 28–31, 72–73, 99, 186, 227–28; Clinton's relations with Democrats in, 170, 183, 191–92; Democrats hoping to regain control of, 155, 197; Democrats in, 127, 186; Democrats losing control of, 145, 183–84; and the economy, 48, 159; and foreign policy, 61, 68, 79–80, 82, 261; and health-care reform, 25; independence of, 2, 5–6; minority members of, 229, 235; in Nixon impeachment process, 178; and NAFTA, 14, 49, 70; oddness of elections for, 6–7; partisanship in, 11, 256–57; relations with presidents, 4, 145–46, 157–59; Republicans in, 26, 71, 116, 170–73, 177; on trade relations with China, 51, 69; and welfare reform, 13, 229. *See also* House of Representatives; impeachment; Senate
Congressional Accountability Act, 172
Congressional Black Caucus, 229, 235
Congressional Hispanic Caucus, 230
conservatism, 252; Clinton's stances on, 191, 193–94; compassionate, 181, 253; ideological, *vs.* operational liberalism, 129; increasing, 2, 151

conservatives, 173; and approval ratings of Clinton, 213, 215, 220; Christian, 208; dissatisfactions with Clinton of, 207, 208, 215; and Nixon's triangulation strategy, 174; and Republicans, 163, 209
Contract for America, 26–28
Contract with America, 171; Democrats rallying with Clinton against, 193; passage of bills, 172–73; and Republican pressure for balanced budget, 51; tax cuts promised in, 116–17
Cook, Suzan D. Johnson, 226
Cornelius, Catherine, 24
Council of Economic Advisers (CEA), 47, 53, 55
courts: not supporting claims of presidential immunity, 39; restricting executive privilege, 11–12, 14. *See also* appointments, judicial
Cox, Archibald, 177–79
crime, policies on, 231; Clinton's, 135, 168, 205; Clinton's conservatism on, 193, 225; and Republicans, 138, 173, 185; rights of victims, 96–97
crime bill: dissatisfactions with, 152, 229; low Democratic support for, 192
critical realignment theory, 150–52, 164–65
*Culture of Disbelief, The* (Carter), 206
culture wars, 203–22
*Culture Wars: The Struggle to Define America* (Hunter), 204–5
Daschle, Thomas, 193
Dayton Accords, for Bosnia, 33, 68
Deaver, Michael, 111
Defense of Marriage Act, 194, 209
defense spending, 57; Clinton cutting, 47, 63; Republicans' proposals for, 51, 72–73
deficit-reduction package, 4, 13, 28, 55; as Clinton victory, 37, 185
deficit reductions, 54, 129; and 1996 budget, 29–31; divisiveness over, 89–90, 173. *See also* budgets, deficits
democracy: Clinton's desire to spread, 61, 63–64; defense of, 69–70; promoting through expansion of NATO, 69–70; role of political ads in, 101; role of polls in, 92
Democratic Leadership Council, 99
Democratic National Committee (DNC): buying ads for Clinton, 9, 101; paying for Clinton's political consultants, 113; reacting against Republican majority, 193; supporting Clinton's policy programs, 188
Democrats: agenda of, 257, 260; areas of strength of, 138, 258; Clinton's relations with,

Democrats *(continued)*
103–4, 121–22; Clinton's relations with congressional, 2–3, 20–21, 170, 191–93, 235; and Clinton's triangulation strategy, 9, 27, 88, 173–74; coalitions of, 148–50, 224, 233; composition of party, 51, 137–38, 190–91, 236, 249–50; in Congress, 26, 235; "dealignment" of, 7; effects of Clinton presidency on, 154–56, 171, 186, 208; effects of Clinton's economic stance on, 42; effects of Clinton's governing style on, 9–10; in elections, 127, 145; factions in, 198–99, 248; and foreign policy, 80; fundraising for, 189–90, 248–49; and Hillary Clinton, 248–49; and Lewinsky scandal, 196–97; liberals in, 107, 163, 248; losing majority in Congress, 155, 184, 228; and minorities, 227, 232–33, 235–37; national party chairmen under Clinton, 187–88; and Nixon, 167, 177–78; nominations to succeed Clinton, 197–98; opposition to Clinton's initiatives, 48; opposition to NAFTA, 14, 49, 70; as presidential party, 183, 185; progressive approach for, 155–56; rareness as two-term presidents of, 6; tax cuts proposed by, 160; unity of, 89–90, 178, 196–97

Department of State, 79

deregulation, 47

divided government: presidents' difficulty with, 228; public splitting tickets to maintain, 7, 194, 197–98, 200, 263–64

Doar, John, 178

Dodd, Christopher, 188

Dole, Bob: effects of welfare reform on election hopes of, 96, 174; presidential campaign of, 36, 173, 177, 190, 241; as senator, 11, 49, 170; and women, 245, 251, 253

Dole, Elizabeth, 254

domestic policy: Clinton's focus on, 5, 8, 104, 169; Clinton's legacy in, 262; Clinton's small initiatives in, 13, 95–96; issues for future presidents, 261; linked with foreign policy, 61–62, 78–80; and Nixon's triangulation strategy, 174

domestic program cuts, 29–30, 42

domestic spending: in budget struggle, 30; Clinton's priorities, 37; Clinton wanting to use budget surpluses for, 57–58; in economic-stimulus package, 47–48; Republicans trying to cut, 29

domestic violence, 240–41

drugs: Clinton's use of, 169; trafficking as foreign policy issue, 78

Early Child Development and Learning Conference, 241

economic policy, in fiscal state, 156–58

economy, 163; and Clinton's deficit reduction package, 13; Clinton's focus on, 29, 45, 128, 224; Clinton's stance on, 41, 53, 168, 260; and Clinton's stimulus package, 11, 29, 42, 47–48; as Democratic Party issue, 138, 209; and domestic policy linked with foreign policy, 62–63, 65–66; effects of stress in, 263–64; effects on Clinton's approval ratings of, 4, 129, 135, 185, 215, 218, 227; and foreign policy, 70–71, 74–75, 78–79, 262; government's role in, 158; growth of, 54, 152, 199–200; growth *vs.* quality issues in, 160, 163–64; importance to voters of, 149, 185; and minorities, 231–33; quality issues in, 160, 163–64, 262; Republicans losing advantage in, 185; U.S. hegemony in, 41, 265

Edelman, Peter, 229

education, 95, 164, 185; and approval ratings for Clinton, 135, 138; Democratic Party favored on, 138; federal aid to, 47, 57, 174; religion in, 209

Ehrlichman, John, 174

Eisenhower, Dwight, as preemptive president, 153–54, 180

Elders, Jocelyn, 171, 207, 230

elections, 41, 185; 1998, 145–46, 181, 186; 2000, 12, 139; Clinton's successes in, 127, 226–27; in critical realignment theory, 150–52; Democratic losses in 1994, 145, 185–86; effects of Latino vote on, 232–33; effects of women's votes in, 239, 251; gender gap in, 244, 251–53; lack of clarity in results of, 4, 257–58; minority support for Clinton in, 224–27; new political cleavages in, 204–5; as plebiscites on economic performance, 159; quirkiness of, in 1990s, 5–7; Republican wins in 1994, 128–29, 181, 184, 209, 241; split-ticket voting in, 158–59, 161, 184, 194; for sub-presidential positions, 184, 194–95; voter turnout for, 4, 225, 241, 248

Electoral College, 7, 185

employment: Clinton's initiatives to benefit women in, 241–42; job growth, 55; work requirements in welfare reform, 26–27

enlargement, strategy of, 60–61, 63–66

environment, 185; as Democratic strength, 138, 155; protecting regulations on, 90, 174; public approval of Clinton's handling of, 135

environmentalists, 104; and Clinton's trade policies, 49–50, 70, 262
Ervin committee: and Watergate, 177
Espy, Mike, 230
Executive Office of the President (EOP), 21, 23
executive privilege, 11–12, 14
extremists: Clinton criticizing, 27; Clinton painting Republicans as, 175–76, 186, 193–94
Falwell, Jerry, 208
families: Clinton's focus on, 95, 138, 239, 251; Clinton taking conservative stances on, 193
Family and Medical Leave Act, 128, 239, 242
family values, Clinton's stance on, 206, 239
fast-track authority, for negotiating trade agreements, 49–50, 71–72, 103–4
Fazio, Vic, 209
federalism, divisiveness among Republicans over, 173
Federal Reserve Board, 46, 159
feminism, and approval ratings of Clinton, 213, 215
filibusters, 11, 48
First Ladies: and popularity of presidents and candidates, 247; possibilities for, 14, 115
fiscal state, 156–59, 164
Forbes, Steve, 139
Ford, Gerald, 178
foreign aid, 71, 80
foreign policy, 5; of Clinton presidency, 60–83; Clinton's accused of double standard, 229; and Clinton's approval ratings, 128, 135; Clinton's legacy in, 38, 74–77, 78–81; development of Clinton's, 32–35; goals of Clinton's, 13–14, 38, 244; influences on Clinton's, 71–72, 262; lack of consensus on, 76, 261–62; opposition to, 70–71; Republican Party advantage in, 138, 185, 194
Fowler, Donald, 187–88
Franklin, John Hope, 226
Freedman, Tom, 101–2
free trade, 58, 75, 91, 199, 262. *See also* trade policy
fundraising, 248; by Clinton, 101, 188–90; by Democrats, 117, 188–89; by Gore, 101, 189; levels of, 146; by opposition to health-care reform, 114; by party organizations, 158, 188–89; by Republicans, 170, 254. *See also* campaign finance scandal
Galbraith, James K., 53–54
GATT. *See* General Agreement on Tariffs and Trade (GATT)

gays. *See* homosexuals
Geertz, Clifford, 32
gender politics, 138, 238–54
General Agreement on Tariffs and Trade (GATT), 49–50, 74–75
Gephardt, Dick, 193, 197
Gergen, David, 24, 112, 170
Gingrich, Newt, 49, 52; and Clinton, 117, 193; Republican leadership by, 6, 171, 193; and Republican revolution, 6, 90, 116; and scandal culture, 4, 11; underrating power of presidency, 172–73, 177; unpopularity of, 177, 178, 253
Ginsburg, Ruth Bader, 208
Glass-Steagall Act of 1933, 46–47
Gore, Albert: character of, 104, 140; effects of Clinton presidency on, 90, 122, 154, 190; effects of scandals on, 122, 189, 233–34, 250; fundraising by, 101, 189; political beliefs of, 59, 122, 197; presidential campaign of, 51, 139, 149, 190; and religion, 207, 222; as vice president, 95, 154, 191
governing by campaigning, 9, 15, 103
Governing Team Day, 171
government: Clinton's views on role of, 87, 91, 260; minorities wanting inclusion in governing process, 232; public keeping divided, 7, 194, 197–98, 200, 263–64; public opposition to, 26, 48, 115; relations between branches of, 11–12, 180; Republicans' view on role of, 26, 90, 155, 173; role of, 38, 158, 213, 240, 250–51, 253; scattered power of, 255, 258; size of, 26, 117, 129, 174. *See also* Congress; presidents
government shutdowns, 6, 11, 52–53, 253; Republicans blamed for, 30, 177, 193–94
governors: Republicans taking over as, 184; Republicans' using good programs of, 170, 172
Gramm, Phil, 47, 173
grand juries: Clinton testifying before, 11; in Watergate investigation, 178
Great Society programs, Reagan's criticism of, 155
Greenberg, Stan, 94, 208
Greenspan, Alan, 4, 46, 185; responsible for economic performance, 54, 58
Grossman, Steve, 187–88
guaranteed annual income, in Nixon's triangulation strategy, 174
Guinier, Lani, 229–30

gun controls, conservatives wanting to deal with, 173
Haiti, 68, 81; Clinton criticizing Bush for policy toward, 32–33; criticism of Clinton's policy on, 128, 229
health care, 138, 185; and approval ratings of Clinton, 213, 215; government role in, 57, 260. *See also* health-care reform
health-care reform, 3, 114, 186; as Clinton defeat, 25–26, 128; Democratic support for, 188, 192; political lessons from defeat of, 37, 115–16; public opinion of, 128, 135, 152
Health Insurance Association of America (HIAA), 114–15
Heclo, Hugh, 19
Herman, Alexis, 230
Hispanics: approval of Clinton by, 212, 216–18, 235–36; complaints about NAFTA's effects of, 230. *See also* Latinos
homosexuals, 208, 224; marriages of, 194, 209; in the military, 23, 127–28, 152, 186, 205
House of Representatives: Democrats in, 186; partisanship in, 11; Republicans in, 6, 171, 186; welfare reform bill of, 28. *See also* Congress; impeachment
human rights: Clinton criticizing Bush on, 32–33, 50; public opposition to interventions for, 70; and trade with China, 50, 69
Humphrey, Hubert, 141
Hunter, James Davison, 204–5
Hussein, Saddam, 68
Hybels, Bill, 207
Hyde, Henry, 234–35
Ickes, Harold, 94–95
immigration: and approval ratings of Clinton, 213–15; Clinton's conservatism on, 194, 210; and Latino voters, 232–33; policy expectations of minorities on, 231; and welfare reform, 28, 96
immunity, and Clinton's legacy on institution of presidency, 38–39
impeachment: aimed at preemptive presidents, 154, 177; effects on Clinton's foreign policy of, 73; factors in Clinton's survival of, 15, 119–20, 133, 178–79, 196–97; House debate on, 11–12; partisanship in, 4, 119, 146, 234–35; public opinion of, 19, 130–32, 186–87; religious groups' response to, 216–20; threat to Clinton presidency from, 31–32
income inequalities, 155; blamed on Reagan, 55; Clinton's tolerance of, 57–59; increasing, 41, 55–57; between women and men, 241–42

incumbents: approval ratings of, 127; and institution of presidency, 19–20
independent counsels, 39; and corruption allegations against cabinet of, 230; low standards for triggering, 99
individualism, *vs.* party affiliation, 162–63
Indonesian government, 189
inflation, 43, 54
information technology, 162
infrastructure, investment in, 47
"institutional thickening," 5, 255–57, 264
institutions, governmental: in fiscal state, 156, 158; presidency disconnecting from other, 21; presidents' politics conflicting with, 2. *See also* presidency, institution of
interest groups: and Congress vs. Clinton presidency, 2, 5; effects of, 255, 257; increasing influence of, 21, 158, 163; on foreign policy, 80–82; opposition to health-care reform, 114–16
interest rates, 43, 47
International Monetary Fund (IMF), 71
interventionism: in Clinton's foreign policy, 35, 38, 64; as legacy of Clinton foreign policy, 74; public opinion on, 70–71, 80–81
investigations, 11. *See also* independent counsels; special prosecutors
Iran-Contra scandal, effects of, 113, 125, 169
Jackson, Jesse, 197, 229
Jews: Clinton's relations with, 204, 206; support for Clinton by, 212, 216–18, 225
jobs. *See* employment
John Paul II, Pope, 31
Johnson, Andrew, as preemptive president, 12, 154
Johnson, Lyndon, 8, 232; scandals of, 132, 179
Jones, Paula, 11, 31
Kean, Thomas H., 226
Kennedy, Edward, 177–78, 229
Kennedy, John F., 132, 179
Kerrey, Bob, 10
Keynesian fiscal policy, 157–61; growth *vs.* quality issues in, 163–64. *See also* "post-Keynesian" macroeconomics
Khachigian, Ken, 176
Kosovo, 33–35, 229, 261; as Clinton legacy, 13–14; effects on approval ratings of intervention in, 133; goals of intervention in, 38, 60; polls in Clinton's strategy in, 9, 81
Kuwait, 68
labor. *See* organized labor

Lake, Anthony, 33, 60, 63–64
Latinos, 234; congressional support by during impeachment, 235; policy expectations of presidents of, 231; relations with Clinton of, 230, 232; support for Clinton in elections by, 225, 226; as voters, 232–33, 236, 260. *See also* Hispanics
law and order. *See* crime
Leopoulos, David, 98
Lerner, Michael, 206
Lewinsky scandal, 11–12; Clinton focusing on foreign policy during, 34; and Clinton's character, 118, 136; Democrats' response to, 196; effects on Clinton's popularity of, 9, 125, 130, 215–17, 245; factors in Clinton's survival of, 3–4, 119–20, 196; Hillary's support during, 3, 245; lessons for Republicans from, 181–82; public opinion of punishment for, 131–32; religious groups' response to, 215–17; threat to Clinton presidency from, 31–32; women's response to, 239, 249. *See also* impeachment
liberalism: approval ratings of Clinton's, 220; Clinton distancing himself from, 153, 168; differences between men and women in, 252; operational, *vs.* ideological conservatism, 129; public opposition to, 186; traditional Democratic, 122, 155–56, 183, 186
liberals: approval ratings of Clinton by, 137–38, 215, 220; Clinton as, 46, 58, 97, 128, 155–56, 186; declining idealism of, 107; in Democratic Party, 149, 163; Democrats trying to escape label of, 99; Hillary Clinton as, 248; and income inequalities, 55–57; judicial appointment of, 234; and Nixon's triangulation strategy, 174; opposition to Clinton's economics from, 53; support for humanitarian interventions by, 14
Lincoln, Abraham, as reconstructive president, 257
line-item veto, 172–73
Livingston, Bob, 234–35
Lott, Trent, 176–77
Lowi, Theodore, 21
Lugar, Richard, 173
macroeconomics, "post-Keynesian," 42, 53, 58
Magaziner, Ira, 25
mandate: Clinton's lack of, 2, 6, 145, 170; economic, 46; and failure of Clinton's health-care reform, 26, 37
market economies, trade policy to increase, 63–64

McCain, John, 64, 139, 165; presidential campaign of, 92, 149
McCurry, Michael, 100, 112
McGovern, George, 176
McInturff, Bill, 102
McLarty, Thomas "Mack," 22, 24
media, 92; advertising by Democratic National Committee, 188–89; Clinton's ads in, 101–2; Clinton's managers of, 112; Clinton's opposition to censorship by, 210; health-care reform in, 114–15; Reagan's image in, 110–11; reductionism in, 88. *See also* press
Medicaid: Clinton protecting, 28, 174; Republicans trying to reduce, 29–30, 176
Medicare, 138; bankruptcy of, 261; Clinton protecting, 174; Clinton's support for, 38, 57, 103; Republicans trying to reduce, 29–30, 101, 116–17, 176, 242
men: alienated by Clinton policies, 251–52; approval ratings for Clinton of, 138; support for Republicans of, 241
Mexico, 71
Mfume, Kweisi, 229
Michel, Bob, 171
Middle East, peace negotiations in, 68
military, 74, 76, 235; Clinton and budget for, 47, 57; Clinton downsizing, 63, 72; Congress *vs.* Clinton on, 72–73; gays in, 23, 127–28, 152, 186, 205, 208; public opposition to interventions by, 70–71. *See also* defense spending
minorities, 7; and affirmative action, 90, 176; appointments of, 23, 225–26, 230, 232; approval ratings of Clinton by, 137, 216, 227, 235; Clinton and racial politics, 223–37; congressional support by during impeachment, 235; dissatisfactions with Clinton, 228–29, 230; policy expectations from presidents, 231–32. *See also* African Americans; Asian Americans; Latinos
Misery Index, of economic factors, 43–44
moderates, favored in 2000 primaries, 139
Mondale, Walter, 57
Morris, Dick, 9, 51, 103; on Clinton's character, 98; influence of, 94–97, 101, 120, 123; remaking of Clinton's image by, 111–12, 117–18; and Republican Medicare cuts proposal, 116–17; and triangulation strategy, 173–74, 193, 209
Moseley-Braun, Carol, 248
Moynihan, Daniel Patrick, 174
Myers, Dee Dee, 22, 24

National Council of Churches, 206
National Economic Council (NEC), 45–47, 48, 51, 79
National Federation of Independent Business (NFIB), 114–15
National Health Care Initiative. *See* health-care reform
National Missile Defense Act, 71
National Policy Forum, 170
national security, 195; Bush's focus on, 169; in Clinton foreign policy, 65; Clinton's advisers on, 32–33, 60; and foreign policy agenda, 78–79
National Urban Policy proposal, 232
Native Americans: dissatisfactions with Clinton of, 230, 232; policy expectations of presidents of, 231; support for Clinton by, 224, 235
NATO (North Atlantic Treaty Organization), 33; expansion of, 68–69; in Kosovo, 13–14, 34
neo-liberals, within Democratic Party, 190–91, 197–99
Neustadt, Richard E., 231
New Deal: coalition for, 107, 148–50, 263; Reagan's support for, 154–55; *vs.* New Vision Economics, 47
New Democrats, 58, 183; Clinton as, 128–29, 153, 168, 191, 224; Clinton as on social issues, 205, 212; and national party chairmen under Clinton, 187–88
New Left/Minority faction within Democratic Party, 191, 197–99
New Market Initiatives, 232
New Vision Economics, 47
Nixon, Richard, 141, 181; and bad relations with press, 100, 112; and Cox as special Watergate prosecutor, 177–78; Democrats' relations with, 167, 177; impeachment proceedings against, 154, 177; political tactics of, 175–76; as preemptive president, 153–54, 154; Republicans' response to, 154; triangulation strategy of, 174
North American Free Trade Agreement (NAFTA), 14, 48, 128, 230; Clinton campaigning for, 70, 170, 192; in Clinton's legacy, 74, 262
North Korea, 128
Nuclear Non-Proliferation Treaty, 73
nuclear test-ban treaty, 71, 104, 180
nuclear weapons, Congress and Clinton's policy on, 73
Nunn, Sam, 99

obstruction of justice. *See* impeachment
Oh, Angela E., 226
Oklahoma City bombing: Clinton's political use of, 97, 175–76; and Clinton's status, 27, 129
Okun, Arthur, 43
O'Leary, Hazel, 230
Omnibus Budget Reconciliation bill (1993), 29
"One America in the Twenty-first Century: The President's Initiative on Race," 223, 225, 234
organized labor, and trade policies, 49–51, 70, 262
Panetta, Leon, 24, 45–46, 51
partisan realignment, 6, 146–52
partisanship, 79, 146, 176; and approval ratings of Clinton, 213, 215, 219–20; campaign finance scandal blamed on, 196; and climate for impeachment, 177–78; in Congress, 11, 256–57; effects on foreign policy of, 261–62; and impeachment, 131–33, 178, 196–97, 234–35; increase in, during economic stress, 263–64; public weariness of, 139, 184, 200. *See also* political parties
party organizations, 158–59. *See also* Democratic National Committee; Republican National Committee
party system, 163–65; changes during Clinton presidency, 151–52; effects of Clinton presidency on, 145–47; "Two Majorities" in, 194
Peña, Federico, 232
Penn, Mark, 9, 94–95, 102
perjury. *See* impeachment
Perot, Ross, 23, 161, 185, 186, 190
Perry, William J., 91
Persian Gulf War, 169
Personal Responsibility and Work Opportunity Reconciliation Act. *See* welfare reform
plebiscites: elections as, 159; through polling, 92
policy: desires and expectations of minorities regarding, 231; difficulties of large-scale changes in, 37, 255–62, 264; in fiscal state, 156; role of poll results in, 93–94. *See also* agendas; domestic policy; foreign policy; trade policy
policy-feedback model, 156–57
policy making: Clinton's governing style of, 9–10; foreign, 78–81
political meetings, politics and policy making in, 95
political parties, 165; affiliation of religious group members with, 221–22; agreement on balanced budgets between, 159–61; in critical

realignment theory, 150–52; decreasing influence of, 21, 200, 256, 263–64; decreasing loyalty to, 3, 187; effects of Clinton presidency on, 145–47; election performance of, with second-term presidents, 186; increasing influence of, 146, 262–63; and preemptive presidents, 154; public skepticism about, 158–59, 161–62; public's perceptions of, 7, 138, 161; public wanting more cooperation between, 139–40; and split-ticket voting, 184, 187, 194, 197–98, 200, 263–64; strength of, 156–59. *See also* partisanship

political process, distrust of, 3

politics, 4, 41; Clinton's, 2–3, 98; Clinton's success in, 8–9, 88; Clinton's tactics in, 89–90, 116–17, 120, 167–68, 180–82; comparison of Clinton's and Nixon's tactics in, 174–76, 178–79, 180; copying of Clinton's tactics in, 108, 122–23; in governing, 88; influence on foreign policy of, 82; minorities wanting inclusion in process of, 232; new culture of, 21, 110; postmodern style of, 259; public skepticism about, 93, 122, 142, 162; public wanting less partisanship in, 139; of Reagan *vs.* Clinton, 113; Republican techniques against Clinton, 114–16; role of, 104; Starr investigation as, 131–33; traditionalist, 218–19. *See also* triangulation strategy

polls: on Clinton legacy, 134–35; Clinton's defense of, 93; Clinton's use of, 8–9, 88–89, 91, 98, 107, 111–12; extent of Clinton's use of, 93–94, 96–97, 114; Gore's lack of dependence on, 104; governing by, 15, 262; increasing use of, 92, 102–3; on opposition to impeachment, 12; influence on foreign policy of, 80–81; during Lewinsky scandal, 118–19, 130–31; on responses to Medicare cuts, 116. *See also* approval ratings; popularity

popularity: of Clinton, 114; of Clintons, 245–47; of Gore, 233–34; presidents' need for, 259; of Reagan and Clinton, 112. *See also* approval ratings

"post-Keynesian" macroeconomics, 42, 53, 58

post-materialism, 41–42, 59

postmodern era: changing expectations of presidents in, 109–11; Clinton as character of, 106–8, 113; and Clinton presidency, 1, 15; Lewinsky scandal, symbolizing, 119–20; political style of, 259

poverty, 41; and expectations of minorities, 231–32; levels of, 56, 233

Powell, Colin, 91, 186

preemptive presidencies. *See* presidents, preemptive

presidency: advantages over Congress of, 30; and Clinton, 11, 99; as communicative role, 36–37; effects of Clinton on, 36–40, 235; effects on incumbents of, 19, 35; and foreign policy, 32–35; institution of, 19, 21; learning curve for, 20, 25, 35–36; limitations of, 26; as necessarily preemptive, 255; status and power of, 31–32, 35, 99, 172–73, 231

*Presidential Power* (Neustadt), 231

presidents, 23, 36; ability to make policy changes, 2, 27, 256–57; acting within institution of presidency, 19; approval ratings for, 92, 125–27, 130; authority to negotiate trade agreements of, 49–50; categorization schemes for, 152–56, 256; changing standards for, 109–11, 125, 149; comparing Misery Index factors under, 43–44; as defenders of public interests, 28, 30; economic policies of, 43, 157–58, 159; effects of first wives on popularity of, 247; effects of institutional thickening on, 5, 255–56; governing styles of, 8, 258–59; immunity from prosecution of, 11–12; leadership by, 8, 20–21, 92–93, 131, 162, 231, 260; moral standards for, 125, 132, 140–42, 149; need for communicativeness in, 36–37, 99–102; not leading parties to congressional majorities, 187; preemptive, 2–3, 12, 39, 180, 259, 264; qualifications for, 5; reconstructive, 2, 121, 256–57, 262–64; relations with Congress, 4, 71–72, 145–46, 157–59, 261; scandals of, 132, 141–42; stability of identities of, 110–11, 259–60; two-term Democratic, 145. *See also* divided government

press: Clinton's relations with, 99–101, 112–13; Nixon's relations with, 112; Reagan's relations with, 112

private sector, character of, 19–20

producer groups, opposition to NAFTA, 70

Protestants: African American, 204, 206, 212–13, 216–18; evangelical, 203, 206–7, 211–12, 216–18; Hispanic, 212; liberal, 203–4, 206; mainline, 211–12, 215, 216, 218

public: Clinton building rapport with, 9–10, 95, 109, 121; Clinton campaigning for support for health-care reform from, 114–16; Clinton's communication style with, 239–40; Clinton's relations with, 89–92, 114, 124–40; Clinton wanting to reach directly, 100, 107–10, 113;

public *(continued)*
  concerns about economy of, 42, 149, 185; dissatisfaction with government of , 26, 171; interest in politicians' character of, 112–13, 216; opposition to impeachment by, 12, 119; opposition to traditional Democratic liberalism by, 186; and party system, 146, 165, 200; presidents responding directly to, 259; skepticism of, 122; splitting tickets to control government by, 186, 194, 197–98, 200, 263–64. *See also* approval ratings; polls; popularity
public appearances, by Clinton, 9
public opinion. *See* approval ratings; polls; popularity; public
quality of life, in progressive Democratic approach, 155
race-initiative advisory board, 226, 230, 234
race relations, approval of Clinton's handling, 135
racial politics, 223–37. *See also* affirmative action; minorities
Reagan, Ronald, 22, 112, 171; approval ratings of, 19, 125; Clinton compared to, 110–13, 125; economic policy of, 41–42, 47, 58; economy under, 43, 55, 57; governing style of, 8, 36; influence of, 2, 162; as last reconstructive president, 256; legacy in judicial appointments of, 234; politicians copying, 117–18, 122–23; support for New Deal by, 154–55
Reaganomics, 47, 58
Reagan presidency, 9, 110, 120–21, 164
realignment theories, and declining loyalty to political parties, 187
recession, 1990–1991, 42
reconstructive presidencies. *See* presidents, reconstructive
Rector, Ricky Ray, 225
Reed, Bruce, 95, 96
referendums, policy changes through, 92, 103
Reform Party, 198
regionalism, 137–38, 191
Reich, Robert, 48, 95
Reischauer, Robert D., 52
Religious Freedom Restoration Act of 1993, 207
religious groups, 221; affiliations of Clintons with, 203–4; approval ratings of Clinton by, 204, 210–15; political party affiliation of members of, 221–22
religious realignment, 208
Rendell, Ed, 188
Reno, Janet, 230

Renshon, Stanley, 98
Republican National Committee, 170
Republican revolution, 116, 121
Republicans, 139, 252; agenda of, 257; attacks on Clinton, 88, 111, 114–16, 118; on budget issues, 28–31, 51–53, 71–72; Clinton coopting issues of, 129, 193; Clinton painting as extremists, 175–76, 186, 193–94; Clinton relying on to pass NAFTA, 70; Clinton's attacks on, 101, 116–17; Clinton's relations with congressional, 2–3, 10, 20–21, 99, 193–94; and Clinton's triangulation strategy, 9, 173–74; coalitions of, 89, 163; and Contract with America, 171–73, 193; control of Congress by, 6, 186, 228; demographics of support for, 207, 236, 241; divisiveness among, 173, 178; and economy, 43, 48, 149; impeachment attempt by, 130, 132–33, 179; influence on Clinton's foreign policy of, 71, 80; mobilizing public opposition to government, 26; and Nixon, 154, 178; opposition to Clinton's policies by, 48, 114–15; relations with Clinton of, 46, 153–54, 167–82; strong areas of, 138, 149, 258; taking over sub-presidential positions by, 184; and taxes, 55, 57, 160; trying to cut entitlements, 13, 159; and welfare reform, 13, 26–28; women's response to, 253
Republican National Committee, 189
Reuss, Henry, 178
Richardson, Bill, 232
Richardson, Elliot, 177
Riley, Richard, 95
Rivlin, Alice, 48, 51
Robb, Charles S., 99
Robertson, Pat, 209
Robinson, Randall, 229
Romer, Roy, 188
Rongji, Zhu, 50
Roosevelt, Franklin, 26, 58; presidency of, 164, 257; scandals of, 132
Rose, Richard, 231
Rubin, Robert, 4, 91; advising on economy, 45–48, 185; and trade policy, 49–50
Russia, 68, 69–70, 76
Rwanda, 68, 229
scandals: Clinton's, 12, 208, 227, 233–34; culture of, 4, 90; public weariness of, 133–34, 139; sexual, 130, 132, 239, 244, 249–50. *See also* campaign finance scandal; Lewinsky scandal
Schlesinger, Arthur, Jr., 92

Schumer, Charles, 248
secular realignment theory, 147–50, 164–65
Senate, 11, 12, 28, 173. *See also* Congress
sexual harassment, 11
Shalala, Donna, 96, 244
Shays, Christopher, 173
Skowronek, Stephen, 153–54
social issues: and approval ratings of Clinton, 213, 215, 219–20; Clinton's focus on women, children, and families, 239–41; Clinton's mixed strategy on, 209–10, 212; Clinton's stance on, 205; of Democrats, 163, 209; partisanship over, 219–20; policy expectations of minorities, 231–32; *vs.* economy, 215; women's greater concern with, 250–51
Social Security, 138; bankruptcy of, 261; Clinton's protection of, 38, 57, 103
soft money, 9, 188–90
Somalia: Clinton's goals in, 38, 67; congressional vote to remove troops from, 72, 261; public dissatisfaction with action in, 33, 128
Sosnik, Douglas, 95, 100
special prosecutors, 39, 177. *See also* Starr, Kenneth
spending: caps on, 37, 54, 57; on foreign aid, 71; Republicans trying to cut, 51. *See also* budgets; domestic spending
Sperling, Gene, 95
Squier, Robert, 95
staff: appointments of women to, 239, 242; Clinton's appointments of, 22–24, 227; improving press relations, 100–1
Staley, Carolyn, 98
Starr, Kenneth, 11–12, 39, 118–19, 216; Cox compared to, 177–79; Democrats unifying against, 196–97; partisanship of, 131–33; public dislike of, 120, 187
Starr Report, 119, 179
state legislatures, 184, 185
states, block grants to, 26–28
Stein, Herbert, 174
Stephanopoulos, George, 22, 24, 42, 51, 109, 177
Stiglitz, Joseph, 47
Stockman, David, 58
strategy of enlargement, 63–65
suburbs, Clinton targeting voters in, 7
Summers, Lawrence, 47
Supreme Court, appointments of women to, 239
swing states, Clinton targeting, 7
swing voters, 102–3; campaigns increasingly focused on, 258–60, 263; Clinton's conservative stances appealing to, 194; Clinton targeting, 7–8, 93, 95
taxes, 30; and Clinton's defeat in Arkansas, 98; Clinton's legacy in, 37–38; cuts, 57, 90, 160, 174, 242; cuts promised by Republicans, 116–17, 172–73; cuts promised to middle-class, 128, 168; increases, 47, 54–55, 57–58, 152, 169, 170; in Omnibus Budget Reconciliation bill, 29; Republicans favored on, 138
Tenpas, Kathryn Dunn, 242–43
term limits, 172, 186
third parties, 185, 263; candidates from, 161–62, 198
third-way politics, dangers of, 180
Thomas, Robert, 226
Thompson, Fred, 190, 196
tobacco legislation, 95, 103–4
trade, 164, 265; foreign policy focus on, 14, 74–75
trade policy, 48–51, 69; under Clinton, 14, 262; fast-track negotiating powers for, 71–72; General Agreement on Tariffs and Trade (GATT), 49–50, 74–75; to increase world market economies, 61, 63–64. *See also* free trade; North American Free Trade Agreement (NAFTA)
traditionalist politics, 218–19
travel office controversy, 24, 114
triangulation strategy, 9, 36, 195; effects of Clinton's, 193, 199, 209; Nixon's, 174; successes of Clinton's, 27–28, 37, 173–74
trickle-down economics, 58–59
Tyler, John, 154
Tyson, Laura, 47, 48
unemployment, 42–43, 48, 54
U.S.: Clinton's view of role of, 91; national interests of, 13–14, 34, 60, 64, 67, 76; role in post–Cold War world of, 33, 71, 75. *See also* interventionism
values: in Clinton's agenda, 95, 129; Clinton's stance on, 117, 206, 239–41; Gore's focus on, 139; postmodern, 107; public concern with, 91, 131, 133, 216; Republican Party favored on, 138; of swing voters, 93
V-chips, 117, 209
Ventura, Jesse, 264
vetoes, Clinton's use of: in budget struggle, 29–31, 52, 159, 177; on partial-birth abortion ban, 210; in welfare reform, 28
vice presidents: Gore as, 122; of preemptive presidents, 154; women nominated for, 253–54

Violence Against Women Act, 241
*Vital Voices* initiative, 244
Volcker, Paul, 54
Voting Rights Act of 1965, 232
wages. *See* income inequalities
Watergate: Democrats learning lessons from, 178–79, 196; influence on Clinton, 167–68, 178–79; partisanship in, 177–78
Watkins, David, 24
Watts, J. C., 235
welfare reform, 13, 26–28, 37, 96, 103; and Clinton painting Republicans as extremists, 176–77; Clinton's conservative stance on, 168, 193, 205; in Clinton's triangulation strategy, 173–74; Democrats divided over, 89–90; effects on Clinton's approval ratings of, 129, 228–29; effects on reelection, 195; minorities' dissatisfaction with, 228–29; support for, 172, 209, 252
Wellstone, Paul, 197
White House Conference on Child Care, 241
White House Office for Women's Initiative and Outreach, 241–42
White House staff, 21–23, 37; and national party chairs, 187, 190; women on, 239
Whitewater investigation, 11, 179
Wilhelm, David, 187–88
Willey, Kathleen, 130
Wilson, Woodrow, 145, 153–54
Winter, William, 226
women: appointments of, 4, 23, 226, 242–44; Clinton's focus on, 253, 260; Clinton targeting as voters, 4, 7, 241; influence on Clinton presidency of, 7; nominated for vice presidency, 253–54; support for Clinton by, 138, 239–41; support for George W. Bush by, 234, 250; violence against, 240–41; voting for Clinton, 224–25, 245, 248. *See also* gender politics
work. *See* employment
World Trade Organization (WTO), 50; protests at talks of, 14, 51, 199, 262; and role of U.S., 75, 265
Yellen, Janet, 53
Zemin, Jiang, 50